The Long Road West

A JOURNEY IN HISTORY

By the same Author

*

MY ONE CONTRIBUTION TO CHESS

DWELLY LANE

THE GREAT NORTH ROAD

THE
LONG ROAD
WEST

A JOURNEY IN HISTORY

Frank Morley

1971

THE DIAL PRESS

NEW YORK

ORIGINALLY PUBLISHED IN ENGLAND
BY CHATTO & WINDUS LTD

FIRST AMERICAN EDITION 1971

LIBRARY OF CONGRESS
CATALOG CARD NUMBER
78-90853

PRINTED IN GREAT BRITAIN

To the memory of
HERBERT READ

Contents

Acknowledgements

Johan Huizinga once exclaimed: 'How much I would like to see a history written of the road!' He explained that he meant the story of a road in its 'cultural function'. I must acknowledge that I took heart from this remark of a great teacher, though I cannot claim that he would have approved of this essay. Grateful and due recognition for granting me means to attempt it must here be given to Bollingen Foundation of New York, which awarded me a Fellowship for three years, and to Relm Foundation of Ann Arbor, Michigan for awarding me a further Fellowship. To both of these generous Foundations I wish to express a lasting gratitude. When even further time out was required (by a man who had far too large a bear by the tail) there were other and private patrons who may, I think, prefer to remain anonymous and yet to whom I insist upon recording my deepfelt recognition.

As regards wise counsel, pre-eminent has always been the kindliness of David Morrice Low, *lumen et decus* of our age; but he and others who have advised me on specific points are not to be blamed for my mistakes. Two friends who have been kind enough to read the whole of the text before it goes to print are Ian M. Parsons and A. L. Hart, Jr. Their many suggestions have been invaluable.

F. V. M.

June 1970

CHAPTER 1

Preamble

A FRIEND of mine in California sent me a newspaper clipping:

> Mrs. Lola Searles, a seventyish widow from Toledo, Ohio, checked into the Hyatt House, near the airport, a few days ago. On Sunday, a lovely day, she decided to indulge in her favourite pastime – walking – little realizing that in the West a pedestrian is looked upon with consternation, if not downright suspicion.

The innocent misdemeanour of Mrs. Searles was promptly halted. I laughed as I read the report (from one of the local papers of the San Francisco Bay area) for at one time (in January 1964, to be precise) I had been picked up by a traffic policeman at the same spot and politely returned to the same hotel for the same offence – walking.

I knew how it felt. Fortunately, to be staying at the Hyatt House was a badge of respectability. In the surburban city of Burlingame, near the airport, it was a hotel well designed for 'executive' types. 'In stride with America's growth' was the announced slogan of the Hyatt House. But the word 'stride' was not to be identified with walking.

After forty-five years I was revisiting California, and on the morning after arrival I set out to stretch the legs and enjoy the sunshine. The mood was exploration. The spirit was perhaps too buoyant: 'California, here I come'. But there was no reason for being uncheerful. Stepping from a cross-street to a handsome highway, there was no hint that walking beside the highway was prohibited.

It was, one noted, a broad highway, six lanes for motor cars, with a wide verge of good earth on either side. The highway itself was busy with cars going in both directions. No pedestrian would attempt to cross such a highway except where there were traffic lights, but the verge looked as if it had been made to be walked on. I remember thinking that from the beginning of roadways a verge had been free space for walkers. I thought of the first and most famous paved road in the world, the Appian Way from ancient Rome. If I remembered rightly that also had an earthen verge on either side for pedestrians and, at intervals, the Appian Way had benches on which wayfarers by foot might sit and contemplate the speedier traffic.

Happily then I walked upon the verge at Burlingame, but not for long. The traffic cop pulled up beside me. He leaned from his car window.

'Where's your automobile?' he said.

'I haven't got one.'

'Thought you must have had a breakdown. What are you doing?'

'Nice day,' I said. 'I'm just walking.'

'Walking?' He seemed incredulous. 'You haven't even got a dog.'

That was true. I had no dog.

'Where did you come from?' said the cop.

'Hyatt House.'

'Get in,' said the cop. 'I'll take you back there.'

Clearly there was to be no use protesting that I did not wish to be taken back to the hotel. I got into the police car. The cop was not in the least unfriendly. I was confused only because I did not understand what law, or what dominant restriction, I had been infringing. Presently I asked the cop. His reply was polite and uncompromising.

'We got to make these roads safe for automobiles.'*

Courteously, the cop did not drive me to the front door of the hotel. We parked just out of sight of the entrance and sat in the police car long enough for each of us to smoke a king-size cigarette. He seemed to be interested to learn that I had been in California long ago. 'Before I was born,' he remarked. 'Guess you'll find a lot of changes.' He used the word 'changes' proudly.

---

* The remark was not confined to 'freeways' or throughways for fast motor traffic. Mr. Lucius Beebe, in his amusing book *The Big Spenders* (Doubleday, New York, 1966) comments on the restrictions on walking in Hillsborough, a residential district of the same Bay area. 'As is true in Beverly Hills, a closely parallel enclave of privilege, there are no sidewalks in Hillsborough. A car, preferably Rolls-Royce or Bentley, is the only thinkable means of locomotion, and pedestrians, unless walking dogs, are automatically suspect, and usually questioned by the police'. Mr. Beebe instances a house guest who was venturesome enough to walk on Hayne Road but was promptly stopped by a squad car; thereafter when he wished to walk he borrowed a standard poodle from his host.

We parted amicably, he to resume his mission and I mine. I found it was possible to make a furtive crossing on foot over the freeway and over the railroad tracks into the business center of the city of Burlingame. It was with reviving spirit that I walked along the sidewalk of Burlingame's Broadway until I came to Bob's Corner. At Burlingame, Bob's Corner is where the east-west Broadway meets the original south-north arterial road of California, El Camino Real.

El Camino Real!

This was what I had been looking for.

On that morning when I revisited El Camino Real at Bob's Corner, it seemed that citizens of Burlingame had come to agree that it would be a civilized occupation just to sit down for a while and gaze at so famous a road. Right there some contemplative thoughtful person had placed a public bench. I sat on the bench to enjoy the sunshine, to look at the splendid avenue of eucalyptus trees, to watch people in their automobiles, and to think about the changes which the road had seen. There were things to be thought of at Bob's Corner, just sitting on that bench, just looking at El Camino Real.

A Greyhound bus stopped suddenly in front of me. The door opened. The driver said 'Get in.'

Startled, I said, 'I don't want to get in.'

'Sit on that bench and you gotta get in,' said the driver.

'Not going to get in.'

'Nut,' said the driver.

I had no retort. The driver slammed his door shut and the bus moved on.

The mood for contemplation had been slightly damaged. Twice I had been cause of disrupting a rigid system. I had broken rules; I had been an alien in a strange land. I got up from the bench and strolled toward San Mateo.

The two mile stretch of El Camino Real from Burlingame to San Mateo passes through a residential area, and the giant eucalyptus trees rising from the side-walks every few yards on both sides of the road form a magnificent shady arcade. There was an elderly feeling about the arcade, and one thought of an elderly word: it is a beautiful ambulatory. My pace slowed in tribute. I say the lofty trees are giants because as I stopped to look, many of them were four or four and a half feet in diameter at the base. Eucalyptus trees are sometimes reputed to be a nuisance. They are littery, careless how they drop their leaves and bark and branches; also the roots spread widely and cause trouble. There were no signs of such nuisance here. Sidewalks and roadway were smooth and tidy, and the shade, pleasing enough in January, might be a blessing in July.

The trees were old; I wondered how old they were and who had planted them. There is a common assumption that the eucalyptus was not indigenous in California and that the tree had originally come from Australia. If so, who brought it? Did the planting begin in the railroad age because the eucalyptus was quick-growing and useful for railroad ties? A sudden demand for railroad ties in the Far West began no more than a century ago. I found I had no idea what was meant by the term 'quick-growing'. To an uninformed eye it seemed these noble trees bordering El Camino Real might have been older than the railroad age. If so, there was a further question: who did originally bring the tree from Australia? It is the old Homeric question which was asked of any stranger – how did he come here? Often in Homer is that question asked and satisfying answer is demanded – 'I doubt if he just came walking on the sea.'

The trees of El Camino Real kept me occupied until I reached the Benjamin Franklin Hotel at San Mateo for lunch. Benjamin Franklin! That struck me oddly, to find an old acquaintance from the east coast lending his name in a far territory which, though he had thought of many things, I warrant he had scarcely thought of.

I stayed at San Mateo for a month, and when dining alone at the Benjamin Franklin I sometimes meditated on such trivial adventures as I have just described. Any visitor anywhere can find himself transgressing local rules and thereby making himself a nuisance. The more interesting question is, how did local rules of life develop, become rigid, even sacrosanct, governing and perhaps repressing individuals more than they are aware of. Bearing in mind that Benjamin Franklin had signed a declaration of independence, what was odd about the explorations from the hotel which bore his name was observance of so much general disposition to accept a narrowly regimented way of life. Regimented by what philosophy? Well, in California I could not help agreeing with Vance Packard that there seemed to be 'Hidden Persuaders' at work to turn individuals, unaware, into consumers of standard products, or customers for any stereotyped idea which could be put over in the name of progress. I am sure the key in that last sentence is the word 'unaware'. From his remarks I don't believe my traffic cop regarded himself as a salesman for a complex notion chiefly profitable to enterprisers in the motorcar industry, cement industry, highway-building industry and the realtor's guild. The cop accepted as if it were his own thought an advertising slogan of General Motors – 'GENERAL MOTORS IS PEOPLE .... Making Better Things For You'. Is that always true? In what sense 'better'? Are we thinking of the same things? I wouldn't wager that the avenue of eucalyptus trees between San Mateo and Bob's Corner will long remain. South of that stretch of El Camino Real and northward into San Francisco most of the trees have been cleared away. Sidewalks disappear for the benefit of drive-in shopping centers, supermarkets, liquor stores and an impressive number of stockyards stocked with second-hand cars. This is not so much for human benefit as for benefit of the imprisoning machinery. El Camino Real is made safe for automobiles.

Cars demand roads, and nobody grudges that cars should have 'freeways'. I was depressed only to watch the spoliation of El Camino Real, a road that at sometime had something to offer to the kind of consciousness that a car does not enjoy. The 'march of progress' in California during the last twenty-five years has caused many people to speak out with exceeding bitterness about the values which have been discarded and beauty which has been defaced. Lewis Mumford mourns what has happened to San Francisco Bay, where the Bay Bridge between San Francisco and Oakland has brought greater damage than benefits to both cities. I share his grief at the elimination of the ferries. That point is hardly arguable, for if you did not know the ferries you do not know what has been lost. But of the Bay Region as it is seen now Mumford writes:

> Once any single feature gets the upper hand sufficiently to suppress urban and regional variety, as we have let the private car and the freeway suppress rapid mass transportation, the ferryboat, and even the pedestrian, it is only a matter of time before the whole region becomes a featureless mess, which is exactly what the bright new fringe areas of the city actually are, though they were built only yesterday. And the faster the identifiable parts of the region coalesce, as they have done along the

throughway that ploughs down the peninsula, the more surely the central city itself will lose its character – indeed, its very reason for existence.[1]

California is now the most populous State in the Union. For the people who have poured in, how shall the way of life be described? Raymond Chandler puts a caustic comment into the mouth of one of his characters:

> Man has always been a venal animal. The growth of populations, the huge cost of wars, the incessant pressure of confiscatory taxation – all these things make him more and more venal. The average man is tired and scared, and in our time we have seen a shocking decline in both public and private morals. You can't expect quality from people whose lives are a subjection to a lack of quality. You can't have quality with mass production. You don't want it because it lasts too long. So you substitute styling, which is a commercial swindle intended to produce artificial obsolescence. Mass production couldn't sell its goods next year unless it made what it sold this year look unfashionable a year from now. We have the whitest kitchens and the most shining bathrooms in the world. But in the lovely white kitchen the average American housewife can't produce a meal fit to eat, and the lovely shining bathroom is mostly a receptacle for deodorants, laxatives, sleeping pills, and the products of that confidence racket called the cosmetic industry. We make the finest packages in the world, Mr. Marlowe. The stuff inside is mostly junk.

The 'Mr. Marlowe' in Raymond Chandler's story (*The Long Goodbye*) sat listening to this diatribe. 'I was sitting there with my mouth open, wondering what made the guy tick. He hated everything.'

Sitting at dinner at the Benjamin Franklin in San Mateo, reading one contemporary American book after another, it seemed to me that a surprising number of writers were expressing a hate for everything. William Whyte's *The Organization Man,* Aldous Huxley's *Brave New World Revisited,* Vance Packard's *The Hidden Persuaders* were among books which came my way at San Mateo, formidable indictments of unhappy trends in our current way of life. These were not writers who could be brushed off. Their indictments had to be considered. The general burden of the complaints was that our traditional system of ethics, in which the individual human retains an importance, was being replaced insidiously by a new social ethic wherein it is the 'group' which is regarded as supreme. In this new ethic men were not to be individuals freely exhibiting variety and eccentricity such as they might have been born with, but within their groups were to be standard products, their actions mechanized, their souls packaged.

Nothing in these indictments which I happened to be reading in San Mateo struck me as peculiar to California. They seemed to be true bills as to pressures in contemporary life, recognizable elsewhere as well. But there was something particularly vivid about the malaise expressed by writers who had lived in California. Therefore the malaise in California seemed to call for particular thought.

Taking a long view of migration of human families, once America had been discovered it came about for many people that 'America was promises'. I am speaking of my part of the Americas, which is North America, and my part of North America, which is the United States. If any individual who had landed upon the Eastern Seaboard felt unduly restricted, there was always the further chance that he might 'Go West'. To put that hope into practice might call for phenomenal exertion – but the hope was always there, that across the wide Missouri there might be something better. There might or might not be gold in 'them thar hills', and there certainly would be hardships, but there would be freedom. It was a noble dream, secretly cherished, I believe, by many Americans; a dream especially cherished perhaps by those who never put it to a wakeful test. Geographically, and to anybody looking for better physical conditions, California was an ultimate promise. Where could there be a lovelier reward than to live in California? Now if it is found that having reached an Ultimate men have chosen to make of it something less than paradise – if life on the Pacific Coast turns sour, then it turns sour with peculiar sourness. That seemed in part to be an explanation of the especially bitter and accusing comments about the condition of modern man which came from writers who had some experience of living on the West Coast.

A part of the malaise, then, was that the end-point of a migration had provided men with nothing different. By reaching California migrants had in no way escaped habits they had carried with them. Details emphasized not more freedom for the individual but more captivity. On the roof of a bank in the business-center of Santa Barbara in Southern California there was a light which, when it was green, showed residents that the Dow-Jones index of stock prices in

New York was up; when the light was red, it showed the New York Stock Exchange was down. Observance of that light was, for some, an important morning's ritual of obedience to an anonymous mastery. I was also thinking of the complex anonymous mastery over the lives of less wealthy people. When Lewis Mumford was speaking of the 'bright new fringe areas' to the south of San Francisco, he may have been thinking of Daly City, an example of the progress in which my traffic cop had pride.

Daly City, on the contours of a wide and spacious brown hillside, was when I saw it a spectacular eruption of long lines of identical boxes, packed as tightly as possible on narrow shelves of concrete. Seen from a distance and considered purely as a geometrical design, Daly City exhibited the kind of beauty that can be seen on a mechanical-drawing board. It gave the kind of pleasure that anyone may feel at rows of tightly packed packages on the shelves of a supermarket. The childhood fascination of toy soldiers was greatest when you could have a whole row of them; the interest of stamp albums or crosswords was when you could fill in tightly every square. But how is Daly City as a design for living? Each box in that tight formation is, supposedly, a home for a human family. There have always been overcrowded living quarters, slave-quarters, slums, in all societies. What is there to be exuberant about in planting a new slum, even if for the moment glossily packaged, in California? In what yesterday was open country, are the identical boxes packed in tight long lines so many individual homes, or so many prison cells? One thing to be said instantly is that the cells in the new slum are not in the least physically shocking, as are older ghettoes of Harlem or Glasgow, or maybe Warsaw or Cairo. Daly City is in no sense whatever to be thought of as a shanty-town. There is status about having an address in Daly City: the status of the new, perhaps the status of tomorrow. Nevertheless what has newly erupted on the brown hill south of San Francisco seems less a product of human life than of insect life. Daly City is clean, aseptic, and dehumanized. It is a crammed together bunch of cells. It is a termitary.

What sort of new homelife was induced in such new suburbs? I read that the chairman of General Foods was happy that Mrs. Consumer was learning to expect 'dinners which can be popped into the oven, heated, served in the pan, and the pan tossed into the trash can

after dinner'. And then? After the children have been evicted from
the television screen, and the $5.95 model kits in which all the parts
are stamped out for the kids have been cleared away by the parents,
what then? For the parents, more television? I was forced to think
that a room of great importance in a home in Daly City would be the
built-in garage; that was the orifice to which the car would bring the
pre-prepared, no-fuss, no-mess (but not inexpensive) meals, and that
was the escape-hatch through which in moments of desperation to get
out. To get out, where to? Wherever the automobile would be safe
and in company with other automobiles.

The observation was not that life in Daly City would seem to be
worse than in many another quarter in many another part of the
world. The sadness I joined in was the sadness of the other writers I
was reading, that at an end of a long trail of human migration, life in
California had succumbed to being the same as in other commer-
cialized societies – the same, or more so.

I said that on arrival in California a first thought was to look at El
Camino Real. This piece of 'royal' road was in a physical way the end-
segment of what had been a very long trail, the result of hard effort
made by men like me, or better men maybe. At San Mateo I fought
against feeling unduly feverish if at the end of the trail the spectacle
was not wholly happy. Regarding the scene around me as the geographical end-stage of a particular human migration, would it not be
better to lay aside opinions about the end-stage until I had somewhat
reviewed the earlier stages of the migration?

What indeed had been the course of the migration that had reached
California? I thought to myself, if I could find it of interest to speculate how eucalyptus trees came to these parts, was it not of more
interest to contemplate how people came, to settle or not to settle, to
thrive or partly thrive? It had taken a long time for people in quantity
to get to California; they had certainly now arrived in quantity; and
that in itself raised the question, how did the westward movement of
people get going? Where did a westward pulse begin? Where did the
migration start? What were the motivating ideas? What were migrants hungering for or momentarily satisfied with? What dominant
ideas had been discarded or altered, or what new ideas had been
adopted on the long trek?

Years ago in Arizona I was afflicted with a sudden physical impression, how similar the Sonora desert was to another desert, Sinai. It was as if the geographical distance of one desert from the other, and any other differences, made no difference. I have not been to Sinai, and I am not fanciful; I am not saying that I was rapt in any dream which might confuse the here and there; but I am saying that physical suggestions in Arizona made me think persistently of Sinai. There was another swift connection which reinforced random feelings. On the way to the airport at Tucson I was taken to glance at a surviving Spanish mission house, planted there (in 1710 I think) by Father Kino, and operative in these days at the edge of the Indian Reservation. You could hardly glance at that white mission house without seeing in the mind's eye the dotted lines of such white houses stretching at one time all the way back to Mexico City. But with a sudden immediacy Father Kino's house on the fringe of Tucson was reminder of something else. It was reminder of the white monastery of St. Catherine planted in that other desert far away in space and time – planted indeed by the Emperor Justinian for Greek monks below the crags of Mount Sinai, and about the planting of that monastery there had been a considerable story – the best of the stories, as a matter of fact, in the long book of Procopius on the buildings of Justinian. The point here is, the one mission house made you think of the other. Fanciful? No, it was a forcible thought. A same and special impulse had created the two missions. Far separate as the houses were, there was a link, something that had not been forgotten as men migrated. It made one think about the transfer from one desert to the other.

Those years ago I did not get very far in tracing the formidable jump that men had made, along an admittedly vast curve of space and time, from the ancient desert of Sinai to the present desert in Arizona. The thought remained in the back of the mind, as one of those things it would be interesting to think about. Naturally I was dissuaded from thinking about it. To attempt to trace the physical and spiritual migration men had made from the eastern end of the ancient Mediterranean to the far west of North America? To attempt to form a notion of all that was simply absurd. The nagging thought remained: men in their generations had caused the journey to be made. The westward push of men and ideas had been an actuality. Migration had occurred.

There had been a pathway made and used, all the more interesting because it was not at all obvious to see how the pathway came about.

To myself I called the pathway The Road West. I was easily enough dissuaded from believing that I could sort out what was to be comprehended in the theme of The Road West. I was easily dissuaded, because if among companions on the Eastern Seaboard of America I exposed a curiosity about the human migration as I thought of it, most of them at once jumped to a more limited assumption. Most of them seemed to assume that it was from the Eastern Seaboard of America that The Road West began. It seemed to be odd to my companions, to be asked to raise their hindsights. Among companions in England, if I were to use the term The Road West, the assumption often was that I was asking about the road from London to Bath. That is a good little road; I have modestly explored it; but it was not what I was now thinking about. My American friends were scarcely less parochial than the British. There seemed to be a fixed idea in the eastern States that The Road West began (perhaps that everything in America began) from the Eastern Seaboard. Of the movement of men and ideas in a westerly direction it seemed to them enough to start with the arrival of the *Sarah Constant* in Virginia or the *Mayflower* at Plymouth Rock.

If there was nothing else to think about than what had happened after men disembarked from such small ships as mentioned, and had taken a look and begun to make trails into the newfoundland, there would of course be plenty of stories of movement to study. Plenty indeed there is to mull over in the intentions of those who made the Old Post Road (Route U.S. 1) or of those who built Conestoga waggons to go west from the Lancaster Pike; or the many great explorations (Lewis and Clark for one famous example, starting from Harper's Ferry – fun to find out about Harper and his ferry, at a trouble-spot where other troubles started). The Road West within North America could include all the westward trails there came to be. And for the migration, not to be hypnotized by names of English origin, there was New France outstretching New England, and Nieuw Amsterdam before it was New York: the migration included all northern European peoples pushing westward from the seaboard. Migrants pushing toward and across the wide Missouri – what was the big idea, what were they going to make of it? Oregon Trail,

Natchez Trace, Santa Fe Trail – wasn't there enough to supply all that anybody needed to visualize westward movement, westering? Were those trails the only ones? There was I at San Mateo, California – Spanish names – and an instant ago I mentioned Santa Fe – it was at Santa Fé in Spain that Columbus received his commission – Columbus, a Genoese. Not forgetting northern Europeans, there were all Mediterranean peoples to be thought of. Because so many peoples were involved in westering there was a wish to find a general picture that would include all of them.

There was more to the migration than that. Peoples had an impulse for westward movement long before the ocean-hopping of Columbus from the Iberian Peninsula. In an Arizona desert I could not forget ancient Sinai. Therefore my conception of The Road West started (at the least) at Sinai. There had been a continuity of movement – despite interruptions the movement had been taken up by different peoples – ever since Sinai. It was the whole westering, or at least something of the story of it, at which I would take a look.

Some of my friends were horrified at such presumption. Modern history was a permissible study, for modern history was about 'us'; ancient history was about a distant 'them' who were long dead. Here one has to argue for the assumption that within the time-span of recorded history people have not changed very much – not basically – make your own allowances about peoples that are disparate and circumstances and ideas that change. I would accept the assumption; a survey of ideas which emerged in an area surrounding the ancient Mediterranean seems to me as real and close as any survey of ideas which have emerged more recently; and vice versa. It was not the time element as such that bothered me in going back so far as ancient Sinai to begin a survey of The Road West; it was the natural compunction which any amateur should feel at venturing into any realm of opinion which has been thoroughly worked over by professional scholars; at daring to take one's own snapshots on an enormous journey and to paste them into one's own album.

Yet the nature of westward migration did seem to be better revealed if one tried to think about the whole of a long journey that men had made. Put it another way, if there had been a consecutive movement you would hardly be aware of other stages of it if you looked at one stage only. The nature of a migration was that you had to take a large view to see it at all. In a preliminary large view it certainly looked as if from Sinai a westward pathway had been made, had happened; a pathway over land and sea, used with many interruptions and delays and yet with continuity. Different peoples took up the traction, different ideas dragged along, and some developed on the way. The baggage that remains is at once our heritage, our exasperation, and our bequest. Yes, I thought, let's take a look at the whole thing.

For one way or another, I think, each of us does form some view of his own of the migration I am talking about. Need there be shame in comparing notes? For my companions who thought that a notebook called The Road West would be concerned with one stage only of the road (perhaps concerned exclusively with cowboys and Indians) I change the title. This is a notebook about a long migration: The Long Road West.

At San Mateo I ruminated about making such a notebook. I did not see that I could form much opinion of the present state of migration unless I took some back-sights, and back-sights might go some way back. For each stretch of the road the traveler needs, of course, professional guides; but in the end it is up to the traveler to make what he can of the journey. I took encouragement from a remark which Sir Maurice Bowra adopted and neatly adapted: 'History is too serious a matter to be left exclusively to professional historians'.[2] But strolling on the sidewalks of El Camino Real (such sidewalks as remained) I was aware that to form coherent notions of how that road came into being would involve me in hard work. Driving in the Santa Clara hills, Bay on one side, Ocean on the other, lakes between, the thought of hard work seemed like too much trouble. In recollection those Santa Clara hills are golden, the sun is shining, the sea and bay and lakes all brightly blue. In the sky (remember?) a sparrow-hawk; towards evening (remember?) deer came down to the lakes for water. Yet at each return to El Camino Real the thought of taking back-sights kept nagging. So the notebook, sketch-book, essay – call it what you will – began.

History is too serious to be left exclusively to the professionals; yet if the amateur's passion is serious he must have licence to follow his quest in his own manner. If on the journey I run too fast – or slow –

consider, each must run the course as best he can. If as we go along you find my knowledge is not half so extensive as your own – or if my thoughts are not nearly so well considered as yours are – that might (who knows?) – give you a superior pleasure. If many of my opinions are uncertain, or worse, if I am ill-informed or seemingly perverse in ignorance – do anything you like to me and my book – as the master of such conversations once said[3] – 'do anything – only keep your temper.'

NOTES

1. Lewis Mumford in *The New Yorker,* December, 1963. Mr. Mumford will forgive me not only for this quotation but for adopting other thoughts of his.

2. Sir Maurice Bowra's remark is the first sentence of his introduction to *From the Silent Earth,* a Report on the Greek Bronze Age, by Joseph Alsop (Harper & Row, New York, 1964).

3. To the plea that Sterne made, I add a note about what might be considered mispellings; e.g. the word 'center' as it has appeared so far is in American spelling, but soon, in ancient or other contexts, it will appear in its other form, 'centre'. I am influenced by the context in choosing between spellings. I trust that causes no offence. Wherever I quote I follow the author's spelling.

   I admit an inconsistency in sometimes using numerals and sometimes spelling numbers out; e.g. in Chapter 9 I refer to 'third century' of our era, whereas in Chapter 10 it became simpler to use '9th century', and so on.

   It is more important to add that references to other books, as made in various notes, refer to the editions which happened to be handy to me. When a book has been separately published in both England and America it would have been polite (but perhaps cumbersome) always to give separate credit to both publishers.

PART ONE
Ancient

CHAPTER 2
Beginning of a Journey

THE Talmud remarks to the man about to make a journey, let him first of all stay and consider the safety. Let him stand in a dark room. Should he see the shadow of a shadow, he may set forth in confidence. But this is not an infallible sign. Perhaps (through not seeing the shadow) his mind will be upset and affect his luck for the worse. Therefore the test, although suggested, should also be avoided.

All that I know of the Talmud is some fragments in modern translation*; but ancient doubts, how to be sure what would happen from a journey, might affect even a chronicler. The instinct of a sixteenth century ballad-monger was to salute the story of an adventure with a fanfare:

> *Both gentlemen, or yoeman bould*
> *Or whatsoever you are,*
> *To have a stately story tould,*
> *Attention now prepare....*

But the oldest and most cunning of all ballad-mongers, and nearer to the period of our beginning, knew better how to set forth upon an epic. Homer simply asks the question: *What was the quarrel?*

The end of a migration can be deferred till it is found, but what *was* the quarrel between Moses and the Egyptians which started off a westward motion of men and ideas?

I cannot find that Egyptians of the period paid much attention to the quarrel.

The Jewish version of the conflict is represented in the Old Testament and in the literature of the Rabbis, and there a first dignity to be recorded is the uncompromising assertion that there is in life a spiritual value superior to any expression accorded to it by Egyptians.

* An excellent compilation in English is *Everyman's Talmud*, a redaction made by the Rev. Dr A. Cohen (Dent, London, 1932). The above advice is found there on p. 314.

The Jewish assertion was that as a people they alone had been chosen to exemplify the workings of the one true God. In the Midrashic narrative the conflict is openly stated in the account of the first interview which took place between the Pharaoh and Moses and Aaron. The Egyptian king is reported as asking reasonably enough, 'Who is your God that I should hearken unto His voice?' They replied, 'The Universe is filled with the might and power of our God', and they went on to repeat that axiom with poetry and passion. Freedom to escape from the bondage of Egypt, to break away and find God somewhere, to receive instruction and to exhibit a corresponding service to Him, is the simple and supreme motive in this scene of the Jewish drama.

The melodramatic elements of the escape of the Israelites from Egypt – the plagues, the Passover, the crossing of the Red Sea, the pillar of fire and pillar of cloud – are so engraved in our memories from earliest childhood that nobody shall dare to tamper with them. I find no reason to tamper:

> *Reason hath moons, and moons not hers,*
> *Lie mirrored on her sea,*
> *Confounding her astronomers,*
> *But, O! delighting me.*

At the same time it is fair to point out that on the Egyptian side of the story no record has been found of theological discussion between Moses, Aaron and the Pharaoh, and the miracles and plagues so much emphasized and relished in the book of *Exodus* are not attributed by Egyptian historians to any special efforts made by a God of the Hebrews. Plagues in the area of the Delta were regarded rather as part of the general nature of things. The special revolt of the Hebrews is, as remarked above, scarcely noticed in the annals of Egypt. The Egyptian priest Manetho does mention the existence of Hebrews as a minor tribe which had squatted near the Bitter Lakes. The impression gathered from Manetho is that various groups of peoples had been accustomed to seep into the Delta country from the north and east, and in a general clearance of the squatters the Hebrews had been merely one of the tribes that fled. Manetho, writing long after the Exodus, flung after them an identifying phrase which came to be bitterly resented by Jewish historians. 'Robbers and lepers' was Manetho's parting insult to the Hebrews, a clear enough expression of an Egyptian feeling of good riddance.*

If the ancient Egyptians regarded the quarrel with the Hebrews as no more than a back-street business, that in no sense detracts from the great drama. Moses himself might have been glad enough to be able to extricate his people furtively, as secretly as possible, challenging no fight. The word passed among them to flee forthwith and at night with such spoils as could be carried with them, tents and clothes and bread that had not had time to rise. The picture of the people who fled with Moses is that of a brave but undisciplined rabble. Escape was only a first act; the further action was safely to cross the desert to a Holy Mount where the secret name of God would be revealed, and where the government of the people, and their future, could be designated.

The peninsula of Sinai is on the map an equilateral triangle which hangs point downward between the enormous land-masses of Africa and Arabia. On a modern map the triangle of Sinai appears as an inconspicuous formation. Each side of the triangle is only about two hundred and fifty miles in length. The side at the top of the triangle stretches directly from the Delta of Egypt toward the land of

---

* *Manetho*, with an English translation by W. G. Waddell, Professor of Classics in Fuad el Awal University, Cairo, is in the Loeb Classical Library (Heinemann, London and Harvard University Press, 1940). To get a few dates in mind, let me accept Professor Waddell's dating of the Exodus *c.* 1445 B.C. According to *O.T.* 1 *Kings* vi. 1, the building of Solomon's Temple was begun 480 years after the Exodus; that is (on this chronology) *c.* 965 B.C. All dates are of course subject to endless argument. The celebrated Manetho (himself a shadowy figure) may have been writing about the middle of the third century B.C. The heterogeneous material in the Talmud, recording earlier oral tradition, derives mainly from a great formative period of Judaism extending from the third century B.C. to the end of the fifth century A.D.

Manetho's description of Israelites is reported in Greek as

πλῆθος τῶν ἀγυρτῶν καὶ λελωβημένων

There is a longer quotation in Josephus, *Contra Apion*, i, 28. There are some flickering sidelights on the ancient quarrel in the *Christian Topography of Cosmas Indicopleustes*, edited by E. O. Winstedt (Cambridge University Press, 1909). Cosmas (another shadowy figure who is called Cosmas Indicopleustes because nobody knows what else to call him) comes into my reading partly because in the sixth century A.D. he entered the monastery at the foot of Mount Sinai which I mentioned in my preamble.

Canaan. The two downward-pointing sides are shaped by the straight narrow gulfs of Suez and of Aqaba. At the extreme southern tip of the triangle are the Sinai mountains, the highest of them reaching upward to more than eight and a half thousand feet.

At the moment of the Exodus it may be that some of the Israelites expected that Moses would lead them straightway along the northerly coastal route toward Canaan, where the path would be shortest and the going relatively easy, within sound of the murmur of surf from the Mediterranean Sea. It was in the tribal tradition that it was by that coastal route that Joseph had come to Egypt, and in the book there is mention that some of the Israelites had an idea of carrying Joseph's sarcophagus, symbol of a time of glory, directly back to the land of his fathers. But it seems that the direct and easy route across the top of the Sinai triangle was deliberately discarded by Moses. We may ponder about the reasoning: it may have been that as an escape route the top of the triangle was altogether too obvious, that Egyptian chariots might all too readily have cut into the Israelites in the coastal plain. It may be that other peoples regarded by Egyptians as 'robbers and lepers' were trying that escape route, and that is why we have not heard of them. Some scholars have said that by taking the coastal route Moses would have run head on into the Philistines – others have said that any mention of the Philistines in Moses' time would be an anachronism, for that 'people of the sea' had at that moment not yet occupied the land of Palestine to which they later gave their name. Dismiss side-arguments: what is agreed is that, for whatever reason, Moses in the first instance walked his people southward, down the Suez side of the Sinai triangle, in what possibly seemed to some of his followers a totally wrong direction.

The book of *Exodus,* as we have it in our Old Testament, divides into two parts. The first half reads like a boys' book: there is the exultation of escape, of outwitting the enemy (with divine help). Then there are the adventures on the route, and disillusionment and discontent with the leadership as the crowd dragged along, short of water, short of food, into a region which was ever worse and rockier. The grumbling increased. 'And they said unto Moses, Because there were no graves in Egypt, hast thou taken us away to die in the wilderness?' A lot of impedimenta may have been discarded on the hard walk southward. We hear no more about the bones of Joseph. We hear little about any heavyweight spoils that might have been filched from the Egyptians – we hear about such gold as might be carried in the form of ear-rings. What we imagine is that when the black tents of Israel were at length set up beside a wadi at the foot of the harsh grey range of Sinai mountains, there were – either resting within the shade of the tents or struggling out to forage – a number of footsore people.

How large a number of people was it, that Moses led away from Egypt? Many centuries later Hebrew scribes use a word which is translated (again many more centuries later) into the word 'multitude'. Somewhere the number of six hundred thousand is mentioned. That would seem a great many. However large the encampment was beneath Mount Sinai, or however small, the second part of the book of *Exodus* is concerned less with a boys' book aspect of the adventures than with a mystery, how the crowd of refugees was brought to discipline and to a proud consciousness of united nationality. That is now the theme. Moses had brought his people through a wilderness to a sacred mountain, where he was now the medium of a revelation which marked a new departure in their religion, and whereby he gave decisions on civil and ceremonial matters which were to form the basis of all their subsequent legislation. Therefore to Moses, under God, Israel owed its national existence.

I borrow those words from an Anglican scholar, Dr. S. L. Brown, writing in Bishop Gore's large *Commentary*.[1] Men of all nations have pondered and go on pondering the work of Moses in that 'forty years' in the wilderness. Goethe was amazed that a man of action such as Moses should have kept his people marking time for so long a period. Daniel-Rops points out that this is exactly the time-span it would take for a generation which hankered for the laxities of Egypt to die out and for another desert-hardened generation to grow up. Many a student, here or elsewhere in the Old Testament, prefers to evade the question whether ancient enumerations are to be regarded as arithmetically exact. If the 'forty years' signifies no more than 'a lengthy time' there nevertheless remains a practical problem. If for a lengthy time a people in any considerable number is contained in a grim desert, receiving the while a deliberate tuition in the Law and in all incidental ceremonial and discipline – how throughout that time did the people manage not only to survive but to prosper?

Prosper they did, according to the second part of *Exodus*. The arrival of the Israelites at Mount Sinai had been presented as a story of adventure and hardship. There was the fight on the way at Rephidim with certain Bedouins (described in *Exodus* as Amalekites) as the people neared the mountains. After arrival at the encampment there is mention that in a wadi, or in more than one of such waterholes, the people found enough water to wash their clothes. What about live-stock and food problems? Hunger is emphasized by the stories of the quails and the manna. Yet after a while Israel's material circumstances seem to become much easier. In the curious episode of the golden calf it is not so much the breaking off of the golden earrings which is impressive, as that by that time the idea of feasting was a natural thought, the sitting down to eat and drink and the rising up to play. Anthropologists tell us that in many another part of the world the poorest of tribes will devise a ceremonial feast with very little equipment; but throughout the second part of *Exodus* consider how the material equipment of the Israelites seems to multiply. As the time came for departure from Mount Sinai, consider the wealth of materials expended on the Ark and the Tabernacle. Are the precious metals mentioned, silver and gold in a quantity transcending a matter of ear-rings – are the rare woods and the trappings to be regarded as a product of poetic licence, supplied by scribes a long time afterwards? Or was there substance behind the story of the second part of *Exodus*? Were the Israelites so very much better off in a material way, as well as in a spiritual way, when they had been in Sinai for a lengthy period than when they had arrived? If so, whence came the prosperity?

Professor Breasted mentioned that long before the time of Moses there had been Egyptian copper-workings in the Sinai Peninsula.[2] There are no doubt many speculations about very ancient traderoutes from Ethiopia and Arabia up the Red Sea to harbourages at Tor and Aqaba. Tor (some think of it as a Phoenician port) certainly became a port for Mount Sinai; a small Greek monastery at Tor was sister to the monastery of St. Catherine's beneath the Holy Mount.* Those monasteries were not founded until about two thousand years after the time of Moses. The copper-works in Sinai might have been

---

* When Cosmas in the 6th century A.D. entered the monastery at Mount Sinai, his friend Menas became a monk at Tor.

working one or two thousand years before Moses; were they at work in his time? Can we skip around on a very large time-scale with any feeling of confidence? At the time of Moses was there a trade-route from Tor, skirting the range of mountains, northward from Mount Sinai to Petra and the oasis of Kadesh, thence into the inward parts of Canaan? I don't see how we can say anything more than that if there had been such a trade-route, and if the Israelites had straddled the route at vital watering-places, that might go some way toward explaining how the people after their initial hardships began to profit either by barter or piracy.

The book of *Exodus* provides no test for this trade-route argument. It was not a purpose of the book to be concerned with our questionings. We might interpret the fight at Rephidim as an objection by the Bedouins to a trespass by the Israelites and interference with an existing traditional carrier-trade. We might skip ahead four or five centuries and ask about the Queen of Sheba – when this foreign Queen visited Jerusalem to test Solomon's wisdom and to exchange with him riddles and other courtesies, by what route did she come? Her name is sometimes transliterated as Bilquis, sometimes (as Kipling has it) Balkis. It is said that she came from Sheba in farthest Arabia, with a brilliant suite and a brave array. 'Her camels carried gold, perfumes and precious stones'. Did she and her retainers travel by boat to Tor, and thence northward by a route past Mount Sinai? When she had been entertained by Solomon and received from him 'all that she could desire' did she return to Arabia by the same trail? If by Sheba's time there was a road fit for a Queen to travel, had the road been a trade-route before the time of Moses? Again I don't see that anyone can say more than that the existence of such a route might have come into Moses' original calculation, that it might help to explain the survival of the Israelites in the wilderness, and that it would prevent any question about the tradition that when Moses was ready to move northward the march was now straightforward beside the mountain range toward Canaan.

It is certainly also in the tradition that when the Israelites moved from Mount Sinai they were no longer a rabble but a confident nation. Josephus, in Book III of his *Jewish Antiquities*, provides a picture of the northward movement from Sinai which is in strong contrast to the picture of the initial southward flight from

Egypt. The march toward Canaan is described as an orderly procession with banners, each banner signifying the command of a chief. Josephus describes the movement as being like the movement of a city.

Josephus is not indefinite about his figures for the marching men of Israel. He says there were 603,650 men between 20 and 50 years of age capable of bearing arms. All these he says were trained to be obedient to the sound of silver trumpets. In the midst of the procession when the Jews took off from Sinai there was guarded the Ark of the Covenant and the six wagons, each with two oxen, which were needed to transport the Tabernacle.

With or without such precise numbering and with or without all the details later and devotedly ascribed to all the panoply, we do believe it was no longer a rabble but a formidable people which trooped away from Sinai, away from the harsh grey mountains of the south, past even more spectacular rock faces, black and purple, northward past the red gorge of Petra to the oasis of Kadesh. There, before the final assault on the Promised Land, they set up their pickets.*

Rehearsing this much of a story familiar to all, and moving cautiously after the Israelites from Egypt in a zigzag toward Canaan, I have made small progress with my announced intention of studying a westward movement, obedient to my title. I have found as yet no geographical westward movement, nor as yet any idea that westering was of importance. I have moved with the ancient Hebrews two hundred and fifty miles south and two hundred and fifty miles north and if anything have lost ground westerly.

Yet the birth of an immense idea is to be traced in the off-hand remark of Josephus, that the movement of the Jews from Sinai was like the movement of a city. The familiarity of the story, the offhandedness of the remark, must not be allowed to obscure the immensity of the idea. It *was* the movement of a city, in the sense of

---

* It can be noticed that I borrow this phrase, and that throughout I follow very closely the narrative as presented by Daniel-Rops in *Israel and the Ancient World*, translated by Kathleen Madge (Eyre & Spottiswoode, London, 1949). I continue to be greatly dependent upon Daniel-Rops. For Josephus I refer to the edition of *Jewish Antiquities* translated by H. St. J. Thackeray in the Loeb Classical Library (1924).

representing a determined search for a city, before in any physical sense the city existed. The physical city had yet to be founded and formed – but the idea had been formed. Israel was on the march to find and make its own City, God's City, Jerusalem. Jerusalem, as the name proclaims: Holy City, City of God. In a physical sense the people marching from a sun-baked wilderness might well be longing for a land of milk and honey and a shady city of palm trees. But the predominant immortal passion is to be summed up in spiritual terms – the establishment of a city worthily representative of 'the might and power of our God'.

So, having followed the Israelites to Kadesh, I have no need to fill my notebook with their local battles with Moabites, Midianites or Philistines. I am not required to pause with Saul and David – except to notice David's selection of the site for the Holy City of Jerusalem. For my purpose what I need to think about is Solomon in all his glory, and what that phrase implied. If my interpretation should be correct, almost immediately after Solomon there was to be an unexpected and dynamic impulse to a dramatic westward movement.

NOTES

1. *A New Commentary on Holy Scripture* (S.P.C.K., London, 1929).
2. I am here turning back to the admirable school-books of Professor James Henry Breasted: *Ancient Times* (Ginn, Boston, 1916) and *The Conquest of Civilization* (Harper, New York, 1926).

CHAPTER 3
Solomon in all his Glory

THE king 'made silver to be in Jerusalem as stone, and cedars made he to be as the sycamore trees that are in the vale, for abundance' (1 *Kings*, x, 27). Whence came the silver? On their return to Canaan the Old Testament emphasizes an immediate admiration of the Jews for the example set by the neighbouring city of Tyre. They were seeking a city; was not Tyre the exemplar of a city? – 'Tyre ... whose merchants are princes, whose traffickers are the honourable of the earth' (*Isaiah*, xxiii, 8).

David had made friends with Hiram, King of Tyre, and Solomon promptly made the closest possible alliance. A daughter of Hiram was solicited as one of Solomon's earliest wives and a treaty with Hiram was one of Solomon's earliest treaties. In the relevant Psalm it is not easy to say which is being celebrated, the daughter or the treaty – 'The king's daughter is all glorious within: her clothing is of wrought gold. She shall be brought unto the king in raiment of needlework: the virgins her companions that follow her shall be brought unto thee' (*Psalms* xlv, 13, 14).

Solomon was to reign for forty years (975–935 B.C. approximately) and Hiram's reign at Tyre was almost exactly contemporary (from about 979 to 946 B.C.). It is supposed that Hiram, slightly the older in his rule, was an immensely influential father-in-law. We must ask who were these Phoenicians, who had apparently immediate influence upon the Jews, for good or ill, when the Jews were setting up their Holy City of Jerusalem.

Phoenix, Phoenicia – the ancient Greek names have a common root.* The complex of root-meanings is not helpful in identifying a specific branch of Semitic people as 'Phoenicians'. Rather the re-

---

* For the complex of root-meanings of Phoenix, Phoenicia, see *The Oxford English Dictionary* (Clarendon Press, Oxford, 1933). A curious little point in connection with the traditional conjecture that traders described as Phoenicians did appear in Britain, and perhaps not only in Cornwall but in the north of the island, is the persistence to this day of the name Fenwick as a

verse: in the beginning, to the Hellenes, when a stranger was called a 'Phoenician' the term may have had no precise ethnic significance – it may have been a term as general as 'Easterner'. One of the root-meanings for 'Phoenicia' is that of a land where dates ripen earliest for eating or for wine-making. The use of dates for wine-making may suggest Mesopotamia and Sumeria, but also Egypt.[1] Another meaning for 'phoenician' is the colour of purple-red or crimson which came to be identified with the famous Tyrian dye. But the richly-coloured bird of legend, the 'phoenix', is often thought of as Arabian, or by some scholars is interpreted generally as an image of the sun – which though it sets, also rises again. Out of this complex of original Greek meanings there emerges one common notion: that to early Hellenes the word 'Phoenician' might mean almost any people or produce or images coming from the part of the world where the sun rises. The increasing localization of the term to the inhabitants of several exchange ports of the Lebanon – Tyre, Sidon, Byblos became the best known – must have been due to an emergence of those ports as dominant in the carrier trade of eastern produce.

In the attempt to assess what it was that most impressed the Jewish people, newly returned from the wilderness, about their new close neighbours in Tyre and Sidon I would look first at an outside view of the peoples of those seaports, such as given by Homer. The respect of the early Hellenes for peoples to the east of them is indicated by the pride taken in Cadmus as the legendary founder of Thebes. Cadmus represented something that Greeks were very eager to absorb. 'If thy country were Phoenicia what reproach is that? Cadmus too, from whom Greece learnt writing, was a Phoenician'.* But the name

---

north-country family name, particularly around Newcastle; and oddly enough, the family name of Fenwick is often associated with tailoring and haberdashery. The family name with various spellings, such as Fenix, Phenix, Phoenix went to America and reappears in many American place-names, such as Phoenix, the capital city of Arizona. I am not suggesting that such trivial thoughts mean anything; at most they are what the Talmud called shadows of a shadow.

* This was a remark in a sepulchral epigram of Zenodotus on Zeno, founder of the school of the Stoics, and therefore a man of the greatest importance in the development of the western world. The point of the quotation is that early or late it was common form among Greeks to regard the legendary Cadmus as originator of their civilization.

'Cadmus' is simply an adoption of the Semitic radicals for 'East'.[2] The myths of Cadmus, of his sister Europa, and of Io, indicate at once how very much mixed up were the affairs of all seafaring peoples of the Eastern Mediterranean. The term 'Phoenician', we have just been warned, could be very general. For the particular tribe of Semites, perhaps blood-brothers of the Hebrews, who had built up Tyre and Sidon and who came to dominate the Mediterranean carrier trade, I don't detect that Hellenes, early or late, had much affection. Respect for the particular peoples of Tyre and Sidon was respect for the purveyors of things eastern, notions from regions as far apart as Egypt and Arabia to the south and the Fertile Crescent to the north. If numbers of ships from Tyre and Sidon appeared upon the sea as early as the time of the Minoan sea-empire, the impression is that they represented no overt threat. The specific Phoenicians who manned the ships did not appear as danger-ous people. The impression is that they appeared as traders, carriers, peddlers.

If the term 'Phoenician' is narrowed to the people of the Lebanon who were neighbours of the returning Jews, the main impression that early Hellenes convey is that those Phoenicians were maritime peddlers. The impression is that they were handy at carrying any-thing. It may be fanciful to think that they transported bulls from Assyria to Crete, but Crete imported livestock from somewhere, and by the time of the Odyssey it is commonplace to mention that Phoe-nicians were transporters of livestock, as well as being sea-peddlers of all kinds. Daniel-Rops puts it colourfully: 'their ships sailed into the ports of the Mediterranean, floating bazaars offering temptation to women. In them they sold cosmopolitan gewgaws, bronze arms, and glass from the Nile, perfumes of Arabia and Egyptian papyrus, Cretan and Mycenaean vases, Lydian and Hittite gold plate, precious stones, and those Asian stuffs to which the purple dye of murex gave so noble a colour. It sometimes happened that, drawing up his anchor without warning, the captain would sail away and sell his beautiful clients as slaves, for the traders were not above being pirates.'

Daniel-Rops supports his description of the sea-traders of Leba-non by referring to the catalogue in Ezekiel of the wealth of ma-terials available to the merchants of Tyre. 'Tarshish was thy merchant by reason of the multitude of all kinds of riches; with silver, iron, tin and lead they traded in thy fairs'. Ionia and the Caucasus traded the 'persons of men and vessels of brass in thy market'. Armenia 'traded in thy fairs with horses and horsemen and mules'. Arabia, in exchange for trash, traded ivory and ebony. Syria traded emeralds, broidered work, fine linen, coral and agate. Judah, the land of Israel, 'were thy merchants; they traded in thy market wheat of Minnith and Pannag, and honey, and oil, and balm'.

The more or less contemporary Homeric view of the Lebanese Phoenicians independently expands the impression. If Greek heroes regarded Phoenicians not so much as warriors but as peddlers, the peddler nevertheless has an importance not to be underestimated. Where the peddler comes from becomes a centre of fashion, and to the early Hellenes their centre of fashion became the Lebanon. Tyre had the name for dyed stuffs, Sidon perhaps more of the reputation for made-up material, but the names are practically interchangeable. The point is that in Homeric times they were both names of potency. In the Sixth Book of the *Iliad* it was regarded by all who listened as the most natural thing in the world for Prince Paris and his highborn Helen to cruise to Tyre and Sidon for their honeymoon. On their way to Troy it was the right thing for them to pick out and take with them embroidered robes, the work of Sidonian women, enough to fill a scented storeroom. Many touches in the *Iliad* show what the listener, in those times, would expect or readily take for granted. The fashionableness of Phoenician wear is not restricted to female fashion only. The helmet of poor Dolops, of which the whole ornament was shorn off and fell in the dust – Homer makes us almost more sad for the helmet than for Dolops, for the ornament was 'fresh Phoenician', the height of fashion. When that ornament had gone what else had Dolops to live for? The princes of Troy took their beauty from Phoenicia; the style was emulated by the Greek warriors; and at home on the mainland of Greece the ordinary clothing for ordinary people was affected by what came from Lebanon. The word *kiton* or *chiton* for the garment universally adopted by the Hellenes was a Phoenician word.

To the Greeks, then, Tyre and Sidon were famous as fashion centres. Whatever linens and cottons were available elsewhere, there was one speciality of treatment invented and refined by the

Phoenicians themselves. This was the dye obtainable from the large sea-snail abundant in the waters off Lebanon, the *murex*. Ancient mounds of the shells of the murex are to be seen at Sidon to this day. There are other notable shell-heaps in other parts of the world: in New England, for example, there are the shell-heaps of the Damaris-cotta in Maine.[3] But nowhere except in the Lebanon are the shell-heaps associated with such refinements of an art which persisted for at least fifteen hundred years; for what the Phoenicians could do with the murex was as famous in the time of Justinian (roundabout 500 A.D.) as it was in the Homeric period. Within the past few years Sir Julian Huxley, contemplating the mounds of murex shells at Sidon and speaking for the moment as a marine biologist, made some interesting remarks about the murex itself. This peculiar sea-snail, he says, is a voracious carnivore. The ancient discovery was that it could be trapped in baited wicker creels like lobster pots; the object of the trapping being the dye-stuff; the source of the dye being a gland in the mantle-cavity of the sea-snail. To a human nostril, says Huxley, the gland stinks; but the purple dye it yields is concentrated and indelible.[4]

Various classical scholars (for instance Bury) have commented that to modern eyes the range of colours available to the ancients in their dyes would seem very limited. But Huxley suggests that the dye from the murex was not confined to the concentrated Tyrian or 'royal' purple. That might well have been, as it were, the most expensive 'liqueur', but with mixtures and dilutions a whole rainbow of colours could have been obtainable. It is conceivable that something in the original quality of the murex played a part as a fixative, analogous to the part played by ambergris in perfumery. At any rate Huxley vis-ualizes that Tyrian dye may have ranged from blackish purple through violet and blue even to orange and red; that with special treatments a green dye might have been fixed, or amethyst or tur-quoise. The more limited the range of other dye-stuffs, the more sought after may have been the range of Tyrian colours. The upshot of Huxley's speculations is that there was considerable choice in the colours of veils and robes available from Tyre and Sidon, and that the recipes for colorations may well have been refined from time to time and jealously regarded as trade secrets.

If Hellenes of the Homeric period thought of the Phoenicians of

Lebanon mainly as traders and carriers and maritime peddlers, to be regarded with some contempt by warriors, there was one manly realm in which they are held to have had a far greater gift than any of the early Greeks. Sea-faring.

A large part of the road west is a sea-road, and how men achieved sufficient mastery of the sea is a mystery less to be swallowed in one gulp than to be stated, and paused at, and returned to. We may easily believe statements that sea-traffic in the Eastern Mediterranean antedated whatever we may know or suppose about Phoenician shipping. We may believe there was open-sea contact between the Minoan civilization and Egypt. But nobody makes it clear that any eastern people explored the Mediterranean to its Far West, by sea, before the Phoenicians; and there is general acceptance that this was what the Phoenicians did. Even by Homeric times the Hellenes were slow to get their feet wet; the fact that Odysseus dared, or was forced, to do so is the dramatic theme of the *Odyssey*. But about that time a commonplace of Phoenician sea-trading is supposedly indicated by the opening phrase of Ezekiel's catalogue about Tyre: 'Tarshish was thy merchant by reason of the multitude of all kinds of riches; with silver, iron, tin and lead they traded in thy fairs'. In that catalogue one might almost pass over Tarshish without thinking; but we are forced to think that Tarshish (with the Hebrew ending) or Tartessos (with the Greek ending) is a part of what is now called Andalusia, in Spain.

We shall have to return to think about this.* Spain is a long way by open sea from Tyre and Sidon. The Mediterranean is not a small sea. As a matter of sea-mileage it is as far from Tyre to the Strait of Gibraltar as it is from Liverpool to Newfoundland. What we are asked to believe is that long before the time of Ezekiel (who apparently took the trade with Spain as an accustomed matter), and before the time of Homer – indeed by the fairly precise date of 1100 B.C. –

* An easy preliminary escape from thinking is to identify the Tarshish of Ezekiel with some place-name nearer to the Lebanon than Spain; it is sometimes suggested that Ezekiel is referring to Tarsus in Cilicia, the 'no mean city' of St. Paul; and this disposes of the whole problem of Phoenicians getting to Spain long before any Greeks got there. But if the capacity of early Phoenicians to sail by open sea to Spain is peremptorily denied, one is led in the end to even greater difficulties than the difficulties (which can't be minimized) of asserting that they could and did.

Phoenicians from the Lebanon had established, among other ports in Spain, the port of Gadeira (Gades, Cadiz) which is west of Gibraltar. We are asked to believe that while other peoples of the Eastern Mediterranean were making relatively short voyages in relatively home waters it was becoming a commonplace for the Phoenicians to navigate to the Atlantic – and back again.

The assertion cannot be swallowed in one gulp, for there are certainly practical difficulties. What time must be allowed for a Phoenician round-trip between the Lebanon and Spain? Hardly less than the best part of a year? I repeat, the Mediterranean is not a small sea, and not by any means always a quiet sea, with steady winds; not so regarded by sailormen nowadays, certainly not so regarded by Homer. The passage of the Strait of Gibraltar from east to west has never been regarded as a simple matter for sailing ships (as Nelson well knew) when currents set in from the Atlantic or when winds are contrary.[5] It is indeed a very considerable assertion to make, that before the end of the second millennium B.C. Phoenicians had established Utica, on the north coast of Africa, as a way-station, and Gadeira, on the Atlantic coast of Spain, as a Phoenician port. Why was Gadeira, on the Atlantic coast, of importance to Phoenician shipmasters? Because (if we are not tired of holding our breath in astonishment) it is held that Phoenician shipmasters were going on to prospect from Gadeira to Portugal, and (again deep in the tradition) northward to Brittany and Cornwall. We must indeed hold breath as to practical considerations of seamanship and navigation.

While reserving judgement about the assertion of extraordinary, arduous and dangerous voyages by early Phoenicians, we can see how acceptance of the assertion would fit in with the story we have been tracing of the Jews. The main motive for the Phoenician voyages is supposed, in one word, to be metals. A combined army of historians and archaeologists who tell you this have a lot of guns on their side. They say in effect that it is up to you to imagine how the Phoenicians managed to establish a carrying trade from West to East in metals – in silver, iron, lead, copper, tin; above all, tin – presumably after a first smelt – from the Iberian Peninsula and perhaps from Cornwall to the faraway Lebanon. But you must imagine such a trade was established to explain at least some of the bronze of the Bronze Age. Tin was scarce in the East, yet tin was vital as an alloy with copper for the making of bronze tools and weapons. Tin was plentiful in the Iberian Peninsula and in Cornwall. Much is explained if tin and other metals came from the West to Lebanon, thus making Sidon, as Homer casually remarks, 'Sidon, smithy of bronze for all the East'.

The picture impressed upon us is that ancient Phoenicians achieved much the same feat that Spaniards achieved twenty-five hundred years later. The Spanish Conquistadors plundered the Americas for precious metals, and thereby altered the economy of Europe. The Phoenicians established a similar pattern by plundering their new western world for the metals available – and thereby altered the economy of the ancient East. The parallel is very striking. We know about the one case, and are the more disposed to accept the other. In their New World, Phoenicians found that there were metals being worked by native tribes with no knowledge of what those metals might be worth in eastern civilizations. For trade-goods of trifling value, ignorant western tribes could be persuaded to work their ores in quantity. Thus the Phoenicians 'made their fortune by bringing together two economic hemispheres, which up till then had remained completely apart, and in which precious metals had very different values'. I borrow the wording and accept the assertion from the distinguished French archaeologists Gilbert and Colette Charles-Picard.[6]

For what at this point I am seeking is explanation of a change of heart among the Jews on their return from the wilderness, a change which many of the faithful have forever lamented. I pictured them as coming to Canaan under command to set up their City of God, and I find them in the neighbourhood of Sidon, centre of fashion and 'smithy of bronze for all the East'; and of Tyre, equally a centre of fashion and, with almost a monopoly of silver, a special banking centre. Tyre and Sidon, one might think, would have formed a heady neighbourhood for people who were building Jerusalem. Hellenes might often be stand-offish to the Phoenicians of the Lebanon, might often treat them with hostility or contempt. But to the Jews, it seems to me that the Semitic people may well have appeared as impressive blood-brothers, elder brothers, wealthy, smart, citified, sophisticated, secure in their self-confidence and immensely worldly-wise.

So far in the journey my credulity has not been strained. Traditions from different sources weave together coherently. I asked to reserve judgement about the Phoenician voyaging, but the immediate admiration of the Jews for the way of life represented by Tyre is an impressive indication of the wealth of Tyre. We have to agree that the influence of Tyre upon the Jews was strong, in order to explain the rapid disintegration of the original firm command that Jerusalem, when built, should be the City of God.

It is not difficult to conjecture why David had made friends with Hiram, King of Tyre, and why Solomon as soon as possible cemented that friendship. The Kings of Israel had to consider the physical safety of their people. Whatever Josephus may have boasted about the numbers of Israel's fighting force, its strength was puny in comparison with the manpower which could be commanded by the Great Kings to the north and east of them, or with the giant strength of Egypt to the south, should that giant choose to wake and not remain inert.

Inland from the Lebanon the Aramaean kingdom of Damascus, with outposts at Palmyra and Aleppo, lay between Hiram and the Assyrian Empire. If Sidon was 'smithy of bronze' it was through the Aramaeans that weapons and tools could pass to the Assyrians, and it was from the Aramaeans that Hiram might learn of Assyrian affairs. It seems that for a long time (from about 1200 B.C. until about 800) the Assyrian armies were preoccupied in warfare with the Hittite Empire to their north and with the restlessness of northern marauders. It was in this long contest that the age of iron began to replace the age of bronze, the iron coming from the northern shores of Asia Minor, and the Assyrian forces, through conquest of that territory, becoming 'the first large armies equipped with weapons of iron'. Breasted emphasizes that; yet soft iron, without the invention of some adequate hardening process, is by itself a poor material for supplying a cutting edge either for weapons or tools, and the availability of iron to the Assyrians was no instant threat to a Phoenician trade in bronze. The physical threat to Sidon and Tyre might come if or when Assyrian war-lords were free from serious conflict to the north of them, and if ever they should choose to move southward to attack the richness of Egypt. That could be hard on any lesser peoples who stood in the way. The Aramaeans were of importance to Hiram because they could ring an alarm bell; and, as regards any threat from the north, for Solomon the alarm bell was Hiram.

In the time of Hiram and Solomon there was no special alarm from the north. There was apparently for Solomon a flutter of fear about Egypt. In the twenty-fourth year of his reign there was in Egypt a sudden invigoration. Sesac, a Libyan, staged a military coup, became Pharaoh, founded the XXIInd Dynasty, and spoke to the world militantly. One may imagine that Hiram was much less impressed than Solomon. Phoenicians, in their home waters, had a tradition of being high-handed with Egyptian envoys. One of the oldest stories of seafaring is *The Voyage of Ouenamon*,* which tells how merchants of Byblos treated an officer of Egypt who put into the port in search for wood – some of the famous cedars of Lebanon, perhaps. The story is that the Phoenician merchants made the envoy wait for the cargo, haggled over the price, teased him with delays, and removed the long steering oar from his ship so that he was unable to depart until he had paid their charges. There may be some more complicated trickery concealed in the story, but the point is that Phoenicians were permitted to appear as high and mighty. At the fancy that Sesac might move northward, Solomon displayed no such haughty behaviour. Solomon at once resorted to his usual diplomacy. He invited the Pharaoh's daughter to come to be his queen of the first rank and to live at Jerusalem in a palace built specially for her. The offer was accepted; as a wedding-gift to Solomon, Sesac conquered and laid waste to Gaza, the last stronghold of the Philistines.

In the lifetime of Solomon and Hiram there was no outside threat to their kingdoms that could not easily be composed, and with no outside threats the two friends prospered. It is clear from the Biblical narrative that from the beginning of their relationship Hiram was Solomon's banker. This upon occasion led to a temporary rift between the two men. At one moment Solomon was seriously in debt and could offer to liquidate only by ceding to Hiram twenty of Israel's towns. Hiram accepted, but with no good grace. Hiram was interested first and foremost in produce, without the nuisance of being a land-

---

* Daniel-Rops quotes *The Voyage of Ouenamon* from Moret, *Rois et Dieux d'Egypte*, p. 228. It is referred to under the name Wenammon in the *Cambridge Ancient History*, II, 193. I have ventured to add the touch about the merchants of Byblos removing the steering oar, for in ancient times that was a usual method for putting a stay upon a ship.

lord. For Solomon there were many incentives to multiply his own trade treaties. One incentive (as with Egypt) was a matter of security; others were a matter of obtaining produce from near and far. It was a customary method with Solomon to accept a new wife with a new treaty. At the height of Solomon's renown, for wealth (for which he drew on Hiram) and for the extravagance and ostentation (for which we must believe he had a natural gift), it is possible that a Queen of Sheba might visit him merely as a mare goes to a notable stud; but the most of Solomon's wives are viewed as representing so many treaties, each bringing trade or protection.

There were dangers to Israel in Solomon's diplomacy. One, as Daniel-Rops suggests, is that he was forced to become 'too fond of building'. If a new wife called for a new house and garden (or call it a palace) with a new shrine or temple representative of her own tradition – if she had to have a retinue of her own followers and priests – that called for barter; and more barter called for more trade treaties, more wives. The number of Solomon's queens in Jerusalem and their rivalries in fashion altered the conception of a city wholly and simply devoted to the service of Yahveh into a cosmopolitan city in which those Jews who remained faithful to the strict law of Moses had perforce to tolerate strange gods. Hence we see the people becoming bitterly divided. In Jerusalem, the Holy City, it was a special outrage to see altars, built by the King himself, for 'Ashtoreth the abomination of the Sidonians, and for Chemosh the abomination of the Moabites, and for Milcom the abomination of the children of Ammon' (2 *Kings*, xxiii, 13). As Solomon's reign went on, Daniel-Rops points out that 'it was no longer even a matter of the local *Baals* of the Canaanites . . . but of foreign deities, carried in by every tide of fashion'.

Did Solomon think that the more pious of his people could be placated by building one great Temple, greater than any other in Jerusalem, to the one and only Most High? Many merchants of Jerusalem may have been momentarily alarmed. They were not discontented with the profits of going to and from Tyre and bringing back the latest fashions. Any alarm was momentary: the greatest-of-all Temple was to be additional, the other temples would remain. There would be no down-grading for the queens in their palaces and for the hangers-on about the royal courts. Many contractors may have been pleased by the size of the additional project. Hiram, as banker, was perhaps most pleased of any. For the building of the Temple, Solomon had once more to go to Hiram. A new treaty was arranged. Hiram was to provide the architects and skilled craftsmen and was to furnish the precious metals and precious woods. The construction of the actual Temple of Yahveh was apparently to be in the hands of unbelievers. By the treaty with Hiram, Solomon was to provide Tyre with quantities of corn, barley, wines and oil – particularly oil. The oil of olives gathered from the tree, not fallen, was specified.*

The Temple itself was to be small – not more than ten or eleven yards in width by forty yards in length – no larger than many a modest modern chapel. But the Temple was to be sumptuous in all its appointments, and it was to gain in dignity by being the sacred centre of an enormously impressive surround. The size of the surround required prodigious labour: a rocky hill had to be hewn, levelled and squared; a supporting wall halfway up the slope was to make it possible to increase the size of the artificial platform on the summit; the hewn stones for the supporting wall were to be cemented together with lead. This was later to become known as the Wailing Wall.

We are told that in Solomon's time, on the wall and on the rest of the workings, there were employed a hundred and fifty thousand labourers, under the direction of three thousand six hundred overseers. While the surround was under construction, for the building of the Temple itself and for its flooring and panelling Hiram was gathering the finest woods wherever available – sandalwood, cedar and cypress. Everything within the Temple was to be of the richest. The curtain which screened the Holy of Holies was to be of immaculate white linen from Egypt, embroidered with purple, violet and gold. In the most secret and sacred part behind the curtain the Ark of the Covenant was forever to reside, in silence and in the protection of total darkness.

Outside the small and precious Temple everything in the spacious forecourts was to be on the largest possible scale. The Altar of Burnt Offerings was to be tended with a perpetual fire; the Sea of Brass, resting on four groups each of three bronze oxen, was to be the

* I rely entirely upon Daniel-Rops for details of Solomon's diplomacy and for the building of the Temple.

immense reservoir of water for the sacrifices. Before the gateway to the inner precincts were to stand twin columns of bronze each about ten yards high. Each of these bronze columns was to bear a name. The name of the one column was to signify *Stability*; the name of the other, *Power*.

The work upon the Temple and its surroundings was completed as planned, in rather more than seven years. Now was Jerusalem, with Temple and shrines and palaces, houses and towers faced with ivory and silver, with shade trees and gardens, a showplace and symbol to be seen afar. If not to every man his idea of a City of God, none was likely to deny it was a City of Glory.

In a world where there might be evilly-intentioned and envious eyes, there was danger to the shining city on the hill-top. If any of the Great Kings of the East should choose to look in the direction of Jerusalem, by the end of Solomon's reign it was a plum ripe for the picking. Perhaps the wisdom of Solomon might turn out to be un-wisdom for Hiram also, for the wealth of the one had made possible the ostentation of the other; if the city on the hill were to attract attention from Assyria, the seaport of Tyre might have even prior visitation. Tyre, as a seaport, had one advantage over Jerusalem if any eastern army should come that way. The treasury and citadel and main city of Tyre were on a convenient island, off-shore, and well-nigh impregnable. There was no approach to Tyre except by boat. If the worst ever came to the worst, Tyre, or some part of it, could take ship and flee. If the worst ever came to the worst for Jerusalem, no flight was possible.

The story of ancient Israel is so familiar that it can do little harm for a faraway note-maker to pick out and emphasize this or that detail to suit his purpose. My purpose is to examine a westward movement of mankind, and what I have been emphasizing is that Solomon made the city of Jerusalem a tempting bait to whatever war-lord, Assyrian, Chaldean, Babylonian, chose to notice it. If a really formidable conqueror were to be attracted to that part of the world, the question immediately pertinent to my purpose is: what was to be the behaviour of Tyre? Here I am in more difficulty, for the drama of the Phoe-nicians is less familiar than the drama of Israel. But I must not let the loud enduring lamentations of Israel prevent me from learning about her enigmatic and less vocal coastal neighbours. For this is the thesis: it was at the time of the same gathering storm which was going to obliterate Jerusalem, that the weather-wise Pygmalion, King of Tyre roundabout the year 814 B.C., said in effect to his sister Dido, 'Go West, young woman' – a move of much importance to our story.

NOTES

1. For the history of wine-making from the earliest times I refer to *Gods, Men and Wine* by William Younger (The Wine and Food Society, London, 1966).
2. *Ancilla to Classical Reading* by Moses Hadas (Columbia University Press, New York, 1954).
3. I owe the shell-heaps of the Damariscotta to *The Discovery of America* by Professor John Fiske (Houghton Mifflin, Boston, 1892).
4. *From an Antique Land* by Julian Huxley (Max Parrish, London, 1954).
5. 'I once spent 3 days trying to beat up to Gibraltar under sail from Almeira Bay' – Ernle Bradford (see Note 10, Ch. 4). For Nelson and Gibraltar, see *Nelson the Sailor* by Captain Russell Grenfell, R.N. (Faber, London, 1949).
6. *Daily Life in Carthage* by Gilbert and Colette Charles-Picard, translated by A. E. Foster (Macmillan, New York, 1961).

CHAPTER 4

Go West, Young Woman

IT was a dramatic moment, in the year 814 B.C. (or thenabouts), when a small fleet set out westward from the quay at Tyre. A summer evening is pictured, when oil lamps were already winking in windows of the town and the stars, which are friends of navigators, were coming out. A gentle and favouring breeze is suggested, for every good omen was needed. The ships held precious cargo.

To picture the sailing at twilight is not fanciful. In ancient days it was a usual sailing time. At the conclusion of a charming idyll in Philostratus[1], Apollonius says to his companion: 'It is now eventide, and about the time of the lighting up of the lamps, and I must set out for the port of Rome, for this is the usual hour at which these ships sail.' The date of Apollonius is about nine centuries later than the date of Dido; no matter, Philostratus makes out that in a previous incarnation Apollonius had been a shipmaster, and he (and Dido's captains also) were obeying very ancient custom.

The more important matter is to recognize the importance of the cargo. The picture is that Pygmalion was sending Dido westward to set up a new city far away on the coast of Africa, close to the trading-post of Utica, which had been established by the Phoenicians three centuries before. The name of the city was to be Kart Hadasht, Carthage, or 'new town'. There is a view that Carthage was 'new' because the trading-post of Utica was so much older.[2] My impression is that Carthage was 'new' in relation to Tyre itself. I do not think Carthage was to be just another trading-post, or a mere colony. I think Carthage was intended to be an actual other half of Tyre; that Tyre, as if by a biological fission, was setting herself up anew, with her old gods, in a new world. The departure of Dido symbolizes not a simple trading expedition but a dramatic effort to preserve the life of Tyre. Tyre as an entity was otherwise destroyed, unless Tyre could set herself up again, new town, new Tyre, with Dido as Queen. It was a vital operation, and one that seems extraordinarily imaginative. In a time of troubles, it is as if Phoenicians said to themselves, why not divide our city, and so shall we be preserved – there is no hindrance – only fifteen hundred miles of open sea separates the old town from the new.

How am I to interpret the Phoenician, and above all his apparently supreme confidence in navigation, whereby the Mediterranean Far West was to him familiar, and the fifteen hundred miles between Tyre and Carthage seemed no hindrance to communication?

The immediate problem is that Phoenicians have left us scarcely a shred of literature about themselves. Hebrews, Greeks, Romans, were plentifully vocal; their characters displayed in their own voices. The Phoenician is almost wholly enigmatic. *Tacuit et fecit*: he unquestionably did things, but he was silent about it. His name is writ in water.

Professor Edward Hallett Carr in his book *What is History?* quotes with enjoyment Catherine Morland's remark about history: 'I often think it odd that it should be so dull, for a great deal of it must be invention' (*Northanger Abbey*, Ch. xiv). Certainly any estimate of the Phoenicians has to be coloured by invention, and with them particularly it behoves anybody to go slow about moulding facts to interpretation and interpretation to facts; which, says Professor Carr, is a proper occupation for the historian. Of 'facts' and of 'interpretation' it is 'impossible to assign primacy to one over the other'.[3] Where it is hard to find agreement about facts, interpretation must be doubly cautious.

But with that caution, I shall begin with Dido. Was Dido an actual identifiable flesh and blood woman, sister of Pygmalion, sent westwards as I have pictured it to become Queen of Carthage, Carthage the other half of Tyre? – or is the Dido story mainly an invention? One would think the story to have been moulded by invention; but that the purpose of the invention was to express an actuality, a real historical event, more concisely and directly by the story than in any other way. Invention is not to be dismissed as 'mere' invention. Flesh and blood women made the voyage from Tyre to Carthage, and Dido is no less flesh and blood if she became also a legendary symbol.

In the Old Testament we see the ladies of Tyre more clearly than the men. There was a Dido (and usually identified as the Dido we are speaking of) who was a great-niece of Jezebel; of a line, that is to say, of distinctively proud princesses.

It was after Solomon's death that the preachers really railed against his example. 'Thou didst bow thy loins unto women, and by the body thou was brought into subjection; thou didst stain thy honour, and pollute thy seed: so that thou broughtest wrath upon thy children, and wast grieved for thy folly' (*Ecclesiasticus*, xlvii, 19). After Solomon's death the kingdom fell apart: Israel in the north with a king of its own in another royal hill-top city, Samaria; and Judah, with Jerusalem, the southern kingdom. The division did not put an end to ostentatious rivalries. What I attend to here is that both Israel and Judah continued to look upon the princesses of Tyre for their queens.

Impartially against the court life of Jerusalem and of Samaria were the fulminations of the prophets, mostly Hebrews of old nomad habits. Daniel-Rops catalogues their performances. He stresses how townsmen saw the prophets 'come and go, clad in a terrible picturesqueness, dressed in the skins of animals, or goats' hair mantles, living in the most extreme simplicity. They respected no worldly convention. The ladies of the court, painted and perfumed, Amos called "cows of Bashan", as a beggar might have called them "bitches". Ezekiel prophesied to them that they would before long be raped. Jeremiah, predicting the Chaldean domination, walked in the streets harnessed like an ass. Isaiah went naked to show what the condition of Israel was to be in the days of wrath'. In this catalogue Daniel-Rops is skipping around with his dates, I would think purposely, to emphasize the capricious yet frequent appearances of the prophets among the city-folk.[4]

Elijah in his goatskins provides the bitterest of the denunciations of a princess of Tyre. It was not altogether Jezebel's 'cortege of idols', and not only the crime of Naboth's vineyard, which made Elijah foretell that the dogs of the street would tear apart her body and feast upon the pieces. Fully as much, it was the feminine snares to which she was accustomed – her vials of perfume, pots of rouge, combs of ivory. Yet a point well noted by Daniel-Rops is that when the time eventually came for Jezebel to meet her predicted doom, she met it with dignity. She was true to her Tyrian standards. Hearing the news of Jehu's arrival, this woman of fashion, no longer young, kept him waiting until she had 'painted her face, and tired her head'. Only then, when properly made up, did Jezebel go to the window to greet her murderer. 'Throw her down', commanded Jehu, and she was thrown down. Jehu was the king who later made obeisance to the Assyrian. Of the two, it is the spirit of Jezebel which is remembered.

Racine, in his drama, makes out with sympathy that Jezebel's spirit survived in her daughter Athaliah. Athaliah was the princess sought for and married by Joram, King of Judah. If Dido represents the same proud line of Tyrian princesses, the statement is supported, that the departure of the ships for Carthage meant something much more complex than the departure of an ordinary trading expedition. It meant departure and transplantation of top people and of the best that they could take with them.

Tyre was dividing herself, but for what cause? Tyre would hardly split into two distant parts without strong reason. The Hebrew prophets tell of the Assyrian menace. Loudly enough, they were ringing an alarm. But the Hebrew prophets were thinking only of their own nation and of its destiny. If God would be using the Assyrians as a rod to chastise the Jewish cities, then presumably Phoenician cities (Tyre, Sidon, Byblos, Aradus) would likewise suffer. The Bible told me nothing about them. In the Bible story there was an awkward time-gap. The Assyrian menace did not seem to manifest itself in brutal actuality upon the Jews until long after 814 B.C. – long after the presumed date of Pygmalion. The time-gap in the Bible story between the predictions of the prophets and the appearance of hostile forces from the East puzzled me very much. I could hardly believe that Pygmalion was so remarkably perceptive as to divide his city in advance of necessity. The departure of Dido represented itself to me as such an upheaval in the affairs of Tyre as to imply some instant and immediate cause, some actual happening that was more precise than I could gather from the forebodings of the Hebrew prophets.

Mr. Donald Harden,[5] with greater wit and competence than I, at once resolved the puzzle of the time-gap. While I was musing over the Biblical story, Mr. Harden went straight to the Assyrians. It is in the Assyrian records that the evidence stands out, as to what was happening to the Phoenicians. Mr. Harden made it clear that before the time of Pygmalion 'the Assyrian menace had arrived', and had arrived with violence, at Tyre:

> In 876 Assurnasirpal, as we learn from his own inscriptions, took tribute from Tyre, Sidon, Byblos and Aradus, among other places – including silver, gold, fine polychrome cloths and ivory. In the next reign (Shalmaneser III, 858—825) we hear of further tribute from Phoenician cities and a defeat of the king of Aradus in battle. The gates of Balawat and the Black Obelisk, both monuments of this king, now in the British Museum, illustrate this. On the former, Phoenician ships bring tribute from Tyre to the mainland, and on the latter many kings of the Levant, including Jehu of Israel, do obeisance before the Assyrian monarch.

Here was the imperative for Tyre to save herself in any way she could. As we look ahead in the Biblical story, we see that Jehu's obeisance was not going to save Samaria. Samaria was razed by the Assyrians in 722 B.C. The armies of Sennacherib were then on their way to Egypt; they by-passed Jerusalem; perhaps their plan was to loot it on the way back. But in the marshes of the Delta pestilence broke the Assyrians. Egypt rejoiced and Judah rejoiced and for nearly a hundred and fifty years there was reprieve for Jerusalem. Then, for many of the Jews, came the apparent end of everything. Nebuchadnezzar was more to be feared than Sennacherib. Judah's self-confidence was unavailing: Jerusalem was sacked, the Temple despoiled, the twin pillars of *Stability* and *Power* scornfully removed. There was the forced march of a captive people to Babylon. An independent Hebrew nation ceased to exist. The city, at one time projected as a visible City of God, was erased.

Tyre was not physically erased by the Assyrians, Chaldeans, Babylonians. Part of Tyre had gone overseas. Tyrian leaders at home became fairly successful collaborators with a succession of Eastern Great Kings. Tyrian and Sidonian seamen were useful to the Persians; as seamen for the Persians they were hated by the Greeks. The island citadel of Tyre was not occupied by any outsider, so far as I could find, before Alexander the Great. Alexander took the island, Arrian says, because he could not occupy Egypt so long as Persian allies commanded the sea.[6] According to Arrian it took Alexander's forces seven months to conquer Tyre; most of the time taken up by construction of the permanent siege-mole from the mainland to the island. When the mole had been built, Tyre was destroyed 'in the archonship at Athens of Anicetus in the month Hecatombaean'. Hecatombaean corresponds nearly to our July, and the year was 332 B.C. That was five centuries after Dido's voyage to Carthage, which to me represents a most remarkable exertion whereby a city tried to save its life.

I take the story of Dido as to some extent symbolic: the purpose being to express the spirit of the effort. Ours is an age in which historians are ill at ease with personifications. There is a tendency to debunk Dido. I would rather try to see why Virgil accepted the story, and what meanings he put into it. Roman Virgil, singing his story of the road west:

> *Ilion falling, Rome arising,*
> *wars, and filial faith, and Dido's pyre*

does not overtly speak of the Assyrian menace to Tyre, which seemed to me such a compulsive cause for Tyre to divide herself and build her other half in Carthage. Virgil, on the face of it, makes out that a sufficient reason for Dido's voyage was a family quarrel. Pygmalion, in Virgil's version, is the grasping tyrant who (and to make it worse, 'before the altars') murders Sychaeus, richest of the Phoenicians in land, regardless of the fact that he is Dido's husband and that Dido loves him. The ghost of Sychaeus, 'unveiling all the secret horror of the house', bids Dido to flee from Tyre, taking old-time treasures with her. Dido assembles all who hate or fear the tyrant. Ships, which by chance were ready, are seized; the wealth of grasping Pygmalion is borne overseas; the leader of this work a woman (*dux femina facti*).

That is Virgil's version of the story; or rather, the version which Virgil makes Venus regard as sufficient for Aeneas to hear; and even Venus, with her particular incentive for arousing interest in Dido, admits it is not the whole story – 'long would be the tale of wrong, long its winding course . . .'. But what is it, if we wish to translate it more cumbersomely into other terms, that Virgil is compactly saying about Tyre? That in a time of monstrous outside pressure the City is in dissension, and the High Command dictates that everything that is of greatest value is subordinated and debased – time-honoured treasures, customs, religion (for Sychaeus was priest, some say High Priest, of Melkarth) – all must yield to the threat. All that spelled the life of Tyre is vanishing; the blood and the spirit is spilled, but the story says that Tyre can live, reborn through its women. Woman, eternal mother of the race, is symbol of the Exodus from Tyre; in this particular desperation of humanity, the leading symbol; all of which, and more, is I think better said and more closely packed in the three words that Virgil emphasizes: *dux femina facti*. The story as Virgil tells it is deeper and more human than my prettified version of a weather-wise ruler of Tyre jauntily saying to his sister, 'Go West, Young Woman'. Virgil's version is more respectful to specifically human valuations than my metaphor that Tyre was trying to save itself by biological fission. The story makes me eager to get on to Carthage, to see what new life is to be born to the Phoenicians.

It is all very well to wish to hurry on, but any serious contemplation of migration along the long road west involves, it seems to me, the physical transportation. Whatever the company of men and women that departed from Tyre to Carthage, departure for some of them must have been a tearing moment. Of those who watched the ships depart, some must have feared the moment as impious: Easterners turning from the sunrise. Others who sailed must have had faith in the stars if they could say: the east is dark, but westward look. Yet the ship-exodus from Tyre should not be dramatized unless it really happened. It could not happen without ships. The ships by chance were ready, says Virgil; *navis, quae forte paratae*. I am curious about the ships.

I pondered on the description of the ships of Tyre as given in *Ezekiel* XXVII:

5. They have made all thy ship boards of fir trees of Senit: they have taken cedars from Lebanon to make masts for thee.

6. Of the oaks of Bashan have they made thine oars; the company of the Ashurites have made thy benches of ivory, brought out of the isles of Chittim.

7. Fine linen with broidered work from Egypt was that which thou spreadeth forth to be thy sail; blue and purple from the isles of Elishah was that which covered thee.

8. The inhabitants of Zidon and Arvad were thy mariners: thy wise men, O Tyrus, that were in thee, were thy pilots.

The description is poetic, by a poet who very likely never sailed the sea, and in the interpretation the uncertainties of translation must also be borne in mind. The effect is somewhat that of being shown a stately barge, into which a princess, with her pots and vials, might be escorted for a pleasure cruise. But unless the description is dismissed altogether, there is a distinct impression of pride in the ships as ships. In the ranging for the best materials for ship construction and in the care displayed for the best furnishing there is a feeling for ships transcending anything that I find in early Greek writers.

A famous impression of the Tyrian trader is given by Matthew Arnold at the conclusion of *The Scholar-Gypsy*:

> *– As some grave Tyrian trader, from the sea,*
> *Descried at sunrise an emerging prow*
> *Lifting the cool-hair'd creepers stealthily,*
> *The fringes of a southward-facing brow*
> *Among the Ægean isles;*
> *And saw the merry Grecian coaster come,*
> *Freighted with amber grapes, and Chian wine,*
> *Green, bursting figs, and tunnies steep'd in brine –*
> *And knew the intruders on his ancient home,*
>
> *The young light-hearted masters of the waves –*
> *And snatch'd his rudder, and shook out more sail,*
> *And day and night held on indignantly*
> *O'er the blue Midland waters with the gale,*
> *Betwixt the Syrtes and soft Sicily,*
> *To where the Atlantic raves*
> *Outside the western straits; and unbent sails*
> *There, where down cloudy cliffs, through sheets of foam,*
> *Shy traffickers, the dark Iberians come;*
> *And on the beach undid his corded bales.*

A comment on this beautiful apostrophe is that Arnold, without bothering too much about the ship herself, superbly conveys the Phoenician's pride in what he alone could do with a ship in the way of long-distance sailing.

But both impressions, as regards the ships and as regards the men who are credited with such a special gift for navigation, call for further pondering.

Hesiod (contemporary with Homer) talks about large ships and small, as it were warning us not to regard Homer's black ships or war galleys as the only kind of ship in his time. As soon as any people took to sea-faring it is obvious to suppose a wish to build long-distance carriers as well as harbour-craft. The only wreck of a craft reasonably identified as early Phoenician (so far as I know) is the wreck investigated by Peter Throckmorton in 1958 at Gelidonya on the Turkish coast.[7] This was a boat about 24 feet long with a cargo of copper and tin ingots; perhaps a coastal trader? The reproductions given by Mr. Harden of Phoenician 'ships' carrying tribute from Tyre's island to the mainland are of small harbour-craft, schematically drawn. I need hardly worry about the existence of Phoenician boats, harbour-craft, coastal craft. It is the large ships hinted at by Hesiod in early times that puzzle everybody. How large? It is worth recalling Hesiod's words. 'If desire for uncomfortable sea-faring seize you' – Hesiod is supposed to be advising his brother – 'if ever you turn your misguided heart to trading', I, who 'have no skill in seafaring nor in ships', can tell you this: 'Admire a small ship, but put your freight in a large one; for the greater the lading, the greater will be your piled gain, if only the winds will keep back their harmful gales.'[8] This is very vague. How large, and decked or undecked, were the ships which Virgil says 'by chance were ready' to take a first expedition from Tyre to Carthage?

There is a wild suggestion that the size of Solomon's Temple might indicate proportions to which Phoenician shipwrights were accustomed to build. I should have wholly dismissed the random thought except for the oddity that as dimensions, the dimensions of the Temple accepted by Daniel-Rops are not far off the measure of the 'round' ship of which the under-water wreckage was examined for five years in the 1950s by Captain Cousteau and his team in the *Calypso*.[9] The wooden building of the Temple was supposedly in the neighbourhood of a length of a hundred and twenty feet and a width of thirty feet or so. The wreckage of the ship found by Cousteau on a deeply submerged ledge of a rock pinnacle known as Grand Congloué, ten sea-miles from Marseilles, indicated that the vessel had been roughly ninety-three feet long, with a beam of twenty-seven feet. The wreck which Cousteau found was dated from the third century B.C., which is a long time later than the early Phoenician period. Nevertheless 'Cousteau's ship' or (from the name of her owner at the moment of her catastrophe), the 'ship of Markos Sestios', may be taken to have been an average cargo-ship of fairly early Mediterranean times; and each must argue backwards as best he can, whether a ship of her size and style represents much earlier customs of shipbuilding.

Details recorded by Cousteau of the ship of Markos Sestios make me wonder which were relatively new-fangled, or which represented old (and perhaps very old) traditions:

> Wooden elements of the wreck made us admire the virtuosity of the shipwrights. They applied differing woods to various structural demands and to intricate dowels and joints. Planking, sheathing, keel and main timbers, knees, ribs and dowels were an interplay of Aleppo pine, Lebanon cedar, and oak . . .
>
> On the starboard side of the main-deck we uncovered leaden sheets, large intact expanses of the shrivelled scraps we had found earlier. This hull sheathing was possibly torn off as the sinking ship scraped the rock. The copper rivets in the sheathing were capped with lead, showing that the ancients understood how to prevent the corrosive action of different metals touching each other in the salty medium.
>
> Other finds added information about the old seamen. We found a heavy marble mortar, a long piece of slate, a thick tile plate, an oar counter-weight, a small earthenware stove, an iron axe, and stout crockery. . . . As we had guessed earlier, this was the stern section of the ship, for ancient crews cooked and ate on the fantail. Here we found a drinking mug. Scratched on the side in crude Greek letters was the legend, 'To your health'. . .

The mention of 'decks', in the wreckage that Cousteau found, caught my attention. That it was common practice, a couple of centuries earlier than the ship of Markos Sestios, for some of the Greek merchant ships to have a solid deck is possibly illustrated by the murder-trial at Athens caused by the disappearance of Herodes.* The

* The trial at Athens for the murder of Herodes took place about 415 B.C. Herodes was a well-to-do Athenian who embarked with companions at Mytilene for passage to the Thracian coast. Bad weather forced the ship that

57

first meaning of the word 'deck' (in the nautical sense) is 'roof' rather than 'floor'; this was so when peoples of northern Europe began to re-invent ships as long-distance carriers, and it is likely that functional developments in 'our' early shipbuilding to some extent mirror earlier developments in the Mediterranean. In our transition from working with open boats to working with decked ships, a temporary covering, tarpaulin or the equivalent, preceded wooden decks that could be walked on. In our ships a solid deck first developed at the stern: English writers of the sixteenth century continue to use *deck* as equivalent to *poop*.* It seems not unlikely, then, that some of the early Phoenician ships had a solid half-deck at the stern, with the waist of the ship open, or protected by temporary coverings.

The coverings at the waist of the ship are suggested by the passage in *Ezekiel*. The coloured covers of 'blue and purple from the isles of Elishah' are vivid to the eye, conveying more gaiety, more love for appearance, than we feel in the North-European usages of tarpaulin; more colour also than is suggested by the 'black ships' of Homer.

---

he was in to run for a bay before leaving the island of Lesbos. In that bay it happened that another ship was already sheltering. Herodes and some of his companions transferred to the other ship with the intention of having a convivial evening. This part of the evidence appears to have been accepted at the trial without question. The intention was natural enough, and so was the reason for the exchange. 'The boat on which we were passengers had no deck, whereas that on which we transhipped had one; and the rain was the reason for the exchange'. It was taken for granted at the trial that there was room enough below deck, in the second ship, for a number to share in a drinking party. But the number is not specified, so there is no estimate of the cubic space below deck; nor is there absolute proof that the deck was solid wood, for the Greek for 'the deck of a ship' is στέγη (taken over in Latin as *stega*), meaning *roof*, whether solid or not. Whatever happened at or after the party was not proved either. It was said that by nightfall Herodes had drunk too much and asserted that he was going ashore; but nothing is certain except that after the party 'below deck' Athens never saw him again. The trial is recorded in the first volume of *Minor Attic Orators*, translated by K. J. Maidment (Loeb Classical Library, 1941).

* It would seem not unnatural for shipmen to think about a half-deck forward just about as early as to think of a half-deck aft, but the Oxford English Dictionary falls rather heavily on Elyot for permitting the word *deck*, in 1538, to be made 'erroneously' an equivalent of *prora*, instead of *puppis*.

There is a factor here to be kept in mind, in forming an estimate of Phoenician character. I think that presently we may be forced to accept that later Phoenician culture, or Carthaginian culture, became predominantly utilitarian; and yet there is an impression, tenuous perhaps, of the peculiar, extra and special feeling that Phoenicians had about ships. It is curious that as regards ships the Greeks, throughout classical times, seem relatively utilitarian; a ship is an implement and nothing more. But there does seem to be something special, perhaps only to be expressed by exaggeration, in the Phoenician feeling for ships. Adornment suggests adoration. It would horrify philologists to say that the phrase 'to deck a ship' could have the same meaning as the phrase 'to deck a woman'; but the confusion is suggested to me by Ezekiel. Possibly an Eastern feeling that the deck of a ship should itself be decorative or decorated persisted in that galley noticed at the Battle of Lepanto whose deck was 'chequered and wroughte marvellous fayre with diuers colours and hystories . . . ingraued and wrought in golde'.* I must not be carried too far by Ezekiel's blue and purple covers. I am led to believe Phoenicians found a special beauty in their ships; but I don't believe they prettified them so much as not to be able to use them. It is the Phoenician use of ships which leads to a next exaggeration.

Ezekiel led to thinking about the ships; Matthew Arnold led to thinking of the men who used them; I must see to the full what I am demanded to believe about the mariners.

If I accept the exodus from Tyre to Carthage more or less as described, I am forced to credit the sea-worthiness of Phoenician ships, and I am forced to accept a confidence in deep-sea sailing and an experience of pressing boldly westward, established *before* the date of the exodus. Objection is: Greek seamanship as described by Homer in the *Odyssey* is in no way adequate to such a demand. I subscribe to the school well represented nowadays by Ernle Bradford, that the *Odyssey* is not in the least to be regarded as wholly a fairy-tale, and that much of Ulysses' voyagings may be traced by a man experienced in small boat work.[10] In the *Odyssey* there is often a glint or glance of mysterious other people who in a more competent

* The Oxford English Dictionary provides the reference to J. Polmon (*c.* 1585?), *Famous Battles*, 320 (Battle of Lepanto).

way had been getting around the western seas before Ulysses. It is not to be disrespectful to the hair-raising and haphazard adventures of Ulysses to think of these other mariners as more competent, but it is a jump to specify them as Phoenicians, and to specify that Phoenician competence was even then enabling them to reach Spain, and return, with regularity. That jump is demanded by my line of thought.

I can state the demand more outrageously. Spain, Hispania, the very name (according to one school of thought) is Phoenician. There is of course another school which denies this, but Virginia Woolf, inclining to the first school, toys very pleasingly with the idea that as *span* in the Phoenician tongue signified the animal that we call rabbit, when the grave Tyrian trader landed in Spain his common seamen with one accord shouted 'Span! Span!' – for rabbits darted from every scrub, from every bush. The land was alive with them. And, says Virginia Woolf, 'where there are rabbits, Providence has ordained there shall be dogs'. So the dogs, almost as instantly to be perceived in full pursuit of the rabbits, were called Spaniels, or rabbit dogs. This train of thought, so gracefully pursued by Virginia Woolf, I have of course exaggerated; even as given by her* it is contested by scholars who have less than her imagination. But in the first place it pleased me to consider that when, after long voyaging, Phoenician seamen landed in Spain they had fresh meat to think of before they uncorded their bales to trade for metals, and in the second place the fancy seemed to be a way of pointing up what I am forced to believe. I can hardly credit the exodus from Tyre to Carthage unless before that time Phoenicians were familiar with the west, and the rabbit story makes me see the full extent of what I have to believe, or explain, if I can. The parable says forcibly that Spain to the Phoenician was just about as reachable as, to the New Yorker of my youth, was Coney Island. It says without equivocation that what time Ulysses was drifting around on his raft from Calypso's island, Phoenicians were already calling Spain their Rabbit Land, their Coney Island.

* In *Flush*, a Biography, by Virginia Woolf (Harcourt, Brace, New York, 1933), p. 11 ff. Mrs. Woolf was there talking about Carthaginian soldiery in Spain and my exaggeration resides in transferring the picture to much earlier times and changing the soldiery into Phoenician seamen. In George Borrow's *The Bible in Spain* (Ch. II) there is a footnote reference to the rabbits and the possible derivation of the name *Hispania* from the Phoenician word for them.

Exaggeration? Yes, to make me face the question, what do we know about early Phoenicians to make it credible that they reached Spain?

The progenitors of the Phoenicians of Tyre must have been landsmen, and I am pushed to the opinion that in the beginning they were a 'carrier people', caravan people; I am pushed to the belief that they learned their navigation on dry land.

The belief that 'navigation' began with the guidance for ships of the desert before the science was further developed for guidance of ships at sea, is a belief which I accept. It is true that there are unbelievers. One authority on the history of sea-faring starts by distinguishing mariners from landsmen:

> The traveller by land, when at a loss for his way, has only to ask some passer-by which road or track to take.

Exaggeration, to emphasize a point, is a device which I have just been indulging; it would ill become me to dispute this remark merely because of the exaggeration; the question is, does one believe the distinction that is being emphasized? True, that in the land-area of which I am thinking, Flinders Petrie pointed out that the early cities of Mesopotamia, as also the early nome capitals of the Delta, were on the average some twenty miles apart: a day's march. A dotted line of friendly towns, offering easy stages of transport, with stores of grain and possible renewal of pack-animals, is an idyllic picture for carriers by caravan. Mumford comments: 'The very closeness of these early towns may well indicate, at the time of their foundation, a state of security and peace not attested by later records of strife and war.'[11] One begins to think then that hostilities could force long-distance carriers to detour from beaten tracks; one sees the safety of a caravan often depending on the ability of its leader to avoid observation and ambush. The Fertile Crescent could hardly be navigated by hugging the range of foot-hills to the north if that meant camping too close to valleys of assassins. It might have been safer to navigate from Baghdad to Damascus by striking out into four hundred miles of trackless desert – if in the trackless desert you could find your way, and find water-holes for the twenty or twenty-five or more days of travel.

It is somewhere along the land-bridge between Mesopotamia and

Egypt that the tribes are first noticed, whose descendants became the Phoenicians of the Lebanon. It is plausible that in that area there was special need for expertise in desert travel. In that area much credence is given to the early works of Babylonian astronomers. Their work is spoken of as priestcraft, but I find it hard to believe that every scrap of ancient craftiness was priestcraft only. If Babylonian magi are exalted, as they seem to be, for exploitation of star-knowledge, did none of the gifts of the magi leak out to those whose great concern was travel?* I don't prolong this part of the discussion; the prime import-ance of using and trusting the stars – the use of the stars by landsmen in this part of the world – is to me sufficiently symbolized in the legend of the Star of Bethlehem. What I could somewhat dwell on as very relevant to my purpose is the relative hardship of desert travel and sea travel; for the case that I wish to make is that a people who had been land-carriers could readily, and indeed joyously, turn to sea-work by preference. If you contrast the slowness, the tedium, the effort and the dangers of caravan work† with the imagined ease of sea-faring

* It would not take a great amount of astronomical expertise for a caravan leader to follow a line of latitude, say from Baghdad to Damascus and back again, provided stars were visible. Without instruments and chronometers to which we have become accustomed, it is hard to see how any early travellers could fix a position precisely; but that problem is exactly the same on sea or land. In deserts where sandstorms could completely alter landmarks, direction-finding has to be granted to those aboriginal skills now largely lost to city-folk. Guidance to be derived from birds and animals is hinted at in plenty of stories, recent or ancient. One thinks with pleasure of the serpents which, according to Ptolemy the son of Lagus, served Alexander's army as guides in the same desert where the sandstorm had destroyed Cambyses; or, as Arrian and Plutarch preferred to say, those guides for Alexander were ravens. (See the Loeb Edition of Plutarch's *Lives*, translated by Bernadotte Perrin, Vol VII, *Alexander*, p. 303, n. 2). But credit to other skills or for-tuitous aids does not diminish the primary importance of the stars.

† Gibbon, in his famous digression about the silk-trade, says 'the caravans traversed the whole latitude of Asia in two hundred and forty-three days from the Chinese ocean to the sea-coast of Syria'. At the western end of that land-navigation there had to be traversed a succession of deserts described at the present day (by an unnamed correspondent in *The Times*, London, September 22, 1962) as 'sheer, glinting rock, gravel, and blazing sand, all afloat in a shimmering, upward-curving sea'. The time allowed by Gibbon for the silk caravans – 243 days – is precise, but makes one wonder how many miles from where to where, at what average speed. What traction for the pack-loads?

you have a powerful recruiting slogan for the sea. You have the incentive, as in that marvellous scene in Xenophon,[12] after the ten thousand Greeks had made their march and reached the Euxine Sea, and the first man to speak up spoke as follows:

'Well, I, for my part, gentlemen,' he said, 'am tired by this time of packing up and walking and running and carrying my arms and being in

---

Camels? I am told that nowadays in a terrain which suits its feet a loaded camel seldom exceeds a speed of $2\frac{1}{2}$ miles an hour (see for instance *The Nile Tributaries of Abyssinia* by Sir Samuel Baker). Pack-horses? I am told from recent experience (*The Wanderer's Guide* by Anthony Stewart) that in suitable terrain where grass is plentiful a good horse should be counted on to take you and your personal gear 25–30 miles a day, and a pack horse (if properly shod and not lamed) will follow; but to keep in condition a horse should be rested not less than one day in seven. The journeys of the silk-caravans in the time of Justinian (5th century A.D.) must have been hard on men and beasts. Not everybody, surely, would willingly become a carrier. But there must have been more attraction to some than to others in the carrier life, and consequently pride, reputation and rivalry in the making of difficult journeys. The 'carrier people' of the silk-trade caravans are shadowy, although so near in time as the 5th century A.D. Shadowy indeed are the much earlier carriers on the land-bridge between Mesopotamia and Egypt. Sometimes there are relevant glimpses in the mirror of the present. Miss Freya Stark (in *The Valleys of the Assassins*) writes of a night of sand-storm in Arabia; it was a night, for her, of solitude and darkness in a mud-walled cubicle:
'In the very early morning I looked out, and saw what appeared to be three little mounds of reddish earth lying in front of my hut. These, in the strengthening light, resolved themselves into the sleeping forms of my retainers, obliterated under desert sand. In the fullness of time they stirred, crawled as from a chrysalis, shook out their turbans, and were ready for tea . . .'
Some animals have more anatomical defences than men against sand-burial: the horned toad has a looped nasal passage which serves to keep sand out of the lungs, and the camel has muscles to close the nostrils (see *Dinosaurs* by Edwin H. Colbert). Wild animals are not manifested as a frightful hazard to early desert travel in the Near East, though the lions so frequently represented in Hittite and Assyrian sculpture can hardly be entirely fanciful. In recent times wolves are sometimes mentioned; the cheetah is mentioned more often. To early Hebrews, when they went on desert journeys, snakes were a worry: there is much mention of them in the Talmud – but the mention is sometimes to make fun. In *Shab.* 110 *a*. 'Let him (who is to sleep in the open) take four cats. Tie them to the four corners of the bed, spread chips of wood round about so that when the cats hear the snake gliding over the chips, one or other of them will devour it' (*Everyman's Talmud* by A. Cohen, p. 275).

line and standing guard and fighting, and what I long for now is to be rid of these toils, since we have the sea, and to sail the rest of the way, and so reach Greece stretched out on my back, like Odysseus.'

Upon hearing those words from Leon of Thurii, how the soldiers shouted! – and another man said the same thing, and in fact all who rose to speak. The wish that I have is to extend that first elation at the benefits of sea-travel to some of the early land-carriers, very much inured as they must have been to the problems and exertions of desert navigation. I feel that I can explain to myself a surcharge of excitement about ships, and explain that special pride in proving what men and ships together could do – I could begin to explain all that I was asked to believe about the early Phoenicians – if I could accept the wishful thinking that they were an off-shoot of a people trained in the wandering and demanding life of desert work. What I had been asked to believe of the early Phoenician was that in a first excitement he was almost a Centaur, half ship and half man; and I thought I caught a glimpse of how I could believe almost that. If so, the main traditional exploits fell into proper order. I could see my Phoenician exulting in ship-invention, in the ship as a part of himself, almost as much alive as any desert-traction animal, superior in speed and durability. I said I could see the early rivalry in exploration suggested by the partnership. I said I could see the exploits in the order demanded – the reaching of the Pillars of Melkarth (so-called long before they were the Pillars of Herakles) and even a taste of the Atlantic came into credibility, and Spain as distant Coney Island came into credibility, before the intimate, familiar knowledge of the African coast which was in turn demanded if one was to feel easy about the exodus from Tyre as represented in the fable of Dido. So I felt with relief that most of the traditional story of the enigmatic Phoenician could be accepted if to begin with he had been one of a wandering tribe accustomed to desert haulage.

If it could be proved that the initially distinctive character of the Phoenician stock was altogether otherwise, the house of cards that I have been building would at once fall down.

One indication of a contrast in character between Phoenician, Hebrew and Greek is given by the alphabet they shared, but of which they made different uses.

For a long time after the invention of writing and of portable material on which to write, paper or tablets and cylinders of clay, the impression is that both writer and reader, at the moment of composition or decipherment, were in some more or less settled place, uninterrupted, able to spend time at the task – not on the move. Both the hieratic script used on paper and the cuneiform writing on clay (and the care to protect the messages on clay within clay envelopes) imply a good deal of leisure at both ends of a correspondence. In cuneiform writing the immense proliferation of individual signs and marks has often caused present-day comment; for instance Luc. H. Grollenberg in his very convenient *Shorter Atlas of the Bible*[13] pauses to refer to a study of cuneiform writing in which are recorded 35,438 different cuneiform signs. 'Happily for us,' says Grollenberg, 'the Elamites, who lived in the mountainous country north of ancient Sumer, also adopted the system and greatly simplified it, leaving only 113 syllabic signs.' The further achievement, usually accredited to the Phoenicians, was to make a workable shorthand method of writing with no more than 22 characters for essential consonants, the vowels to be supplied by the reader according to context. Everyone now remembers that this wonderful and practical simplified alphabet became the alphabet adopted by the Hellenes (who added signs for their vowels) and by the Romans and in due course by the whole of the western world; a remarkable instance of the transfer of a serviceable piece of equipment from one people to another along the whole length of the long road west.

It is not so much the alphabet itself as the way in which it was used by the Greeks, Phoenicians and Hebrews which is relevant here. Credit for the invention of the short alphabet was commonly ascribed by the Greeks to the Phoenicians, but as 'Phoenician' could be used as a very general term, no precise origin is, or perhaps could be, pinpointed. What seems clear is that the Greeks, from the time they were presented by Phoenicians with the new toy of writing, eagerly experimented with the letters. Some Greeks used the letters in the way they were handed to them, and wrote from right to left; others reversed the order and wrote from left to right; or experimented vertically, up and down. There was quick interest in calligraphy, in giving the letters a particular Greek style; and then, among the Greeks, the standardization of writing from left to right, for the ready

65

communicability of every form of literature so zestfully invented by them. Whoever it was, along the land-bridge between Mesopotamia and Egypt, who first managed to codify the short alphabet,* one sees it used by both Hebrews and Phoenicians. From the start both peoples continued to write from right to left in horizontal lines, but the difference in the calligraphy is curious. The Hebrew calligraphy suggests a close and scrupulous attention to the lettering and a desire to beautify it in their own way; by contrast, Phoenician lettering seems almost scornfully scratchy and careless. Furthermore, the early Phoenician letters gradually became longer and thinner, whereas early Hebrew letters became increasingly thicker and shorter. If one elects to be fanciful, the difference in the letters themselves almost suggests a contrast in the peoples' characters – a contrast as of gadabouts and stay-at-homes.

Such contrast between Phoenicians and Hebrews is supported factually, in that early Hebrew inscriptions are reported (in Dr. Diringer's survey) 'almost exclusively in Palestine', while Phoenician inscriptions spread over the whole of the Mediterranean map: a Phoenician–Hittite bilingual inscription is among those reported in eastern Cilicia, and 'finds' of the Phoenician writing are spotted not alone in 'Phoenicia' but in Cyprus, Greece, North Africa, Malta, Sicily, Sardinia, Marseilles and Spain. Such literate traces far transcend the unlettered traces of the gipsy type – the patrin or patteran such as many wanderers leave to show to their kin a way that has been travelled. Yet the mystery remains, that in contrast to his coevals the Phoenician continued to be illiterate. The gift of writing most marvellously added to the burgeoning and excitement of communal life in Greece. The gift as nurtured by the stay-at-home Hebrew became the means, throughout oppression and dispersal, of keeping a ring of fire around his permanent faith. No equivalent excitement, no equivalent faith, is expressed in Phoenician writing. Perhaps the technological equipment which enabled the Phoenician to go where he would, inhibited other forms of self-expression. Be that as it may, apart from the inscrutability of his fidgetty lettering the Phoenician did write his name in water, and the water that now concerns us is the fifteen hundred sea miles between Tyre and Carthage.

* The most comprehensive and authoritative work in English is *The Book of the Alphabet* by David Diringer (Hutchinson, London, Revised Edition 1968).

In that leap westward there seems to be promised a new way of life, yet of a fashion not divorced from an ancient heritage. Communication over the sea miles could be kept up. There was as yet no enemy more vicious than winds and weather to threaten transportation between the new town and the old.

NOTES

1. *Philostratus, The Life of Apollonius of Tyana,* translated by F. C. Conybeare (Loeb Classical Library, 1926) II, 191.
2. The view that Carthage was 'new' in relation to Utica is represented in the first volume of the monumental 12-volume *Historia de España,* dirigida por Ramón Menéndez Pidal (Espasa-Calpe, S. A. Madrid, 1952).
3. *What is History?* by Edward Hallett Carr (Knopf, New York, 1962).
4. The references to Daniel-Rops are again to his *Israel in the Ancient World.*
5. *The Phoenicians* by Donald Harden (Thames & Hudson, London, 1962), pp. 52, 53.
6. Arrian, *Anabasis Alexandri,* translated by E. Iliff Robson (Loeb Classical Library, 1954).
7. *History Under the Sea* by Alexander McKee (Hutchinson, London, 1969). For more detail, see *Archaeology Under Water* by George F. Bass (Thames & Hudson, London, 1966).
8. Hesiod, *Works and Days,* 618–649. I have followed the quotation, with her condensation of it, from Professor E. G. R. Taylor's *The Haven-Finding Art* (Hollis and Carter, London, 1956).
9. *The Living Sea* by Captain J. Y. Cousteau, with James Dugan (Hamish Hamilton, London, 1963). My quotations are from Chapters 4 and 5.
10. *Ulysses Found* by Ernle Bradford (Hodder & Stoughton, London, 1963).
11. *The City in History* by Lewis Mumford (Harcourt, Brace & World, New York, 1961), p. 73.
12. Xenophon, *Anabasis,* at the beginning of Book V. I quote from the translation by Carleton L. Brownson (Loeb Classical Library, 1932).
13. *The Shorter Atlas of the Bible* by Luc. H. Grollenberg, O.P., translated by Mary F. Hedlund (Nelson, London, 1959), p. 45.

CHAPTER 5

The New Town and the Old

WITH the arrival of the Phoenicians at Carthage I have accomplished a quarter of the distance, and perhaps a sixth of the time on the time-scale, of my journey from Ancient Sinai to modern California.

What I have been watching so far is an original Hebrew enthusiasm for setting up a city as a Holy City, a City of God – God, not a mere tribal god, but God, whose might and power filled the Universe. The singlemindedness of a nation in service to the Almighty seemed to be the harder to maintain, in that Jerusalem was planted close to Tyre; it was the interaction of Tyre and Jerusalem that I was trying to watch. Together they achieved a prosperity which was observed by Great Kings of the East. I envisaged that Tyre, if unable to fight off a large enemy, was at least technologically equipped to divide herself and set up another city.

I pictured Hebrews and Phoenicians as being closely kin, heirs of a same Semitic flesh, but I was puzzled by behaviours which seemed distinctive. They shared a common alphabet, but I had reached a curious distinction in the way each used it. Perhaps the Jews, in their most bitter time of trouble, had no ligature to bind them except the written word. Insofar as Ezra was the man who saw the need for the writings which preserved communion among a homeless and divided people, a very special reverence is due to Ezra. Even the calligraphy of the Talmud, as versions were written down in the exchange of faith, expressed a sharing of devotion. The act of lettering was in itself an action of religious service, as witnessed by the writing room at Qarân: the long tables on which the Dead Sea scrolls were written had hollows in them for the water in which to dip the fingers before writing the sacred name of God. No doubt it was only upon sacred writings that there was lavished such extreme care; but the distinction which was puzzling is that while Jews preserved themselves in faith through writing, there was no evidence whatever that Phoenicians chose to do more with this instrument than to leave 'tiny fidgetty letters scrambling hurriedly across tiny stones'.*

That forced me back to the impression that at the time of physical attack by eastern Kings the spiritual crisis for the Phoenician was not at all the same as for the Jew. I had touched upon the fact that there was no physical obliteration of Tyre. In that city the twin pillars of the temple of Melkarth were not thrown down. I had indeed been led to think that before the Assyrian menace arrived Phoenicians had been aware that at the faraway western end of a large watery demesne there were other twin pillars – Calpe (the Rock of Gibraltar) and Abyla (Mount Hacko on the North African coast) – which they had also named Pillars of Melkarth. 'My Lord, Melkarth, Lord of Tyre' extended a guardianship to more than one far secret haven. If I read the legend of Dido rightly, there was for her a choice of sites for Carthage. The problem of sustaining his faith, for Jew and Phoenician, was wholly different. The one had failed in service to the Lord of the Universe; from the consequent humiliation there was no escape. The other had not yet been failed by the tribal Lord of Tyre; Melkarth offered protection elsewhere. It is possible to identify Melkarth. At Malta (in the Phoenician language Maleth or Malet, and precious then and later as 'the navel of the sea') a bilingual inscription in which the other language is Greek, equates the names 'Melkarth' and 'Herakles'.† Herakles, or Hercules, was not depicted by other

---

* I do not know the originator of this expressive phrase. It is given as a quotation in *Daily Life in Carthage* by Gilbert and Colette Charles-Picard (Macmillan, New York, 1961) p. 70.

† It has seemed to me that in the beginning the Herakles of Greek mythology was borrowed from Melkarth (or else both borrowed from some prototype). The early Herakles of Homer is to some extent a sea-pioneer: he goes to the gates of Hell to carry off Cerberus, and the entry to the nether world is in Homer associated with the Pillars of Herakles. The Herakles of Homer also fights with a sea-monster. As the character of Herakles captured Greek imaginations – the character as hero whose prodigious labours entitled him to immortality and simultaneously the character as god who would particularly help those who worked to help themselves – many another story was added by the later writers. Of the 12 labours usually admitted to the canon the only one mentioned by Homer is the adventure of the nether world. In the beginning, then, Melkarth and Herakles seem very much the same; but the Lord of Tyre appears to remain a relatively static character, whereas among the Greeks Herakles alters and shrinks or enlarges according to who is talking.

peoples as the one and only God; but part Hero and part God, he was supreme in helping people to perform unheard of feats by physical energy. If Tyre relied on Melkarth as her special deity, that reinforces the impression that acts of worship were not so much spelled out in letters, but rather such as could be manifested by the instrument of ships.

More and more the distinction is borne in upon me, that as Jews became a people of the Book, Phoenicians became a people of the Ship; and there is a way of looking at it which makes it likely that excessive devotion to the ship could be a positive hindrance to the development of writing. Agreed, that a move from Tyre to Carthage implies continuance of communication over a long stretch of sea; but how did the tedious circumlocution of writing come into that problem? There are people who prefer word of mouth to writing; and in what way is the trusted ship-borne messenger inferior to the scribe? For Tyrian or Carthaginian the ship was instrument, the ship was the far-carrier of speech, the ship, to them, was telephone. As nowadays the telephone is sometimes more valued than writing, one sees there may have been an attitude among Phoenicians for their dismissal of the art of writing. An art of annotation sufficient for practical purposes must certainly be credited; but the peculiar pride remained in

---

Herakles continued to be worshipped throughout all Greece both as a god and as a hero; in both, his character is one of physical strength and energy. Plutarch, in his Life of Alexander, makes play with the awareness, among the Tyrians, that Melkarth was identical with Herakles. Plutarch has fun retelling the tale that during the siege of Tyre, when Alexander announced that Herakles was on his side, the Tyrians at once rushed to their statue of Melkarth and 'as if the god had been a common deserter caught in the act of going over to the enemy, they encircled his colossal figure with cords and nailed it down to its pedestal, calling him an Alexandrist'. In those days Tyre's faith in the Lord of Tyre was degenerate; there was acceptance that the Greeks had stolen Melkarth and renamed him. But at the time of the founding of Carthage I would believe the Tyrian faith in Melkarth was strong; the Greeks as yet were hardly on the scene; as soon as they were, they were sufficiently aware of Melkarth to wish to steal him. As in due course Rome wrenched him from the Greeks, crediting him with other labours and, oddly, trying to connect him with the Muses. Rome represented Hercules often with a lyre, of which there is no trace in the Greek conception of Herakles, and none at all in the original Phoenician conception of Melkarth – unless Phoenicians raised their anchors with sea-chanteys.

Carthage, of proving what could be done without writing, rather than with it. One way of looking at the story of Carthage is to see that so long as ships were of excessive importance they were in effect a danger to development. But that is a matter of hindsight: none of the founders of the new city of Carthage was likely to feel that a people of the ship was worse off than a people of the book.

I was looking at the voyage of Dido as symbolic of a genuine fission of Tyre: men and women made the voyage. I am not going to speculate how long the voyage took, or how many pots of *dibis* were used up on the way by Dido and her companions.* I shall return to Dido, but wish to see first what men did about a harbour at Carthage. We pretty well know what the harbour was like eventually (that is to say

* *Dibis* I understand to be a face cream used by desert women, and presumably anciently used; a preparation of date juice looking like mud, but I would hope effective against the salt spray of the Mediterranean.

As for the route of the voyage, Professor E. G. R. Taylor in *The Haven-Finding Art* (Hollis and Carter, London, 1956) argues cogently that a large amount of Phoenician shipwork must have involved direct deep-sea navigation. 'Historians, confronted with the fact that voyages were actually made, coined the phrase that, before he had the magnetic compass, the sailor "hugged the shore", and crept coastwise from port to port by roundabout routes. It is true, of course, that there was coastwise sailing, but every sailor has a wholesome dread of being driven on to a lee-shore, and stands well out to sea to avoid the dangers of hidden rock and sand-bank, of breakers and tide-rips, which are characteristic of inshore waters. In some current Admiralty sailing directions, for example, the sailor making for the south-west past Brittany is told concisely: "Ushant must not be sighted", for if he is as near in as that, the powerful on-shore set may sweep him on the rocks'.

'Ushant must not be sighted' is clear enough indication that whoever carried tin by sea from Cornwall to Spain could not safely have done so by hugging the coastline. Deny that Phoenician shipmasters ever voyaged so far as Cornwall, you still have the problem of their voyages to and from Spain. Deny voyages to Spain until after the founding of Carthage, you still have the problem of routes between Tyre and Carthage.

There is of course plenty of sea-room for several schools of thought. One school dismisses Dido altogether and, pursuing a story of Herodotus, suggests that Phoenicians founded Carthage by starting from the Red Sea, hugging the coast all the way round Africa, and entering the Mediterranean from the west. On balance of credibilities I prefer to plump for a mainly open-sea route between Tyre and Carthage. But how they managed to make their landfalls I don't know.

by the time of the wars with Rome), for Appian obtained a description from Polybius, and we trust Polybius as an eye-witness. By his time the main harbour at Carthage was a double harbour, with two basins, the first rectangular, the second circular:

> The harbours were so arranged that ships could pass from one to the other. The entrance from the sea was 70 feet wide and could be closed by iron chains. The first harbour, reserved for merchant ships, had a large selection of berths. In the centre of the inner harbour was an island which, like the harbour, was lined with quays, along the whole length of which were boat-houses providing accommodation for 220 ships; above these were lofts for storing the rigging. In front of each boat-house stood two Ionic columns, so that the perimeter of the harbour and of the island looked like a portico. On the island itself stood a small building used as headquarters for the Admiral and as a post for the trumpeters and heralds. The island was just opposite the entrance of the harbour and rose steeply from the water, so that while the Admiral could see what was happening outside, little could be seen of the interior of the harbour from the open sea. Even from incoming merchant ships, the arsenals remained hidden, for they were surrounded by a double wall and men from the merchant vessels passed from the first harbour into the town without going through the arsenals.[1]

That was the main harbour after several centuries of work upon it. As archaeologists, the Charles-Picards report that during the centuries the Carthaginians had scooped out the basins, first the rectangular one, then the naval base with entry which swerved from the sea-entrance sharply to the right, so that the base was close to the sea-wall and the Admiral's quarters on the central island had unimpeded view. When the circular naval basin had been dug, apparently the bottom of the basin was paved, the island built up and bridged to the mainland, the stone foundations for the bridge bonded together, like the Wailing Wall at Jerusalem, with lead. The picture, with the boat-houses and Ionic columns which Polybius described as a circular portico, and the island with its pilot-house for Admiral and trumpeters, makes one accept the Charles-Picards' statement that the heart of Carthage was always its harbour; the feeling is indeed that the harbour was the Temple for the men of Carthage.

The double harbour as described had taken time to build; but from the beginning a harbour was worked on and was looked upon to make

Carthage Queen of the Western Seas. Promptly the men of the New Town began to over-run land territory to bring back goods for export. The land territory that was explored was enormous. In addition to the coastal strip of North Africa from Cyrenaica to the Atlantic, Carthage came into a trade-control of the southern half of Spain, the small islands of Majorca and Minorca, the large islands of Sardinia and Corsica, the western half (or more than half) of Sicily. Voyagers skirted the bulge of Africa at least as far as the Cameroons, where Hanno's seamen chased 'women' with shaggy bodies – possibly chimpanzees or baboons.[2] There were land expeditions across the Sahara all the way to the Niger; several desert routes toward the Gold Coast are described by the Charles-Picards as chariot routes; and it is averred that weighty raw materials, such as ivory, were brought back overland to Carthage, as well as gold. The chief impression of the men of early Carthage is of their energy and speed in ransacking the new world, not so much for martial conquest as for trade. And the dominant idea of the trade was the export, from Carthage, of raw materials. The pattern of trade as set at the beginning was the barter of cheap goods for raw materials; the raw materials to be trans-shipped to workshops of the East; whence in return there came a flow of further cheap goods for the further barter. Trade so established was so successful that there was no apparent reason for altering the pattern; at least there is little evidence that Carthaginians were ever much inclined to set up or improve their own crafts, workshops or manufactures.

In Tyre one saw the women more clearly than the men; in Carthage that statement is reversed. We share the excitements of the men in their new world, and in the rapid increase of their entrepôt-trade. What of the women? I said I would return to Dido, for I imagined that if there were princesses of the royal line of Tyre who shared the expedition, they would not easily accept nonentity. I pondered the words that Virgil emphasizes, *dux femina facti*, and I found some suggestions in Virgil as to what happened. Recall that as regards the earliest days of Carthage, Virgil makes Venus observe that 'Tyrian maids are wont to wear the quiver, and bind their ankles high with the purple buskin'. In other words, ladies of fashion accepted frontier conditions but still hankered after the purple: I would not lightly pass over that word 'purple', for it has significance in the history of

73

Carthage. At Tyre, the purple represented the powerful attraction of style, whereby Tyre had become fashion centre for the Greeks; the purple represented the very noticeable attraction that princesses of Tyre exerted upon Kings of Israel and Judah. The reason we see the women of Tyre so clearly is that Jews wrote so much about them. When thinking of the Jews, I stressed the impact made by Tyre upon Jerusalem; I must not forget that Jerusalem provided ladies of Tyre with admirers to dress for. At Carthage, planted on the coast of Africa, there were no neighbouring principalities. Among Libyans, Numidians or lesser peoples it is hard to think of any who would elicit a fashion show. The isolation of Carthage makes it plausible for Virgil to describe Dido as in a flutter at the surprising arrival of a personable stranger.

The dress by day for a Tyrian maid of Dido's time might be that of a huntress: robes tied in a knot around the waist, bare knees, hunting boots above the calf – but the boots had to be purple. I assume the dye had to be as nearly as possible the real thing, the real Tyrian murex, the real 'fresh Phoenician' which had been so much loved by Dolops; the best 'oyster', as Plato said, which was his way of referring to murex.* I am sure that a very early disappointment at Carthage was the absence there of a real murex with its precious mantle-gland. The murex of Tyre and Sidon does not breed in the western Mediterranean. In the western waters there was only a lesser species, yielding a much inferior dye. Shell-heaps of the inferior species remain near Carthage; it was not for lack of trying that the Carthaginian murex industry failed. I insisted that 'purple' was of importance. A search for quality in other realms of life might more easily be given up, but about true and false purples anyone from Tyre knew the difference. It is symbolic of much of Carthaginian history that a substitute purple, though known to be inferior, came to be accepted as good enough. The substitute was found among the seaweeds. After much searching among dye-producing lichens of the sea-rocks, the best that could be found was what came to be known, in modern times, as the orchilla weed. The Carthaginians sought for the weed as far as their mysterious 'Purple Isles', which are mentioned in Horace, and which one may conjecture to have been the Canaries or the Cape Verdes. In Roman times the Carthaginian weed came to be known as

* *Republic* iv, 420 c.

fucus, and it was recognized as something deceitfully passed off as pretence for real 'Phoenician'. Quintilian remarks that wool dyed with fucus pleases less than real purple, but that is a relatively faint condemnation. Horace uses the term *fucus* at a moment of utmost anger to express what is characteristic of the Carthaginian and also what is false about him.* Yet it came to be that this inferior dye was what the ladies of the upper town of Carthage had to put up with, and it is not inappropriate to select this particular example as representative of other losses of pride. There is a bitterness in the words *dux femina facti*, for the women of Carthage lost heart sooner than the men. The men can hardly be exonerated, for women might have continued to dress well, had anyone cared. But the deterioration of women's fashions in Carthage is demonstrable. Before they left their old world Phoenician women had given fashion to the Greeks; their descendents in the new world sank to accepting second-hand Greek fashions, the fashions not of Athens but of Corinth.

The upper town of Carthage spread on the hills behind the harbour, and court and government and social life are represented in the upper town. The town spread into rural suburbs, dwellings with gardens, farmhouses with fields. Here the portrait of Carthage seems remarkably modern. The Charles-Picards speak of finding in one suburb (Kerkouane) a house with 'an admirably equipped bathroom complete with slipper-bath and a wash-basin which allowed its owner to wash his face while sitting in the bath'. This, they say, was a Greek technique: 'The bathroom is lined with fine waterproof cement and is just like one found in a house in Corinth of the same period.' It was about 650 B.C. that the workshops of Corinth, in particular, began to be busy servicing Carthage with goods not good enough by the best Greek standards but very acceptable, it seems, in Carthage. I was looking at the effort to maintain the production of dye-stuffs (including cosmetics) but as for rings, bangles, necklaces, collars and diadems, it seems that Greek ornaments came to be accepted as stylish. So it was with table-ware. In short, in the attempt to estimate what sort of social life accompanied that private bathroom at Kerkouane, I am forced to feel that even in the heyday of that life, before

* *Odes* III. v. (the ode about Regulus). The sense is, no one who has yielded for a moment to the taint of Carthaginian dye (fucus) can ever reassume the true colour of a Roman. There is an echo here of *Republic* iv, 430.

any of the wars that ruined Carthage, there was lacking some thrust of its own; one looks in vain for some *élan vital*. At Carthage of the seventh century B.C. I see a people lucky enough and spirited enough to have made a notable leap westward; but as soon as the new city had been set up there seems to be a falling-off of creativity in social life. There seems to be less spontaneous creativity than spontaneous deterioration.

No theatres, no public games, are mentioned in accounts of Carthage during its rise to power and prosperity. Public feasts given by political candidates and severe religious festivals appear to have been the main ceremonies. Melkarth is not reported to have been a particularly cruel god, but two gods of the upper town, Tanit and Baal Hammon, are mentioned as demanding human sacrifices either when necessary to avert misfortune from the people as a whole, or to make expiation for some general misfortune. Thus when the Sicilian Agathocles invaded Africa, and for four years kept the citizens of Carthage in terror, in that extremity it is said that public sacrifice was made of 500 children, chosen from the most noble families. A gloss upon this story is that the obligation to Baal Hammon was regarded as a ritual obligation which could be met by the substitution of young slaves for the real children of the nobility. The Charles-Picards draw an inference: 'In such transactions with their gods, the Carthaginians resorted to the same sharp practices as they employed in human affairs and were delighted when they could manage to get the better of the dreaded Baal.' I have no means of knowing whether the story or the gloss is literally true; both are of a type which could be invented. The attack by Agathocles was fairly late in the story of Carthage (310–307 B.C.) and by then Carthaginians had perhaps earned a good deal of hostile propaganda. The inference drawn by the Charles-Picards seems, however, justified; for 'sharp practice' could on occasion be true amongst most peoples. What seems certain is that religion among Carthaginians remained of a harsh, Old Testament kind. The charitable Plutarch says that they were always a stern people, peculiarly hostile to pleasures and amusements.

The fertility of the land in the neighbourhood of Carthage, in ancient times, cannot be overlooked. If the social life of Carthage was arid, at least the land was not. Carthaginian potters did not make good table-ware, but they made good drain-pipes and good use was made of them for town and agriculture. At the time of the Punic wars Romans carefully copied Carthaginian ship-design, and no less carefully studied Carthaginian methods of husbandry. The Carthaginians had invented a threshing-machine, which Romans called the 'Punic cart'; and the one Carthaginian book toward which Romans paid notable respect was Mago's treatise on farming. By this time, six centuries after the founding of Carthage, Carthaginians were beginning to use their alphabet. A 'great library of Punic literature known to have existed at Carthage in 146', when the Romans burned parts of the town, is mentioned by Harden on the authority of Gsell. It is not easy to believe in the existence of a great library of general literature without some other evidence of interest in calligraphy; but Mago's writings on husbandry were in themselves almost a library – there were 28 volumes of them. Those rolls were saved, at the taking of Carthage, by Scipio, and were presented to the Roman senate. They were translated into Greek by Cassius Dionysius of Utica, and into Latin by order of the Roman senate, although Cato (the same who repeatedly said *Delenda est Carthago*) had already written copiously upon the subject. The Romans, according to Lemprière, 'consulted the writings of Mago with greater earnestness than the books of the Sibylline verses'. Hesiod's *Works and Days* played its part in stimulating Greek literature, and had there been a Mago at Carthage's beginning rather than at the end, a more exciting social life might have blossomed. There is no evidence, though, of any lyrical feeling in Mago's writings; late or early, the Carthaginian attention to farming seems to have been for food alone. There was no particular development of vineyards and no wine-making of repute. For wine, as for most other manufactured products, Carthage in its prosperity depended on the Greeks.

Polybius, musing upon the decline of Carthage and the rise of Rome, gives his analysis in political terms:

> The constitution of Carthage seems to me to have been originally well contrived as regards its most distinctive points. For there were kings, and the house of Elders was an aristocratical force, and the people were supreme in matters proper to them, the entire frame of the state much resembling that of Rome and Sparta. But at the time when they entered on the Hannibalic War, the Carthaginian constitution had degenerated, and that of Rome was better. For as every body or state or action has its

natural periods first of growth, then of prime, and finally of decay, and as everything in them is at its best when they are in their prime, it was for this reason that the difference between the two states manifested itself at this time. For by as much as the power and prosperity of Carthage had been earlier than that of Rome, by so much had Carthage already begun to decline; while Rome was exactly at her prime, as far at least as her system of government was concerned. Consequently the multitude at Carthage had already acquired the chief voice in deliberations; while at Rome the senate still retained this; and hence, as in one case the masses deliberated and in the other the most eminent men, the Roman decisions on public affairs were superior, so that although they met with complete disaster, they were finally by the wisdom of their counsels victorious over the Carthaginians in the war.[3]

At Carthage there may have been from the start an adulteration of civility (to use the word which Dr. Johnson preferred to 'civilization'), and there may have been the gradual decay in relations of populace and Senate (that Polybius chooses Sparta for comparison is interesting); but these are criticisms which for two or three centuries seem to have been masked from Carthaginians themselves. Long before Rome put an end to their power and prosperity, the people who first shook the Carthaginians were the Athenians.

Far ahead of anyone else, the Phoenicians had raced into the far west of the Mediterranean and into the Atlantic, and the secrets of where they found what they valued (metals in particular) were to be kept to themselves. I find this view, expressed by others, easy to accept. 'Any Periplous or Pilot for the area,' Ernle Bradford comments, 'and any information passed by word of mouth from one sea-captain to another was for Phoenicians alone. Certainly none of it would have been revealed to the Greek traders.' The same thing has happened throughout the whole history of maritime discovery, Bradford continues, and instances the much later conduct of the fifteenth century Portuguese in concealing their West African discoveries and putting it about that seas in which they navigated were wholly innavigable.[4] When thinking of the Atlantic voyages of the Carthaginians, of Himilco from Gadeira to the north or of Hanno to the south, one bears in mind that part of the business was to hand out, especially to the Greeks, false information. We believe, then, that the innavigability of the Atlantic was a story successfully passed off to the

Greeks, with considerable results in later history. Yet without denying to the Carthaginians an exquisite satisfaction in concealing the sources of treasure in bullion, the cunning began to be much overmatched when Greeks invented their own and effective use of the bullion, when or as they could lay hands on it. So long as Carthaginians continued to do the hard and dangerous work of providing the raw metal, the sources were of relatively small importance to the Greeks; for the Greeks were the first within the Western world to make the bullion nimble by the invention of coinage. Coinage was of itself a pregnant invention, in that it began the anarchic development of money, banking, credit. Thus, it is felt, began the economic revolution which worked much more to the advantage of the Greeks than to the Carthaginians. When (about 485 B.C.) Athenians found their own silver mines near Cape Sunium, these state-owned mines (leased separately to highest bidders) were a major source of Athens' wealth, and except for wheat, Athens was relatively independent of anybody else. But long before that, Carthage had drifted into its considerable dependence on Greek manufactures.

I drew a melancholy picture of Carthaginian women losing heart as fashion deteriorated; but I do not suppose that what seemed to me to be deterioration was always admitted to be so by them. Nor would I think that men of Carthage in its prime recognized any inferiority. In their explorations, barter may have been the primary aim rather than military conquest; but they had been able to reduce some of the intractible Libyans and Numidians to slavery; they had been able to conciliate Spaniards; and if Greeks provided them with manufactured goods, all that implied was that Greeks seemed servile. Before the Carthaginians and Athenians came into bitter warfare, I do not think a wealthy Melkarth felt any need to fear an infant Herakles. Conflicts between Carthaginians and Athenians began at sea, and each naturally blamed the other. The route for the Athenian grain ships from Egypt cut straight across the Carthaginian traffic with Tyre. Athenians (for instance Thucydides) were forever vocal about Phoenician pirates, but the voice is one of the pot calling the kettle black. Of the two, it is even possible to feel sympathy with Carthaginian indignation when a cargo on the way to Tyre was intercepted. Supremacy at sea was their prerogative, and it was challenged. Much as Francis Drake provoked the Spaniards of the sixteenth century, I feel that Carthaginians were provoked by Athenian piracy; and much as Drake's provocation played its part in the assembly of the Spanish Armada for the suppression of England, so I would believe the provocative piracy of the Hellenes caused Phoenicians to egg on first Darius and then Xerxes to crush the pestilential Athenians once and for all. There were many other factors, I don't doubt, in the fifth century wars of Persians on Greece; but I would not regard Phoenician shipmen as mere hirelings in those wars, but active instigators.

The combined effort to subdue the Hellenes was the first widespread military exertion in which Phoenicians were concerned; and as the world knows, Athenians led in the repulsion of the threat. It was no half-hearted threat; it was an organized and simultaneous triple action against Hellas; and for the moment Hellas united to respond at all three battlefields. First, the direct assaults of the Great Kings from Asia Minor were defeated by the Greek Confederation, and this involved complete humiliation of the Phoenician ships at Salamis by the Athenians. Second, in Sicily, Gelon of Syracuse defeated the Carthaginian army of Hamilcar the Magonid in the battle of Himera, fought, it is said, on the same day as the battle of Salamis (in 480 B.C.). Third, in Italy, the Etruscan allies of the Carthaginians lost control of Campania and Latium through combined actions of the Greeks of Cumae and Italians who sided with them. The uplift to the Greeks in their success was immeasurable. The corresponding depression of Carthage has been less noted by the world. Their pride had been engaged in all three actions, and in all three had been humiliated. It was not pride alone, but their economy, which suffered. 'One thing is certain', say the Charles-Picards in summarizing the archaeological records:

> One thing is certain. These defeats brought about a serious economic recession in Carthage. Precise archaeological evidence of this has been found. Graphs drawn by Vercoutter and Cintas show that at this time, amulets of Egyptian origin disappeared almost completely. It was the same with Greek vases. Black-figured vases made in Corinth or Attica figured extensively in our collections, but red-figured vases, whose production started about 520, are completely absent. Etruscan articles also vanished. Carthage had thus suddenly ceased all purchases of finished products from allies and enemies alike.[5]

After the defeats a new idea seems to become increasingly dominant in the story of Carthage: the idea of revenge. The alternation of periods of Spartan austerity and then of periods of warfare for which the strongest motive seems to be revenge, is the story which I need not pursue until the pattern alters from revenge against the Greeks to revenge against the Romans. Perhaps an original mistake was made when the other half of Tyre was planted so far away. It showed a wonderful faith in ships; but the excessive attention to shipwork may have meant the failure of Carthage, at its prime, to be more than an opulent suburb. Wind and weather over the long route to the East gave an advantage to Corinth, perhaps, as a place from which Carthage could fetch the goods she failed to manufacture for herself. After the battle of Salamis, Athenian maritime supremacy from the Straits of Messina to Egypt then hampered Carthage's trade with Greece as well as with the East. With her eastward sea-links damaged, Carthage invested more and more in Sicily; and there in due course the conflict for possession of Messina (or in Roman tongue Messana) was the immediate cause of the first Punic war with Rome (264 B.C.). Revenge for that war was held to be the cause for Hannibal's great effort, and for such support as merchants of Carthage could give him. In the end those merchants, no longer merchant princes, could be caricatured by Plautus; who to a ribald Roman audience could present the Carthaginian merchant as a *gugga*, a 'little rat' or 'desert rat', bringing to Rome his offerings of spoons, drainpipes, walnuts, and panthers for the public games.

NOTES

1. I borrow the translation of Appian's report of Polybius' description of the harbour at Carthage from *Daily Life in Carthage* by Gilbert and Colette Charles-Picard; the harbour is also discussed in *The Phoenicians* by Donald Harden.
2. A translation of Hanno's narrative is provided by Harden, pp. 170–177, with suitable cautionary comment, for all that one has for text is a Greek version of possibly the tenth-century A.D.
3. Polybius, *The Histories*, translated by W. R. Paton (Loeb Classical Library, 1923) vol. III, p. 385.

4. Ernle Bradford, op. cit. p. 111. Himilco seems to have been particularly good at professing the terrors of the ocean, to keep his own routes to himself; see Professor A. Garcia Y Belldo in the *Historia de España*, vol. I, p. 289. I gather that the name Hanno might refer to one or other of several Carthaginian explorers.

5. Charles-Picard, op. cit.

CHAPTER 6

The Rock Pool

NOW, if I am studying the making of the Road West, I must
look at what delayed its making. The Phoenicians had to be
studied, for they advanced my narrative; and about Phoenicians you may more or less think as you please, for their own
writings will not contradict you. I cannot be so free and easy with the
Greeks, but here it is my theme which saves me. By and large, the
early Greeks did little to advance a physical pathway westward. My
question is, why not?

Though Herodotus might be writing in the then western world of
Italy, he took it for granted (in the fifth century B.C.) that West had
meant little, and East had meant everything, in the inspiration of the
Greeks. 'Everything' (Gods, customs) came to Hellas from Egypt,
says Herodotus.[1] Plato takes it as a matter of course that every intelligent Greek, be he Athenian, Spartan or Cretan, will have inspected
the great works of Egypt 'on the spot'. Not to go to school with the
Egyptians, not to learn how they teach mathematics 'with a good deal
of fun and amusement', not to dispel one's own ignorance – 'such
ignorance', when he had been made aware of it, seemed to the narrator
in Plato's *Laws* 'more worthy of a stupid beast like the hog than of a
human being'. It was in recalling his Egyptian travels that the Athenian said: 'I blushed not for myself alone, but for our whole Hellenic
world.' So over the doorway of his apartment in the Academia at
Athens Plato placed the inscription

ΜΗΔΕΙΣ ΑΓΕΩΜΕΤΡΗΤΟΣ ΕΙΣΙΤΩ

which latter-day mathematicians have sometimes translated literally
– 'Let no one unacquainted with geometry enter.' I wonder if there
are not other meanings entwined in that compact word 'non-geo-
meter'. Without delving into mystical interpretations, there is a suggestion that 'earth-measuring', in the sense of 'travel', teaches. For if
Plato often suggests that foreign travel should be restricted to people
of maturity (lest the good customs of one's own city be corrupted by

foreign notions too readily accepted by the impressionable young) he does not tire of talking about Egypt, nor did he hesitate to go westward to Sicily. But as to the direction of travel, there is to Plato this distinction: go eastward to learn, to borrow what inspires you, and then return home to shape and improve upon what you have borrowed – go westward not to learn but to impose what you have learned. If over-crowding in Hellas forces the setting up of new cities to the westward,* make sure they have the fairest of constitutions and are in every way best governed – such is a large part of Plato's teaching and of Aristotle's after him.

Go west, but not too far west, continued to be the feeling of the Hellenes as the colonizing spread in Italy, and as far afield as Massilia (Marseilles) and even as far as Barcino (Barcelona). The thoughts of Pindar (522–442 B.C.) were not to be disobeyed, and it is very impressive how centripetal his thoughts are. No Greek should travel to any excessive distance or set up a city so far away that freeborn men (and any talented athletes in their households) could not return home with regularity for the important Games. Perpetually, Pindar is welcoming home the not too far-flung colonists, and abjuring them never to venture away from the self-contained rock pool beside which is the light and ornament of the world, the centre for refreshment of the spirit, 'Athens, city divine!'

Pindar was not untravelled; he celebrates voyaging; he spent some time at the western court of Hiero at Syracuse; that may have induced his younger competitor, Bacchylides, to do the same. But as for sailing farther to the westward, Pindar firmly says no. Never attempt to pass the Pillars of Herakles – those Pillars are 'the utmost verge'. 'All beyond that bourne cannot be approached either by the wise or the unwise.' I said Pindar celebrates voyaging, but mainly toward the rising sun. Eastward is the direction he commends – 'even unto Troy'. The Euxine may be open to you only in the summer, but winter sailings may be made to Egypt. Bacchylides also rises to the theme of

* At the peak of the strength of Athens (431 B.C.) Gomme estimates the population to have been, Citizens, 172,000; Metics, 28,500; Slaves, 115,000. A 'metic' might perhaps be described as a resident alien. In a good year, and in peacetime, the soil of Attica was then producing enough cereals, it is estimated, for 75,000 people. Hence the importance to Athens of wheatships, and also the pressure to form colonies.

Egypt: 'over sunlit sea wheatships bring wealth untold from Egypt'. But again, so far as ambitious westward exploration – no. It is all right for Greek ships to sail to the colonies of the Near-West, but never right to dare the Pillars. To Pindar, any such dare was simply illegitimate: his prohibition is absolute. The Pillars of Herakles are 'the farthest limit of voyaging ... the limits of the land'. 'Let none pursue prowess that passes beyond that bound'. 'Beyond Gadeira toward the gloom we must not pass: turn back thy ship.'

You may say that Pindar and Bacchylides were primarily sports-writers; it was their speciality to applaud the Games – Olympian, Pythian, Nemean and Isthmian – to attend particularly to that 'big' circuit, and to centralize attention. They were indeed metropolitan sports-writers: Pindar could celebrate even such a sophisticated ban-queting game as 'flinging the cottabus'. But Pindar is not inventing the complete and absolute taboo which the Greeks placed on the Pillars of Herakles. Pindar is only accepting and confirming the taboo which had been firmly established by Homer. That taboo was a mat-ter of religion. I would agree with Ernle Bradford that in the 'Under-world' section of the *Odyssey* Homer 'introduced from some Phoenician source the geographical *fact* of the Gibraltar Strait and of the Atlantic beyond it', and I would agree with Bradford's further observation that Homer was aware of the Phoenician myth that Mel-karth, in his capacity as Lord of the Underworld, dwelt by the Pil-lars:

... In this place, which nature had fashioned like a giant archetype of the twin pillars of his temple in the Phoenician city of Tyre, dwelt Melkarth, god of the darkness beyond the world's limits.

Once this Phoenician legend is understood it is easy to see why Circe should have sent Ulysses to the Strait of Gibraltar, for it was here that the god of the Underworld had his domain. Beyond the Strait lies the realm of Ocean (Circe's grandfather), the place where the Sun (Circe's father) sinks nightly into the unknown west.[2]

Mr. Bradford is expressing the point that mythology, far from being merely a pleasant way of telling fairytales, is 'a kind of shorthand designed to record certain truths about nature, and man, and his place in nature'; and though nobody need look for an actual place on the Atlantic coast beyond the Pillars where Ulysses dug his trench and poured libations to the dead, the representation in Homer is that the action of passing the Pillars stands figuratively for Death. There may be people who feel a death-wish. Let them who feel it sail into the westward ocean – such feeling is taboo for Greeks. And so from Homer onwards, not merely in Pindar but as one dips elsewhere, classical Greek literature is full of warnings: *our* life is on the midland sea; there is nothing to the west of it. Euripides, for instance, refers to the Pillars of Herakles as a natural marker beyond which 'lies the end of voyaging, and the Ruler of Ocean no longer permits mariners to sail the purple sea'.

This Greek taboo was real enough for us to notice, though it never prevented fancy or speculation about the untouched realm of Ocean. Aristotle remarks that if earth is a sphere and if you sailed right round it, clearly you could be brought back again to the port whence you started. Plato advances a practical rather than a superstitious reason for the innavigability of the Atlantic. In his parable about Atlantis, the old man of Egypt whom Plato is pretending to quote, tells him that in the very ancient days before the Flood the Atlantic *was* navigable, and there was an island situated 'in front of the straits which are by you called the Pillars of Herakles':

> The island was larger than Libya and Asia put together, and was the way to other islands, and from these you might pass to the whole of the opposite continent which surrounded the true ocean, for this sea which is within the Straits of Herakles is only a harbour, having a narrow entrance, but that other is a real sea, and the land surrounding it on every side may be most truly called a boundless continent.

But, said the old man, in the time of great earthquakes and floods the island of Atlantis sank and 'disappeared in the depths of the sea'.

> For which reason the sea in those parts is impassable and impenetrable, because there is a shoal of mud in the way, and this was caused by the subsidence of the island.[3]

From the Homeric period until after the death of Plato (347 B.C.) no account of a Greek ship venturing into the Atlantic stimulates Greek literature. The Pillars of Herakles were a natural limitation, signifying stoppage. Whether it was the Homeric taboo, or whether it was the fanciful shoal of mud, or whether it was tall stories put about by Carthaginians, adventurous Greeks were not interested in any Atlantic seaway. A Road West, in the sense that I use the term, was of no interest to Greeks in their heyday.

I am sure that Carthaginians were delighted, perhaps scornful, and as near to being gleeful as Carthaginians could ever get, at this peculiar Greek timidity, this absence of desire for 'westering'. Yet it was the Greeks who had the real laugh, not the Carthaginians. Why should a Hellene wish to use a gateway to go outside the Midland Sea? The Greeks had the gift of making their own rock pool far too interesting for any of their best men to wish to leave it.

I remember that Virgil, when he had finished with Carthage, turned at once to the subject of Games; and for any single theme, whereby to remind ourselves of the life created by the Greeks, I don't see any theme that is better. A contrast with the Carthaginians is emphasized at once. At the time that the Carthaginians were excavating their harbour, the Greeks were building stadiums for athletic events. It is amazing how quickly there came to be standardization in the competitive events. At Olympia a set programme for runners, and necessary rules, were codified early in the eighth century B.C. and adopted (with few variations) at Isthmia, Nemea, Athens, Epidaurus, Argos, Plataea and elsewhere. Wrestling, the Pentathlon, Boxing and the Race in Armour, came in before the end of the sixth century. Competition from all parts of the Greek world was intense; the rewards in glory, prizes and prize-money were of importance; and athletes from the colonies (and their supporters) streamed regularly back across the sea from east or west to the four games which were most famous. Training was rigorous, not only at home but after arrival: would-be competitors at Olympia were required to put in a month's training at Elis before the Festival. The dates of the famous Games were staggered: each year there was something going on.

Within the Grecian world such competitive activity was far more thrilling than exploring a dull seaway to Gadeira, or possibly duller parts of the world beyond. It was not that it was impossible to flout the prohibition of sailing beyond the Pillars of Herakles; it was merely comparatively uninteresting. Fairly late, towards the end of the fourth century, it did occur to Pytheas of Massilia to pass the Pillars and sail as far as he could into the northern seas. There is no particular reason to doubt that he did what he claimed, which, by interpretation, is that he sailed round Britain, discovered another island (which he called Thule), and entered another sea, supposedly the Baltic. He asserted that the tides of the Atlantic were in some way connected with the moon, and established a distinction of climate by the lengths of days and nights; and when his report was talked of in Athens he was naturally regarded as a great liar. Discussion of the periplus (or 'sailing-round') of Pytheas was relatively ill-informed, for the reason given by Aristotle in the *Nichomachean Ethics*: 'We dispute about the navigation of ships more than about the training of athletes, because it has been less well organized as a science.'

The phrase 'well organized as a science' means, I take it, that the training of athletes fitted in with the spontaneous organic life of the community. It was in its conscious all-round quickening that Athens was 'city divine'. Navigation fitted less directly than athletics;* insofar as the gods took pleasure in the same things as mortals, display of physical excellence was godlike; but not the only service that was godlike. With that singular Greek capacity for combining everything that was lively, the athletic Games were not divorced from other aspects of full social life. The growth of Games and Festivals was organic and integral. A point well made by Professor Harris in his book on *Greek Athletes and Athletics*[4] is that for us, drama and athletics seem to have little in common: the one chiefly an indoor entertainment for the evening, the other often an outdoor daylight pursuit. In the Greek world they were closely bound together, in a same daytime.

> The Greek word 'theatron' simply meant 'place for viewing a spectacle' and was used of the spectators' banking in the stadium as well as that in the dramatic theatre.

The gods took pleasure in many things, and every kind of spectacle and contest in Greece began to grow up together. A name heard in one sphere gained music when heard in another. Pythagoras, from

---

* In Greek education scorn was rather fostered (perhaps on both sides) between the educated man and the practical seaman. Even Aristotle, despite his conversations with fishermen, makes use of a scornful phrase – 'the sea-faring rabble'. Much later, Philostratus was one of the Greeks who carried to Rome the Greek opinion of the low position, in society, of a ship's captain.

Samos, was first known in the mainland when, in his 18th year, he won the Olympic crown for wrestling. A young Athenian called Aristocles competed in the Isthmian Games at Corinth, also as a wrestler: he earned the nickname Plato, the 'broad-shouldered', and by that nickname, and for works other than wrestling, is remembered. Most of the intellectuals of Greece were present at the Games as spectators, if not competitors. The only occasion on which Socrates ever left Athens except on military service was when he went to Corinth for the Isthmian Games. Aristotle is not recorded as competing, but is recorded as a promoter; he is said to have paid the expenses of Philammon of Athens, an Olympic victor in boxing.[5]

One difficulty in the organization of the Games was what to do about women. In all athletic events, including boxing, wrestling and the 'all-in' combination called the pankration, it was the custom for contestants to be completely naked. 'The Greeks always regarded their own readiness to appear naked before their fellows as one of the traits which marked them out from the barbarians.' There were games for girls and women up to a marriageable age: girls ran naked in the public games at Sparta. But outside of Sparta the Greeks came not to care for that custom, so in the large official public Games females were forbidden to contend. As a side effect, this removed women from competition in contests which were non-athletic; a ruling of which Pindar, it is said, took advantage. Pindar, at Thebes, was five times defeated by Corinna in the contest for a poetical prize, which, 'according to some' – I am here quoting Lemprière – 'was adjudged rather to the charms of her person, than to the brilliancy of her genius, or the superiority of her composition'. Be that as it may, Pindar moved on to the four most famous festivals, where women were not permitted to compete.

In the first rush of Greek lyric verse women were as quick to get off the mark, and fully as expert as men: witness Sappho. Or, for the influence which could be exerted in Athens by a woman of genius and taste, witness Aspasia. But co-education (though there were many, for instance Plato, who stood up for it) was hampered by the identification of schooling with the gymnasium. The 'gymnasium', which means literally a place where you exercise naked, with its palaestra or practice-ground and bath-house attached, provided at once a schooling and a club-life from which girls and women were excluded. The inheritance in modern life from the teaching that went on in the Academia of Athens (favoured by Socrates and Plato), the Lyceum (favoured by Aristotle) and the other gymnasia of Greece is indicated by the repetition of the names: gymnasien for schools in Teutonic countries, lycées in France, and academies all over the world. In Greek times, the natural connection of sport and soldiering is also indicated by Professor Harris, when he reminds us that 'two of Alexander's generals took their portable cover for a training track with them on the king's expedition'.[6]

Within Greece, it is painfully observable that rivalry in sports was not enough to satisfy competitive instincts. The initial squabblings of Athens and Sparta started not unlike Red Indian warfare in America, the object not so much to destroy the other tribe as to score off them, and count coups. Thucydides gives that picture, at the beginning: about 449 B.C. 'the Lacedaemonians undertook the so-called sacred war, and getting possession of the temple at Delphi, delivered it to the Delphians; and afterwards, when they had withdrawn, the Athenians made an expedition, got possession of it, and delivered it again to the Phocians'. But Thucydides makes it very clear that one aggression led to another. When Spartans invaded Attica they developed a habit of cutting down the olive trees. To destroy a cereal crop was relatively fair game, but it takes as much as forty years to replace olive trees. So instead of both sides engaging only in ritual encounters and the winners putting up trophies and then going home, the tradition grew of doing as much damage as possible, and that became serious. The Peloponnesian war began in earnest in the year 431, and it lasted for 28 years. By the end the population figures for Athens, as noted earlier for the year 431, are practically halved; the Athenian treasuries were exhausted, and the temples stripped of their silver and gold.

The general pleasures of peaceable life and the periodic excitement of the Festivals and Games were thus insufficient to prevent the Greeks from bitter and self-destructive internecine war; but no matter how many times Attica was invaded, the Peloponnesian war was never for Athens a total preoccupation. One might nowadays steep one's self in a good deal of imperishable Athenian literature with hardly any recognition that it was produced in wartime, or in a supposedly exhausted aftermath of war. The Peloponnesian war went on

for 28 years, and there was much mutual savagery. In 430, the second
year of the war, there was the destructive plague at Athens – some say
it was a virulent form of measles, and some, that it was a direct result
of too many people crowding into the city from the ravaged country-
side, and consequent breakdown both of food supply and sanitation.
Particularly in the early years of the war Attica was frequently ravaged by the Spartans; a fragment of Andocides pictures the feelings
of an Athenian:

> May we never again see the charcoal-burners and their waggons ar-
> riving in Athens from the mountains, nor sheep and cattle and helpless
> women, no, nor old men and labourers arming for battle. May we never
> again eat wild herbs and chervil.[7]

Perhaps the chronology of those war years is best followed by
thinking of the life of an individual. 429 was the third year of the war,
the year of the death of Pericles and of the birth of Plato. When Plato
was a baby of 2, in the year of the 4th invasion of Attica, Athenians
were under the stringency of eating wild herbs and chervil, and it was
in that year of austerity that Aristophanes first won the competition
as a comic poet. When Plato was 5 (a year when Socrates and Xenophon were with the troops at Delium) Aristophanes produced the
Knights. There is a short passage in the *Knights* which has given
pleasure to other people in other wartimes:

> *Demosthenes.* My poor old mate, how d'ye feel?
> *Nicias.*　　　 Bad, as bad as you do.

It is immediately after that companionable exchange that Demos-
thenes says: 'Then come here, and let's pipe Olympus' nome of woe
in concert', and the comrades hum a few bars. Aristotle has a comment about the musical compositions of Olympus, that they 'carry us
away, an effect which is a condition of the character of the soul'. It
was in the character of the Athenian soul to keep the Festivals going,
no matter what. When Plato was 15 (in the 18th year of the
war) the Athenians mounted their ill-fated expedition to Sicily;
Aristophanes at Athens produced the *Birds*. As the war dragged on
from its 20th to 27th year (and Plato aged from 17 to 24) Euripides
and Sophocles were rivals at the Festivals, and in the last year Aristophanes was lively as ever with the *Frogs*. The year 404 was the 28th

and last year of the Peloponnesian war: Athens was bankrupt, capitulated to Lysander, and Athenian democracy as such was abolished.

The bankruptcy and defeat of Athens and the continuing fertility of Athenian spirit are contradictions which have to be reconciled; at least, Athenians managed to reconcile them, and from the discussions as reported by Plato you would scarcely deduce that he had grown up in hard times. If you are of the school which maintains that Plato was born not at Athens but at the neighbouring Aegina, you may say that Plato in childhood missed the worst of the city hardships, and it was only after he had won the crown for wrestling at the Nemean Games that he came, in his 20th year, to be a devoted attendant of Socrates in Athens. It may be true that Plato never had to run around town with poor boys eating nothing but green stuff, but from his account of Socrates (or Xenophon's independent account of Socrates) there is no feeling that Socrates ever exhibited (either for himself or for Athens) any kind of excuse or self-pity. The Age of Pericles passed away with regret but without much moan; the music of the Athenians went on piping; and an example of Athenian democracy continuing to work was shown in Xenophon's *Anabasis*. That was a book which played its part in exciting the great adventure of Alexander the Great, and, without being too paradoxical, I hope to show that the example of Alexander had much to do with the reshaping of the pathway that I am studying – the westward pathway which had been started by the Phoenicians but which had apparently stopped at Carthage.

One has to have as many eyes as Argus to see things which happened to shape the Long Road West. My simple idea of tracing a human movement in a westward direction came to a halt at Carthage; it was not mere physical movement that I was attempting to study, but the westward movement of something that could be called, according to preference, 'civilization' or 'civility'. At Carthage I could see a people who had made an immense stride westward in mileage, but the life that they created seemed dull, particularly when compared with what the Greeks were doing. While Greeks were busy with their own fightings, Carthage recovered from her defeats, conquered most of Sicily (closing that western source of grain supplies to Greece), and unrest on both sides of the Straits of Messina began to attract attention as far away as Rome. One eye needs only to note that at the beginning of the 4th century B.C. Rome was as yet remote, and the Senate not as yet much concerned with other than local problems. Another eye notices that in Greece, immediately after the Peloponnesian war, there was impulse for individuals to break away from the rock pool and serve as mercenary soldiers elsewhere. The 10,000 who engaged to serve the Persian Cyrus, at first under Spartan leadership but later under the leadership of Xenophon, came from all over the Grecian world; and what that little band of Greek soldiers did was to prove, to Philip of Macedon, how vulnerable the Great Kings of the East really were. Philip was no friend to Athens or Sparta; he had won a crown at the Olympic Games, but there was greater glory to be won by conquering the ancient enemies, the wealthy Persians. Philip, as it happened, was killed in a flare-up of tempers while preparing for the invasion of Asia. The young Alexander at once took over, assumed command, and with a force (it is said) of 32,000 foot and 5,000 horse, set out to attack the East. If the figures are correct, Alexander's force was smaller than the force with which Caesar later invaded Britain. The smallness of his striking force did not prevent, or perhaps enabled, Alexander to become Alexander the Great.

Nothing caused so much astonishment in the ancient Western World as the phenomenal career of Alexander. It seems to me that there were three ways in which the example of Alexander affected the westward movement of civilization. There is no need to rehearse Alexander's career in detail: the active fighting in the rougher parts of Asia Minor, the humiliation of Tyre, Egypt's capitulation, the conquests of Media, Syria, Persia, the impact on the borders of India and on the inner parts of Scythia – and then Alexander's retirement to Babylon and his death at the age of 32 or 33. There is less need to dwell upon the detail; it is the general impression upon which one has to pause, the deduction from Alexander's career of a then world-wide feeling, in the 4th century B.C., that powers at one time great were universally sick and weak and that a new order could be welcome and accepted. When I say we may skip the details of Alexander's career I do not mean that the details are unimportant. Egypt, for instance, capitulating without a blow: one must remember how, before the 4th century, Egypt had been a symbol in the Mediterranean world for all that meant stability.* Alexander, a mere upstart from the rascally state of Macedonia – that in wise and ancient Egypt he should be accepted as a god, was a prodigious portent. That was the first striking indication that a ruler of a western state might rule the world.

One of the influences of Alexander's eastward adventures in the creation of a Road West was commented on by Plutarch. Plutarch, reflecting at leisure at his home in Chaeronea, in a reasonably serene period of the *pax Romana*, was not thinking primarily of the geographical transplanting of ideas (such as my theme demands). Life in Boeotia was placid at the time that he was writing (some time about A.D. 118) and he was reflecting on the blessings of the *pax Romana*. But the very conception of such a universal peace was due, he felt, to the example of Alexander. 'Knowing himself used by the gods to be the lawgiver to all, and to reconcile humanity, he [Alexander] desired that all men should regard the entire world as a single fatherland.' According to Plutarch, Alexander's military undertakings were only means to this great aim. It had to be admitted that not much of this idea of a world-polity survived Alexander's death in 323 B.C. All the world that Alexander had conquered promptly fell apart; yet the effective idea of one united world-empire, containing different peoples in one peaceful combination, was not lost. It emerged again in Rome, and (according to Plutarch) directly from Alexander's example. That is what I meant by the apparent paradox, that Alexander's adventures in the east contributed to westward movement. The idea of empire had taken a long westward course when it was put into effect by Rome.

The funeral pyre of Dido is a symbol that whatever had been the Tyrian idea of a 'great society' simply and of itself burnt out; but the

* I was thinking of the lament of Hermes Trismegistus: 'O Aegypte, Aegypte, religionum tuarum solae supererunt fabulae, eaeque incredibiles posteris tuis; solaque supererunt verba lapidibus incisa, tua pia facta narrantibus'. ('O Egypt, Egypt, of thy religious rites nought will survive but idle tales which thy childrens' children will not believe; nought will survive but words graven upon stones that tell of thy piety'). (The Latin Asclepius III, 25, in W. Scott, *Hermetica*, i., p. 342). What Plato had been impressing upon Greeks was the permanence of Egypt; the much later lament reflects a change of feeling which was not expressed until after Alexander.

funeral pyre of Alexander at Babylon is symbol of a flame which others (and now in the west) attempted to relight. The most obvious of the immediate imitators of Alexander were the would-be rivals for military glory and the consequent personal rewards. The impersonal ambition of creating one whole world at peace – the ambition as ascribed to Alexander by the benevolent Plutarch – is not much observable in Pyrrhus, pretender to the throne of Macedonia, and conscious imitator of Alexander 'in arms and action'.* And Pyrrhus is of importance to my narrative, for very distinctly it was Pyrrhus who first stirred Rome to arms and action on a larger than local scale.

Before about 340 B.C. the Roman military organization was regarded by nobody as an instrument of foreign conquest. Rome appears as self-contained, deliberative about its own self-government, industriously cultivating the olive and the vine – Rome, an entity, a unity, hostile to immediate neighbours, not liked by them and not much concerned to be liked. Nobody playing around in the Greek rock pool seemed to be much aware of Rome, nor were early Romans much excited by Greek sports. I do not read of Roman competitors at the early Olympic Games. Perhaps they were not admitted; I do not know; but whether admitted or not, there is no sign that they much cared. The Greek towns of lower Italy cared at that time very much about the Games. In the period 596–300 B.C., the Greek colony of Taras (or, in Latin, Tarentum) and her neighbour-city Croton scored a total of 29 victories at Olympia; Sparta in the same period scored 13. And at the period after the Peloponnesian war, when Alexander burst out of the rock pool to the east, a similar centrifugal explosiveness seems to show in the Greek colonies. The voyage of Pytheas from Massilia occurs at that time; but more to the point, in the year 334, the same year in which Alexander started on his eastern campaigns, the Tarentines attacked the Romans.

The Roman response to this attack from the south is what seems to

---

* The phrase is from Plutarch. 'The other kings, the Macedonians said, represented Alexander with their purple robes, their body-guards, the inclination of their necks, and their louder tones in conversation; but Pyrrhus, and Pyrrhus alone, in arms and action' (*Life of Pyrrhus*). According to Plutarch, Hannibal 'declared that the foremost of all generals in experience and ability was Pyrrhus, that Scipio was second, and he himself third'.

me of special interest. Romans began methodically to build a stone-paved road in the direction of the enemy. Efficient military organization was demanded, so they turned a businesslike attention to that; and the most businesslike of the inventions, it seems to me, was that paved road, the Appian Way (Rome to Tarracina and Capua), begun in the year 312. A paved road, with *coloniae* at strategic points, gave all-weather mobility to Roman troops. There was, it would seem, no concern that it might lead enemy troops in; it was a statement rather of determination that if there was going to be warfare to the south, Rome would push out to meet it. Rome had manpower to build a paved road, a solid permanent investment; where Rome pushed, she would push for keeps. I harp upon this road because it was an indication of a spirit which was distinctively non-Greek. 'Is not the road to Athens made for conversation?' was a remark of Plato; there was not much attention to the dull job of making it a paved road. The road from Rome was professionally paved for permanence; and it signified that if it was going to be used for war, that war would not be just a momentary game of hit and run.

The Tarentines, who are described by Plutarch as a people not so much notable for constancy of purpose as for liveliness, and fiestas, and brilliancy by fits and starts, in due course countered what seemed to them a plodding dour spirit of the Romans by engaging Pyrrhus. At the moment, of all the kingly Greeks he was the most at leisure, with reputation as the most formidable general, and one who at nights was given to dreaming of cordial conversations with Alexander the Great. Pyrrhus 'thought it tedious to the point of nausea if he were not inflicting mischief on others or suffering it at others' hands, and like Achilles could not endure idleness,

> "but ate his heart away
> Remaining there, and pined for war-cry and battle" '

It was in character therefore, Plutarch says, for Pyrrhus to accept the invitation of the Tarentines. Despite shipwreck on the way, he managed to land in Italy with a small contingent of Indian elephants; and in his first engagement the elephants were of advantage, and he out-manoeuvred the Romans. Both sides suffered heavily in that first battle; the Romans were compelled to abandon the field, and Pyrrhus marched to within '300 furlongs' distance' from Rome, at which point he offered terms. By ordinary rules Rome should have acknowledged his victory; but the Senate refused. In further and very hard-fought trials of strength there were the same 'Pyrrhic victories'; and finally Pyrrhus was unable to impose his will upon a people who despite their losses would not admit defeat. During his six years in Italy, Pyrrhus made a side-incursion into Sicily; there he tested Carthaginian enmity, and as he was leaving, made the prophetic remark 'My friends, what a wrestling ground for Carthaginians and Romans we are leaving behind us!'

In 275 B.C. Pyrrhus sailed away and, for the second time, fought himself into the throne of Macedonia. The Tarentines were much worse off than before, for Rome, hitherto not much inclined toward distant military action, had been stung into action by Pyrrhus. Plutarch points out that Rome now had troops in hand, who, from fighting off the greatest warrior since Alexander, had themselves acquired 'high courage and power and a reputation for invincibility', and 'they at once got control of Italy, and soon afterward of Sicily'.

The Roman Senate, not in the least Empire-minded, continued as it were to make Rome into a solid block of concrete. I search in vain for a metaphor better than that, simultaneously to express the firmness and solidity for which the ancient Romans had such gift, and their feeling for steady, heavy, industrious building. The power of the phrase *civis Romanus sum* was so strong a cement in the laws of the Roman Republic as not to crumble in later Dictatorships or later Empire. In thinking about the Greek way of life, I felt competent only to select one strand as relevant to my theme; and for Rome likewise I shall be no more daring than to select what my theme calls for. I shall have need of the Roman conception of Law, and the firmness of its application, and of the gradual extension outwards of Roman citizenship. Also what I need to watch in the early Republic is the emphasis on team-work in engineering. Romans were interested in aqueducts when Pyrrhus came along to interrupt. The first aqueduct, the Aqua Appia, had been less than a mile in length; when Pyrrhus had been driven away the Anio Vetus was completed, which brought water 40 miles to Rome from the Sabine Hills. The sting applied by Pyrrhus was, it seems, interpreted as requiring an orgy of road-making. The Appian Way was pushed on from Capua

south-eastward towards Tarentum and Brundisium; other paved
roads began to tie Italy tightly together – the Via Latina, the Via
Flaminia, and the Via Aurelia along the coast to Tuscany and Pisae.
The spirit of the road-building seems to be that of making the whole
of peninsular Italy into one compact defensible unit. There is not
much impression of quick greedy haste for military aggression. The
manpower available for the road-making is impressive; and, as Plutarch was observing, there was also a high-spirited manpower remaining under arms after the final brush which dismissed Pyrrhus. It was
natural that before the troops were disbanded they should be used to
punish the Tarentines. There was a further call from Messana for the
aid of invincible Roman troops against the Carthaginians. Without
much special clamour about it in Rome, the military aid was granted
to Messana; and so, in 264 B.C., the first Punic war began. Sicily became, as Pyrrhus had predicted, the wrestling ground for Rome and
Carthage. Pyrrhus, imitator of Alexander, and as it were the catalytic
agent of the first Punic war, did not live to hear about it. Three years
after his return to Macedonia he was attacking Argos, and there was
killed, in the 46th year of his age, by a woman who snatched a tile
from the house-top and hurled it on his head.

Polybius in his *Histories* devotes much detailed study to the importance of the Punic wars in shaping and increasing the determined
spirit of the Romans. Nothing I think is more impressive (and nobody
since has written about it any better than Polybius) than the way the
Romans methodically set about learning sea-warfare. Land-fighting
was more natural to them; Polybius expresses the unshakeable
confidence in Rome that no matter how the war dragged on in Sicily,
their own home-grown soldiery would in the end master any of the
mercenaries, Numidian or Libyan, which Carthage might employ.
But Carthage at the beginning and for several years of the war had
complete control of the sea. The Romans had no ships of their own,
nor any experience in ship-building, nor any home-grown mariners.
None the less they set to work to build a navy. A decked ship of the
Carthaginians had run aground; it was seized by the Romans and
used as a pattern, from which was fabricated a whole fleet. While the
fleet was building, rowers were collected and drilled in the art of
rowing, using benches on dry land. Their first experiments at sea
were thoroughly unhappy. Roman ships and oarsmen were easily out-

classed by Carthaginians; but the Romans concentrated on one theory: if in calm water an enemy ship should come close enough to be grappled and held alongside, in the hand to hand fighting they would have superiority. Someone, Polybius says, suggested the engines which came to be called 'ravens'. Polybius (himself a soldier) describes in detail these cumbersome, top-heavy, crane-like structures which were to grab the enemy ships and make a sea-battle 'just like a fight on land'. In a first and fortunate encounter the ravens worked; they astonished the Carthaginians, who lost 50 ships. This sea-fight at Mylae (off the northeast point of Sicily) caused immense jubilation in Rome: Gaius Duilius received the first triumph ever accorded for a naval victory. In Roman opinion the war was as good as over. The war went on for another 16 years. Premature elation about sea-fighting was soon dashed, chiefly because Roman commanders had no patience to be weather-wise. In the course of the war 700 of their largest ships (quinqueremes) were lost, mainly from storm damage. But the Roman economy could afford replacements, and Roman manpower was not exhausted, and after 23 years from the beginning, the first Punic war was in fact ended by a sea-battle.

The general exhaustion of Carthage toward the end of the long war is observable, but it is a reversal of faith which seems significant. To state it baldly: Carthage lost faith in the sea. The mere statement does not measure what I am trying to say; which is, that an age-old central faith departed from this sea-port city, whose harbour had always been the heart. About any city other than Carthage, the statement I have made would have less meaning. Unless all my surmisings have been altogether wrong, sea-water was the blood of Carthage, seafaring was the interstitial tissue. To detect a falling-off in shipping and a lack of upkeep for the ships is, for Carthage, to pronounce a fatal diagnosis. That lack of upkeep, that loss of pride in ships, is diagnosed some time before the end of the long war; by the 21st or 22nd year of the war the signs are obvious. Polybius reads less meaning into the signs than I do. He says the Carthaginians allowed their ships to become unserviceable, their maritime equipment to run down, their crews to be untrained, through an unwise contempt for the Romans. Thus, in the final sea-fight, the Carthaginians were short of both men and serviceable ships. The final sea-fight certainly proved the Carthaginian deterioration; but the deterioration had set in before that; and was, I would think, due less to contempt of the Romans than to exhaustion within Carthage itself. Whether there was shortage of materials for ship-replacement, whether all the best men had been killed off, whatever the causes or excuses, when exhaustion in Carthage touched the harbour, the disease was fatal. I instanced an early loss of heart for the women of Carthage, when 'purple' lost its tone and women put up with inferiority; a swift loss of spirit in the men is manifested when the harbour at Carthage lost its tone. It was a religion that had gone; Melkarth had turned away, and had been seen to turn away. There was a short time left for men of Carthage to search for other gods, but when sea-service failed them it can be noticed that they never again found a proud unity of spirit.

For a short time only, this diagnosis was concealed. Melkarth had turned away, was stolen by the Romans, was renamed Hercules; very well, the Carthaginians might steal Mars. The initial jubilation at Rome after the sea-fight at Mylae was premature, but it was justified: it was at sea that the war was won by Romans. On land, and contrary to every Roman expectation, contrary to effort, stubbornness, courage and far superior manpower, the Romans were unable to subdue the Carthaginians in Sicily. 'The general to whom the palm must be given both for daring and for genius,' says Polybius, 'is Hamilcar called Barcas, the actual father of that Hannibal who afterwards made war on the Romans.' It was the unbeaten Hamilcar who was instructed from ship-weary Carthage to make peace in the year 241, at the humiliating terms of total evacuation of Sicily, the ceding to Rome of Sardinia and Corsica, and the payment of more than fifty tons of silver; the silver to be produced within twenty years.

Anyone who has sympathy with Hamilcar or with the Carthaginians is handicapped by their illiteracy. Within Carthage there may have been a peace-party; there was a western world still open to Carthaginians; they could forget about Sicily, they had an Africa, they had a New Carthage in Spain. It was about this time that Mago seems to have been writing his works on farming; that suggests that even if faith in sea-supremacy had departed, there were some who had faith in their lands. There was no time granted for peaceable hopes to develop. It was not the loss of Sicily but the return of the army to Carthage, there to be paid off, which caused the trouble. Carthage, for troops to fight on land, had always had to depend on mercenaries; the men who fought with Hamilcar in Sicily were a mixed lot of Iberians, Greeks, Numidians and Libyans; united, though, in pride that it was they who had humiliated Rome. They had done their job, and done it well, and returned to Carthage for their pay. There was clamour within Carthage not to pay them, and they were not paid. Since most of the mercenary troops were Libyans, the new war that Carthage was quickly forced to fight was called the Libyan war. It was no momentary flare-up. The Libyan war lasted three years and four months and 'far excelled all wars we know of in cruelty and defiance of principle', says Polybius; but the point here is not to dwell upon the horrors of it, but to say that Carthage only got out of that war by entrusting itself entirely to Hamilcar Barcas. Hamilcar in turn cared little for the life of Carthage. When the North African scene was at length restored to a resentful and uneasy peace, Hamilcar withdrew to Spain, taking with him his son Hannibal, then about nine years of age.

Hannibal was trained in Spain to be a soldier of fortune, in the same direct line of ambition which Pyrrhus had derived from Alexander. Hannibal saw his father reduce 'many Iberian tribes to obedience either by force of arms or by diplomacy', but the steady purpose for which alliances were made and Iberian soldiery enlisted had less to do with benefiting Carthage than with providing Hannibal with force for the revenge which he was sworn to take on Rome. Thus, and rightly, Polybius declines to speak of the wars yet to come as 'Punic' wars. He calls them the Hannibalic wars: wars to appease his father's feelings, and for a personal success in the endeavour in which his father had not been beaten, and in which Pyrrhus had almost succeeded. To hell with what happened to Carthage: Hannibal was going to conquer Rome.

Now I can be less detailed, and look at the result. What I have seen is this: after dealing with Pyrrhus, Rome had some troops in hand, and without as yet much thought of Empire, engaged in a small war for Sicily. I followed that war; I need not follow the Hannibalic wars; merely note in passing the complete ruin imposed on Carthage at the end; and – which is of importance for my Road West – the flight of Hannibal himself eastward, over the old original Phoenician sea-route, to join Antiochus, King of Syria. Was Hannibal, now the arch-enemy of the Roman people and the Roman Senate, to escape? Rome had more troops in hand than after Pyrrhus, and lest Hannibal raise head in far off Syria, for the first time there was movement of Roman troops eastward. Greece, Macedonia, happened to be in the way and there were some scores to settle; but the trigger for the eastward movement was to threaten Antiochus into giving up Hannibal. Frightened by the Roman threat, Antiochus sent the old war-criminal (Hannibal by then was approaching 70) farther on to the King of Bithynia. Thus the Roman Senate learned geography, and threats were made against Bithynia. Hannibal took the poison from the ring on his finger, and so far as concerns my theme, his fame passes; but he had been the agent whereby the short Appian Way became a long sea-road.

NOTES

1. Herodotus (Book II, 48–50). I rely on the translation by A. D. Godley in the Loeb Classical Library. I would like to put in a layman's tribute to the Loeb Classical Library: it does enable a layman to enter the otherwise walled garden of the Classics, with a ticket to range freely. It enables one to read the writings at the natural pace for which they were designed, and to get some measure of a work in its entirety; but with the text, which is ever the real thing, side by side, for as much close attention as one's senses are equipped to give it (or to receive from it). As to translations in general, naturally one acquires preferences. The reference to inspecting the great works of Egypt 'on the spot' is to Plato's *Laws* (11, 656, e). For the *Laws* I personally prefer the translation by A. E. Taylor, available in Everyman's Library, also conveniently reprinted in *Plato's Collected Dialogues*, edited by Hamilton and Cairns. Plato refers to the Atlantis myth in two dialogues, *Timaeus* and *Critias*. For these 'poetical' passages I prefer Jowett's translation.
   For Pindar I shall rely on the translation by Sir John Sandys in the Loeb Classical Library.

2. Bradford, op. cit., pp. 112, 113.

3. *Timaeus* (Jowett's translation). See Ronald Schiller (*Reader's Digest* December, 1967) for the suggestion that the Santorini eruption of

about 1400 B.C., which eliminated the island of Stronghyli (70 miles north of Crete), may have started, or reinforced, the Atlantis story.

4. *Greek Athletes and Athletics* by H. A. Harris (Hutchinson, London, 1964).

5. Harris, p. 38. For the Greek 'readiness to appear naked', see Harris p. 65. For the comment on Pindar's defeats by Corinna, see *Lemprière's Classical Dictionary* (Routledge, London, 1949).

6. According to Harris (pp. 40, 41), Alexander's generals, Perdiccas and Craterus, carried on their campaigns a huge marquee 200 yards long, to enable training to be continued under all conditions of weather: 'perhaps the earliest example of indoor athletics'. Wherever the Greeks went (even to India) there was spread of enthusiasm for athletic contests. Unexpected enthusiasm, says Professor Harris, 'is to be found in the complaint of the author of *Maccabees* in the second century B.C. that the young priests in Jerusalem were neglecting their temple duties in order to practice discus throwing'.

7. *Minor Attic Orators,* translated by K. J. Maidment (Loeb Classical Library), vol. I, p. 583.

CHAPTER 7

Civis Romanus Sum

I AM increasingly puzzled about the nature of the thing I set out to study. A human migration and the pathway that it took are not matters to be thought of separately. There is perpetual interplay: the tribe makes a road, and use of the road then alters the tribe. The interaction of tribal spirit with other man-made instruments is also very much observable, but road-making, insofar as road-making asserts itself as an identifiable factor, is for me here a sufficient mystery. I had a nebulous view of what happened to Phoenicians when they took to sea-faring. What happened to Rome when the Appian Way had stretched out to join the main sea-highway of the Mediterranean is more distinct.

By unexpected reflex actions the road itself appears as an active participant in Roman affairs. Consider Rome in the beginning, when it was a parochial kingdom; under the Tarquins a noticeable characteristic was the interest of Romans in solid building, stonework, masonry. Centuries later, one Tarquin's 'simple edifices' were a continuing part of Rome's heritage. Another Tarquin made the term *Rex* a word that was continuingly shameful: Rome prospered more as a Republic, Senate and populace retaining faith in the Sibylline Books, in the XII Tables of Law, and continuing to express prosperity in solid building. Such is a simplified impression of parochial Rome, remote as yet from the east-west seaway of the Mediterranean. I had been watching that seaway: the sea-paths as it were marked, established, taken for granted, squabbled over by different tribes of people, from Syria to Carthage, from Greece to southern Italy. I had been watching the traffic on the Mediterranean long before Rome sent out a tentacle which might or might not touch the sea-routes. I look at that tentacle, the Appian Way, with increasing astonishment. There was nothing tentative about its physical construction. The direction, the aim, the purpose of the road – all that – seems relatively casual. Rome to Capua: the immediate demands of traffic would seem to call for no more than a by-road. Not so to the Roman builder – nothing

less than a stone-paved causeway, an amazingly solid piece of engineering, no problem avoided, no detail incomplete, the whole professionally polished – nothing less than that was made of this
small piece of road when Rome was but a small Republic sitting on
its seven hills. The display of energy in the building of the Appian
Way seems wholly excessive. What that stone causeway wrote upon
the domestic landscape between Rome and Capua carried a surplus
of significance. It was a statement as legible as the writings
on the bronze pillars of Solomon's Temple; it was a Roman statement, seemingly inerasable, of the stability and power of the young
Republic.

But a road, a pathway (land, sea, air or space), is more than a
passive instrument. The heavier the investment in the pathway, the
more apt it seems to turn upon its makers. I have to look at that first
piece of Appian Way as if it were a stone-muscle – it is not easy to
find a right metaphor – as something that was going to have a flexing
power far beyond the expectation of the Appius Claudius who gave it
his name. First I watch the stone-muscle pushing outward from the
Porta Capena; later I watch what the muscle pulls in by reflex
through that same gate of Rome. So far I have seen only the first of
the outward pushings. I made out that Rome had been irritated by
the Tarentines; that as part of the reaction the Appian Way stretched
out, an angry arm, a paw with claws. The paw reached on for Sicily,
the claws (Polybius called them ravens) splashed into sea-water. That
is what is to be noticed, rather than the Punic War as such. The
Appian Way had stretched into a new element.

Not just in idle curiosity but with awareness which has moments of
horror, I watch the road stretching out from Rome as if it were a
muscle. There is no appropriate metaphor – it is only a road, provided you see a road as something which grows and flexes and acts.
It is to express the activity that one strives for the metaphor. This
Roman road, for sure, was active. It was alive, it could be hurt, it
could be severed. Hannibal cut it off: Hannibal's men, some of them
Spaniards, some of them Greeks, sat and feasted at Capua. That was
as horrible for Rome as an arm torn off at the shoulder. The limb had
power of renewal. The limb indeed was not torn off: the claws were
fastened to Hannibal. As Hannibal moved away the road dragged
after him, but not as if it were a lifeless thing. The arm was stronger,

stronger now than Hannibal. Hannibal moved to Carthage, and this time there was no reprieve for Carthage. There was no reprieve for Hannibal – it was his blood the claws were after. Hannibal fled from Carthage by sea, over the old Phoenician sea-way to the East. It was that flight of Hannibal which drew the Romans after him, and so attached the road which had started as a by-road, the former short stone-muscle of the Appian Way, to the more ancient fluid highway of the Midland Sea.

Now what I must perceive is the complete and thorough manner in which the east-west Mediterranean sea-way, although a sea-way, became a Roman road. Generations of men have been so impressed by the remains of hard-paved Roman roads on land, that when a 'Roman road' is mentioned, it is a land-road that is thought of. The making of a Roman through-way over the Midland Sea was fully as methodical. As I watched the first Punic war, the spectacle of Romans tackling the sea, as if a sea-road could be sighted ahead with boning-rods, as if its path could be hacked out with two-toothed mattocks, seemed to me comical. They paid a price in ships and men for their thought that winds and water would succumb to engineering. But in the end it was at sea that they beat the Carthaginians; and after Hannibal had fled eastward – Hannibal, who had injured and angered Romans more than anyone would have thought possible – the process was almost automatic, whereby the eastward sea should become a marching road for Roman legions. The process was in fact complicated: Greeks who had sided with Hannibal were due for punishment, and that became a process in itself. Yet taking a large view, what is important to watch is the steady growth of the eastward sea-route, the Romans making a sea-road that should be theirs and nobody else's. The death of Hannibal in Bithynia scarcely mattered; he had activated a procedure of sea-roadmaking that was self-continuing. The Greek states were in such a condition of dismembering themselves as rather to invite than to impede eastward troop movement. Except for Macedonia there was small organized resistance, and after the battle of Pydna (168 B.C.) there was no fight left in Macedonia. Again what I attend to is not so much the submission of all Greece, as the increasing growth of Roman-controlled sea-traffic. I have to see not only the outward pulse of the strong road-muscle, but the reflex action. What came back along the sea-routes to Brundisium and travelled up the Appian Way to the Porta Capena had much to do with altering the way of life within the walls of Rome.

The decay of the Roman Republic, the alteration of life in Rome, is far too wide a theme to be measured by road-study; but in the wide theme the flexing of the sea-road constantly turns up. One cannot say that the Roman sea-road caused the downfall of the Republic, but it is easy to perceive instances of its active participation.

Caesar was born about 100 B.C. By that time the east-west sea-highway was carrying so many cargoes to Rome that piracy, upon the sea, was of itself an organized and formidable profession. Safety of travel upon the Roman land-roads was a matter of concern, familiar enough to Senate and populace. On the Appian Way within a day's travel from Rome there was a particular grasshopper-hill called Aricia, notorious for unexpected appearances of thieves and marauders, *lazaroni* or *lepros*. More serious and dangerous was the outbreak of the gladiators under Spartacus; the escape of the desperate men from the gladiatorial school at Capua caused a well-warranted fear about road-traffic. Whether for casual highwaymen or for rebellion such as organized by Spartacus, all land-roads demanded police-work. Crassus did the hard work of suppressing Spartacus, but the more popular hero Pompey turned up from Spain to steal the credit. Interruptions to traffic on the sea-highway were as frequent, and more difficult to cope with. Action to make sea-travel safe for Romans was demanded. Caesar, for instance, as a young man of 22 set out, in a way regarded as normal for a young man born to the purple, to sail to Rhodes to study oratory. On the voyage he was captured by pirates, and, for release, had to pay 50 talents. Indignant Caesar had his revenge; those particular pirates were crucified; the episode calls for mention only as an instance of an awareness, which increased in Rome, of a need for harsh policing of the seas. In a short ten years after Caesar's adventure I can guess at many repetitions. Need for police-work at sea was so vivid a concern in Rome, or could be played up as such, as to cause the Roman Senate to entrust to Pompey a total of 500 ships, fully manned for active warfare, to make the Mediterranean seaways safe from piracy.

This is a moment at which to pause. There ought to be an apprehensiveness that the strong stone-muscle of the Appian Way, extending now into the sea, might in fact stimulate action in reverse.

It was not long before this time that Sulla, having the seaway at his command, had returned from Greece and imposed his will on Rome by force of arms. As if the recent proscriptions of Sulla had been forgotten, the force of warships allotted by the Senate to Pompey's sole command was formidable. It was a naval force greater than had been assembled, at any one moment, for use against Carthage. The proclaimed purpose was to put down piracy, wherever it occurred; to make the whole of the Mediterranean a Roman lake. The year for this programme was 67 B.C., twelve years after Sulla had relinquished his dictatorship. Pompey's age, when entrusted with unprecedented sea-power, was 39. Caesar at this time was 33.

Pompey's police-work was rapid and effective. He divided the whole of the sea and the adjacent coasts into 13 districts; for each district there was a commander, responsible directly to him. 'In forty days all told,' Plutarch reports, Pompey had cleared all pirates from the Tyrrhenian Sea, the Libyan Sea, and the sea about Sardinia, Corsica and Sicily. 'This was owing to his own tireless energy and the zeal of his lieutenants'. The citizens of Rome expressed excited jubilation: with unhoped for rapidity of change, the market was now 'filled to overflowing' with provisions. A residue of piratical ships escaped Pompey's network around Italy; they were reported to have 'sought their hive' in far away Cilicia. Against Cilicia therefore, Pompey proceeded in person. Now the temptation for Pompey to abuse his power became a little clearer. The Roman law had presented Pompey with dominion over the whole of the sea and over all the rim of mainland to the distance of four hundred furlongs from the sea; within the year this had been interpreted by Pompey to add to his personal conquests the territories of Phrygia, Lycaonia, Galatia, Cappadocia, Cilicia, Upper Colchis, and Armenia. With the same exuberance with which within Italy he had stolen the credit from Crassus for the suppression of Spartacus, he borrowed, as soon as he was in the East, legions which had been sent there for the fighting with Mithridates and Tigranes. Now were some Senators in Rome beginning to be seriously alarmed. The power given to Pompey 'to take the sea away from the pirates' was being interpreted (so Plutarch puts it) as 'not an admiralty, but an out-and-out monarchy and irresponsible power over all men'. Reports from Pompey divided senatorial opinion. At his own whim Pompey had turned southward, demonstrating his strength to Alexandria, conquering Jerusalem in 64, and remaining (until 62) in his headquarters in Syria, which *he* proclaimed a province.

That Pompey had now made the east-west seaway of the Mediterranean into a solid Roman road, solid and safe for Roman travel, is sufficiently indicated by an anecdote, otherwise trivial, in Plutarch's life of Cicero. One of the Metellus family enters Plutarch's narrative because he happened to be a butt for one of Cicero's many sarcasms. To characterize this Metellus Nepos, Plutarch says he was 'a fickle sort of man', and what defines his fickleness is that 'he once suddenly deserted his office of tribune and sailed off to join Pompey in Syria, and then came back from there with even less reason'. That was in the year 62. I derive from the anecdote that by 62 an end-to-end return journey, over the seaway between Rome and Syria, could be arranged at short notice, with no particular hazard of pirates. It is taken for granted that the long seaway is viable. It is taken for granted that the whole route is a Roman road, extension of the Appian Way. That had been achieved by Pompey's power. What next for Pompey? Was he, the armed commander of the seaway, intending to return with greater strength than Sulla to rule all Italy and Rome itself? There was more point to the 'fickleness' of Metellus than Plutarch chose to make out. Rome itself – the Roman Republic – was becoming fickle, changeable, avid for excitement.

The tentacle of the Appian Way had now branched out into the many tentacles that spread over the Midland Sea, and which made that sea, from end to end, Roman. The reflex action of the greater seaways begins to be observable. I go back to Sulla in 83 B.C. as a first example: a Roman official, sent to Greece to serve Rome, returns to use his troops to subdue Rome itself, imposing his individual will upon the institutions which had long been collectively built up in the Republic. The political institutions of Rome were strong enough not to be wholly altered in the three years of Sulla's dictatorship, but the reflex action of the roadway to Greece was not confined to the sending back of a temporary dictator. One naturally pays attention to the impact Sulla made on the governance of Rome; one pays attention also to a more general contagion carried in from Greece. I am thinking not only of material things which seeped into Rome by way of loot, plunder or trade; I am thinking of Grecian ideas and a gradual crumbling of the old Roman religion. Later on, and through the participation of a road other than the road to Greece, the successive replacements of the old religion (as extolled, say, by Polybius), become dramatic. Premonitions of the drama are noticeable in the time of Sulla. When Sulla fought his fellow-Romans and seized the City, an incident in the fighting was that the Capitol was burned. In that conflagration there perished the Sibylline Books. Whatever the cryptic guidance that had been provided by the Sibylline verses, it had been a home-grown guidance; whatever the superstition, it had been a superstition that was of Roman tradition, guarded by a Roman college of priests. Now that those books were gone, it is to be observed that commissioners were hastily sent over the seaway to Greece. The search in Greece for material from which to reconstruct Sibylline verses was unsuccessful, but that is not the point. The point is that at an occasion of distress that particular wound to Roman piety was not regarded as self-healing: comfort was looked for from an outside source. Much earlier than the time of Sulla various thoroughly-Roman Romans had individually struggled with the impact of Greek thinkings. Cato the Elder, vehement in youth against all Greek influences, in age had turned to studying the Greeks. Cato the Younger, no less a thoroughly-Roman Roman, welded with his Roman piety a Stoicism consciously derived from Greece; and when (in struggles that we shall come to) he detected nothing in Crassus, Pompey, or Caesar but political opportunism – when Cato for his own part chose suicide, his death was after a pattern that was Greek.* At the time when the tentacle of sea-road to Greece flexed and threw back Sulla to become Dictator, much of Roman thinking had become Hellenized; and Sulla, when he brought Apellicon's library from Athens (including most of the works of Aristotle) was following an established intellectual trend. But for the orthodox college of priests in Rome to consult with Greece on a matter of religious ritual suggests a wider emotional disturbance. A little more, and as other tentacles of seaway strengthen, we may see a situation within Rome similar to the situation within Jerusalem, when each of Solomon's trade treaties brought with it a strange god. After the time of Sulla I watch the sea-

---

* I see no reason to doubt the story that Cato spent the night before he killed himself, reading and thinking about Plato's *Phaedo*.

roads not merely for their participation in providing Rome with new conquerors but also with new deities.

Switching now from the earlier highway to Greece to the lengthier new Roman road to Syria, as soon as Romans pondered on Pompey's achievements, it was expected that on his return he would imitate Sulla's example. In 62 B.C. Pompey's return was heralded. 'All sorts of stories about Pompey kept travelling to Rome before him,' says Plutarch, 'and there was much commotion there, where it was thought that he would straightway lead his army against the city, and that a monarchy would be securely established.' Pompey's first gesture astonished those who feared him. On arrival at Brundisium, he disbanded his army. His soldiers were sent home, or appeased with land-grants, and told to remember to come together again for the celebration of his triumph. As the conqueror of Asia journeyed along to Rome unarmed, as though returning from an ordinary sojourn abroad, the people streamed forth to show their good will; and Plutarch observes that if at that moment Pompey had purposed any revolutionary changes at Rome, he would have had no need of the army that he had disbanded. His exaltation was refreshed by his triumph, gloriously celebrated in 61. In the display there were reminders of Pompey's two previous triumphs for his services in Libya and in Europe, and it seemed indeed that by adding the conquest of Asia, one man had conquered the whole world.

My theme does not at all require a detailed study of the next decade. What is sufficient to observe is that the road to the East, considered as a participator in human affairs, has repeated the pattern of sending back a Roman with sufficient power to alter Roman institutions, at his own wish. If Pompey's nature was to fritter away the power accorded to him, that power was certainly such as to arouse Caesar's envy. The picture which is unforgettable, in the decade after Pompey's triumph, is that of Caesar turning from matters of politics to mastery of soldiering. Caesar, who until after Pompey's triumph had no experience of commanding troops in action – we cannot avoid watching Caesar (now past the age of 40) leaving Rome, constantly in the field, at the lean and hungry business of practising, perpetually practising, his active fighting against northern sparring-partners. Whilst attending to the vivid picture of Caesar in the north training himself to become a soldier, one tends almost to forget the roadway to the East. That road might seem, for the decade, to be vegetating; and so it was, if you recall that the Roman word *vegetare* meant to be active or lively. In 58 it was the road to Syria which attracted the bright and dashing young Mark Antony and introduced him to what became his Oriental cast of mind. But it is after Caesar had returned from the north and crossed the Rubicon, and after Pompey chose to retreat from Rome, that the Road East comes into full visible activity. For, as it had been with Sulla and the road to Greece, the reflex action of the Road East upon Rome was not confined to the sending back of this or that soldier to govern. More profound was the sending back of alien conceptions of what should govern governments: in other words, the sending back and the acceptance in Rome of a different idea of Deity. I am watching the process by which there comes into the life of Rome the possessive conception of a man-god, an idea never hitherto permitted in Roman religion.

It is after Caesar crossed the Rubicon that the seaway to the East manifests itself suddenly, unexpectedly, as if by accident. At the Rubicon one thinks of Caesar primarily as a soldier: first things come first, he has to win his battles. At the battle of Pharsalus, in the year 48, he is the soldier who, and suddenly, has won. What then? The actuality of such a moment, is it ever as preconceived? 'They would have it thus', said Caesar, as he gazed upon the Roman dead at Pharsalus; and, if I follow Professor Syme's interpretation, Caesar said it 'half in patriot grief for the havoc of civil war, half in impatience and resentment'.[1] Resentment, because the very men upon whose cooperation the restoration of Rome depended, were dead on the field, or scattered in implacable hostility. After the battle I see Pompey himself in flight, over the seaway, making for Egypt. Caesar I then see in full sail after him. It is as accidentally as that, that the sea-road to the East returns to view, and with enlarged importance. The accidents continue. Pompey never reached Alexandria; he was murdered before landing, his body left unburied on an Egyptian beach, his head shown to Caesar on Caesar's arrival. That settled that. The murderers were executed. Again one asks, what then? One cannot pry into Caesar's thoughts, but one may see his actions. What account do you make of Caesar's actions for the ensuing weeks and months, after Pompey the Great is dead and done with? Rome, sometime, will have to be restored. Caesar appears to let that wait. Caesar stays on for months at Alexandria.

I do not feel that the lingering with Cleopatra is of itself the explanation of Caesar's stay at Alexandria. The impression I derive is that at Alexandria he had been received not as a mere human conqueror but as an actual god. The deification may even have startled Caesar, though according to Eastern conceptions it was natural. Alexander had been received as a god in Egypt, his divinity formally celebrated. The full and complete apotheosis of a conqueror or a king, while the man himself was still and palpably a living man, was part of an Eastern heritage. Perhaps the divine honours and the actual worship within Egypt of each Ptolemy as saviour and preserver (*Soter*) had diminished by the time of the 12th Ptolemy to whom, jointly with his sister Cleopatra, the sovereign power had in Caesar's time descended; but the spirit had not departed whereby government depended upon acceptance of the ruler as in truth a god. The apotheosis was accepted by both governor and governed. I read of no formal ceremony for the deification of Caesar in Egypt, such as had occurred in an older time for Alexander; but from an Egyptian point of view, when Caesar appeared upon the scene as a conqueror outranking all other conquerors, since he outranked Ptolemy and Cleopatra in mortal power, it was a necessity for him to outrank them in the divine quality as well. Whether he liked it or not, in Egyptian opinion Caesar was a god. The presumption is, he liked it. The status of *deus*, and of an outranking *deus,* was of itself an automatic reason for Cleopatra to crave a son by him to elevate the dynasty of Egypt; it was of itself an excuse to keep his soldiers busy, according to Cleopatra's desire, in the elimination of her brother Ptolemy. The business of the Alexandrine war which Caesar conducted till the end of March 47 seems less of a side-issue if Caesar is regarded as really enjoying, at Alexandria, the temporary status of man-god.

Caesar might dally awhile as *deus* in Alexandria. He might prolong the temporary status, but Rome had to be faced in the end. There is no hint that Caesar ever expected Rome to accept the governance of a divine king – a king perhaps, but a warrior-king, not a divinity. Romans were Romans still; the Civil War had not been ended by Pharsalus; Scipio, Cato, and Pompey's sons and allies, were alive and active. How the tremendous strength of Rome was to be harnessed and governed was the abiding unsolved question. When, after the months in Alexandria, Caesar made up his mind to return to Rome it is not at all clear what he would do about government. It is very clear that when returning to Rome in 47 he was still putting first things first from the point of view of a soldier. Rome was first to be conquered by force. The way chosen for return was through Pompey's Syria and Asia Minor. The superior ease of his victory over Pharnaces in Pontus gave Caesar opportunity of sending to the Roman Senate the famous three-word telegram:

CAME, SAW, CONQUERED!

There was menace in that. Caesar promptly followed up the telegram, sailing with his troops from Ephesus. On arrival in Italy there was no nonsense about dismissal of troops or of obeying the ancient law of the Senate that a commander should lay down his arms before entering Rome. Caesar entered Rome in September, 47; he was away again, and with his troops, to Africa before the end of the month. The defeat of Scipio and Cato in Africa occupied Caesar until July, 46. That same autumn he was off again to fight the two sons of Pompey in Spain. They were eliminated, one killed and one escaping, in the spring of 45. In September, 45, Caesar returned to Rome.

The long abiding question had now to be answered. Some durable form of government, adaptable to Rome, had to be shaped. In the seven months from September until the Ides of March nothing of permanent shape was settled. Caesar, for all his genius, could not decide what title to assume or to accept, as ruler of Rome and of the world. At his triumph in September he appeared to be toying with the title of *Rex*. In February 44, at the festival of the Lupercalia, there was the curious pantomine when Antony (possibly behaving as devil's advocate) repeatedly offered Caesar the diadem, which Caesar, at that moment, repeatedly declined. The assassination was exactly a month later. Caesar knew that there were plots against his life. He had foreseen the likelihood of his assassination, and had remarked only that 'his removal would be no remedy but a source of greater ills to the Commonwealth'. During the last months of his uneasy rule, in which those who were close to him noted his irritability and melancholy, he made one firm decision; in his will he named none of those who counted on the undefined succession – Antony, for one, seems to have counted on it – but named as heir his great-nephew, the boy then variously called Octavius or Octavian, who in March 44 was not yet 19 years of age. Immediately after the assassination, and before it could be meditated what effect the title might have upon Caesar's successor, the Senate conferred upon Caesar, dead, the title of *Deus*.

'The deification of Man was not a natural process of the Roman mind', Warde Fowler said; and yet it was found to fit with 'the float-ing ideas' in 'that strange time'.[2] It was not through the living Caesar that 'the *dominus* and *deus* of the Orient found his way into the *urbs aeterna*'. If Caesar, recognizing that perfect faith in a governor was a desirable instrument of statecraft, wished that his fellow-Romans would deify him, it would seem that he dismissed the wish as idle. After his death, the unnatural process of deification was promptly accorded by the Senate, and in the summer it was arranged that Octavian should sponsor public games in Rome in honour of the apotheosis. At that time Caesar's deification 'convinced the City as a whole', says Suetonius; 'if only because', he goes on to remark, 'on the first day of the Games a comet appeared about an hour before sunset and shone for seven days running. This was held to be Caesar's soul, elevated to Heaven'.* Pliny records the same episode of the comet and of the impression it made. One wonders about the impression made upon the boy Octavian.

Caesar's prediction of 'greater ills to the Commonwealth' after his removal was promptly fulfilled. For 17 years after the assassination there was continuous fighting about the rulership of Rome and the Roman world. Then emerges the management by Octavian (under the new name of Augustus) of the peaceful reign which (contrasting with Caesar's reign of 7 months) lasted for 40 years. In this transition I continue to watch the participation of the Mediterranean seaway.

I see that during the years of uncertainty about the rulership of Rome the sea-road to the East continued to go on working. Carrier-trade did not die, and Rome controlled the road no matter what

---

* I am using the translation of Suetonius (*The Twelve Caesars*, Penguin Books, 1957) by Robert Graves. Pliny, in the passage referred to (*N.H.* ii. 94), is precise about the belief: the soul of Caesar was received 'among the god-head of the immortal gods'.

uncertainty there was about the control of Rome. I see some of the 'floating ideas' that Fowler mentioned, and I don't see how they could float except on the sea-road. But it is in the year 30 B.C. that the road manifests itself in a visual and dramatic way. The motions of the major *dramatis personae* over the sea-road are extraordinarily repetitive of the motions after the battle of Pharsalus. This time it is Antony who flees to Alexandria, and Octavian who sails in pursuit. In the year 30, Octavian is no longer the boy who watched the comet at the Games for Caesar's deification; then he was rising 19, now he is rising 33. Antony is twenty years older than Octavian; Cleopatra (though the son she had borne to the first Caesar was now 17 years old) is not to be regarded as elderly at the age of 39. The point for me is not the violent actions in Alexandria; the point is that after the actions, when Antony and Cleopatra and Cleopatra's son Caesarion are all dead, the problem which then puts itself to Octavian is a repetition of the same problem which, at Alexandria, had faced the first Caesar. Now that Octavian had conquered his chief individual enemy, in what guise was he to present himself at Rome?

I was sufficiently baffled in the impertinent effort of discussing Caesar, and would be more baffled to make any remarks about Octavian, who became Augustus. A characterization which might hold at one moment of his long career might not hold at another. As regards a distinction between Caesar's conduct and Octavian's when faced, at Alexandria, with the same problem of returning, as ruler, to Rome, Suetonius attends to one small detail which possibly has significance. Suetonius mentions the seal with which Octavian sealed his letters from Alexandria. It was Octavian's habit not only to date each letter that he wrote, but also to enter the exact hour of the day or night when it was composed, whether the document was private or for public view. Octavian sealed each letter from Alexandria, and the seal that he chose to use, noted by Suetonius because no doubt it was noticed by others, was a replica of the Egyptian Sphinx. Here is a contrast: Caesar announcing his return to Rome with the menace of the *Veni, vidi, vici* and Octavian, who had put a summary end to the dynasty of the Ptolemies and reduced Egypt to a Roman province, making no declaration about himself, except the sphinxlike declaration of declaring nothing. Caesar's final battle, before he returned to Rome, had been in Spain; it is curious that Octavian also had to be fighting in Spain before he could settle in Rome. Repetition in some of the events emphasizes a change in the climate of ideas. After Octavian's conquest in Spain, in 27 B.C., a title such as had eluded Caesar was conferred upon Octavian by a grateful Roman Senate. *Augustus!*

'Augustus' was a word originally belonging to the language of religion. Augustus had hitherto no specific connotation as a title. During the next forty years, as title for so remarkable an administrator, Augustus gradually took on the meaning *Majesty* or *Imperial Majesty*, and as a surname for the man himself it completely replaced the name Octavian. At some time, Suetonius goes on to note, Augustus changed the seal by which he had previously sealed his letters. The new seal was no longer a Sphinx; it was a head of Alexander the Great. The new seal might convey several meanings. We noticed how Alexander had been regarded by some purely as the model of a military conqueror; we noticed Alexander regarded by Plutarch as Father of a world Fatherland; we also noticed Alexander as a man who during his lifetime was deified. Of these particular three interpretations, Augustus moderated the first, enlarged the second, and as to the third, remained sphinxlike. Many who were grateful for the *pax Romana* were ready to apply to the living Augustus the term which Virgil used – *Deus nobis haec otia fecit* – 'it is a god who wrought for us this peace'. Augustus did not repress Virgil for his application of the word *Deus*; he did perhaps punish Ovid for his mockery of gods; but to penetrate his inward feelings is all guesswork. In the fullness of years Augustus made one final change in his personal and official seal. The head of Alexander joined the Sphinx as a discard. The seal used to the end by Augustus was his own head, as portrayed by Dioscurides. After his death (A.D. 14) the official deification of Augustus was proclaimed at once, and his portrait was used by succeeding Emperors as the official seal of state.

I withdraw from further probing into Roman conceptions of Deity.* What I was attempting to report was that the sea-road to the East quickly participated in the death of the Republic, returning

* Reference might be made to the succinct discussion in *Horace and his Lyric Poetry* by L. P. Wilkinson (Cambridge University Press, paperback edition 1968) pp. 24–34.

Roman conquerors with the political aspect of tyrants yet also, in an aspect larger and more difficult to define, tyrants elevated to a status potentially more than mortal. Rome was no longer the Rome of seven hills; the Rome of Caesar was coextensive with the habitable world, the Rome of Augustus was coextensive with a whole world at peace. So it might seem, at any rate to Roman eyes, throughout the long reign of Augustus. It was the animating spirit at the centre of the huge organism upon which all depended. It was the office of Emperor which required utmost veneration, and under Augustus, for a long time, achieved it. Augustus with his formula of *Pax et Princeps* appeared to have defined the office of Emperor as the office of Chief Magistrate, and official deification of Augustus after his death could be taken as a proper overspill of worship to a man who, though not infallible, had served a supreme office well. By ratifying such a deification a Senator had to exhibit somewhat of an official disrespect for Deity, and the extent of permissible disrespect was soon tested. Gibbon surveys the immediate successors of Augustus in a famous sentence near the beginning of *The Decline and Fall of the Roman Empire* – a sentence famous for the choice of epithets – 'the dark unrelenting Tiberius, the furious Caligula, the feeble Claudius, the profligate and cruel Nero, the beastly Vitellius, and the timid inhuman Domitian. . . .' Of the six names selected by Gibbon it is noticeable that only one – the name of Claudius – represents an Emperor who was officially deified after death. Such slight cohesive power of denial was almost all the power that was retained by the once proud and powerful Senate of Rome: the power of denying that a despicable tyrant should, after his death, be worshipped.

During the lifetime of a tyrannical Emperor the hopelessness of any individual resistance to his caprice was only emphasized by the size and the cohesion of the Roman Empire. Augustus emphasized the cohesion by setting up the Golden Milestone (*milliarum aureum*) in the Roman Forum, symbolic point toward which all the great roads of a well-policed empire should converge and terminate. Gibbon, who takes his stance at the centre of things and writes as if with the sentiments of a patrician Roman, exposes that the golden milestone could easily become a symbol of terror:

. . . the empire of the Romans filled the world, and, when that empire fell into the hands of a single person, the world became a safe and dreary prison for his enemies. The slave of Imperial despotism, whether he was condemned to drag his gilded chain in Rome and the senate, or to wear out a life of exile on the barren rock of Seriphus, or the frozen banks of the Danube, expected his fate in silent despair. To resist was fatal, and it was impossible to flee. On every side he was encompassed with a vast extent of sea and land, which he could never hope to traverse without being discovered, seized, and restored to his irritated master. Beyond the frontiers his anxious view could discover nothing, except the ocean, inhospitable deserts, hostile tribes of barbarians, of fierce manners and unknown language, or dependent kings, who would gladly purchase the emperor's protection by the sacrifice of an obnoxious fugitive. 'Wherever you are', said Cicero to the exiled Marcellus, 'remember that you are equally within the power of the conqueror'.

Gibbon, looking from the centre outwards, is abundantly impressive about the power given by the roads to an emperor. Even the moderate Augustus could be tempted to fling away to the circumference, there to languish among barbarians, anyone whom he disliked. In the passage just quoted, Gibbon's mention of the frozen banks of the Danube is a reminder of the fate of Ovid, banished to the town of Tomi, in the region where the mouths of the Danube pour into the Euxine Sea. With a flick of the wrist of an emperor, a man who appeared to mock at Roman gods could be thrown out of Rome, although a Roman citizen of standing, a patrician and a lawyer too. Ovid was forever banished; his appeals unto Caesar were of no help; and the example of Ovid makes it the more interesting to wonder how it came about that a certain provincial citizen, known to us as Paul the Apostle, could use a legal claim effectively to be wafted from the circumference of empire directly to the centre. Looking at the network of roads not from the centre outwards but from the outside inwards is to be impressed by the power, opposite to that which Gibbon emphasizes, of their reflex action. I have been looking at examples of the eastward sea-road throwing back upon Rome notable Roman adventurers with notable armed forces. What I have now to look at is the sea-road as an instrument equally available to a man who, without physical force, had the genius to seize upon it. It was, to say the least of it, an act of genius for Paul to compel Romans to carry him from Jerusalem straight to the centre of Rome. I should be careful and correct the statement. Paul was not carried instantly to the central symbol of empire, the Golden Milestone in the Forum. No, it was to the more ancient Porta Capena that Paul was conducted by the Centurion. Within the gate by which the Appian Way originally emerged, Paul was permitted to dwell and talk with the brethren about a wholly new manner of conquering the Eternal City. That seems to me the most portentous of all the many reflex actions of the stone-tentacle which had pushed out from Rome.

The land-bridge of Asia Minor is pictured as having been perpetually fought over from earliest times. After Alexander, ordinary daily life in, say, Cilicia, is dominated by Greek customs. At Tarsus one sees a gymnasium; it was a centre for Greek Games. In the second century B.C. the conquest of Macedonia by Aemilius Paulus brought into Asia Minor both the virtues and the vices of the Roman Republic. Polybius considers that the success of Paulus at the battle of Pydna (168 B.C.) was the beginning of Rome's world empire.* It was the behaviour of Paulus after the battle and the contrast of his generosity with the conduct of the defeated king of Macedonia which won a general respect for Romans as, in that part of the world, the new conquerors. One of the merits of Paulus that was most appreciated was that whereas he reduced the previous taxes and extortions expected from Greek rulers, he did his best to expand what he respected of the Greek heritage : the books, the general culture, and the

---

* One of the most marvellous paragraphs in the English language is that in which De Quincey discusses the defeat of the Greeks by the Romans ; that is to say, the failure of a 'little rascally system' of internecine warfare to withstand the intrusion of a wholly different idea. De Quincey argues that the 'unity' of Romans was one cause of superiority and 'better military institutions' another : 'better' in the sense that the legion was an instrument more flexible and business-like than the 'holiday arrangement, tournament arrangement' of one 'fastidious phalanx' set up against another. De Quincey's paragraph is I say marvellous for its swift evocation of the contrast of ideas, as to what warfare (and life and death and all the rest of it) was all about; marvellous for the way it excites a reader's mind toward perception of other contrasts of ideas, at other times, and now as well as then ; and marvellous just for itself – a paragraph which is one of the very best of De Quincey's superb performances. I wish it could be quoted in full – but the paragraph covers, irrepressibly, several pages. It may be found in *The Posthumous Works of Thomas De Quincey*, edited by Alexander H. Japp, Vol. II (Heinemann, London, 1893), in De Quincey's review of 'Mr. Finlay's History of Greece'.

Games. Paulus appeared to represent respect for all things Greek except Greek morals; an attitude later expressed by Cicero, in his remark that he granted to the Greeks all manner of skills, yet that race never understood or cared for the sacred binding force of testimony given in a court of law.[3] What the conquest of Paulus offered to Asia Minor was the best prospect of a Graeco-Roman world: Greek skills plus Roman Law. No wonder that there was both an instant and continued respect for the name 'Paul' in Asia Minor, and that as Roman citizenship came to be extended to provincials, and valued as providing important legal protection, among the new citizens 'Paul' became a popular and customary name. In the later time of Augustus the name remains to be used in a Jewish family of Tarsus. We bear in mind that the apostle, the 'Saul who was also Paul', was both 'a Hebrew sprung from Hebrews' and also from birth a Roman citizen, sprung from forbears who had acquired that citizenship; and we need not dismiss Lemprière's suggestion that as a boy at the Tarsus gymnasium 'his full name may very possibly have been Gaius Julius Paulus'.

The name of Paulus may have continued in Asia Minor to connote respect for the magnanimity of an early Roman conqueror but by the time that Pompey was gobbling up Asian territories in the name of the Roman Republic, Roman greed is more conspicuous than Roman magnanimity.* With provinces rapidly new-formed there was rapid increase of business dealings in the Roman Forum, and Warde Fowler finds it hard to say which type of business under the Republic wrought the most mischief in the provinces, the joint-stock companies which operated as tax-farmers or the money-lenders. The example of personal 'abstinentia' as originally set by Aemilius Paulus was not imitated by all provincial governors, and when a governor was strict enough to prevent extortion, he could readily be attacked in Rome. 'There are many repulsive things in the exquisite poetry of Catullus', Warde Fowler remarks, but goes on to say that none of them jar on him so much as the attacks by Catullus on a provincial governor 'in whose suite he had gone to Bithynia in the hope of enriching himself, and under whose just administration he had failed to do so'. That was in 57 B.C. When Cicero was called upon to rule

* This is one of the themes discussed in *Social Life at Rome in the Age of Cicero* by W. Warde Fowler (Macmillan, London, 1908).

Cilicia for the year 51 he found the people 'quite unable to pay their taxes and driven into the hands of the middle-man in order to do so'. One of Cicero's beliefs was that the mission of Rome was to make the world safe for property, and that belief was under much tension while he was in Cilicia. There was the pull of genuine sympathy for the unfortunate provincials; there was the opposite pull of his banker Atticus and other friends in Rome, shareholders in the tax-companies; these conflicting interests are exhibited in Cicero's letters written during his year in Tarsus. Cicero was not particularly concerned to feather his own nest; his year as governor netted him a paltry sum*; though there was some distress when the total of his emoluments, while still on deposit at Ephesus, was seized by Pompey's men during the Civil War.

Under ordinary circumstances the term of service for a Proconsul ran only for the year from the day of his arrival at a chief town of his province. It was customary for him to arrive in pomp, displaying himself in the robe of military commander, accompanied by his twelve Lictors, his Quaestor and Legati and a numerous staff. More than one shipload of Roman intruders is suggested, for whom lodging and forage was requisitioned. Tarsus had been in Roman hands since about 80 B.C. and there, as elsewhere, a continuity of arrangements depended on the conversion of reliable local inhabitants into willing collaborators. Hence the convenience for a Proconsul to extend an outright Roman citizenship to such provincials as he chose. Such provincial citizenship promised to the individual (and presumably to his heirs) an immediate right of appeal to the governor in all legal disputes, and, in any criminal cause, a theoretical right of appeal (*provocatio*) to Rome. The services rendered, or the fee imposed, for purchase of citizenship, are largely unrecorded. The privileges are a matter of speculation. At the time of the Civil Wars a right of appeal from a province to Rome had dubious value. The welcome of the Augustan Age to Romans in the provinces is stressed by Warde Fowler. 'Provincial governors were made more really responsible, and a scientific census revealed the actual tax-paying capacity of the

---

* Warde Fowler estimated the sum to be the equivalent, in 1908, of £17,500. In the currency of 1968 the arithmetical equivalent needs to be adjusted upwards; but still, as Fowler says, a paltry sum in contrast to the extortions of some Roman Proconsuls.

provincials; tax-farming was more closely superintended and gradually disappeared'. *Pax et Princeps* seemed indeed a welcome formula. For any Roman citizen involved in serious trouble, 'I appeal unto Caesar' might seem to mean something. I have to think about what it meant for Paul the Apostle.

The dual loyalties of Paul's youthtime in Tarsus stand out: the strictness of the Hebrew traditions and the simultaneous participation in an education traditional in the Graeco-Roman world. Lemprière suggested that he was enrolled in the gymnasium as Gaius Julius Paulus; Professor Harris, in his *Greek Athletes and Athletics,* suggests that he was an ardent schoolboy supporter and perhaps even a contender at athletic events at the Tarsus stadium:

> The evidence for the belief that in his boyhood the great apostle was a lover of athletics, is, of course, to be found in the way in which the language of athletics constantly springs to his pen, and in that habit of his mind by which time and time again the Christian life is visualized as an athletic contest. The effects of this are deeply marked in Christian thought and language. The soul must be trained as the athlete trains – the word 'ascetic' is the Greek for an athlete in full training – and the reward for the Christian life is the prize, the crown or the palm, the reward of the victorious athlete in the games. . . .

Professor Harris admits it is unlikely that Paul took an active part in athletics after his schooldays; while still young he went to Jerusalem to study theology. But when Paul was no longer young, consider, says Professor Harris, the terms in which he writes his boast to the Corinthians:

> Five times the Jews have given me the thirty-nine strokes; three times have I been beaten with rods; once I was stoned; three times I have been shipwrecked, and for twenty-four hours I was adrift on the open sea. I have been constantly on the road; I have met dangers from rivers, dangers from robbers, dangers from my fellow-countrymen, dangers from foreigners, dangers in towns, dangers in the country, dangers at sea, dangers from false friends. I have toiled and drudged, I have often gone without sleep; hungry and thirsty, I have often gone fasting; and I have suffered from cold and exposure.

'The man who could write that', says Professor Harris, 'was tough by any standards'. And Professor Harris makes a guess at the particular form of sport wherein Paul as a schoolboy had practised for such toughness. Though not without knowledge of boxing and wrestling, where Paul's heart really lay, with his small stature, was in distance running. Professor Harris, who prefers the *New English Bible* for his quotations, points to two more of the immortal statements:

> For myself, I set no store by life; I only want to finish the race and complete the task which the Lord Jesus assigned to me.

And again, in the summing up:

> I have run the great race, I have finished the course, I have kept faith.

I am pondering the remark made by Paul Winter[4] that from a legal point of view, the trial of Paul the Apostle presented Roman authorities with a more complicated problem than the trial of Jesus. What I am considering is how the legal complications were used by Paul to further his fixed intention.

The original instruction to the Apostles, as recorded in *Acts* 1, 8, was to be 'witnesses unto me both in Jerusalem, and in all Judaea, and in Samaria, and unto the uttermost part of the earth'. Perhaps some of the Twelve originally regarded their special work as witnesses as limited to Jerusalem, Judaea and Samaria, and others thought specially of 'the uttermost part of the earth'. Luke's part in the writing of the *Acts* 'was to give a coherent picture of the spread of the Church from Jerusalem to Rome'.[5] The first thing that one notices is that the powerful name of Rome comes into the narration not with a bang, but quietly. In the *Acts* it is gradually though steadily developed that Paul's special instruction is to be Apostle to the Gentiles: from the first message through Ananias (Chapter IX) that he is 'to bear my name before the Gentiles, and kings, and the children of Israel' to Paul's own report (in Chapter XXVI) to king Agrippa that he had heard direct from the voice of Jesus that the Gentiles were to be his special province. There is at first no particular identification of 'Gentiles' and the 'West' but there is steady pace toward such identification. On the first missionary tour of Paul and Barnabas in Cyprus the Gentiles are 'local' Gentiles. There is the importance of the Church at Antioch: the appeal to 'Grecians' – *lo, we turn to the Gentiles* – the mission is now spoken of as 'unto the ends of the earth'.

Paul's second tour is towards Greece. The vision at Troas, *Come over
into Macedonia, and help us,* is taken by many to mark the origin of
Christendom in Europe. It is a remarkable step westward, but the
mission as yet, within the Roman Empire, remains provincial. The
heart of empire, Rome, has hardly been mentioned.

But it is in the chapter of the *Acts* from which I have just been
quoting (Chapter XVI) that Paul makes special and effective use of
his particular prerogative: the Roman citizenship that was thoroughly
native to him. That Paul was equally and consciously Roman as well
as Jew has not been stressed in the narrative. It is brought in suddenly, with the incident at Thyatira, perhaps a suburb of Philippi, a
Roman colony. There Paul and Silas were caught and drawn 'into the
marketplace unto the rulers' with the complaint that 'these men, being Jews, do exceedingly trouble our city, and teach customs, which
are not lawful for us to receive, neither to observe, being Romans'.
The multitude rose up together against them, and the magistrates in
haste performed the ritual rending of clothes and 'commanded to beat
them'. So Paul and Silas were beaten with many stripes and cast into
prison. Slaves could legally be beaten uncondemned, and were customarily examined under torture; but not Roman citizens. It was
after the miracle at midnight and the conversion of the keeper of the
prison, that Paul was moved to use the illegality of the magistrates'
action:

> And when it was day, the magistrates sent the serjeants, saying, 'Let
> those men go'. And the keeper of the prison told this saying to Paul, 'The
> magistrates have sent to let you go: now therefore depart, and go in
> peace'. But Paul said unto them. 'They have beaten us openly uncon-
> demned, being Romans, and have cast us into prison; and now do they
> thrust us out privily? nay verily; but let them come themselves and fetch
> us out'. And the serjeants told these words unto the magistrates: and
> they feared, when they heard that they were Romans. And they came
> and besought them, and brought them out, and desired them to depart
> out of the city.

A minor detail about the incident is puzzling: how did Paul in
faraway Philippi instantly establish that he was a Roman citizen?
Before accepting their own misdemeanour, one might expect the
magistrates to have sought more identification than an oral statement.
In the subsequent episode at Jerusalem (*Acts* xxii) where there was

much more uproar than at Philippi, the conversation is reported between Paul and the chief captain at the castle:

> Then the chief captain came, and said unto him, 'Tell me, art thou a Roman?' He said, 'Yea'. And the chief captain answered, 'With a great sum obtained I this freedom'. And Paul said, 'But I was free born'.

My mentor in such matters tells me that a Roman soldier was entitled to a diploma (a folding bronze tablet) which, if appropriate, could carry confirmation of Roman citizenship; but what diploma, tessera or token Paul might have carried on his journeys to prove he was a freeborn Roman remains a minor mystery.[6] But that intrusion is a very minor one; the more important observation is the use that Paul made of his status as a Roman.

I was quoting from Paul Winter, that from a legal point of view the examination of the ambivalent 'Saul, who also is called Paul' was a complicated problem:

> The defendant claimed Roman citizenship. He was not a Palestinian resident and had been in Judaea only about a fortnight. Some of the offences with which he was charged had been committed outside Judaean territory. Even those allegedly committed in Jerusalem were of a controversial nature; some may have come under Jewish jurisdiction, whilst others were subject to Roman Law. The defendant had been in Roman detention since the day of his apprehension and had remained in such detention for a prolonged period of time. Paul was never under sentence by the Sanhedrin. . . . Paul himself expressed his preference for a trial by a Roman judge. Under these circumstances – after long uncertainty – the question of judicial competence was decided in favour of the stronger party.

To be tried by a Roman judge, for a cause which would entitle an appeal to Caesar, was what Paul seems to have methodically designed, after the success in Macedonia and the ill-success at Athens and the long stay at Corinth. He must 'bear witness also at Rome'. At Rome, and as a Roman citizen; for if Rome said to the world 'Wherever you are, remember that you are equally within the power of the conqueror', it also said to its citizens 'Wherever you are, your testimony may be tested at the empire's heart and centre'. From

Jerusalem to Rome the road was open to Paul, not for clandestine use, but for open use, and with a Roman escort.

Paul's final visit to Jerusalem seems to exhibit the consciously-formed and fixed intention of an ultimate interpretation of the phrase: 'Depart: for I will send thee far hence unto the Gentiles'. It seems that the 'Gentiles' in Paul's mind were now those specifically of the Far West. The visiting of Rome was not a sudden thought: there was the modest Church already there, the small mixed group (predominantly Gentile-Christian but including a strong Jewish element) which Paul had told that he would visit – he had indeed projected (*Romans* xv, 24) a further journey to Spain. At the time of writing the epistle to the Romans the actual manner of the journeying remains unspecified. What is foreshadowed by the episode at Philippi is Paul's capacity to become master of a dangerous event at the swift instant of its happening. At the intense moment of the final visit to Jerusalem it is this capacity which shows forth to the fullest. In the riot in the Temple he was already about to be killed by the violence of the people, when rescued, lifted over the heads of the riot squad of Roman soldiers, and carried through the tumult to the castle. From the stairs of the castle, with Roman guards surrounding, he spoke once more, and when he uttered the word *Gentiles* there was such Jewish uproar that there was no possible Roman action except instant imprisonment of Paul. To look on coldly, to say that such a moment was contrived, would be an utmost travesty; what one is watching is the impress of genius on events at the instant moment. The courage is so manifest as almost to be taken for granted; it is, if I may use so poor a word, the wit, which strikes as deeply. After the arrest there was the question of juridical competence: the examination before the Sanhedrin, then that before Roman authority; the deferment by Felix, the arrival of Festus, the appeal of Festus to Agrippa. Throughout the long delays the 'Passion of St. Paul' is presented at length by Luke, with the indication that no composition of the legal dispute, or acceptance of dubious liberty within Judaea, would accord with Paul's intention. *Hast thou appealed unto Caesar?* said Festus. Agrippa was forced into agreement: *Unto Caesar shalt thou go*. The Augustan police, 'the royal cohort', were to escort him on the sea-road.

Luke, most gifted of recorders, was permitted to go with Paul.

Bishop Gore points out that Luke has a love for parallels, and suggests that in the narrative of the sea journey Luke possibly has in mind the parallel, and contrast, of Paul and Jonah – 'Jonah refuses to go to the imperial capital of Nineveh because he hates the oppressors of his people, and desires their destruction; St. Paul goes willingly to Rome on his mission of salvation'. Jonah's presence threatens his mariners with destruction; Paul's presence saves them. In the narration of the voyage and shipwreck, blended with symbolic touches there are certainly touches of direct first-hand experience and observation.* The arrival at Puteoli, the meeting there with brethren, the

* The ship which put into Malta, rescued those who had been shipwrecked and carried them forward, was a 'ship of Alexandria . . . whose sign was Castor and Pollux'. When did ships begin to be given individual names? In Luke's time it was hardly as yet a general custom. The Greeks had frequently distinguished between the specific nature (ἰδιώματα) of a person or thing in contra-distinction to the generic nature, but they seem to have been slow in applying or recording individuality to a ship. All earliest 'names' I can think of (*Ark*, *Argo*) are generic terms. There are no individual names in Homer for the black or red-prowed or blue-prowed ships which sailed for Troy. Later terms at Athens for official messenger-ships (Paralos and Salaminia) also seem functional. There is nothing subtle about that distinction: in New York you might cross the Hudson River in a ferry-boat, and speak of it from its function as simply the ferry. But even a ferry-boat is in modern times apt to have an individual name.

Mascots or signs for recognition ('We be of one tribe') or for protection of the deity whose sign was carried seem with most sea-faring peoples to precede the custom of attributing an individual name to an individual ship. The ocean-going canoes which raced in the Pacific to make landfall at New Zealand are said to have had 'names' (*Arawa, Tainui, Tokomaru, Aotea, Mattaatua, Kurahaupe, Takitimu*); but the pride of a modern Maori in tracing his lineage to one of these names suggests that these are tribal names – that within each of seven groups there might be several individual canoes, each bearing the same tribal sign. In the Mediterranean at the beginning of the Christian Era there were many ships of Alexandria bearing the sign of Isis, and many more from Alexandria or other ports, bearing at one and the same moment the sign of Castor-Pollux. Castor and Pollux were to the Romans the most popular of the protectors for seamen. By recording that the 'sign' of the relief ship was Castor and Pollux Luke is indicating that the travellers are now just about within the embrace of Rome; as within a few more verses they actually are.

But I do not think the *New English Bible* improves upon older translations by saying 'the Castor and Pollux of Alexandria' as if that were her name and port of registry. Catullus (in his poem numbered IV) comes almost up to the point of according an individual name to the particular ship for which he is travel up the Appian Way, the friendly reception at 'the three taverns', is variously computed to have taken place in one or other year roundabout 62 A.D. Within the gate of Rome Paul 'was suffered to dwell by himself' and though under restriction began to receive 'all that came . . . no man forbidding him'.

The legal appeal, and the road, had each been instruments for the forthcoming alteration of Rome.

NOTES

1. *The Roman Revolution* by Professor (now Sir) Ronald Syme (Oxford University Press, 1939).

2. *Roman Ideas of Deity* by W. Warde Fowler (Macmillan, London, 1914).

3. *Pro Flacco* 4. 9., quoted by W. Warde Fowler, *Social Life at Rome in the Age of Cicero* (Macmillan, London, 1908), p. 183.

4. *On the Trial of Jesus* by Paul Winter (Walter de Gruyter, Berlin, 1961), p. 87.

5. E. J. Bicknell, in his commentary on the *Acts* in *A New Commentary on Holy Scripture,* edited by Bishop Gore, (S.P.C.K., London, 1929).

6. Individual identification tags are reported in various dictionaries of Roman Antiquities. Ramsay indicates that in early times in Italy it was customary for each boy-child, accepted by his father to be legitimate, to be given a name and 'a hollow disk called *Bulla,* made of gold, silver, or, in the case of the poor, of leather'. The *Bulla* slung round the neck, might contain a charm against the Evil Eye, and was presumably an identity disc; before the close of the Republic the *Bulla* was 'assumed by all *Ingenui*'. Was an official *Bulla* issued to the provincial to whom Roman citizenship had been granted or sold? There would seem to have been opportunities for fraud. When Paul was held for examination at

---

expressing communicable affection: he almost names her, but not quite; she is one of the nameless under the sign of Castor-Pollux. It is in the next generation after Catullus that Virgil distinguishes the ships which race against each other (*Aeneid*, Book V) with individual names. *Pristis* (which might mean 'Sawfish' or possibly 'Whale'), *Chimaera, Centaur* and sea-blue *Scylla* – I have not run across proper names for ships accorded earlier than those by Virgil.

Jerusalem there was ample time for the status which he claimed to be verified. A traveller in unfamiliar territory might carry a token, called *tessera hospitalis,* which would be honoured by the full protection of his *hospes,* if the alliance of *hospitium* had been previously arranged; because such an alliance was regarded as sacred and binding, there was careful scrutiny of the tessera and of the individual who presented it. The theme of mistaken identities is certainly complex.

CHAPTER 8
The Delta

I MUST now speed up with westward motion; but how can you hurry Romans of the early Empire away from their preoccupations, their amusements? Sometimes they seem to regard their City as if nothing in it mattered except, in Juvenal's phrase, bread and circuses; or, for some, cake and circuses. It was the sea-road from the East which provided things of most excitement; for a long time the road from Alexandria influenced Rome, almost as if Rome itself had become a portion of the Delta of the Nile.

When Rome began to go westering, what were her main offensive weapons? Her legions, yes: and wine. For the conquest of barbarian peoples, it has been argued that wine was one of Rome's chief weapons. There is the comment of Diodorus Siculus, written at some time about 44 B.C. Don't give all of your attention to Caesar's military conquests, says Diodorus; notice also the fact that the Gauls had little resistance to wine. Gauls had no knowledge of the grape; they had never been able to make anything better than a poor kind of ale and a poor kind of mead. Quickly enough the Romans found that they were

> . . . exceedingly addicted to the use of wine and fill themselves with the wine which is brought into their country by merchants, drinking it unmixed, and since they partake of this drink without moderation by reason of their craving for it, when they are drunken they fall into a stupor or a state of madness.
>
> Consequently many of the Italian traders, induced by the love of money which characterizes them, believe that the love of wine of these Gauls is their own godsend. For these transport the wine on the navigable rivers by means of boats and through the level plain on wagons, and receive for it an incredible price; for in exchange for a jar of wine they receive a slave.*

*I quote the translation of Diodorus Siculus as given in William Younger's *Gods, Men and Wine*. Lemprière warns us that Diodorus is 'too credulous in some of his narrations', but there is no reason to doubt this particular observation. The use of rotgut liquor and 'trade gin' on 'savages' is a familiar story;

So, by conquest of the legions or conquest by wine, slaves from Gaul were brought to Rome, and a profitable trade it was, by all accounts, when they were put up for sale by the *mangones* or *venalitii* – slaves of less value auctioned in open market, and those of higher quality reserved for private shops (*tabernae*).

I could easily lose myself in thinking of the Roman slave-trade, and it would be no departure from my theme: a considerable amount of Roman exploration to the north and west was due to the demand for slaves. Those dragged to Rome and sold in the market were stripped and exhibited in a wooden cage (called *catasta*) where purchasers might examine them; a label (*titulus*) was attached to the neck of each. The estimated age of the individual, his country, qualities and defects were noted on the label, and whether he or she was new or had been trained to servitude. The second-hand slave was considered of less value, from the suspicion that he was more likely to be idle and cunning. If representations on the *titulus* were afterwards discovered to be false, the purchaser had grounds for legal action against the seller. With Rome's rapid rise to power, the trade in slaves was large and well organized by law and custom. If the seller declined to give any warranty, the slave was exposed for sale with a cap on his head. When put up to auction, the specimen was made to stand upon the slave-block, to be visible to all. If newly imported from abroad, his feet were whitened with chalk.

The roads which stretched from Rome into Europe provided Romans with servants, with unskilled labour, and with an increasing

---

alcohol as a weapon has been rather especially used by northern European peoples. In the New World there was relatively little use of the weapon by Spaniards, but the conquest of the North American Indians, particularly the Plains Indians, was achieved as much by firewater as by firearms. The capture of the last of the notable Apaches was largely a matter of food and drink. At so late a date as 1891, General Nelson A. Miles had the unenviable task of pursuing Geronimo, over the border into Old Mexico, up again into Arizona. 'Tiresome work and very difficult', the General wrote to his wife. 'They have been followed rapidly for about one thousand miles.' Heliographs set up on mountain-tops were used to trace the fugitives, but it was an unguarded frontier saloon which captured Geronimo. He was forced to agree to terms before he had recovered from his hangover: the honourable terms offered by Miles were later dishonoured in Washington. See *An Unregimented General* (Biography of Nelson A. Miles) by Virginia Weisel Johnson (Houghton Mifflin, Boston, 1962).

supply of auxiliary troops. Wine played its part in the levelling and surfacing of roads. The regular ration of wine for legionaries, in addition to the bread and cheese, meant business for the Italian *caupones,* chapmen, wine-traders of whom Diodorus made early mention. When there came to be standing armies, they were regular customers; and in the time of Augustus and Tiberius, when many Roman legions were tied down in Spain, the vineyards within Spain became serious competitors, to the hot indignation of Italian winegrowers. For the Italian traders it was a happy movement when troops were shifted to the east and the Italian wines moved with them to be consumed in Pannonia and the Danubian provinces. To the north and west it was principally from Campania and partly from Tuscany that Italian wines – and roads on which to move them – went into Gaul.

Martial remarks that it was the vine-rod which was the centurion's emblem of power; where in the beginning did it come from? – from 'treacherous Nile', *fallax Nile.* Ever since Sappho's brother Charaxus was seduced from Lesbos to learn about the wine business in the city of the Delta, and remained there with the hostess of whom Sappho strongly disapproved, Egypt had retained a reputation (among all other reputations) for every kind of tempting depravity. As for winedrinking, Greeks in general did not rush to follow Charaxus; they disliked Egyptian etiquette in wine-drinking; all information about Greeks of the classical period is that they were reasonably simple in their tastes. To wine which by accident or design already contained resin, they were content to add sea-water and honey and perhaps a few 'perfumes', but nothing much that was elaborately exotic. They were also somewhat restrained in eating-habits. Greek lips might smack at the feasts as described in the *Iliad,* but so far as one learns, the well-to-do Athenian was more or less content with a normal Mediterranean triad of lentils or grain, oil and dilute wine – vegetables and fish, fresh, dried or salted, might be added, and for an occasional treat one reads about hog's pudding or haggis. A hodgepodge stew of vegetables, meat and fruits (later to be called *gáron*) is also spoken of, as eaten by both Greeks and Carthaginians. The *gáron* of Gadeira is judged to have been especially tasty, in that it was imported to Rome by Romans searching for novelty.

A novelty in table pleasures sought by the Greeks resided less in the

fare than in the talk and in the games and floor-shows at a good
dinner. At least, in the symposiums described by Plato and Xenophon
there is far less mention of the food and drink than of the other
entertainments. Periodical drunkenness was agreed as part of the
Dionysian festivals; and after the Greeks had started viticulture and
vineyards in the south of Italy, Romans could be seduced by wine
(according to Lemprière) as easily as the Gauls were later (according
to Diodorus). Lemprière, who occasionally indulges the thrill of hin-
ting at unmentionable orgies, speaks of the eager initiation of Greek
revels in the supposedly disciplined era of the early Roman Republic.
An early Roman enthusiasm for worship of the god of wine, with all
of the attendant 'impure actions and indulgencies', called aloud for
the interference of the senate. At the time spoken of the population of
Rome was small, but it was a sizeable portion that could go crazy at
the festivals. 'The disorder and pollution which was practised with
impunity by no less than 7,000 votaries of either sex, were beheld
with horror and astonishment by the consuls, and the Bacchanalia
were forever banished from Rome'. Prohibition, self-imposed in the
early Roman Republic, was imposed from outside by Hannibal when
his troops took charge of the wine-centre, Capua. There, says Lemprière, it was in turn Hannibal who suffered from the wine-weapon.
At Capua 'the Carthaginian soldiers soon forgot to conquer in the
pleasures and riot of this luxurious city. From that circumstance it
has been said, and with propriety, that Capua was his Cannae.'

By and large, it was not in the Greek temperament to misuse the art
of wine which had been learned from Egypt, nor was there much that
was peculiarly excessive in such customs as Rome derived direct
from Greece. It was when Rome's sea-road by-passed Greece and
went on to Alexandria, that the social rot (so much excoriated by
Juvenal) really set in. Pompey, Caesar, Antony, Augustus – none of
them had valued Athens so much as Alexandria. After Augustus, a
visit to Alexandria was the Grand Tour for a young patrician; parade
of tastes acquired at Alexandria became a lasting fashion. The drugs
and spices to be used in livening Italian wines originated from Egypt
and Syria, and Capua, as depot for domestic vintages, became the
chief centre of the art of mixing perfumes with them. Oil (meaning
olive oil) was the best known vehicle for odorous essences; hence
spices of every description went under the general name of unguents;

and a district of Capua (called Seplasia) was occupied by the *Unguentarii*. Rivalry in novel mixtures of oils and wine meant variety of choice for Roman banquets, and mixtures strange to modern palates, and extra shells and jars and alabaster boxes of extra-special unguents, were regularly travelling from Capua over the well-worn stones of Via Appia, Queen of roads – as Statius called it, honouring it more for bringing wines to Imperial Rome than for having brought St. Paul.

I was thinking that Greek table-manners were less elaborate than the fashion was in Egypt, yet the banqueting ritual of the Greeks was elaborate enough to appeal to Romans, with Egyptian luxuries super-added. The Greek custom at private banquets of feeding whilst reclining on low couches was, so far as concerned eating and drinking, one that demanded considerable physical contortion. By all accounts Romans from Sulla onwards were pleased to imitate the custom. A banqueter *A* at the head of a couch, reclining on his left elbow, his body propped with cushions, was required to stretch his legs at full length behind the body of banqueter *B*, whose head came up to the breast of *A*. Banqueter *B* was similarly impeded by banqueter *C* – and so on, on the other couches, round the room. For prolonged eating and drinking, the procedure seems awkward; but there is no doubt that it became a fashion of the Empire. Dishes were served from the centre of the banqueting room; the most elaborate of dishes were those most highly prized; the service itself was a floor-show. The *carptor* or carver was esteemed for his flourishes and for his solo dance-steps; the house-slaves who served the food and wine were meant to be looked at, appraised, discussed by those diners who remained capable of doing so. Such banquets were often, perhaps deliberately, endurance tests. With the dismissal of the dishes, the serious drinking began; and after entertainment of further floor-shows by dancing girls or acrobatic tumblers, the wind-up was frequently the game of *cottabus*.

'Cottabus' was a banqueting game which Romans took over from Greeks. It consisted of throwing at a target the last drops of wine in the wineglass, and the art was that the thrower had to remain recumbent, and fling the wine-drops with a practised flick of the right wrist. In Greece it had been a game as far back as Pindar's time, and there were as many variations as could be suggested by the master of the revels, or *symposiarch*. I gather that what won applause among Romans was not dexterity alone, but sometimes the costliness of what was flung away. The wine-glasses most valued in Rome were the *vasa murrhina* imported from Alexandria; and if there was any complaint that the wine-bowl was not sufficiently perfumed, the host who could not add some special unguent was disparaged. (In later times it is still asked if a punch-bowl has been well 'spiked', a usage which reflects the Roman taste for spikenard). The opulent citizen of Rome might very well hold in reserve, to be broken into the banqueting-bowl, the same sort of 'alabaster box of very precious ointment' that was broken on one occasion to anoint Our Lord's feet.

A point of lingering over a few of the customs of Rome at the time of Paul's entry is that it helps in the estimate, how easy or how hard was his mission.

Silk was coming into Imperial Rome at the time of Paul's journey. Silk and sex have been so much allied in social history that it is an almost startling thought that in early days of Tyrian fashion or at the court of Solomon, silk was unknown. Gibbon remarks that Virgil is the most ancient of western writers 'who expressly mentions the soft wool which was combed from the trees of the Seres or Chinese; and this natural error, less marvellous than the truth, was slowly corrected by the knowledge of a valuable insect, the first artificer of the luxury of nations'. Gibbon continues:

> That rare and elegant luxury was censured, in the reign of Tiberius, by the gravest of the Romans; and Pliny, in affected though forcible language has condemned the thirst of gain, which explored the last confines of the earth for the pernicious purpose of exposing to the public eye naked draperies and transparent matrons. A dress which shews the turn of the limbs and colour of the skin might gratify vanity or provoke desire; the silks which had been closely woven in China were sometimes unravelled by the Phoenician women, and the precious materials were multiplied by a looser texture and the intermixture of linen threads. Two hundred years after the age of Pliny, the use of pure or even of mixed silks was confined to the female sex, till the opulent citizens of Rome and the provinces were insensibly familiarized with the example of Elagabalus, the first who, by this effeminate habit, had sullied the dignity of an emperor and a man.

When Peter, after his last customary swim in the waters of the

Lebanon, embarked at Byblos for this final visit to the Church in
Rome, it is likely that the same ship carried examples of Phoenician
fashion. The Tyrian art had been revived by silk. The same road
which brought rare and elegant luxuries from the East also brought
a faith which was divorced from earthly luxuries, and there is a speculation which in part reconciles the apparent incongruity. The gravest
of the Romans might shake their heads at the silks and other luxuries,
but Rome had long outgrown her own religious controls. The falling-
off of home-bred religion in later days of the Republic was
accompanied by search for religious reinforcement from Greece, and
then, as soon as sea-travel encouraged it, from Syria and Egypt. The
worship of Isis was one of the early imports. Four times in a single
decade, in 58, 53, 50 and 48 B.C., the worship of Isis was suppressed in
Rome; but many Romans continued to become converts to Isis.
Strabo's *Geography,* compiled about the time of the birth of Christ,
laid much emphasis on the value to Rome of what was to be found in
the East. The loss of grip of home-bred virtues lent to some Romans
an added desire to import the more ancient wisdoms which, as well as
wealth and luxuries, were available in the East in rich profusion.
Eastern Gnostics provided a 'know-how' which was in satisfactory
accord with universal wishfulness for health and wealth and favourable fortune. Eastern messages about the vanity of human wishes
could call for equal respect, and for the same reason: the East could
speak with accents of experience. Egypt in particular, Egypt of the
mighty monuments, had known about things for a very long time.
The worship of Isis had the colourful appeal of a ritual so ancient that
to participate was by that fact a comfort. The readiness of the Romans of his moment to accept almost any Eastern philosophy is ridiculed by Juvenal.

I must remember, to keep my time-scale in order, that Juvenal –
sturdy and stubborn in Roman virtues – was born at the time that
Paul was entering Rome and that Peter was returning to the small
group of Roman Christians. Juvenal gives a picture, none better, of
the Rome of his moment, stirred by influences from the Nile. The
fifteenth satire, for example, is an attack on acceptance of disgusting
cults from Egypt, for no reason better than that they were Egyptian;
an attack which Juvenal would hardly have bothered about without
cause.

The cult of Isis in Rome had been one of those to survive early repressions. Apparently many eastern 'mystery' cults could readily come to terms with Roman wealth and fashion; much the more readily were cults accepted if the source of luxuries also seemed source of wisdom. I am harping also upon the reverse: Eastern philosophies which rejected earthly vanities, Stoicism for example, had the same extra appeal, in Rome, in that they were eastern. Ideas applicable in civilized life, ideals of civility, were less expected to emerge from Gaul, or the forests of Germany, or foggy Britain, or from Spain than from the eastern end of the Roman lake. If the early Christian brethren in Rome came together in circumstances that seemed unpromising, there was at least this much advantage – their message came from a right direction.

The thought of Paul arriving in Rome in custody, and the conjecture that the ship from Byblos which carried Peter also carried the latest samples of Tyrian silks, were reminders of an all-round contest which a small Christian group would have – one of the innumerable contests that anyone could look at in Rome's great Vanity Fair. One of the noticeable contrasts between 'the glory that was Greece' and 'the grandeur that was Rome' resides in the games which were played by Greeks and the contests staged for the excitement of Romans. When Greeks in their short heyday commanded their rock pool, colonists were regularly drawn back to the centre for the Festivals and Games, and a noticeable number of, so to speak, 'everybody', took part in competitions which have ever since been regarded by other peoples as civilized. There were limitations of 'everybody': there was the troublesome difference of sexes, there was the anomalous situation of strangers (the *metics*), there was the separateness of slaves. Yet for as many as could compete, competitions were 'open', and that was the fun of it – this Greek bloodied that Greek. The rules therefore were moderated. The Greek Games fitted with a philosophy of 'nothing to excess'. The contrast exhibited by the Roman Circus, as Rome came to power, was 'everything to excess'. In the arena for sports, instead of Roman contending with Roman, an exhibition more expressive of Conquest was that of men or animals brought from distant countries and forced to fight each other. Since these were servile contests, there was no limit to the amount of bloodshed. There are records of the quantity of butchering which Romans could stomach. I quote Sir William Ramsay:

> The number of animals destroyed on many occasions almost transcends belief. In the second consulship of Pompey, 55 B.C., 500 lions, 410 panthers and leopards, and 18 elephants, were killed in five days; Julius Caesar turned 400 lions loose all at once; Caligula, at a festival in honour of Drusilla, caused 500 bears to be put to death in one day; and in the games celebrated on the return of Trajan from Dacia, 11,000 wild animals were butchered.

Of all the feelings which such a paragraph arouses, I would dwell for a moment on the audience reaction. A thought is, that the death-contests staged between animals and animals, or animals and men, or men and men, indicate that the audience was capable of considerable callous detachment. 'Safe up there on the benches, they could enjoy the horror and death, and they laughed because it wasn't happening to them'.* When some of the torments were exhibited, such as the martyrdoms of Christians, presumably the planners wished the audience to feel that similar torture might readily happen to them if they misbehaved; but what remains of interest about Romans who flocked to circuses of their own volition is their vicarious thrill at watching any novel fight, and in betting on the moment when the Emperor's thumb would go down or up. The reflection is that the circus-going Roman was to this extent tolerant to any strangers who might be brought to Rome: it was not their feelings or beliefs that mattered, but whether they put up a fight.

Another reflection which bears on my theme is that the lions, panthers, leopards and elephants, mentioned in the above quotation, did not obligingly walk to Rome of their own accord. The quantities of animals mentioned make one think of the ship-work involved: elephants mean biggish ships. I have commented before on the bias of some scholars in making out that Romans 'never became addicted to maritime pursuits'. Nonsense! All that is meant by such a remark is that there was a fashion among literate Romans for writing disparagingly of the sea. We shall come to that, but consider first that for hauling anything to Rome it was as much within the nature of some Romans to show rashness as it was for others to show phobia. When Juvenal coined the phrase 'bread and circuses' the first word was as

* Nigel Kneale, letter to *The Times*, August 9, 1968.

important as the last. Three important sources of Rome's wheat-supply were Sicily, Tunisia (not then the dust-bowl it later became), and Egypt. At sea there was storm-damage: Paul's shipwreck is one example, and in that episode a Roman rescue-ship came along as a matter of course. There is another shipwreck which also serves to illustrate a Roman attentiveness to 'maritime pursuits'. At Ostia, Claudius is supposed to have caused the pharos, or lighthouse, to have been built on the submarine foundation formed by the wreckage of a large ship. The ship, from Alexandria, had nearly reached her desti-nation. She was waiting in the roads, perhaps, for a berth. She was loaded with some heavy Egyptian obelisks with which Claudius was intending to mark the harbour entrance at Ostia, in imitation of the two granite obelisks which had been set up at the harbour entrance of Alexandria. The Alexandrian obelisks (each of which had its own long history) are known today as Cleopatra's Needles. They were taken away from Alexandria and re-erected, one on the Victoria Em-bankment in London in 1878, the other, in 1881, in Central Park, New York. The 19th century transportation of the Alexandrian ob-elisks was regarded as a wonderful maritime achievement. The par-ticular needle which got to London is 68½ feet high and weighs 186 tons. If the obelisks which sank at Ostia are to be credited with any size commensurate with that, it was a notable feat of maritime-minded Romans to have got them so nearly to the designated site. They were not put ashore at Ostia. By accident, or possibly by design, the ship was sunk at the mouth of the Tiber. That was not the finish of the story. In the soft bottom of river-mud the wreckage could form a hard foundation. The story concludes with the building of the Roman lighthouse over the wreckage, with an inscription in firm Roman let-tering to assert the purpose – 'benefit of sailors'.

It might be accurate, I think to say that Roman interest in ships and seamen was predominantly utilitarian. The Roman who went to the Circus was becoming habituated to watching other peoples' per-formances; for housework and fieldwork there was increasing use of slaves; the legions of the Empire were increasingly made up of mer-cenaries. So, as regards ships and shipping, I would imagine that adventuring for the mere sake of adventuring, was a performance of small social standing. The products of shipwork, though, provided social standing. Rare foods, hauled across the sea to Rome, are much discussed. Many of the delicacies came in, automatically, by air. There were the vast number of thrushes, quails, millet-fowl, beccaficoes and other birds of passage which were caught alive by fowlers and kept in cages to be fattened for the market: Varro mentions one large bird-cage out of which 5,000 thrushes were sold in a single season. But fish were of as much importance as birds. The stocking and re-stocking of the salt-water ponds of the villas on the Campanian coast must have called for a good deal of boatwork, in or out of the summer season. Hirrus, one of those whom Cicero sarcastically nicknames *piscinarii*, obtained six million sesterces (roughly equivalent to £100,000 or about $250,000 today) for a villa of no special value except the quantity of fish in the salt ponds. This is the Hirrus who handed over several thousand *muraenae* to Caesar, to garnish his triumphal banquets. Those eels were specially large, Pliny suggests, because they had been fed on human slaves. Juvenal's skit about the giant turbot, too large to be offered to anybody but Domitian, may serve as sufficient example of the Roman esteem for fish. Many were the sea-coasts praised for being *pisculent,* abounding in fish; I cannot tell which specific promontory Solinus had in mind, when he coined for it a delightful word of highest praise, *pisculentissimum.*

In schooldays I obtained an impression that Romans scarcely ever attempted to keep to the sea during winter, but were wont to haul up (*subducere*) their vessels on dry land in autumn, and not haul them down (*deducere*) to sea until the gales of spring were past. But the giant turbot that Juvenal mentions came to the fisherman's net in winter: it was the frost, in days before refrigeration, which kept it fresh. It will also be remembered that one of the expert gustators brought in to advise about the turbot was the man who could tell by taste whether an oyster had been bred at Circeii, or on the Lucrine rocks, or at the beds of Rutupiae. Rutupiae is now Richborough, in Kent: it is to British oysters that Juvenal is referring. There is no surprise in that – everyone knows that British oysters were shipped from Rutupiae and eaten by epicures in Rome. The mystery comes in, if you ask how the oysters got there. It is still traditional for us to follow the Roman custom of avoiding oysters in the summer, when there is (in our calendar) no 'R' in the month. What about the transportation? – was that a matter (as with Juvenal's turbot) of waiting for the winter? And what about containers for the live oysters on the long journey? Did the oysters travel in little casks, first over the Narrow Sea, then overland to Rome – the water in the casks refreshed from time to time with brine, the oysters fed from time to time with some equivalent of oatmeal? The journey from Britain was a long one, 1,200 miles or so, yet some of the oysters appeared to have reached Rome more or less alive. Or were the oysters shipped all the way by sea from Britain? On ship, it might have been easier to keep the oysters refreshed; but then, one has to think about ships, and navigation, and the Bay of Biscay, not in summer.

British oysters in Rome remain a puzzlement. Part of the esteem, no doubt, was that they were a rarity. But any oyster that did reach Rome suggests that there was somebody who was not subducering his sea-boat at the first breath of autumn; and even the urbane poets who exaggerate the terrors of the sea reveal, when one looks closely, the noticeable amount of all-year-round maritime activity. A pleasure-loving Roman may have hired others to do the shipwork, and thought the worse of them for doing it; but the pharos at Ostia was alight not only in summer; wheat-ships were not all laid up in winter; and there were some Roman merchants on sea-roads to Syria or to Gades, eager enough to gain advantage from the timidity of others. Gades was becoming the newer, and familiar, name for the ancient Gadeira. The Roman merchant roved the whole Roman lake with eagerness: why then are there so few hints that any Roman cared to think about Atlantic exploration? Romans had ships and men and had the money too, for the mounting of sea-expeditions to the westward. As a matter of course they sailed to Gades. In the time of Nero, Apollonius of Tyana was a passenger to Gades as if such voyage were wholly ordinary. So far as passage was concerned, Paul could have got to Spain without difficulty. The ordinary answer, that beyond the Atlantic coast of Spain there was no hint of profitable merchandise, is insufficient. I will not say that there were hints galore, but there were certainly hints that exploration of the Atlantic might be profitable. I must return to those hints later, remarking here only that Roman enterprise, if left to its own devices, showed much capacity to act on very small hints. That oyster-trade! The oysters of Portugal were green, the oysters of Britanny not much better: very well, oysters then from England, shipped from Richborough. What a ridiculous amount of trouble, over a minor curiosity! At the time when Seneca was talking of a new world (*nova orbis*) at the other side of the Atlantic! If Seneca had suggested there were oysters in the new world, Romans might have raided it.

A large part of the explanation, why Romans did not sail westward into the Atlantic, is provided in the *Life* of that same Apollonius whose journey to Spain has just been mentioned. In the *Life of Apollonius* it is reported that the city of Gadeira or Gades 'is situated at the extreme end of Europe, and its inhabitants are excessively given to religion; so much so that they have set up an altar to old age, and unlike any other race they sing hymns in honour of death'.

This seems a very important clue. In Imperial Rome the ancient Greek taboo about the West was strongly working. It was a written taboo. It was in the books. I am not belittling all the other things which came to Rome from the Delta of the Nile, but one of the most important items was books. The Roman temper which could over-indulge the use of unguents and pepper, could also succumb to Alexandrian book-habits.

Noticeable, in the heyday of Greece, are the warnings about not overdoing the use of books. Books are not good for learners, says Socrates (*Phaedrus* 274 d. ff.): they 'will create forgetfulness in the learners' souls, because they will not use their memories; they will trust to the external written characters and not remember of themselves'. Socrates is quoted (Xenophon's *Memorabilia*) as implying more than that: books are all right only insofar as you bring to bear a mature judgement. The emphasis for learners is to attend not to extracts but to the wholeness of what is said, and not only to remember, but to think for yourself. So throughout Plato and Aristotle and in the education of the classic period in Greece there was insistence that mere book-learning could be contemptible, and too much of it, a depravity.

'Tell me, Euthydemus, am I rightly informed that you have a large collection of books written by the wise men of the past, as they are called? – By Zeus, yes, Socrates, answered he, and I am still adding to it, to make it as complete as possible'. Professor Moses Hadas[1] (from whom I borrow this quotation and much else) comments that Socrates was able to disabuse Euthydemus of his excessive pride in book-collecting; but the habit spread. It spread according to the temper of those who took it up, and that is what I am looking for – the different tempers displayed towards their books by Athenians of the classic age, by the Alexandrians, and by the Romans. The one verse of Homer which Socrates said was above all others always dear to him, was:[2]

Whate'er of good and ill has come to you at home

and as a bald quotation (taken from other meanings that it has within its context) it is supposed that Socrates was emphasizing heavily the last two words. The power of a book to strike home and to influence a student's life and character made it an instrument of which to be wary, and an ungoverned book collection could be as dangerous as an unguarded arsenal. There are hints in Plato's writings that the choice of books, in any library of his, would not have been indiscriminate. There is no estimate of the number of books in Aristotle's library; there is more evidence that they were carefully arranged; at least, the legend is that Theophrastus, the heir to Aristotle's library and successor to the presidency of the Lyceum, influenced the contemporary Ptolemy of Egypt to become interested in the collection and arrangement of a library of his own. The direct influence of Athens upon Alexandria was extended when Demetrius Phalereus, disciple of Theophrastus and 'last of the Attic orators worthy of the name', was exiled, took flight to Egypt, and was there 'assigned large sums of money with a view to collecting, if possible, all the books in the world'.[3] This would have been about 307 B.C., and what seems to be quickly accepted at Alexandria is the valuation of a library for the quantity of its titles and for its completeness.

One report has it, that when Ptolemy Philadelphus asked how many books Demetrius had collected, Demetrius answered: 'Above two hundred thousand, Your Majesty; and in a short while I shall exert every effort for the remainder, to round out the number of half a million.' Professor Hadas finds other estimates for what the size of the library at Alexandria came to be; the estimates range from 100,000 to 700,000 volumes. Greeks predominate in the succession of curators; one of the most industrious, at the beginning of the Christian Era, was Didymus, surnamed Chalcenterus or Brazen Guts, for his unwearied capacity for writing and reading. The 'reading' at the library at Alexandria calls for special attention, in that throughout antiquity and long thereafter, as Professor Hadas reminds us, 'even private readers regularly pronounced the words of their text aloud, in prose as well as poetry'. I find it hard to believe that Plato and Aristotle had been incapable, had they so wished, of reading silently, or that Euclid could not do sums in his head; but I do have to believe that the practice of reading aloud, and of not relying on the inward ear, was general. There is the passage in St. Augustine's *Confessions* which records Ambrose's custom of silent reading as a strange anomaly: 'But when he was reading his eye glided over the pages and his heart searched out the sense, but his voice and tongue were at rest.' Visitors, Professor Hadas comments, 'came to watch this prodigy. . . .' The habit of reading aloud certainly persisted: medieval scriptoria are described as noisy places filled with the sounds of the copyists reciting their texts. Whether or no the habit had been approved at Athens, I would believe it to have been fostered at Alexandria; and if Didymus of the Brazen Guts was reading aloud each of his new acquisitions, and simultaneously each book-borrower vociferously mastering a different text, the sneer of the Skeptic Timon is readily explained, that the scholars of Alexandria were 'chatterers in a bird coop'. The exodus of eremites to solitude in the Thebaid is seen as a desire to hear one's self think.

The library at Alexandria was famous before there were many Romans of affluence or leisure, and when there was a quickening toward such excitement as there might be in books, it was to Alexandria, rather than to impoverished Athens, that most Romans turned. It may be wise then to remember that the literature and science, which in time past had been a wine of life in Athens, was for the most part offered to Romans as it had been adulterated in Alexandria. The 'doctoring' of Greek writings at the Alexandrian library possibly, for Rome, increased their potency. The original Caesar had derived from Alexandria the conception of a public library for Rome. That project died with him; it was revived by Augustus. By the time of Trajan there were 28 'public' libraries in Rome. The multiplication had taken place in the thirty years since Vespasian (69–79) had appointed Quintilian as Rome's first director of education – Quintilian, the ardent Spaniard whose first law was that a boy of the Roman Empire should learn Greek before his mother tongue, and who gave the first and fullest place in the curriculum of reading to Homer. Books written in Greek were thus to provide no obstacle in Rome. Domitian, not otherwise noted for encouragement of liberal studies, sent scribes to Alexandria to transcribe copies for the replenishment of the public libraries. The individual benefactor, says Professor Hadas, came to provide a library for his provincial town as customarily as he might provide a school or a public bath; he instances the younger Pliny, who had studied under Quintilian, and who gave a library to his native Como.

Public libraries in Rome had been long preceded by the private book collections. By Nero's day private libraries had become as common in the houses of the rich as were banqueting rooms. Many were the contemporary gibes at those who claimed pride of possession in handsome volumes, without much habit of unrolling them. The gibes may be ignored: it is the reading habits of the Romans who did read books, in private or in public libraries, which is in my theme. What, broadly speaking, did books mean to Romans? What did they cotton on to, from whatever it was that Alexandria taught? What was it that Alexandria offered, and what did Romans absorb?

The first thing usually noticed about the library at Alexandria was the tendency there to become 'academic', in a sense of the word which might have been much deplored by Socrates and Plato. As far back as Ptolemy Philadelphus, in a decade roundabout 20 B.C., the task had been given to Zenodotus and two colleagues, to collect and edit all the Greek poets. It was Zenodotus who produced a standard edition of Homer. The copying, emending and recopying of Homer at Alexandria came to produce what Professor Hadas calls 'freakish' amusements. Thus 'Tryphiodorus wrote a "lipogrammatic" *Odyssey*; that is, the poem was rewritten so that in each book the use of the letter by which the book was numbered was avoided: there was no alpha in Book I, no beta in Book II, and so on. We hear too that one Timolaos wrote a Troica by inserting a line of his own after each line of the *Iliad*. Suidas says Idaos doubled Homer by adding alternate lines of his own.' If such and other donnish games came to be enjoyed by those who strolled in the precincts of the library at Alexandria it does not necessarily indicate a total disrespect for Homer; it may indicate the reverse – you had to be very familiar with a text before you got fun out of making a game of it. But these were games for scholars only, private games, and they suggest a wide division between people of the library and people of the world outside. It is easy to feel that Homer might have preferred the rough and tumble company of Greek-speaking seamen of the port – progeny of Sappho's brother and the woman Sappho did not like – but at Alexandria the shade of Homer was being buttoned up and kept within the cloisters.

It is likely that Virgil read Homer in an Alexandrian edition, and it is likely that an Alexandrian edition had reached Quintilian at his birthplace (Calagurris, now Calahorra) before he came to Rome (about the time that Paul arrived) to win all prizes for his eloquence. Neither Virgil nor Quintilian regarded Homer as a distant 'classic', remote in circumstance of place and time; each in his way took fire from the text. It is the fire and excitement communicated to the Mantuan and the Spaniard which is so noticeable; the flame licked out at them despite the asbestos coverings of some of the Alexandrians. Though Virgil was a Mantuan and Quintilian came from Calagurris, both were Romans, and set about it to provide for Rome such shout of spirit as they heard in Homer. Quintilian took Homer straight into the Forum, making Homer the model and inspiration for every kind of oratory; and what may seem extraordinary is that Quintilian's zeal was, among Romans, contagious.* But it was easier for Quintilian to see through the assiduous pedantry of Alexandria and get to the heart of Homer than to prevent, among his followers, the growth of a similar pedantry. It was, I think, extraordinary that Romans could be swayed into making Homer their cornerstone of education and into making Greek a compulsory language; but what Quintilian may not have intended was that enthusiasm for Homer could lead insensibly to acceptance in Rome of some of the ancient ideas which, except for the authority of Homer, might have been seen to be out-moded. Nothing whatever in Homer about the nature of humanity was out-moded; but Homer's authority as to what was

* I should have liked to quote the superb appreciation of Homer as expressed by Quintilian (10. 1. 46–51), but it is too long for quotation in full. There is an excellent translation in Hadas, *Ancilla to Classical Reading*, pp. 143, 144.

invariant could carry over into acceptance of his authority in all matters. Human feelings had not much changed since Homer's day; therefore it was eminently rational that Grecian conventions of rhetoric should apply also in Rome; but along with them came other Greek conventions, the product of temporary circumstance.

The point I wish to put is that Romans knew with their own eyes much more about geography than Homer ever knew, and yet it came about that they could accept a Homeric statement about geography long after such a statement was contradictable. I am referring to the hesitation of Romans to send their ships beyond the Pillars of Hercules. No doubt it would be too simple to ascribe the hesitation directly to Homer's taboo, but what one looks for are the indirect effects in Rome of adopting Grecian views. One looks to see what books were saying. A trivial instance is to note that at a moment when Rome's merchant marine was doing all the things I was talking about, an often repeated theme of Horace's *Odes* is terror of the sea. I am confident that Horace, so to speak, knew better. He was not talking of the sea which served Rome daily; he was composing odes, and consciously echoing Pindar; as Pindar, in turn, had been consciously echoing Homer. With this kind of doubled reflection there came into Roman poetry, and into schooling, a 'literary' sea which was not at all the same as the sea of the working seaman. This of itself is a trivial instance, but what it indicates are the social separations in Rome's great transformation scene. Social separations would have happened anyway, but often they follow a Greek pattern. This is attributable in part to the teaching of Greek books.

The separation which concerns me is that between the landsman and the seafarer; I watch how books promote such separation. The original type of Roman farmer is Cincinnatus; when forced to do so he can come to Rome, but what he prefers is the smell of the soil. He can spit on his hands and hold his own plough. In that same Roman tradition, farmwork, as late as Cato's time, is rough and ready; there is not much absentee ownership of farmland; there is good farming or bad, but farming of itself creates no elaborate social distinctions. As Rome goes in for foreign conquests and as wealth accumulates, an atmosphere of country life is seen to change. Cicero had a powerful friend whose native Roman name was Pomponius: it was an Athenian influence which caused the change of name from Pomponius to Atticus. Atticus plays a large part in establishing that it is possession of a country estate which marks a Roman as a gentleman – a Grecian kind of literate gentleman. In the Augustan Age this Grecian mode is greatly promoted by Virgil and Horace. It is now a matter of social distinction to be a *ruris amator*, an amateur countryman as praised by Horace, who in a pleasant season gets him to his little farm and vineyard (*O rus, quando te aspiciam!*). Pliny's pleasure in praising his farm, with its cornfields and meadowland, vineyard and woodland, orchard and pasture, beehives and flowers, is in great part a carefully nurtured literary pleasure. This accretion of pleasure, not natively Roman, is powerful; it persists in such a figure as Rufus Festus Avienus at the end of the fourth century; and has persisted ever since.

With Roman education based on Greek texts and many Roman writers fostering Grecian modes of thought, concurrent with increase of status for the landed proprietor came the opposite Greek scorn for the seafarer. To the pleasure of Augustus, Virgil praised the husbandman; for the pleasure of a later Empress (the wife of Severus, whose reign was 193–211) there was prepared the *Life of Apollonius of Tyana*. In this *Life* there is much of interest; only one small and incidental item concerns me here. Apollonius, it should be said, is being set up as a Messiah more congenial to the then Roman Court than Jesus, and at the point that I quote he is being interviewed by an interlocutor, Iarchus. The interlocutor had asked Apollonius about his previous incarnation, and Apollonius had replied that his former life had been 'an ignoble episode'. Iarchus therefore took him up and said: 'Then you think it ignoble to have been the pilot of an Egyptian vessel, for I perceive that this is what you were?'

'What you say', said Apollonius, 'is true, Iarchus; for that is really what I was; but I consider this profession not only inglorious but also detestable, and though of as much value to humanity as that of a prince or the leader of an army, nevertheless it bears an evil repute by reason of those who follow the sea. . . .'[4]

As Roman social life sorted itself, the down-grading of the seafarer is as noticeable as is the up-grading of the farmer. In Roman genes there may have been a native predilection for this; if so, the predilection was encouraged by what Romans chose to listen to from Greeks. Philostratus, the writer of the *Life of Apollonius*, was a

Greek at the court of the Roman Empress. The 'evil repute' of the seamen that he offered was natural to him. At the Roman Court or in the Forum there was no social advantage to be achieved by the reputation of sailing beyond the Pillars of Hercules. Nobody but a seaman might think of doing that. But all the capillary ways by which hostility to the Atlantic entered into Roman education reach back, I think, to the heart of the matter; to the persistence of Homer's 'Ocean', identified as death.

The 'doctoring' of Greek texts at Alexandria and the freakish amusements sometimes indulged in at the great Library did not prevent Rome from receiving the direct impact of Grecian poetry. At about the same time as the martyrdom of Peter and Paul, Nero forced Seneca to suicide. The Christian message was not as yet attracting wide attention; Seneca drew much attention to Greek classics, and I have alluded to the great impulse, in the same direction, of Quintilian, who at the time of Seneca's death was in his twenties. It is curious that Seneca and Quintilian, who so notably caught and conveyed Greek techniques of rhetoric, were both of Spanish origin. The books which emanated from Alexandria had become an instrument whereby provincial men of genius could rise to power in Rome. Thus grammar was akin to glamour; the freakish scholarship at Alexandria did not conceal that the Library was a power-house. In 'literature' the freakishness was seen through; in 'science' it was not. Romans have often been castigated for their lack of interest in Greek science; but here it is worth remembering how that department of Greek heritage was exceedingly hedged about at Alexandria.

It was in their passion for mathematics that Greeks themselves, in classical times, broke their own precept of 'nothing to excess'. Story after story repeats the rapture to be found, superior to any other activity, in 'pure' intellectual exercise. In the realm of astronomy, the stories illustrate religious rapture: from the early example of the tale which Plato tells with humour, of the maid-servant rallying Thales, to the late example of Ptolemy's epigram – 'I know that I am mortal and the creature of a day; but when I search out the massed wheeling circles of the stars, my feet no longer touch the earth, but, side by side with Zeus himself, I take my fill of ambrosia, the food of the gods.' It is not only toward astronomy, said Aristotle, that intellect should be directed, but toward all living things – there is a pantheism to be seen in all – and so he looks at a great variety of 'small' life-histories: insects in their many kinds, bees and wasps and moths and cicadas, and the cuttle-fish, crabs, eels, and the other fishes which he discusses with the fishermen in his long holiday on the island of Mytilene. It is in a culminating paragraph in his book about *Animals*, that Aristotle expresses his purpose:

> The glory, doubtless, of the heavenly bodies fills us with more delight than the contemplation of these lowly things; for the sun and stars are born not, neither do they decay, but are eternal and divine. But the heavens are high and afar off, and of celestial things the knowledge that our senses give us is scanty and dim. The living creatures, on the other hand, are at our door, and if we so desire it we may gain ample and certain knowledge of each and all. We take pleasure in the beauty of a statue, shall not then the living fill us with delight; and all the more if in spirit of philosophy we search for causes and recognize the evidence of design. Then will nature's purpose and her deep-seated laws be everywhere revealed, all tending in her multitudinous work to one form or another of the Beautiful.

It was in mathematics, I was saying, that Greeks found a peculiar ecstasy, expressed in the many stories from that of Pythagoras sacrificing a hecatomb of oxen in gratitude for seeing the proof of the right-triangle theorem, through the late symbolic episode of the death of Archimedes – so absorbed in the study of a geometrical diagram that, when captured at Syracuse by a Roman soldier, he did not at once obey orders and was killed. In the classical Greek attitude towards mathematics there is a chemical mixture of feelings: there is in the mixture something of utility, something of a game, something of priestcraft, and all are blended. The quasi-monastic movement initiated by Pythagoras exhibits itself as a secret society with considerable ritual: pure mathematicians serve God in the interior court, learners are lay-brothers on the outside, not all at once entrusted with the inner worship but at first only with subordinate routines. The mystical element in the mathematics of Pythagoras is regarded by some as an Eastern taint, caught during the years in which he had been expatriate from Greece. According to Iamblichus, Pythagoras had been 'reborn in Syria as an initiate in all the Syrian religious rites; he then shared in Egyptian priestcraft for 22 years, and for 12 more years was a student of the Magi in Babylon. The peculiar genius of mathematicians later than Pythagoras was to throw away (so Cumont says) the 'fantastic rubbish' of the Eastern superstitious ideas; then (as Heath put it) 'the Greek genius could take an independent upward course'. Plato is held to have been praising Greek freethinking, in his proud boast in the *Epinomis*: 'Let us take it as an axiom that, whatever the Greeks take from the barbarians, they bring it to fuller perfection.'

There is no doubt of the beautiful game that the Greeks developed in mathematics, but it is wrong to say that their passion for mathematics was devoid of mystical element. To look at the context in which Plato was making the above-quoted boast, what Plato was saying is that the stars are to be regarded as animate beings, with a soul indwelling in each body. The 'fuller perfection' which Greeks brought to science was less a matter of eliminating mystique, than of expressing their own mystique in scientific study. There is a story of a lecture of Plato's on 'The Good' which Aristotle was fond of telling: 'Everyone went there with the idea that he would be put in the way of getting one or other of the things in human life which are usually accounted good, such as Riches, Health, Strength, or, generally, any extraordinary gift of fortune. But when they found that Plato discoursed about mathematics, arithmetic, geometry and astronomy, and finally declared the One to be the Good, no wonder they were altogether taken by surprise; insomuch that in the end some of the audience were inclined to scoff at the whole thing, while others objected to it altogether.'

Plato's comprehensive interest in mathematics could dwell upon small and homely practical procedures, as Aristotle's interest in science could dwell upon the anatomy of cuttlefish. Plato noticed arithmetical questions involved in the game of knuckle-bones, the game which in the Homeric period had involved Patroclus in trouble. Plato puzzled over the theoretical principles of all the games he watched in Egypt – games with pebbles, with bowls of different sizes, the arrangement of the draw for tournaments, methods of handicapping, probabilities in the throwing of dice. Plato was friendly with Archytas of the mechanical devices – the dove made of wood which would fly, and the rattle to be given to the children to occupy them and keep them from breaking things about the house. Aristotle also highly approved of that rattle, 'for the young are incapable of keeping still'. Yet in the whole variety of outward matters looked at, behind the instant curiosity appears the latent passion. The passion exhibited by Aristotle as by Plato and which informed their roving curiosity, was to find laws behind instances, the laws themselves exhibiting a beauty that was worshipful. In the Lyceum as in the Academy worship was infused in the exhibition of 'one form or another of the Beautiful'. The Hebrew axiom ('The Universe is filled with the might and power of our God') is equally an axiom in Athens of the classical period. The Greek theism unfolds in its own way; the mysteries of geometry and numbers, or of the cuttlefish, exemplify the embrace.

In mathematics, a change to be observed at Alexandria is the development of priestcraft; the Euclidean school, by defining the cult, also narrowed it. At Athens 'utility' had never been proclaimed as the sole object of the study, nor had utility been wholly dismissed; at the school in Alexandria, one of the spiritual merits of ' pure' mathematics was its complete divorce from wordly matters. What Professor Whitehead calls 'a celibacy of intellect' took charge of Euclid's school. There is a story told by Stobaeus:

> Someone who had begun to read geometry with Euclid, when he had learned the first theorem, asked Euclid, 'What shall I get by learning these things?' Euclid called his slave and said, 'Give him threepence, since he must make gain out of what he learns.'

I would say that Stobaeus, writing in a late period (about A.D. 405) is copying a cheap retort, an 'academic' invention very much later than Euclid, and unworthy to be fathered upon Euclid himself. The tone is wrong; the tone of a man close to the source of inspiration is given by Peter ('Silver and gold have I none, but of such as I have I will give you'); and that Euclid's period (around 300 B.C.) was one of real mathematical inspiration is clear from the beauty and the power of the works ascribed to him and his immediate successors. For early Greeks, the geometric dance that could be done with line and circle was a dromenon, a pattern of dynamic expression; and numbers had a therapeutic rhythm; and aesthetic consummation was the perfect union of theorem and proof. In the aspect of a game, an individual performance was sometimes pretty enough to be given a familiar name, such as the 'flower' or 'bloom' of Thymaridas, or the 'sieve' of

Eratosthenes, or the 'reductio ad absurdum', as a device much favoured by Euclid came later to be called. Some ingenuities in simple plane geometry came down to us as nicknames: the 'lunes' of Hippocrates, the *salinon* (presumably 'salt-cellar') and *arbelos* (or 'shoemaker's knife') of Archimedes. In the aspect of a profession, there was hard and proper thinking to capture the wild species ('irrational' numbers, and other notorious problems and paradoxes). But in the early inspiration, the warmth of mathematics was in the fusion of the dance and game, technique and mystery. From Euclid's time until the death of Archimedes that warmth lasted; mathematics was a form of worship felt by many; but the mention of Archimedes is a reminder that the form of worship was one not readily recognized by the Roman soldier.

At Alexandria the warmth was going out of mathematics long before the sea-road brought Romans to the Library. While Archimedes was studying at Alexandria (before 200 B.C.) he was not above dabbling in practical matters; he invented the Archimedean screw as a means of pumping water; when later defending Syracuse against the Romans he invented catapults, quick-firing mechanisms, and cranes and grapples for the overset of enemy ships – perhaps the very 'ravens' which were adopted by the Romans. But to the pure mathematicians of Alexandria, to those who were rigid conformists to their definition of the Euclidean school, Archimedes was forced to apologize. The apology, probably foisted upon him, was that practical inventions were merely the 'diversions of geometry at play'; according to Plutarch:

> ... though these inventions had obtained for him the renown of more than human sagacity, he yet would not even deign to leave behind him any written word on such subjects, but, regarding as ignoble and sordid the business of mechanics and every sort of art which is directed to use and profit, he placed his whole ambition in those speculations the beauty and subtlety of which is untainted by any admixture of the common needs of life.

Centuries later (at the end of the third century A.D.) Pappus of Alexandria did gently rise to defend the application of geometry to practical arts: 'for geometry is in no wise injured, nay it is by nature capable of giving substance to many arts by being associated with them, and, so far from being injured, it may be said, while itself advancing those arts, to be honoured and adorned by them in return'. Heron (also in the third century A.D.) was encyclopedic in his collection of applied mathematics. He wrote about surveying, and the restoration of boundaries in a flood-area when all except two or three marks had been obliterated. He wrote about a hodometer for measuring distances traversed by a wheeled vehicle, and more generally about the transmission of mechanical power by interacting toothed wheels. He wrote about the astrolabe, water-clocks, automata for the theatre, and many devices for employing the force of compressed air, water, and steam. Siphons, 'Heron's fountain', slot machines, and many elementary steam-engines are found in Heron's *Pneumatica*; and having dealt with the mechanical powers of wheel and axle, lever, pulley, wedge and screw, he is indefatigable in drawing attention to applications in daily life: e.g. 'Why does a stick break sooner when one puts one's knee against it in the middle?, Why do people use pincers rather than the hand to draw a tooth?, Why are great ships turned by a rudder although it is so small?'

At the time that leisured Romans were prepared to raid the storehouse of ideas at Alexandria, mathematics was no longer there exhibited as the dromenon it once had been. A first excitement at the discoveries in a realm symbolic of the law and order of the universe, a first delight in unexpected revelations, was hardly to be preserved by the mere preservation of an established mathematical curriculum. Without the refreshment of new perceptions there came to be conscious schism in the Alexandrian school, between purists and would-be innovators. By the time that Romans came to find what was offered, the exhibition of mathematics at Alexandria may have seemed somewhat like the exhibition at Laputa, when visited, in Swift's description, by Gulliver. Romans at the time of the Punic war had been interested in Archimedes' grappling-irons and catapults; but it was this 'applied' mathematics which was scorned by the purists. Heron's encyclopedia of applications, scorned or not at Alexandria, was of some interest to the invading Romans: there were tricks and novelties to be copied. Heron's pulleys were useful, and Rome picked up the idea of slot machines. On the level of tricks and pastimes, there were at Alexandria plenty of 'mathematical recreations' to be restated in terms that were amusing in Rome.

There are many examples: e.g. one pipe by itself fills a bath in one day, a second in two, a third in three – how long will it take all three running together to fill it? Another problem which amused Rome was that of the will made by a dying man: his wife being with child, his will is that if she gives birth to a son, the son shall receive two-thirds and the widow one third of his estate; if a daughter is born, she shall receive one third and the widow two-thirds. The man then dies, but the devil of it is that the widow is delivered of twins, boy and girl. How shall the estate be divided so as to satisfy the will? The Roman jurist, Salvianus Julianus, made a name for himself by his solution of this poser.[5]

Perhaps the excitement of 'pure' mathematics was too much hedged about by the purists at Alexandria to be conveyable to in-coming Romans. With regard to Aristotle's interest in natural science there was a similar lack of communication. In Aristotle's *Historia Animalium* (as his compilation came to be called) there were plenty of trivial anecdotes and strange stories – the goats that breathe through their ears, the vulture impregnated by the wind, the eagle that chooses to die of hunger, the stag caught by music, the salamander that walks through fire, the unicorn, the manticore – these were stock items not originated by Aristotle, and recorded by him rather as matters which had not as yet been investigated. The life-history of the cuttlefish, to which Aristotle gave acute examination, is an instance in which he had been able to rid of extraneous myth. From Homeric times, the peculiar craftiness of the cuttlefish, which when alarmed squirts black ink into the water and so disappears from vision, had roused Greek admiration; the cuttlefish, whose own whiteness was so fused with power of blackness, was special symbol of the sea-goddess Thetis, the ultimate creator (mingling beauty with trickery and guile) of the sea-world. The replacement of Alcman's kind of wonder at the symbolic cuttlefish by Aristotle's kind of wonder at the sufficiently remarkable life-history of the little animal itself, lasted while Aristotle was alive; but gradually the scientific interest reverted. One does not read of laboratories at Alexandria, and when Romans came in search of won-ders, Aristotle's matter-of-fact examinations were not in favour. Cer-tainly Pliny, when inspired to write his own *Historia Naturalis*, was more interested in phenomena which seemed strange and spectacular, than at the mysteries which Aristotle had pointed out, near at hand.

Without the vision that laws fundamental in the universe were as excitingly revealed in homely as in far-off things, it was hard to maintain investigations such as Aristotle started; and without vision of some transcendent meaning the interest in geometry and numbers slackened when it seemed that most of what could be learned was all well-known. In the third century A.D. there were still such men as Pappus and Diophantus who could see beyond the boundaries of existing knowledge, and there were those to come (Augustine, Boethius) who could see in mathematics what the ancient Greeks had seen. For the Roman tourist in Alexandria, if it seemed that what pleased him was meretricious marvels, they could be supplied. In science, manticore and unicorn could be exhibited, with Aristotle's name stamped on them. In mathematics, Alexandria could easily produce some cheap debasements. Diophantus has just been mentioned, one of the last of the great creators. About the time of Boethius, a Greek called Metrodorus collected for Roman consumption a Greek anthology of arithmetical epigrams. Diophantus was mocked by Metrodorus in the following pastiche: the boyhood of Diophantus (says Metrodorus) lasted one sixth of his life, his beard grew after one twelfth more, he married after one seventh more, his son was born five years later; the son lived to half his father's age, and the father died four years after his son. How old was Diophantus when he died?

The crudity of that little puzzle was a return to the crudeness from which Greeks had elevated arithmetic ten times longer ago than the length of the lifetime thus ascribed to Diophantus.[6] It is to the eternal credit of Boethius, that 'last of the Romans', that he could see through the tawdry presentations of such vendors as Metrodorus. But the real reason, I think, why earlier Romans failed to catch on to the Greek mathematics, was that their introduction to Alexandria was at a moment when the best minds in Alexandria were all ablaze with a different fire. Theology closer to the heart and passions was what was stirring in some Romans and some Alexandrians alike, before the beginning and after the beginning of the Christian Era. The startling influence from the Delta upon Rome shows not in the realms of literature or science, but in the acceptance of Christian theology.

NOTES

Chapter 8:

1. *Ancilla to Classical Reading* by Moses Hadas (Columbia University Press, New York, 1954).
2. *The Attic Nights of Aulus Gellius,* translated by John C. Rolfe (Loeb Classical Library, 1927). Vol. III, pp. 46, 47.
3. Hadas, p. 23.
4. *Philostratus: The Life of Apollonius of Tyana,* translated by F. C. Conybeare (Loeb Classical Library, 1921), Vol. I, pp. 277–9.
5. Salvianus Julianus divided the estate into 7 parts, allotting 4 parts to the son, 2 to the mother, 1 to the daughter.
6. The age of Diophantus (call it x) is given by
$$x/6 + x/12 + x/7 + 5 + x/2 + 4 = x$$
whence, without the pleasure of much ingenuity, $x = 84$.

CHAPTER 9

The City of God

THERE now returns into the story of westward migration the impulse with which we started – the conception, although very much altered, of the City Of God.

Professor Charles Norris Cochrane, whose *Christianity and Classical Culture* is my chief guide through the troubled period immediately ahead, divides the first three centuries of the Roman Empire (with the customary caution that distinctions of this kind are largely arbitrary) into a first century of adjustment, a second of fruition, and a third of disintegration and decay. These are the centuries roughly corresponding in date with the first three centuries of the Christian Era.[1]

The ministry of Paul and Peter at Rome was one side of a pincers movement upon Rome's noisy populace. The other side of the pincers is represented by Philo of Alexandria, born a very few years earlier of a distinguished Jewish sacerdotal family, possibly of the sect of the Pharisees. He had been educated not only in the subjects usually studied by a Jew of his standing, but also in the Greek philosophies, and he was especially a follower of Plato. At Alexandria, his theology became more Greek than Jewish; and his effort to reconcile the Mosaic revelation with the Platonic philosophy was of lasting effect in early Christian thinking. 'The Epistle to the Hebrews and the Fourth Gospel are unintelligible,' Dean Inge remarked, 'without some knowledge of Philo.' Philo was as eminent for his eloquence as for his learning, and was sent as ambassador of his nation to Caligula in A.D. 40. The Roman state-religion required the worship of the emperor as a god, and there was a quarrel at that moment with the Jews over their refusal to place statues of the emperor in their temples. It was a refusal shared by Jews and Christians, for which both were to suffer.

Philo was unsuccessful in his embassy to Rome, yet in the book which he wrote to defend the Jews his rhetoric was so impressive, and met with such applause in the Roman senate, where he read it publicly, that it was permitted to be given circulation in the public libraries, and he was openly spoken of as 'the Jewish Plato'. If Philo could not prevent the renewed destruction of the Holy City of the Jews in A.D. 70, what he did by presenting Jewish and Greek thinking as an amalgam, was an example to the Christian apologists of the second century. With them the appeal for the toleration of Christians is on the ground that the best Greek philosophers taught very much the same as the Christians. I borrow some references from Dean Inge:

> 'We teach the same as the Greeks,' says Justin Martyr, 'though we alone are hated for what we teach.' 'Some among us,' says Tertullian, 'who are versed in ancient literature, have written books to prove that we have embraced no tenets for which we have not the support of common and public literature.' 'The teachings of Plato,' says Justin again, 'are not alien to those of Christ; and the same is true of the Stoics.' 'Heracleitus and Socrates lived in accordance with the divine Logos', and should be reckoned as Christians. Clement says that Plato wrote 'by inspiration of God'.[2]

Augustine, much later, was to say that 'only a few words and phrases' need be changed to bring Platonism into complete accord with Christianity; but that is in a different context, and Augustine is not suggesting that the words and phrases are insignificant or to be glossed over. It was in the early days of the effort to obtain toleration for the Christian church in Rome that apologists insisted that their thought was orthodox Greek thinking; and this apology was indeed so much accepted that it is possible, by taking a distant view, for Dean Inge to assert that 'the Christian Church was the last great creative achievement of the classical culture'.

If the Citadel of Imperial Rome was to be penetrated it could hardly have been done by vaunting the impiety of the intrusion. The nature of the concord binding the Roman philosophy of the state, as described by Virgil, was not a shallow intellectual compact but 'a union of hearts'; not a sentimental rapture over 'wheat and woodland, tilth and vineyard, hive and horse and herd', but a call to work for the realization of moral values associated with the life of the farm, and a call to exert just and righteous domination over those among whom these qualities existed in lesser degree. There is in the Virgilian picture a powerful sense that with the rise of Rome fate has given birth

to something wholly new in the evolution of peoples. Professor Cochrane suggests[3] that we shall best understand the spirit expressed by
Virgil 'if we think of the Romans as having achieved in the Old World
precisely that to which men of European stock were to set their hands
in the New'. In the first century 'the state and empire of Rome depend fundamentally on will: virtue is not so much knowledge as
character; and its fruits are seen in activity rather than in repose or
contemplation. Aeneas is thus the pilgrim father of antiquity . . .'.

The point on which I am concentrating is the human endeavour
whereby the Christian church obtained an entry and then a domination in this pagan Roman world, seemingly so confident in itself.

If you had conversed with Plutarch in his sleepy, sunny old Boeo-
tian town in the early days of the Pax Romana, it might have been
easy to admit that 'in Stoicism the mind of antiquity had not only
reached in some respects its highest expression, but that expression
had become popular in a way unparalleled in the history of any other
school'.[4] If there were any questioning, Plutarch might well have
quoted to you his revered father, who said: 'You seem to me to be
handling a very great and dangerous subject, or rather to be raising
questions which ought not to be raised at all, when you question the
opinion we hold about the gods, and ask reasons and proofs for everything. The ancient and ancestral faith is enough; and if on one point
its fixed and traditional character be disturbed, it will be undermined
and no one will trust it.' Stoicism 'teaches men to venerate and obey
natural law; to accept with proud equanimity the misfortunes of life;
to be beneficent, but to inhibit the emotion of pity; to be self-reliant
and self-contained; to practice self-denial for the sake of self-
conquest; and to regard this life as a stern school of moral discipline'.

This I believe to have been a dominant attitude of the devout
pagan of the first century. A Roman man of the world like the
younger Pliny had only the vaguest notion what Jews or Christians
were until he came across them as the governor of an outlying province, and then he disliked them not as individuals, nor for their private superstitions, but for public impiety. The Holy City of the
Jews was erased for what Rome regarded as public impiety. The
Christians in Pliny's experience were a meek people in comparison
with the Jews, but their Gospel was worse: the Gospel was impious

even in its original homeland. The Gospel was, as Paul said, a wholly new creation. To the cultivated Roman it was doubly impious, for its direct questioning and for its direct assertion; and if in Rome a notable man like Flavius Clemens, Domitian's cousin, was won to the new community of Christians he withdrew at once from the world's eyes.

What I therefore described as a pincers' movement was the double approach upon Rome of an underground message which was politically subversive, and a simultaneous intellectual apology that the new theology was only the fruition of the best Greek thinking. It was the double approach which gradually exerted a prodigious grip. What could be extracted from Plato, and was extracted at Alexandria and brought from Egypt to Rome by Plotinus, was an exposition of the whole prologue of St John's Gospel, with the exception of the one essential fact that the Word became flesh and dwelt among us; and to that revelation Paul was in every way a comprehending witness. So the appearance and immediate popularity of Plotinus in Rome widened his upper-class part of the message that philosophical truth could be known, though he gave no means of attaining it; but Paul had given the message that seeped upwards from the lowly that the very truth as preached by Plotinus had 'already been revealed to men by God and made available by a divine authority which made it unnecessary for their feeble reasons to exhaust themselves in long study.' Thus St. Paul's Christianity made it possible 'for the Platonism of the mind to become a thing of the heart, for the Platonism of theory to become practice'.[5] Equally, the academic respectability of Platonism assisted Paul's mission.

I am impressed by the 'pincers' argument, but wish to see the sort of people on whom the pincers were to work. It is difficult not to run ahead in the time-scale, and I must remind myself that Plotinus did not achieve his great popularity in Rome until the latter part of the third century, when the complacency of *Romanitas* was not what it had been. Here I would look at three provincial men of talent, attracted to Rome in the prosperous second century before the complacency was altogether shaken. These are Galen, the physician; Apuleius, an adventurer; and Philostratus, the author of the *Life of Apollonius of Tyana*.

I bring in Galen chiefly for his picture of the easy-going, sociable and pleasure-loving society in which he moved. Galen was born about A.D. 129, at Pergamum in Asia Minor. He studied medicine at Pergamum, at Smyrna, at Corinth and at Alexandria. He went to Rome in his thirties and became court physician to Marcus Aurelius and to that very different character, the Emperor Commodus. He was frequently accused by his rivals of using magic arts, and had his temper been less equable or his friends less powerful the accusations would have been dangerous. Magic had been proscribed in Rome ever since the original XII Tables of Law. Magic had been proscribed, but it had never been easy to define: black magic or white magic, who was to draw the line?

Galen gives us a picture of Roman society, which I follow in Thorndike's transcription:

> Not only physicians but men generally begin the day with salutations and calls, then separate again, some to the market-place and law courts, others to watch the dancers or charioteers. Others play at dice or pursue love affairs, or pass the hours at the baths or in eating and drinking or some other bodily pleasure. In the evening they all come together again at symposia which bear no resemblance to the intellectual feasts of Socrates and Plato but are mere drinking bouts. Galen had no objection, however, to the use of wine in moderation and mentions the varieties from different parts of the Mediterranean world which were especially noted for their medicinal properties. He believed that drinking wine discreetly relieved the mind from all worry and melancholy and refreshed it. 'For we use it every day'. He affirmed that taken in moderation wine aided digestion and the blood. He classed wines with such boons to humanity as medicines, 'a sober and decent mode of life', and 'the study of literature and liberal disciplines'.[6]

Thorndike finds that Galen in his few allusions to the followers of Moses and Christ scarcely distinguished between them and speaks of them 'rather lightly, not to say contemptuously'. In one allusion to the use of vague and unintelligible language, Galen says that it is 'as if one had come to a school of Moses and Christ and had heard undemonstrated laws'. In another place where criticizing opposing sects for their obstinacy Galen remarks sardonically that it would be easier to win over the followers of Moses and Christ.

Apart from these allusions there is little reference to Christians or

Jews in the voluminous writings of this court physician. Professor Latourette remarks that Marcus Aurelius 'heartily disliked Christians, possibly because he thought of them as undermining the structure of civilization which he was labouring to maintain against domestic and foreign threats, and during his reign persecutions occurred. . . . Under Commodus, the unworthy son of Marcus Aurelius, persecution, at first continued, was later relaxed because of the intervention of his favourite, Marcia'.[7] But there is nothing seriously hostile in the tone of Galen's references, and there is the implication that 'schools' of Jews or Christians were at any rate sometimes open to a general, if condescending, public. In Rome 'free speech', in the sense of preaching sedition, had been proscribed along with black magic, from the time of the original XII Tables. So far as Galen's testimony is concerned, in the time of Marcus Aurelius and Commodus persecution in Rome of Jews or Christians, either on grounds of religion or grounds of subversion, would seem to have been no more than half-hearted. Galen is alert to many things but not interested in Christianity. Galen's friends do not as yet feel either side of the Christian pincers. As is perhaps natural for a court physician, he is more concerned about sharp practices with drugs.

The perennial interest in magic and witchcraft is sometimes held responsible for the survival of one of the most interesting books of the second century, *The Golden Ass* of Apuleius. This is a book which in the guise of straightforward narrative falls into three parts, three acts of the Human Comedy as seen at that time. It is a serious comedy, which should be considered as a whole; commentators have too frequently dismembered it. It is a pilgrim's progress, the first act a journey through a wild valley of witchcraft, demonology and gnosticism; the second a beautiful recollection of Hellenic spirit, typified in the story (apparently invented by Apuleius) of Cupid and Psyche; the third a welcome for the narrator into the mystery-religion of Isis and Osiris, with consequent prosperous career to be looked forward to in Rome.

Dean Inge regards the thanksgiving to Isis at the end as 'very beautiful in itself, though it is an odd termination of a licentious novel'.[8] Thorndike is interested only in the first part, for its details of magical practice. Others have torn out the lovely story of Cupid and

Psyche, which entered into European folklore as progenitor of Cinderella stories (wicked sisters and all) and details of which (the performance of unfair and impossible tasks through the assistance of friendly animals) are imitated in many a delightful fairy-tale. But I repeat, *The Golden Ass* is worth looking at as a whole. It is a very artful piece of work, and as for being a licentious novel, that's as your taste may be. St. Augustine did not disdain to read it, and I am dwelling on it partly because it brings us close to the world in which *The City of God* was written.

Carthage, as a Roman colony, was steadily regaining importance by the second century A.D.; and the port of Hippo, a little to the west, and the nearby inland towns of Thagaste and Madauros, all appear intimately in the life of Augustine two centuries later. Apuleius was born at Madauros, his father presumably a Greek and his mother reputedly a direct descendant of Plutarch; which, if true, is interesting: for Plutarch's placid contentment with the Stoicism of his time is not at all represented by Apuleius. Madauros was on the border of Numidia and Gaetulia, which is why he later sometimes described himself as half a Numidian and half a Gaetulian. He appears always to have been given to semi-humorous leg-pulls and mystifications. That he was quick-witted, and that he read early and voraciously among Greek authors, may be reasonably deduced. Also I see no reason to suppose that the Latin language was any less native to him than it was, later on, to Augustine, growing up in the same territory. I mention this because scholars have sometimes been bothered by the unusual Latin style in which *The Golden Ass* was written. Stephen Gaselee (who is very generous in his appreciation of Apuleius) expresses the problem:

> Apuleius is by no means an easy author, delightful as he is, to read in the original Latin. Latin was not his native or natural language, and when he mastered it he worked out for himself a most extraordinary style, which seems to contain the genius of some quite other tongue clothed in a Latin dress. He would make use of rare and outlandish words, as well as reviving others which had dropped out of the ordinary language since pre-classical times, and combined the whole into a curious mosaic, not at all unsuitable, indeed, to the weird and jolly stories that he had to tell, but disconcerting to those accustomed to the sobriety and regularity of classical Latin.[9]

I would not be disposed to think that this quirk of Apuleius was due to native ignorance of Latin, or innocence. The Preface of Apuleius to his son 'and unto the readers' is fair warning of a leg-pull, and after the mock apology for his 'rude and rustic utterance' there is a hint of his deliberate intention – 'And verily this new alteration of speech doth correspond to the enterprised matter whereof I purpose to entreat: I will set forth unto you a pleasant Grecian jest.' The device of style in *The Golden Ass* is suited to the intent of keeping the reader guessing: what is this strangely presented Grecian jest? Augustine, in *The City of God*, points to the tension the reader of Apuleius is supposed to be in: 'bee it a lie or a truth that hee writeth?'

I have made it very difficult for myself to summarize in a few sentences the narrative of *The Golden Ass*, for I look at it as a comedy simultaneously on two levels, and if you see it on either level only, you do not see the whole. A bald summary would miss the mark as much as *Don Quixote* would be missed by a bald summary; and, incidentally, there is much in *Don Quixote*, in mood and episode, comparable with *The Golden Ass*. Yet if a reader should be unfamiliar with Apuleius, or unable to run with speed to the Loeb Classical Library for a good translation, I must give some indication why I think it comes into my story of The Road.

Let it be agreed, then, that *The Golden Ass* makes mockery of, successively, three ways of thinking which were strong in the second century. It was perhaps easier for Cervantes to choose the theme of knight-errantry as the pretended basis for his sport, for knight-errantry as such was by his time only spuriously alive in the romances; but the manners and modes of thinking with which Apuleius was concerned were very much modes and manners of active practice. First, the Gnostic opinion, uniting a body of superstitions from many sources, some of them Hermetic, Babylonian, Egyptian, Persian, some of them Greek, Etrurian and African, represented an essentially practical attitude toward life, toward accident, and toward the fear of death. Astrology, demonology, witchcraft were all methods of knowing or influencing your luck. The important thing was somehow and secretly to *know* your daemon – this *knowing* was a part of gnōsis. A very practical business: a twentieth century translation might be, *gnōsis* equals *know-how*.

At the beginning of *The Golden Ass* the narrator, Lucius, goes to the midst of Thessaly, which, by common report of all the world, is the birthplace of sorceries and enchantments. Lucius is well received in Thessaly, by virtue of his mother Salvia, whom he much resembles, and by virtue of his descent from Plutarch. In all this there is a considerable pretence of verisimilitude – the first name of Apuleius was in fact Lucius, his mother's name is supposed really to have been Salvia, the descent from Plutarch is at any rate plausible. The verisimilitude prepares us for the pleasing tension that Augustine noted. What the Lucius of the narrative covets and craves is the know-how of witchcraft. In the house where he is staying he has some uninhibited dalliance with the handmaid Fotis, who is persuaded to give him a private view of her mistress (an active witch) in the act of anointing herself with an unguent which, before his eyes, turns her into an owl – and away she flies to do whatever she will. This so delights Lucius that he persuades Fotis to steal the box of magic ointment for him; but Fotis steals the wrong ointment and he is transformed into an ass. This is not irremediable: Lucius can regain his human form if he can find and eat some roses. But roses, for an ass, are hard to come by, and throughout many misadventures Lucius has to continue to suffer the fate of asses for his dabbling in witchcraft.

Yet throughout the career of Lucius in the shape of an ass, as Augustine remarks, 'had he his humane reason still', and his long ears can overhear and he can understand what humans say. He overhears (this is the second act of the comedy) the beautiful consolatory tale of Cupid and Psyche, which loses none of its beauty though it is told by a wretched and drunken old woman to a woebegone captive bride who has lost both home and husband. The beauty of the story is not lost upon Lucius, but a Greek perception of the beautiful and good seems remote if it remains unshareable, in this sordid world; and the old dispensation of Greek gods and beliefs is poor consolation to Lucius as he goes on finding ugliness and trouble. Worse than that, when his physical luck changes and he is well-fed and well-caparisoned, there is forced upon him behaviour which even as an ass he regards with both loathing and fear.

In an extremity of misery (and this is the third act) he breaks away, reaches the sea-shore, plunges his head seven times into the water, and prays to the unknown mother of all things for deliverance. The natural mother of all things, divinity for all the world here and hereafter, appears to him and invites him to be bound forever to an eternal religion. She may bear different names in different countries, but her true name is Isis. On the morrow he joins a religious procession in her honour; a priest offers him roses to eat, which he does with utmost reverence, and regains his human form. Now, and with elaborate ritual, is Lucius received into the order of Isis. With true devotion he rises in the order, and by the exhortation of the goddess goes by ship to Rome. There he rises still further to the highest of the orders, as a priest not only of Isis but also of Osiris, and he executes that office with a shaven crown, not covering or hiding the tonsure, but showing it openly to all persons. He had already begun to gain much money in the pleading of causes in the courts, and his religious advancement is apparently coupled with the promise 'that I should now get me great glory by being an advocate'. Since Lucius had previously and most emphatically denounced lawyers and advocates as the lowest of people, and 'all judges sell their judgements for money', the 'happy ending' seems to be double-edged – another metamorphosis.

Such is at any rate my interpretation of this interesting book. Other information about Apuleius is derived from his *Apology*,[10] his own rambling defence when he was on trial for the practice of magic. The speech of Apuleius appears to have been preserved more or less as it was delivered, perhaps as taken down by shorthand writers. The occasion of the trial was that Apuleius, voyaging along the African coast, stopped off at Oea and married a presumably wealthy widow. This was a shock to her relations, who brought suit before the Roman proconsul. The widow, they said, was sixty years of age, already affianced to a suitable citizen of Oea, and they claimed that Apuleius, as a known practitioner of black magic, would be certain to do away with the lady. In substantiation they asserted that another woman, in the presence of Apuleius, had fallen into an epileptic fit. The proconsul at this point intervened to ask whether the woman died, or what good was her having a fit supposed to do for Apuleius? The prosecution dropped that charge and passed on to others, that in addition to practising medicine Apuleius practised dentistry, that Apuleius had invented a tooth-powder and in this connection searched for strange fish, including shell-fish, and that he used mirrors. Apuleius, vain and voluble, then harangued the court in his own defence.

In the second century, unless you were as well protected as Galen, charges of the black arts were dangerous. Outside the walls of the Library at Alexandria, the word 'mathematician' (mathematikos) meant any calculator who, with Chaldean cunning, would compute a horoscope and fix up the prophecy, 'as they usually do, to suit the person consulting them'. So says Apuleius, in his defence, as a counter-charge that his accusers have consulted Chaldeans for their prediction that his wife might die. But he defends his marriage as in every way honourable and natural: he produces records to show that she is 'not much over forty' and alleges that the husband proposed by her relatives is 'a decrepit old man'. He is conscious of his own good looks and invites the court to admire him.* And, as real magi have often been accused of being false magicians, he wished the court to know that he really was a wise man: he could deliver half a speech in Greek and finish it in Latin; he could write poems, satires, riddles, histories, scientific treatises, orations and philosophical dialogues with equal facility in either language. He instances Epimenides, Orpheus, Pythagoras, Ostanes, Empedocles, Socrates and Plato as all having been at times accused of the 'calumny of magic'; at this trial he is but sharing the suspicion of 'so many and such great men'. He rejects the charges about his tooth powder: he procures all kinds of fish in order to study them scientifically, as did Aristotle, Theophrastus, Eudemus, Lycon and others. He is writing a book on *Natural Questions* in both Greek and Latin, and has passages from the section on fishes read aloud in court. The charge of using mirrors starts him off on an optical disquisition about solid, flat and convex mirrors; he cites the *Catoptrica* of Archimedes; and he cites the familiar story – also told by Aristotle, Pliny and Aelian – how the crocodile opens its jaws to have its teeth picked by a friendly bird.

What Apuleius seems here to be defending is his use of an instrument familiar enough nowadays – the dental mirror. To Apuleius the

* To be fair to Apuleius, it should be noted that it is only within the last 300 years that the Western World has disapproved expression of self-praise. 'The ancients, and the Greeks more than the Romans, and again the Middle Ages and the Renaissance tolerated it, and so did the Moslem world'. (*Medieval Islam* by Gustave E. von Grunebaum, University of Chicago Press, p. 265). Professor von Grunebaum singles out Plutarch as approving judicious self-praise, and we should bear in mind that Apuleius made out that he was descended from Plutarch.

accusation of his using a dental mirror could mean death, if the use were defined as black magic. Against the opinion that the only proper and permissible conduct for a dentist was to feel around behind the teeth with his fingers, Apuleius appears to have defended himself jauntily and successfully. On the main charge also the accusation was dismissed as 'not proven'.

But pleased as I was to find this pother about the dental mirror, and comic as I felt the whole trial to be, it was not for that purpose that I brought in Apuleius. I brought him in for *The Golden Ass* and for the picture of (I would think) a highly intelligent adventurer capable of representing in his jesting novel the emptiness of three main Roman systems of belief. There is not a word about Christianity in Apuleius, nor any reason to suppose that he might not have been equally sarcastic towards Christianity. What he exposes about the Rome of his period is that there was an inner vacuum, waiting to be filled. Apuleius would be the first to scoff if I laid too heavy a burden on his Grecian jest; but his intellectual hunger for a positive faith was what made him of interest, I think, to Augustine.

No expectation was intimated by Galen that Christianity might ever become the state religion of Rome. His attitude, like that of Tacitus, was that the Christian sect could be ignored. Apuleius indicated that a more likely state religion for Rome was the religion of Isis, who could say: 'my name, my divinity is adored throughout all the world, in diverse manners, in variable customs, and by many names'. On that passage of *The Golden Ass*, Inge commented: 'This more than tolerant hospitality of the spirit seemed to the mixed population of the empire the logical recognition of the actual political situation, and those who deliberately stood outside it were at least potentially enemies of society. This was the real quarrel between the Church and the empire.'[11]

My view is that Apuleius was mocking all three systems of belief, Gnostic, Stoic and the 'more than tolerant' ritual of Isis; saying in other words that there was no worthy religion. The significance of Philostratus is the indication of an upper-class awareness that the vacuum as exposed by Apuleius was noticeably being filled by the Christian Church; that the Christian impulse was impressive enough, early in the third century, to warrant upper-class propaganda against it, including the propaganda that if Christ had won his way by magic, others had done so too, and shown a spiritual conduct equally good and far less revolutionary.

Philostratus was a Greek from Lemnos who came to Rome by way of Athens some fifty years after Apuleius. He became attached to the literary circle of the Empress Julia Domna, wife of Septimius Severus, and with her encouragement produced, round about A.D. 217, *The Life of Apollonius of Tyana*. There is to this day controversy about the book. The story is that the empress had come into possession of documents about Apollonius and commissioned Philostratus to write the *Life*; the controversial part of the story is whether or not the book was deliberately put forward as being descriptive of a godlike man whose example was eminently more acceptable to Graeco–Roman culture than the example of Jesus.

Apollonius was born about the same time as Jesus, at Tyana in Cappadocia, and his birth was supposedly attended with miracles and portents. As a boy he knew all languages without ever having learned them, and knew the thoughts of birds and animals as well as the inmost thoughts of men. He remembered a former incarnation, and had the power of predicting the future. He foreswore marriage, practised a rigid asceticism, carried no money on his person but begged his way to Persia and India, converting by his conversation all wise men to his views, and performing miracles whenever required. He performed many more miracles than Jesus. He returned from India to visit Egypt and went up the Nile to acquaint himself with the Gymnosophists or naked philosophers. He returned to Alexandria and traversed the length and breadth of the Mediterranean by sea. He was wordly-wise and spiritually perfect, and a good counsellor to Kings and Emperors. There were some Roman emperors he did not get on with (Nero, Domitian) and he was often in danger of prosecution, but Nerva honoured him. He died serenely at an advanced age and then ascended bodily to heaven, appearing after death to promise future life and redemption to those who believed him.

The view that Philostratus intended his *Life of Apollonius* 'as a counterblast to that of the Christian gospel' is 'utterly unwarrantable', says Conybeare in his preface to the Loeb edition of Philostratus: 'The best scholars of this generation are opposed to this view.'[12] These are strong words, and a layman is hardly inclined to demur. Yet the point would seem to be whether the relatively easy doctrine of salvation with a minimum of sacrifice was not to be more readily accepted by the upper class in third century Rome than the doctrine of the Christians. Whether Philostratus intended a counterblast is an academic question: our question is, was the book taken as such? At the end of the third century, when the fight was really bitter as to what should be the state religion of Rome, and the persecutions of the Christians under Diocletian were not in the least half-hearted, one finds Lactantius assailing what had been 'vomited forth' by a follower of Apollonius, and Eusebius felt it necessary to write a treatise to explain that Apollonius was a mere charlatan, and if a magician at all, then it was thanks only to evil spirits. A century later than that, Augustine mentions in one of his letters (Ep. 136) that Apollonius and Apuleius were both men who had been addicted to the magic arts and pagans had said of them that they had performed miracles greater than those of Christ. But Augustine, whose time we have now reached, had to deal with matters much more imperative than byegone controversies. Philostratus had been forgotten. A Christian concept of a City of God had been established. But the earthly City, in Augustine's time, was ruined.

Mr. Stewart Perowne[13] reminds us that it was while Antoninus was emperor, in the year 145, 'that a Greek orator from Smyrna, called Aelius Aristides, came to Rome for the city's birthday, which was celebrated, as it still is, on April 21. He delivered an oration in praise of Rome, in the course of which he said that Rome was better not only than Persia, but better even than the old Greek polities, for the Athenians and the rest of the Greeks were good at resisting aggression, and defeating the Persians and spending their revenue for the public good and putting up with hardship, but they had not training in government, in which they proved failures.'

'How different was Rome. In her world "neither sea nor land is a bar to citizenship, and Asia is treated exactly the same as Europe. In your empire every avenue of advancement is open to everyone. . . . A civil world-community has been set up as a free republic, under a single ruler, the best ruler and teacher of order".'

This was the age which Gibbon chose: 'during which the condition of the human race was most happy and prosperous'.

Carthage is a window from which to view that world.

In Roman times some of the notable observers of the Roman scene wrote from Carthage. Between the scoffing Apuleius and the careworn Augustine there are two notable Christians of fiery temperament, both concerned for the state of government: Tertullian and Cyprian. To Tertullian the peaceful and prosperous state of the empire under Septimius, Caracalla and Geta (say from A.D. 193 to 217) seemed 'to warrant the belief that it was favoured by divine providence and that it would endure till the end of time':

> What reforms [Tertullian declares] has this age not witnessed! Think of the cities which the threefold virtue of our present sovereignty had built, augmented, or restored, God bestowing his blessing on so many Augusti as on one! The censuses they have taken! The peoples they have driven back! The classes of society they have honoured! The barbarians they have kept in check! In very truth, this empire has become the garden of the world![14]

Within a generation Cyprian was writing: 'Behold the roads closed by brigands, the sea blocked by pirates, the bloodshed and horror of universal strife. The world drips with mutual slaughter, and homicide, considered a crime when perpetrated by individuals, is regarded as virtuous when committed publicly.'

The unexpectedness of the crisis of the third century, the rapidity and magnitude of the collapse of the confidence which had seemed to Tertullian so solid, requires the full scale and detail of Gibbon's treatment, or at the least, the extent of analysis provided by Cochrane. 'The *débâcle*,' in Cochrane's view, 'was not merely economic or social or political, or rather it was all of these because it was something more. For what here confronts us is, in the last analysis, a moral and intellectual failure, a failure of the Graeco–Roman mind.' Perhaps all that I need to quote here is part of one of Cochrane's paragraphs:

> Of the magnitude of that crisis there can be little doubt. It was, indeed, a prelude to the long agony of the decline and fall; and, though the Roman world, by a heroic effort of reconstruction, was to survive the disasters of the time, it was to do so only by submitting to revolutionary changes as a result of which the principles of Graeco-Roman polity were hopelessly defaced and mutilated, if not utterly destroyed. Complete collapse of the imperial fabric was averted only by the services

of the fighting Illyrian emperors, the last of whom, with some show of right, merited the title of *restitutor orbis*. But in salvaging the poor remains of *Romanitas*, Diocletian transformed it almost beyond recognition. Under the bureaucratic and militarized régime which he established, the empire experienced the ultimate nemesis of the political idea. In order to meet the insatiable demands of the fisc, this so-called 'Camillus of the lower empire' introduced a harsh and brutal regimentation of social life which reduced the subject to a condition of virtual peonage. The taxpayer, his ranks thinned by constant defection, staggered under an intolerable financial burden, while sovereignty, now finally transferred from camp to palace as it had earlier been transferred from senate-house to camp, claimed adoration in the person of the imperial *dominus et deus*. Such was the economically and morally bankrupt system which, in the dynastic troubles succeeding the abdication of Diocletian, was to pass into the hands of Constantine.[15]

The high hopes of the year 313, marking the conversion of Constantine to the Christian faith, and the year 325, marking the doctrinal formulation of the Nicene Creed, were immediately heartening to the faithful. During the preceding three centuries there had been, on the whole, little for Christians to do except 'to accentuate the elements of opposition between the Church and the world'. Now, after the cruelty of Diocletian, there was guarantee of freedom for Christians to profess their faith without hindrance; there was doctrinal formulation of the faith; and there was a third and utterly novel idea which came after the Council of Nicaea, that there was to be one vast Christian commonwealth in which the ruler, although 'Emperor by divine right', was also a member of the Church and subject to the Church in matters of conscience. Now indeed there might be visible fulfilment of peace throughout the world, and with peace, righteousness. Yet before the end of Constantine's career, how much peace was there? Eusebius, who had sat upon the right hand of Constantine at the Council of Nicaea, who never lost his faith, was nevertheless forced to become apologetic. 'The most conspicuous quality of Constantine,' he declares, 'was that of benevolence. On this account he was frequently imposed upon by the violence of rapacious and unprincipled men who preyed upon all classes of society alike, and by the scandalous hypocrisy of those who wormed their way into the Church, assuming the name, without the character, of Christians.'[16]

Within the Empire violence did not disappear, although it changed direction. Within the Church there was to be violence, if necessary torture and death, for heretics, though the Arian heresy and the rebellion of the Donatists were not readily put down by persecution. Outside of doctrinal quarrels, an enormous amount of legislation under Constantine 'neither aimed at nor achieved any radical alteration in the constitution of imperial society'. In the frantic pursuit of revenue 'the dreaded indictions of Diocletian and Maximian were continued, without appreciable change either of spirit or method' except that 'illogical privileges' were extended to orthodox churchmen 'as opposed to Jews, pagans, and heretics, whose condition was to become progressively worse with the lapse of time'.

The climax of Constantine's achievement was 'New Rome' – Constantinople – dedicated May 11, 330. The new capital 'was adorned with venerable objects of art, such as the Delphian tripod, which were torn from the feeble communities of Greece'. New Rome was to be unique, 'for it was to be the wholly Christian capital of a prince devoted to the faith'. But I am concentrating on Old Rome.

However high were the hopes of the Church, one can only catalogue an increasing woe among the sincerely pious, an increasing scepticism, and an apparently ever-increasing taxation. Disturbances were empire-wide. On the fringes of the empire barbarians were increasingly moving in. By the middle of the fourth century Franks, Alamans and Saxons were invading Gaul. Julian, nephew of Constantine, born in Constantinople, secretly drawn to pagan views by study at Athens, as commander in many battles and in particular by his victory at Strasburg in 357, temporarily saved Gaul. In 360 Julian was proclaimed Emperor at Paris, and to the shock of all Christians then revealed his 'Apostasy'. In 363, in an effort to defend the East, Julian was defeated and killed by Sassanid Persians in Mesopotamia. In 364 there was a new invasion of Gaul by the Alamans, repulsed by Valentinian; from 365 to 371 there was continual war against the Goths. From 372 to 375, in Africa, the Berber chief Firmus was in revolt. In 378 Valens was defeated and killed by Goths at the battle of Adrianople. In 380, by the Edict of Thessalonica, Christianity was fully affirmed and restored as the official religion of the Roman Empire. That made small difference to the barbarian invasions. In 392 there were further waves of Huns: Vandals were driven westwards by Alamans, who followed them. In 395 the Roman Empire was formally divided into two empires of West and East. From 395 to 408, the Vandal Stilicho, as regent for Honorius, ruled the West. In 409 the Vandals and Suevi swept on from Gaul to enter Spain. Rome seemed to be incapable even of self-defence. Honorius withdrew his court to Ravenna. In the summer of 410 (the date is said to have been the 24th of August) Old Rome herself was captured by the Visigoths under Alaric.

Augustine was born in 354. He was 26 years old, unorthodox (a Manichee), and supporting his mistress and his 8 year old son by teaching Rhetoric at Carthage, at the time of the Edict of Thessalonica. In 383 Augustine abandoned Manicheeism, and became a Professor of Rhetoric at Rome and subsequently at Milan. In 386, when he was 32, there occurred his conversion. In 387 his mother died at Rome. A year later Augustine departed for Africa and for three years was in monastic life at Thagaste; during this period his son died. Although reluctant to take 'orders', at the age of 36 he did not abstain from nomination and ordination as priest at Hippo, where a few years later he was consecrated bishop. For the remainder of his life, that is to say for about thirty-five more years, he and his friend Aurelius (Primate of Carthage) directed the work of the African Church. From the two main ports of Africa the two friends watched the tally of appalling events in Rome; where, after the capture by Alaric, Christians turned upon Christians. 'The enmity of the Christians towards each other,' remarked Ammianus, 'surpassed the fury of savage beasts against man.' Not only Rome had been despoiled by the barbarians, but the whole 'garden of the world'. Hippo, Augustine's own city, was besieged by the uncontrollable Vandals. In 430, in the third month of the siege, Augustine died. He was in his seventy-sixth year when he was released, as Gibbon says, 'from the actual and impending calamities of his country'.

Catalogues of distant griefs mean little. From the record of catastrophes, one turns to see Augustine's interpretation, and his actions. After the shock of the fall of Rome – after the shock that the Eternal City, 'Rome the founder, the mistress and the capital of the Empire, had fallen' – one of Augustine's actions was to write a news-letter. *The City of God* was a news-letter to intimates, friends, and to fugitives and waverers, to any who might fear that the collapse of the physical City was in any way the result of its adoption of Christianity. It announced from the beginning a positive statement of faith transcending even the immediate occasion of the fall of Rome. The title for Augustine's serial letter was an old one: it was old, and it was not peculiarly Christian – it was a phrase old to the Hebrews and to the Stoics, old when Marcus Aurelius had cried out: 'the poet saith, "Dear City of Cecrops", but wilt thou not say, "Dear City of God?"'.

The 'news' that Augustine promised opens (in Healey's translation) as follows:

> That most glorious society and celestial city of God's faithful, which is partly seated in the course of these declining times, wherein 'he that liveth by faith', is a pilgrim amongst the wicked; and partly in that solid estate of eternity, which as yet the other part doth patiently expect, until 'righteousness be turned unto judgement' . . ., have I undertaken to defend in this work . . .

The work appeared, section by section, at intervals, over a period of thirteen years, transcribed in the midst of other writings and in the midst of interruptions. I obtrude no comment on the text, but having quoted the first sentence, may quote the end. 'I think,' says Augustine at the conclusion of Book XXII and after thirteen years of compilation, 'I have discharged the debt of this great work by the help of God.'

> Let them which think I have done too little, and them which think I have done too much, grant me a favourable pardon: but let them which think I have performed enough, accepting it with a kind congratulation, give no thanks unto me, but 'unto the Lord with me'. Amen. Amen.

I note a paragraph in Cochrane:

> In seeking to describe the 'greatness' of Augustine, the author of the biography in Hastings, *Encyclopedia of Religion and Ethics*, ascribes to him a significant contribution to Catholic theology, pre-eminently as the 'doctor of grace'; while, at the same time, he regards him as the spiritual ancestor of Protestantism, considered, on its dogmatic side, as a triumph for the doctrine that grace is 'free'. To Augustine, also, he attributes the origin of Platonic Christianity, which embodies a mysticism derived from Plato as opposed to Aristotelian rationalism. Besides this,

Augustine is credited with having inspired, through the *De Civitate Dei*, conceptions underlying the Medieval Church and empire; in confirmation of which it is recorded that Charlemagne habitually slept with a copy of this work beneath his pillow. As though this were not enough, it is supposed also that he influenced the development of Cartesianism, with its basis in 'clear and distinct ideas'; while, through his 'romanticism', his 'self-assured subjectivity', and his 'penetrating psychological insight', he anticipated certain distinctive aspects of what is called modernism. Finally, he is said to have been the first thinker to undertake a philosophy of history.[17]

'By thus revealing something of what posterity has discovered in Augustine,' Cochrane remarks, 'this statement excites attention as to the source of such extraordinary influence.' We could add Professor Carruccio's observation about the renewal of scientific thinking after the period of the ancient Greeks. 'The idea of starting a new period in the history of scientific thought with St Augustine is justified,' says Professor Carruccio, and he proceeds to justify the statement.

My study of the Road West leads me to pay a different tribute to Augustine. I see him, in hindsight, as a man who, when a great pathway came to a dead end, revived it, set off again with further animation. From this particular point of view the story of Rome itself subsides, immense and permanent though that story be. The story that I trace is not the tale of Rome but of the Road. I had seen Hannibal provoking the extension of Rome's Appian Way, and watched the sea-pathway from the East transforming into a highway, becoming a Roman road. The road itself was nothing but an instrument; yet a most active and participating instrument, setting into motion men and what they carried with them. Watching the intake into Rome, with an almost pardonable paralogism I could say it was the road which forced a sequence of transformation scenes within the city. One of the most inexplicable of such transformations was the partial capitulation of the capital of Empire to Christian faith. At no time was the capitulation more than partial; to have any sort of insight into that transformation, I should study at least every page of Burckhardt's *The Age of Constantine*: for my more narrow purpose I sketched only three resistors, they and their like momentarily overcome by those whose faith was that Old Rome might yet become a shining city, shining with such light as had once been designed for

Jerusalem. If Old Rome could be seen as Holy City, City of God, then all roads might lead to Rome and end there. But Old Rome, almost as soon as nominally Christian, collapsed and fell, and here again no pencil-sketch expresses the confusion, no sketch in any frame smaller than that of a Burckhardt or a Gibbon. Yet in the turmoil, what Augustine formed was the restatement that the City of Christian desire was no earthly city; the Christian was a pilgrim, this earth no more than a road.

The power of mighty Rome had been magnetic and centripetal, pulling everything in; so far as any one man serves as symbol, Augustine stands for the restart of roads away from Rome, for the outward push of Christian impulse. The planting of monasteries, for example, was one centrifugal result. But the repetitive exhortation in *The City of God* could be interpreted as meaning that the whole body of the Christian Church was a pilgrim society. Living by faith and looking to the Hereafter, the Church itself was an itinerant, and on the move. In subsequent ages, differing eyes have seen many different encouragements in the text of *The City of God*. It is the firmness of the man, at the moment of disaster, that I am emphasizing. That Christianity had not according to human definition 'saved' Rome – to explain such an admission at that moment was not easy. Yet with Rome damaged and his own Carthage doomed, Augustine managed to maintain his permanent assertion: no sombre circumstance whatever, no pain on earth, destroyed the attachment of his life to that of the Celestial City. This Carthaginian of Berber fatherhood stood to his station, by his conduct proving that as God called them, men might stand or move; and, largely, his words put the Church to further motion.*

Strange, I thought, that my survey had revealed one Carthaginian, Hannibal, drawing a roadway out of Rome, eastward; and now

---

* Was Saint Augustine black or white? The question is sometimes raised by modern commentators, e.g. Henri Marrou, *St. Augustine* (Harper, New York, 1958). It is a question which, in ancient times, nobody bothered about. The colour of a man's skin was a matter of indifference. Augustine speaks of his mother, but of his father there is only the remark in the *Confessions* that he was a Berber. In the context the term Berber may have meant nothing more explicit than 'non-Christian'. It is not at all easy to determine what Berber does mean. In a footnote (in Bury's edition, vol. V. p. 469) Gibbon divides the history of the word *Barbar* or *Berber* into four periods. 1. In the

another Carthaginian, Augustine, lending enormous impetus to the Road West. Rome's pounce upon the East was quick; 'westering', for a long while to come, seems a slow process. There are thirty generations of human life to think of, before the Iberian Peninsula can be seen as springboard for westerners to use in leaping the Atlantic. But when I do begin to see migrants passing from Europe into North America, I need not forget that among the cities there set up, the city of longest standing commemorates the name of Saint Augustine.

NOTES

1. *Christianity and Classical Culture* by Charles Norris Cochrane (Oxford University Press, 1944).

2. The references in this chapter to Dean Inge are to his article on *Religion* in *The Legacy of Greece,* edited by R. W. Livingstone (Oxford University Press, 1922). This quotation is from p. 31.

---

time of Homer, the name as an imitative sound was applied to 'the ruder tribes, whose pronunciation was most harsh, whose grammar was most defective'. 2. From the time of Herodotus the term was extended to *all* the nations who were strangers to the language and manners of the Greeks. 3. In the age of Plautus 'the Romans submitted to the insult and freely gave themselves the name of barbarians. They insensibly claimed an exemption for Italy and her subject provinces; and at length removed the disgraceful appellation to the savage or hostile nations beyond the pale of the empire'. 4. 'In every sense it was due to the Moors; the familiar word was borrowed from the Latin provincials by the Arabian conquerors, and has justly settled as a local denomination (Barbary) along the northern coast of Africa'.

To that note by Gibbon, Bury adds a gloss: 'In Moorish history, the Berbers (Moors proper) are clearly distinguished from the Arabs who ruled, and were afterwards mastered by, them'. Nowadays, the *Encyclopedia Britannica* suggests that *Berber* means one of a number of peoples discontinuously distributed all over northern Africa. It speaks of many Berber subgroups, some of them nomadic, and of most tribes a 'brunet pigmentation' is suggested. It suggests that the position of women is higher among Berbers than among Arabs.

Augustine's father, one gathers from Augustine, was no nomad, but a townsman. Except for Marrou's phrase about 'pure Berber stock' (p. 11), I would not have thought that *Berber*, in Augustine's time, was a term conveying any specific racial meaning. The *Encyclopedia* is properly concerned with how the term is used by present-day ethnologists; Gibbon is possibly nearer the mark as to what the term connoted when the *Confessions* were written.

3. Cochrane, pp. 64, 65.

4. *Hellenism and Christianity* by Edwyn Bevan (Allen & Unwin, London, 1921), pp. 68, 72. For Plutarch's 'revered father', see Inge, p. 30; for Flavius Clemens, see Bevan, p. 66.

5. *The Christian Philosophy of Saint Augustine* by Etienne Gilson, translated by L. E. M. Lynch (Random House, New York), p. 233.

6. *A History of Magic and Experimental Science by* Lynn Thorndike (Macmillan, London, 1923), I. 1. Ch. 4. Thorndike discusses Apuleius and Philostratus in Chapters 7 and 8 of the same book.

7. *A History of Christianity* by Kenneth Scott Latourette (Harper, New York and Eyre & Spottiswoode, London, n.d.), p. 86.

8. Inge, p. 50.

9. *The Golden Ass* by Apuleius, translated by W. Adlington, introduced and edited by S. Gaselee (Loeb Classical Library, 1924). Gaselee's reference to Augustine is to Healey's translation (with Elizabethan spelling) of *The Citie of God*, xviii, 18 (17).

10. A comprehensive discussion of the *Apology* of Apuleius is in Thorndike, op. cit., I. 1. 7.

11. Inge, p. 34.

12. *The Life of Apollonius of Tyana* by Philostratus, translated by F. C. Conybeare (Loeb Classical Library, 1927). A point that Conybeare is making is that it was not so much against Philostratus as against Hierocles, a later anti-Christian writer who 'vomited forth' in praise of Apollonius, that the Christian Fathers, Lactantius and Eusebius, went into action.

13. I have drawn upon two pieces by Mr. Stewart Perowne in *The Times* (London) under the dates of July 20, 1963 and August 17, 1964.

14. Tertullian is quoted from Cochrane, p. 155; Cyprian, *ibid.,* p. 154.

15. Cochrane, p. 151.

16. Cochrane, p. 208.

17. Cochrane, p. 377. For Professor Carruchio's observations, see *Mathematics and Logic in History and in Contemporary Thought* by Ettore Carrucio, translated by Isabel Quigly (Faber, London, 1964).

CHAPTER 10

Cross and Crescent

OUT of the general picture of things falling to pieces as Rome's strength failed, my task is to select details such as provide momentum for a renewed Road West. The figure of Saint Augustine stood out for me as a very remarkable activator of such momentum.* A 'world-rejecting' attitude leads automatically to geographical exploration. I shall pursue the question, how the Christian Church came (if I may use a term loosely) to canonize ocean-voyaging. That, in effect, is what slowly happened. It captures my imagination to find a religious factor helpful towards sea-faring, and a factor so large and important as has not been seen since the dimly perceived incitement to the Phoenicians of the worship of Melkarth.

But the intrusion which affects everything is the sudden rise of Islam.

The contest of Cross and Crescent is of itself almost sufficient to explain the emergence, as a by-product, of a sea-road from the Iberian Peninsula to the Far West of the Americas. I am wrong, of course, to apply the emblem of *crescent* to the early Saracens or to the Moors of Spain†, but I follow a common usage in so doing. The Crescent here is representative of Islam in general. It is the general impact of medieval Islam upon Latin Christendom of which I have to form some notion; though, fortunately for me, the only details that I need are those relevant to the Western Ocean.

'If the decline of the Roman empire was hastened by the conversion of Constantine, his victorious religion,' says Gibbon, 'broke the violence of the fall, and mollified the ferocious temper of the conquerors.' The second part of that remark is heavily ironical, for I would not suppose that Gibbon thought of the 'barbarian proselytes

---

* I should like to pay special tribute to *The Political and Social Ideas of St. Augustine* by Herbert A. Deane (Columbia University Press, 1963).

† Specifically, *crescent* was a military symbol of Turkish sultans in Turkish dominions.

of the North' as turning soft when they turned Christian. From the confusion of their strenuous and hard in-fightings as tribal rivalries flared in most parts of the Continent (most parts then as beautiful a Wild West as can be well imagined), Gibbon turns with undisguised relief to the episode which prompted a measure of teamwork against an unexpected enemy from outside. Saracens (i.e., Strangers) appeared, a spearhead of them thrown from Spain into the very heartland of Gaul. Charles Martel, or Charles 'the Hammer', had the satisfaction of uniting, for the moment, a force of Franks and Teutons sufficient for the occasion. The battle which was fought at Tours, in central France, in 732, retains great meaning for the part it played in shaping the conception of a Western Christendom. The battle of Tours was won, but it brought home to peoples of inland Europe that there was a new reality to be thought of – Islam. The Saracen threat was repeated: three years after the battle of Tours, another invasion from Spain captured the cities of Arles and Avignon. Once again the thrust was repulsed; the Arabs were evicted from the French cities, and henceforth, except for border raids, could be regarded as contained behind the Pyrenees. Yet the fact remained that Spain was now an outpost of the new, vast and mysterious Islamic empire.

The initial effect of Islam upon Medieval Europe was enhanced by the speed with which that empire had materialized. Gibbon expresses the swiftness: the rise of Mahomet, 'with the sword in one hand and the Koran in the other'. Gibbon makes due allowance for the weakness of Mahomet's enemies; except for that weakness, 'the torrent of fanaticism might have been obscurely lost in the sands of Arabia'. Gibbon traces the beginnings, before the faith became a torrent, and then, and with mounting excitement, shows how successive conquests encouraged 'a fiercer and more sanguinary tone'. The Prophet died in 632; within twenty years his followers had achieved greater and more lasting conquests in the East than Alexander. Persia was in the complete control of the Mahommedans; the Northwest of India received the new faith, and emperors of China felt cause to solicit the friendship of the Arabs. So far, the direction of the Arabian conquests makes them of little consequence to Latin Christendom; the subsequent part played by notions percolating westward from the Far East does not as yet appear. But in the Near East successes of Arab armies were an instant threat. Whatever the internal rifts between

Rome and Constantinople, it was a shock to both when Syria was conquered by the common enemy and when Jerusalem surrendered to the Caliph Omar.

Gibbon enjoys the description of Omar entering the Holy City. To the devout Muslims, Jerusalem was to be revered almost as much as Mecca and Medina; for Christians, it was an extra humiliation to observe that the capture was celebrated by Omar with the kind of mockery which later on became a pattern for Western Chivalry to imitate. Omar, when Jerusalem had been forced to surrender, disdained all pomp and ostentation in his formal entry. For his approach he was mounted on a red camel, which carried also a bag of corn, a bag of dates, a wooden dish, and a leathern bottle of water. Gibbon says that this modest entry of the great conqueror into Jerusalem took place in the year 637; Bury corrects the date to 636; von Grunebaum corrects it again to 638 – no matter, it is the impression made upon the West which counts, and not the precise year. Rumour of Arab victories soon had more to work on. One of Omar's officers, Amrou, moved west from Palestine; with an army of 4,000 he dared to invade Egypt. His success was preposterous: he crossed the Nile, captured Memphis, and, with reinforcements, besieged and subdued Alexandria itself. Alexandria! – 'the great city of the West', as Amrou exclaimed to his Caliph, recording that Alexandria now suddenly provided Islam with another 4,000 palaces, 4,000 public baths, 400 theatres or places of amusement, 12,000 shops for sale of vegetable food, and 40,000 tributary Jews.

Gibbon rejected the story, as being a much later and biased invention, that the Saracens burned the contents of the famous library of Alexandria. The suggestion is rather that there was greater activity in studying the remnants of Greek learning than Romans had displayed. But the Arab conquest of Alexandria was only a beginning; the further progress of the Arabs across the north of Africa to the Atlantic was methodical. By 670, soldiers of the caliph had advanced into what is today Tunisia and founded the city of Qairawan; by 700 the Byzantine garrisons of seacoast towns had been wiped out; and tribe by tribe the native Berbers were either converted or subdued. As the Arabs moved forward, Sicily and Spain received 'a sizeable percentage' of the Hellenized or Latinized population of the African seaports.[1] The organized fanatical ambition of the Muslim was the theme of many tales spread by the refugees; Gibbon selects episodes which feed that theme; one episode concerns the impetuous warrior, Akbah, whose conduct admitted no check until he was suddenly confronted by the one phenomenon that was unconquerable – Ocean. Even at that moment, says Gibbon:

> He spurred his horse into the waves, and, raising his eyes to heaven, exclaimed with the tone of a fanatic: 'Great God! If my course were not stopped by this sea, I would still go on, to the unknown kingdoms of the West, preaching the unity of thy holy name, and putting to the sword the rebellious nations who worship any other gods than thee'.

The snapshot of Akbah on horseback, accepting stoppage by 'the great Sea-Ocean that compasseth all the world about', gives me an opportunity to clarify the thought which is the drawstring for this chapter. Akbah is a worthy representative of early Mohammedan conquest. I contrast an early Christian hero, purposely going far afield to the Irish abbot, Brendan – later, in *The Golden Legend*, spoken of as Saint Brandon.

The contrast is that Akbah accepted stoppage by Ocean, whereas Brendan, who was the earlier by some two hundred years, was famous for his ocean voyages. Part of the contrast is merely circumstantial: Akbah is a landsman, Brendan an islander, from birth accustomed to the sea. I would draw more into the contrast than that. What I am noticing is that within a century after the death of Augustine the monastery-impulse had spread across Europe to the far northern coasts; that Brendan, born at Tralee, had become a Christian monk. Put it the other way, I see it as natural that a chaplain with some gift of sea-knowledge should set forth in faith to demonstrate that all parts of the wide Sea-Ocean were of Christ's domain.

For five centuries or more Northmen, Pagan and Christian alike, continued to sail beyond sight of land with ridiculously few developments in maritime technology. It is as if ocean-conquest remained a sport for which improvements were not needed, or an action the more valued if performed by faith alone. In all those centuries there is skill and daring; there is luck; there is, among the northerners, very little organized science.

Five centuries after Akbah, men of his faith had acquired knowledge of immense potentiality for the alteration of sea-faring. Name what you like that Northmen lacked – magnetic compass, stern-post rudder, astrolabe and numerals convenient for star-tables, instinct and capacity for compiling almanacs and charts – add, if you wish, offensive weapons – you see that these potentials come into the West not among Christians but among Muslims. In the 12th century they are all in rudimentary form in or around what it pleased Mohammedans to call the Central Sea. You see that a know-how, such as might be developed for the conquest of Sea-Ocean, exists within Islam at a period when seamen of the western seaboard of Christendom seem to be stubbornly disinterested in know-how.

I am looking for the start of an Ocean Road. I see a Medieval Islam which is displaying marvellous capacity for organizing science; yet Islam appears to have no special interest in Ocean. I see some seamen of Europe's western seaboard who display a single-minded special interest in Ocean; yet who have less science.

The value of Brendan to my story is that he links Ocean with the Church; and so, for my story, I become interested in the Church and the Courts of Chivalry insofar as they are the agencies within which an intelligence develops to snatch from Islam that part of Islam's science which applies to Ocean.

Akbah and Brendan signify ahead of time what episodes I should be looking for in the crunch between Islam and Western Christendom. The men themselves may be of doubtful historicity. Some have doubted if Akbah (or Okba ibn Nafi) ever really reached Tangier or the Atlantic. Others are uncertain if Brendan or Brandan or Brandon was born in the precise year 494 or the precise place of Tralee in County Kerry. It would be worse, to doubt the power of legend. It is the growth and form of feelings toward Ocean that I must watch. I accept Akbah and Brendan into evidence, as representing certain early feelings about Ocean, in Islam and in Christendom respectively. Even their names suggest them as Exhibits A and B.

In the year 710, Arabs had captured the African coast; Gibraltar to the north was in full view; therefore it was to Spain that Mahomet's option was next offered – the Koran, the tribute, or the sword. With an objective in full sight, wavelets presented no obstacle. At the opposite end of the Central Sea, and almost simultaneously with this attack upon Gibraltar, a navy made the narrow waters of the Bos-

porus protective for Constantinople. There, the fiercest of Mohammedan attacks were withstood by the courage of Leo the Isaurian
and his sea-galleys armed with 'Greek fire'; but here, in the Straits of
Gibraltar, there were no Spanish galleys to blockade Tangier or
Ceuta. Gibbon says four vessels were considered a sufficient fleet to
make the unopposed crossing to Spain. The vessels carried 'one
hundred Arabs, and four hundred Africans' – the 'Arabs' here means
horses, and the 'Africans' means whatever company of men it was
which followed Abu Zora Tarif or Tarik ibn Ziyad on the reconnaissance. I mention both names (following Gibbon's spellings, as I
do throughout when quoting him) because Gibbon ascribes the derivation of the name 'Gibraltar' on one page to Tarif and on the next
page to Tarik.* The swift result of the reconnaissance was the complete conquest of the Iberian Peninsula.

In the first excitement of reporting this success to the Caliph (then
in Damascus), one of the Arabian generals, Musa, proposed to return
eastward from Spain by way of Italy, and down the Danube to the
Euxine, and thus to overthrow Constantinople from the rear. Musa
proposed to set out as Hannibal had done, and proposed on the way
to conquer Rome and preach the faith of Mahomet 'at the altar of the
Vatican'. The pleasing idea of attacking the idols of the Christians at
Rome was put into effect in a Saracen raid upon Rome a hundred
years later, but at Musa's moment, and to Musa's disappointment,
the Caliph did not approve the zealous grand design of the complete
encirclement of the Central Sea. Administrative difficulties of holding
together an empire which already stretched from Persia throughout
North Africa to Spain may possibly explain the Caliph's caution;
whatever the reasons, it was left for a new Caliph, Hashem, and
another general, Abderame, to test the fighting power of western
Christians by the invasion from the Pyrenees.

The fanatical assaults on Constantinople in 717 and 718 had been
beaten off by Leo. Abderame discovered that Christians in the west
could also fight. His sudden appearance in the wild and open country
revealed the astonishment, rather than the timidity, of scattered
Europeans. Abderame's onset is summed up by Gibbon: 'his standards were planted on the walls, or at least before the gates, of Tours

* Gibbon (Bury's edition, V, 474, 475). Bury in a note remarks that the
derivation of 'Gibraltar' seems doubtful, though commonly accepted.

and Sens; and his detachments overspread the kingdom of Burgundy, as far as the well-known cities of Lyons and Besançon. The memory of these devastations, for Abderame did not spare the country or the people, was long preserved by tradition; and the invasion of France by the Moors or Mahometans affords the groundwork of those fables which have been so wildly disfigured in the romances of chivalry'. The penetration into the heartland of Europe from the south and west – it is over a thousand miles from the rock of Gibraltar to the banks of the Loire – is a tribute to the initial thrusting power of Islam; but in the end what the raid evoked was a fighting power in Western Christendom sufficient at first to resist and then to retaliate. Charles Martel proved capable of organizing the Franks, and in the fields between Tours and Poitiers, in the October of 732, Abderame was killed, and his various emirs made their separate retreats to the mountains. Except when called upon to deal with the further raids at Avignon and Arles, Charles 'the Hammer' and Charlemagne after him do not seem to have been peculiarly worried about Islam as a military menace; but a very lasting effect in Europe was the impetus towards combination and the curiosity as to what might be going on behind the mountain-curtain of the Pyrenees.

'Barbarian proselytes of the North,' surrounded by monuments of what had once been meant by 'Romanitas', had no other civilization to compare with that presented by Latin Christendom. When 'the Saracen hove in sight', there was another way of living, that of Islam, with which to make comparison. I keep an eye for the release, in Europeans, of feelings for which the Latin fathers were not catering. Gibbon is right, in suggesting immediate attention to 'those fables' which sprang into being after the raid of Abderame. One of the first Arabian customs to be adopted was probably that which boys could use in a new version of the game of cops and robbers: the Arab device of riding *à la gineta*, with short stirrups, as modern jockeys continue to do. Presently the attractiveness of things Arabian to young people is causing concern to their Latinized teachers; the concern persists; by 854 the monk Alvaro is writing:

> My fellow-Christians delight in the poems and romances of the Arabs; they study the works of Mohammedan theologians and philosophers, not in order to refute them, but to acquire a correct and elegant Arabic style. Where today can a layman be found who reads the

Latin commentaries on Holy Scriptures? Who is there that studies the gospels, the Prophets, the Apostles? Alas! the young Christians who are most conspicuous for their talents have no knowledge of any literature or language save the Arabic; they read and study with avidity Arabian books; they amass whole libraries of them at a vast cost, and they everywhere sing the praise of Arabian lore. On the other hand, at the mention of Christian books they disdainfully protest that such works are unworthy of their notice. The pity of it! Christians have forgotten their own tongue and scarce one in a thousand can be found able to compose in fair Latin a letter to a friend! But when it comes to writing Arabic, how many there are who can express themselves in that language with the greatest elegance, and even compose verses which surpass in formal correctness those of the Arabs themselves.[2]

As early as 756, Moorish Spain had become a regional administration. It was part of Islam's far-flung stretch of spiritual unity, but it was independent of strict political control. In the same way the Caliph's writ, as such, was no longer valid in the 9th century in North Africa. Yet the political fragmentation of the Caliphate did not diminish the over-all unity of spirit. Islam's distinctive syncretism of ideas, of style in manners and forms, whether of architecture and gardening, of fieldwork or manufacture, of literature and language – in short, anything within the whole range of culture which might be the rage in any other part of Islam – appears likewise in Spain. The royal legion of Damascus had at the outset been planted at Cordova, and the Ommiades who ruled in that kingdom were not disposed to allow the life of Cordova to become merely parochial.

According to Gibbon, the first of the new rulers of Cordova welcomed the support of Jews and Christians. As Gibbon puts it: 'The disciples of Abraham, of Moses, and of Jesus were solemnly invited to accept the more *perfect* revelation of Mahomet; but, if they preferred the payment of a moderate tribute, they were entitled to the freedom of conscience and religious worship.' How liberal the conduct of the Ommiades in Spain, and how moderate the taxation, is not the question. I am attempting to assess the rumours about Moorish Spain which spread across the Pyrenees and stimulated the excitement that Alvaro was deploring. A first rumour was that Cordova was prosperous. Gibbon reports that its ruler derived from his subjects an annual sum 'which, in the tenth century, most probably surpassed the united revenues of the Christian monarchs. His royal seat of Cordova contained six hunded moschs, nine hundred baths, and two hundred thousand houses: he gave laws to eighty cities of the first, to three hundred of the second and third order; and the fertile banks of the Guadalquiver were adorned with twelve thousand villages and hamlets.' At that point Gibbon comments that 'the Arabs might exaggerate the truth'; but if the repute of Cordova was partly due to boasting, nevertheless the reputation spread. 'The splendour of Cordova', in Professor von Grunebaum's words, 'dazzled the eyes and stirred the imagination of the Latin world'. As far away as Gandersheim the nun Hrosvitha (who died about the year 1002) was writing of Cordova as one of the fairest of the world's ornaments, partly because Cordova was 'especially abounding in the seven streams of knowledge'. So a second impression is that the glamour of Cordova presented itself not merely as that of a prosperous provincial city, but as that of an independent capital of the vast fresh empire which stretched from Spain to Persia. Cordova presented itself as representative of a proud, superior and animated culture, in which her share was equal, not inferior, to that of Damascus or Baghdad.

Thus one feels the range of interests and excitements communicated by Cordova to Alvaro's fellow-Christians. The excitements were more than momentary. The stimulus of Islam may have worked by fits and starts, but repeated its workings vigorously in realms both of passion and of intellect.

Although the orthodoxies of Islam and Western Christendom remained in firm opposition, heresies within the one had power of trespass into the other. There is a striking paragraph in Denis de Rougemont's *Passion and Society*:

There occurred during the twelfth century in Languedoc and in the Limousin one of the most extraordinary spiritual confluences of history. On the one hand, a strong Manichaean religious current, which had taken its rise in Persia, flowed through Asia Minor and the Balkans as far as Italy and France, bearing the esoteric doctrines of Maria Sophia and of love for the Form of Light. On the other hand, a highly refined rhetoric, with its set forms, themes, and characters, its ambiguities invariably recurring in the same places, and indeed its symbolism, pushes out from Irak and the Sufis, who were inclined alike to Platonism and

Manichaeism, and reaches Arabic Spain, then, leaping over the Pyrenees, it comes in the south of France upon a society that seems to have but awaited its arrival in order to *state* what it had not dared and had not been able to avow either in the clerical tongue or in the common vernacular. Courtly lyrical poetry was the offspring of that encounter.[3]

At a first reading of that paragraph, torn from context, the concluding sentence might seem a comedown. Two streams of heretical passion come to Europe from the East, and 'courtly lyrical poetry' seems an unimpressive result. In the context of M. de Rougemont's study, the effective workings, in terms of social action, are swiftly shown: the rhetoric of passion-love is one of the triggers of a change large enough to be called a psychical revolution. The chain-reaction of Courtly Love, Chivalry, and the Crusades, is the vast pageantry which will involve a good deal of practical attentiveness to sea-faring. But that returns me to the puzzle: how, within Latin Christendom, the consensus grew not merely for recapturing a piece of physical territory from the Saracen, but for something which comes into being as a new idea – the idea that Ocean (that strange outside surrounder of the world) is an available instrument. For the construction of an Ocean-road I have to see how all the necessary lesser instruments were gathered to make it possible to use Ocean; but the greatest of changes that came about was in the conception which led to the gathering of the lesser equipment. As stated before, by the 12th century most of the technological equipment for Ocean-faring was in the hands of Islam, but Ocean-going use of it remained inhibited. The stealings of the equipment by Christendom is an interesting, though relatively minor, matter. The large question is, how was it that Christendom came to the view that Ocean itself was *usable*. For the beginnings of that attitude to Ocean, I continue to seek clues in M. de Rougemont's *Passion and Society*.

The rhetoric of passion-love, which by the 12th century had become a trigger to violent commotions, had been taken by the Arabs largely from Greek poets. In the beginning the Greek 'love-poetry' was often ridiculed in Islam. One of the early mockeries is not too long, I think, to quote. The Caliph Mutawakkil (847–861) is talking with Abû, l-'Anbas:

'Tell me about your ass and his death and the poetry which he recited to you in a dream'.

'Yes, O Prince of the Faithful: my ass had more sense than all the qâdîs together; 'twas not in him to run away or stumble. Suddenly he fell ill and died. Afterwards I saw him in a dream and said to him, "O my ass, did not I make thy water cool and thy barley clean, and show thee the utmost kindness? Why didst thou die so suddenly? What was the matter with thee?"

' "True", he answered, "but the day you stopped to converse with so-and-so the perfumer about such-and-such an affair, a beautiful she-ass passed by: I saw her and lost my heart and loved so passionately that I died of grief, pining for her".

' "O my ass", said I, "didst thou make a poem on the subject?" "Yes", he said; and then he chanted:

> I was frenzied by a she-ass
> at the door of a perfumer.
> She enthralled me, smiling coyly,
>   showing me her lovely side-teeth,
> Charmed me with a pair of soft cheeks
>   Coloured like the *shaiqurânî.*
> For her sake I died; and had I
> lived, then great were my dishonour!

'I said: "O my ass, what is the *shaiqurânî?*" "This", he replied, "is one of the strange and uncommon words in the language of the asses" '.

Mutawakkil was delighted and ordered the minstrels to set the poem of the ass to music and sing it on that day. No one had ever seen him so gay and joyous before. He redoubled his marks of favour to Abû'l-'Anbas and loaded him with gifts.*

Joking apart, the rhetoric of rapturous love continued to be cultivated within Islam, and the mystical poets, with every secret double meaning of erotico-religious language, succeeded in communicating passions far too strong and permanent to be brushed away by ridicule or suppressed by persecution. Most of the intake of mystical poetry seems to have come from the Greek sources. The Song of Solomon, about which Jews and Christians alike had been much troubled – whether or not to retain it in their respective canons – appears to have been less directly influential in the visions of 'the Belovèd' and the

---

* Quoted from *Medieval Islam* by Gustave E. von Grunebaum (University of Chicago Press, 1961), pp. 312, 313. The delicious translation is attributed to R. A. Nicholson, *Translations of Eastern Poetry and Prose* (Cambridge, 1922).

eulogies of Love, and in the eulogy of death-for-love which was the perfect consummation of pure and chaste desire. By the 12th century the guardians of the Koran were driven to suppress, with what violence they could, 'Grecian' feelings released in the continuing Arabian Canticles of service to The Lady of Thoughts and The Veiled Idea. Two of the chief writers of this kind of poetry, Al Hallaj and Suhrawardi, were impeached, condemned and executed. Their symbolic language exposed them to a charge which, for its own wording, I find worth mentioning. The accusation was: 'These adore God with a physical love, through the magnetic attraction of iron to iron, and their particles of light are impelled like a magnet back towards the focus of light whence they came.'[4] It is recorded of Al Hallaj that he went to execution laughing; such martyrdom was the summit of *ioy d'amor*. Any paleness connoted by the phrase 'Platonic love' is shown, in the Arab world of the 12th century, to be the paleness of a white-hot flame; the Arab name was 'Ohdri love' from the name of the respected tribe which had most notably exalted chaste desire to the ultimate of ecstatic death. As M. de Rougemont was pointing out, it was the 'Ohdri love' of Andalusia which affected in the south of France, and later in the north, the formation of 'Courtly love'.

I am in trouble here, not to get lost amidst the emotional phenomena that appear in Europe's 'First Renaissance'. The 'powerful and almost universal rise of Love and of the cult of Idealized Woman' presents temptations which could lure me far from my theme. Courtliness, Chivalry, Crusades are all certainly relevant as providing explanation, how medieval landsmen came to think in a practical way about sea-routes to and from the Holy Land. Yet Crusades, as military operations, did not of themselves create a new feeling, such as I am looking for, about Ocean. There was nothing particularly new, and no deep taboo to be overcome, in the crossing or recrossing of the Central Sea; there was nothing in that type of sea-faring that was unconscionably strange. What I have to continue to contend with is the consideration that to Mediterranean peoples, Christian or Mohammedan alike, the outside Sea-Ocean was still, in the 12th century, and by every classical tradition, completely strange. I have to see how that tradition was overcome, the tradition that Ocean was Untouchable. There were individual acts of daring heresy to touch the untouchable, such as the suicidal voyage of Ugolino in 1291, which I shall mention later; great honour must be given to Ugolino, but his experiment was unsuccessful, and did not of itself effect the change that I am seeking – the change which brings science to bear on oceanography. I have to look for an enormous general change in medieval thinking, to see how it is that Ocean comes into the picture at all, to see how Ocean was, so to speak, brought to earth. Mohammedan thinking failed to do that, and Christian thinking did. Was medieval Christian thinking more flexible toward heresy? I must look that far into the psychic background.

One supreme example of a change beginning in the 12th century is the innovation of worship of the Virgin. The urge for such worship was communal. Not for centuries was intellectual sanction to be officially recorded by the Papacy, but in the 12th century Mary popularly receives the title of *Regina Coeli*, 'and it is as a queen that from that time art has depicted her'. In part, M. de Rougemont links the enthronement of the Virgin directly with the emotion of Courtly love. 'For the Lady of Thoughts of *cortezia* there was substituted Our Lady.' Courtliness, however, was but one of the many manifestations of the period which in various ways and in varying proportions were exalting Purity, bodily mortification, contempt for mortal ties, encouragement of Love contrary to marriage, and at the same time, encouragement of chastity. The largest popular movement of emotional mysticism – the congregation of the Goodmen, or Cathars – was so ferociously attacked by orthodox churchmen in 1209 that the slaughter of 'the Albigensian crusade' stands out as the first genocide in 'Christian' western history. If one were to take no more than a coldy distant view, the terrible turmoil of the time only emphasizes the magnitude of the change in orthodox churchly thinking whereby the worship of the Virgin, arising partially as a palliative to heresy, was in the end formally adopted and canonized. I fail to see any equal example of a flexibility on that scale in Islam's orthodox thinking. I am speaking beyond my scope, and therefore with timidity; but subject to correction the contrast suggests itself, that within Islam the heresy for which Al Hallaj was executed remained a heresy, whereas within Christendom, such mystical expression came to be approved.

I venture no farther into the psychic background than to see that by encouraging the worship of the Virgin, the Latin Church demonstrated a capacity for accepting and acclimatizing thoughts that had hitherto been exotic. Attention to thinking about *Regina Coeli* was forced upon the Church (if you accept de Rougemont's argument) by the extraordinary urge that welled up on all sides to have such a Queen. Exaltation of a 'feminine principle' may have been triggered, in the 12th century, by Arabic and eastern impulses, but the explosion released feelings that were deeply indigenous, though hitherto relatively inarticulate, in European peoples. Rituals of religions and witchcrafts, more anciently embedded than the newer offerings of either Christianity or Mohammedanism, exerted spontaneous revival.* It was in the recognition of these deep forces in the nature of their 'barbarian proselytes' (and acknowledgement of the same forces in themselves) that the medieval Roman Churchmen displayed a flexibility of thinking. The 'scholasticism' of St. Thomas Aquinas (1225?–74) appears as an exciting recognition that the world in which men were then living was a 'new' world, new in the sense that it was other than the world hitherto studied; and, in correction of Augustinian rejection of the world, the new world was to be accepted. It is to the general capacity within the Church to rearrange its thinking that I ascribe a large part of the slow process of bringing Ocean first into the realm of discourse, and then of scientific study.

There was no such instant pressure for a medieval churchman to think about Ocean, to be in any way compared with the emotional pressures to which I have been alluding; and yet as the weight (or power or strength or whatever you choose to call it) of Christendom shifts from the Mediterranean northward, the Ocean-Sea, and what

* A curious item of change in the 12th century is noticed by M. de Rougemont: it occurs in the game of chess. Instead of the four kings which had dominated the game in its first eastern form, the alteration is that a Lady (or Queen) assumes precedence over all the other pieces, save the King; and the King is actually reduced to the smallest possibility of real action, even though he remains the final stake and the consecrated figure. This alteration makes one wonder, what hidden persuasion was at work; one's thoughts turn perhaps to *The Golden Bough*, to Miss Weston's *From Ritual to Romance*, and to the writings of Dr. Margaret Murray. The possibly pagan Lady of Chess does not prevent the game from being played in monasteries. Instances of chess being banned appear to be otherwise explained: the game could be too absorbing, and (sadly) could lead to quarrels.

men feel about it, increasingly asserts itself. As Ocean comes gradually into discourse, we may watch for the gossamer thoughts which
start the process. As the thoughts take shape in a time of emotional
turmoil, we are prepared for differences of feelings. In the substratum
of old religions of the north, taboos are opposite to those of southern
peoples; Ocean, by Northmen, has always been accepted as actual,
not wholly supernatural, environment. Saxons, Angles, Jutes had
physically sailed across a western sea to a New World (Britain), and
found that New World habitable. Vikings took to their sea-boats
without mystery: the richest of pluckings were to the south, but there
were lesser dividends in Iceland, Greenland, Vinland.* Ocean was not
a Sea of Darkness to all Northmen, and for all coastal peoples who
dared to follow the whalepath (Britons, Bretons or Biscayans), the
symbol 'West' entirely reversed some of its Classical meanings.
Ocean as *Mare Tenebrosum* and 'West' as a death symbol had often
been infused with contrary meanings; beyond the sight of men there
was at the same time mournful Elysium and Happy Isles, or Islands
of the Blest. In the turmoil of the middle ages there is increased
struggle to reconcile meanings of 'west', and for landsmen to absorb
what seamen and sea-traders have to say. Within the Church, the
habitual location for fabulous reverent stories had always been in the
East. It is fascinating to watch the change of placement: the legend of
St. Brandon reverences the Western Ocean, the legend of the Welsh
Prince Madoc sails him westward to a Promised Land. The 'date'
ascribed to Madoc is about 1170; the legend of St. Brandon has been
for centuries so irrepressible that it is put into *The Golden Legend,*
circulated for lay-reading in the 13th century. So, simultaneously
with its other struggles to widen its embrace, the Church demon-
strates that is is beginning to think about Ocean.

I said that as to the way in which medieval men – landsmen – began
to think about Ocean, I should have to be dealing with gossamer
thoughts. Some tiny lights illumine the unknown Ocean-World. I
mean that; I am thinking of the tiny lights of fireflies. When did the
firefly first appear in Europe, and where did it come from? I have not

---

* I am certainly not disregarding Northmen as having been independent,
pre-Columbian, discoverers of a North American coast, though I can't find
that any early plantings ever really took root. The name Vinland can hardly
have any connection (except to Latin ears) with *vines* or grapes.

yet found a reference to it in ancient classical writing, though I cannot believe that ancient poets would have ignored the firefly, had it been within sight on summer evenings. I throw myself open to correction, but I find no mention of the firefly anywhere, until there it suddenly is, winking with its small fairy-light, in Canto XXVI of the *Inferno*. How, in fact, did the firefly come to Italy? If it was not in the Mediterranean area in classical times, where did it come from? More to my immediate point, where did Dante think it came from? Was it just accepted as a spontaneous appearance, or was it a little messenger, a tiny harbinger – from where? – that is the question. It is a strange little problem, a gossamer thought indeed, and one which breaks at any slightest weight. Yet this much weight I shall place, and possibly return to: Dante is using the firefly in the particular Canto where Ocean, and Ocean-voyaging, and Otherworld are in his mind. Perhaps the firefly was supposed to have come to Italy from the Canaries, or somewhere Oversea. I don't know; there's no weight on the thought; I am only surmising that Ocean arrives, in medieval consciousness, in ways that we can only see by half-seen glimpses.

But Dante is 14th century; a number of wills-o'-the-wisp had been gathering by then. Ocean was sufficiently and practically in mind by the time of Richard Coeur de Lion (1189–99) for an Ocean-road to be made the instrument of an attack upon the Holy Land, by sea, from Britain. Before running ahead, I must return to watch the gathering of some of the 'utensils' for that Ocean-road construction.

The quotation from Alvaro (p. 188) showed that in the 9th century the brightest of his fellow-Christians were excited by Arabian 'lore' as well as by Arabian 'romances'. The very notable (though rather shadowy and half-seen) Gerbert of Aurillac appears in the next century: a Frenchman from the Auvergne, drawn as a youth to study in Spain by the reputation spreading from Cordova. In the year 999 he became Pope Sylvester II, the 'magician Pope'. His attainments in mathematics and the physical sciences have been variously recorded. In the 18th century, in the discourse preliminary to the great French *Encyclopedia,* D'Alembert regarded Gerbert as comparable with Archimedes; nowadays, Arthur Koestler has credited him with reinstating the belief that the earth was round. These are true statements, not in the sense that anybody has evidence of Gerbert's personal proficiency or of his opinions, but in the sense that he indisputedly triggered off in Europe the process whereby Graeco-Arabic science was transferred, and understood, and put to use. The stature of Gerbert is less to be measured by any remnants of manuscript, than by the excitement that he released. A deserved greatness is thrust upon him by those (and shortly there were many) who indicate that it was Gerbert who set them off to study arithmetic, geometry, music, and (since in medieval times *mathesis* is a term which may mean either mathematics or divination) astrology as well as astronomy. In the 'First Renaissance' there was excitability in the realm of intellect as well as in the realm of passion; excitement aroused by the 'magician Pope' flared up in England. Gerbert's posthumous reputation for magic seems to start with William of Malmesbury in the first half of the 12th century,* but before that Adelard of Bath catches the desire for Arabian learning and by travel into Mohammedan lands, learns Arabic, and returns to England with a store of information. Adelard is not concerned with magic, and expresses very well his conception of the quest for knowledge:

> It is worth while to visit learned men of different nations, and to remember whatever you find is most excellent in each case. For what the schools of Gaul do not know, those beyond the Alps reveal; what you do not learn among the Latins, well-informed Greece will teach you.[5]

The Norman Court in England was apparently especially interested in Adelard's translations from the Arabic. His treatise on the astrolabe seems to be dedicated to Prince Henry Plantagenet; his earlier translation (perhaps in 1126) of the astronomical tables of Al-Khowarizmi possibly provides the germ of the idea of an English nautical almanac; the Pipe Roll for 1130 suggests that in that year Adelard drew for his services a royalty of four shillings and sixpence.

* Thorndike's *History of Magic and Experimental Science* shows the continuation of Gerbert's reputation for pious 'white' magic. Early in the 13th century Michael Scot makes out that when Gerbert had borrowed an astrolabe, demons explained its purpose to him, taught him how to use it, and how to make another one. In another 13th century manuscript 'Gerbert became archbishop and pope by demon aid and had a spirit enclosed in a golden head whom he consulted as to knotty problems in composing his commentary on arithmetic. When the demon expounded a certain difficult place badly, Gerbert skipped it, and hence that unexplained passage is called the *Saltus Gilberti*'. Thorndike gives references to other medieval stories about Gerbert.

Adelard of Bath, like Gerbert, remains 'a dim and shadowy figure'. Other discoverers of eastern science are dimly seen in western cloisters and at princely courts; in England by about 1250 there is almost a class of such figures, known as 'Egipte clerkes ... hem lerede, witterlike, Astronomisie and arsmetike'.[6] But in the lively period of this first Renaissance, inquisitiveness about Arabian inventions was not confined to adventurers who were intellectual by profession. One of the individuals who comes to life most clearly is a boy who was born roundabout the year 1170 in Pisa – the famous tower of Pisa was then already rising, though not yet leaning. The father of this particular boy was named Bonaccio, so, though the boy was baptised as Leonardo, he was usually called Fibonacci, 'Bonaccio's kid'. The father became a customs official at a trading station in Algeria, and sent for his kid to join him. There, and it is not known in what precise circumstances, the boy saw an Arab clerk doing something like this:

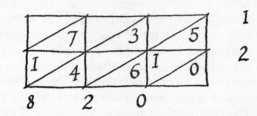

I say the circumstances which produced such a diagram are not precisely known – whether the diagram was made 'with a cane pen upon a small black board with a white, thinly liquid paint which made marks that could be easily erased' – or whether the diagram was made 'upon a white tablet, less than a foot square, strewn with red flour', so that the figures appeared white on a red ground – whether the figures were at all like those in my diagram (which they probably were not) – whether the performance was specially designed for Fibonacci's instruction, or whether it was a performance that he just happened to notice – these circumstances are unknown.[7] But however the pattern was presented, Fibonacci looked at it; and some little demon in his head agreed that it showed a neat way of multiplying $12 \times 735 = 8820$. Or, as the demon perceived, the diagram was a ready reckoner which would apply to other sums.

The art of reckoning 'by a marvellous method through the nine figures of the Indians' was how Fibonacci described this in the preface of his book *Liber Abaci,* issued first at Pisa in 1202. Between the time he first saw the nine figures (and noticed the use of zero) and his book-writing, Fibonacci had scoured around Egypt, Syria, Greece and Sicily, comparing different methods of calculation. That the nine 'Arabic' figures were of Hindu origin was generally agreed; what Arabs (or Syrians) had supplied was the 'marvellous' dexterity in use. The dexterity, as demonstrated in *Liber Abaci,* appealed to the Emperor Frederic II; Fibonacci, addressed in more dignified style as Leonardo of Pisa, became himself a figure at the royal Court; Florentine merchants and bankers adopted the Arabic numerals for bookkeeping. Before the end of the century a serious hitch developed. The catch about Arabic numerals was that different people wrote them in different ways, which led to confusion and fraud. The absence of standard practice had already been deplored in many of the monasteries of Europe, wherein house-rules differed. In manuscripts that have been found in different places, dating from Gerbert's time onward, Arabic figures display much independence of behaviour: the 7 upright in some places, in others lies prone or supine, and 5 is a particularly freakish jester. 'Noumbres of augrim' had advantage over the Roman notation for the marking of degrees on astrolabes and for the compilation of star-tables; but the idiosyncracies of the figures called for witterlike copy-clerks. In due course it was the printing-press (that mechanical copycad*) which contributed to standardization.

The rhetoric of which the Arab mystics had made inflammatory use was mainly of Grecian origin, and so was the science which the Europeans were now beginning to explore. To what had been inherited from Greece, Islam had added devices from far-eastern sources; the numerals are the outstanding example. The impression is that Arabs (using the term loosely, for those who wrote in Arabic) took hold of Hindu numerals, stripped them of mystical significance,

* The spelling 'copycat' is, I believe, a corruption which conceals the origin of the expression. The term is unlikely to derive from the animal, for a cat is not noticeably imitative. But 'cad' (short for 'cadet') was I think a common usage for the junior clerk, the cadet whose status was that of a copyist only. Hence I have preferred the spelling 'copycad'.

played with them, paraded them in new formations. I don't suppose it could be said that the manipulative skill with numbers exceeded the skill of the Greeks; but there is an expertise which seems distinct, a style which is Islamic. In medieval Islam there is also an increase of interest in instruments, and instruments incite experimentation. But in Islam's science one sees that if some inhibitions have been discarded (zero admitted to a place in ciphering, instruments approved, not frowned on), other inhibitions seem to be retained, or sometimes imposed. The alchemist is allowed great play with his alembic, but not every Jinn that comes out of a bottle is a good Jinn, and some are proscribed. Research for the Elixir of Life is questionable; on a lower level, the distillation of alcohol is discovered, and the drinking of it banned. The beauty and the meaning of a discovery are not interpreted in terms of instant utility. I drew attention to the charge made against Al Hallaj in the 12th century (p. 193), for it shows that knowledge of the magnet was then familiar enough for mention in theological court-room argument; the interest there expressed bears no relation to the utility of the magnet as a direction-finder for travellers. At that very period it seems fairly certain that a low-grade use was being made of the mariners' needle, very possibly in a form borrowed by Arab seamen from Chinese seamen – the floating fish. But is it fanciful on my part to feel that in 12th century Islam a mystical interpretation of the magnet was, so to speak, proper, but any utility the magnet might have for mariners, a matter of less respect?

Islam took up a residence in the Iberian Peninsula; some of Islam's most knowledgeable men had opportunity to look westward at the mystery of Ocean. I can find references to speculations, but find no indication that any of Islam's scientists ever set out to try to sail the sea. There is a strong temptation to conclude that the old taboo on Ocean which Homer had anciently expressed, retained its hold unchanged upon Mohammedans. The snapshot of Akbah stopping at the Ocean is understandable; more deeply surprising is that the technological equipment as gathered by Akbah's descendants was not used against Ocean. I think I have begun to see Westerners obtaining some ideas of using Ocean and I have come to see the beginning of the borrowing of the equipment. There is a long way yet to go before I can see more exactly how it was that the Iberian

Peninsula, rather than any other place, became the launching pad from which a rocket went to a new New World.

The long-continued contest of Cross and Crescent in the Mediterranean area plays its gradual part in the construction of the new road west; such details as I have attended to, suggest that Westerners will build a sea-road. As contestants, Islam at first seemed stronger and better organized; of the two disjointed parts of Christendom, the Latin Christendom with which I was concerned was hard to think of as an entity. Later the relative powers of Cross and Crescent become reversed. Despite all qualifications, something that can begin to be called a European spirit comes into being in the First Renaissance, and both in passion and in intellect that spirit then seems to outdo Islam in active creativity. I do not think I need examine (even if I could) the acquisition by Europeans of each item of Islamic technology: the things I hinted at – numerals, magnetic compass, stern-post rudder, astrolabe, star-tables, almanacs, charts – these, and gun-powder and the brass cannon, and the printing press also (wherever *that* notion originated) – will all be necessary before a real and routine Ocean-road can be established; but I can be content with glimpses of them, after Europe has captured them and, in European hands, they become self-developing. The 'ancient' period of my narrative ends, in one sense, with the First Renaissance; though the end is more spectacularly marked when, in the last half of the 15th century, Cross and Crescent each lose and gain one of the two great outposts at either end of the Central Sea. The capture of Constantinople by the Turks in 1453 was certainly regarded, by all contemporaries, as the end of an epoch. The capture of Granada by Ferdinand in 1492 is fully as evident to us, as the turning-point for something new to happen.

Gathered together at Santa Fé in Spain, awaiting the surrender of Granada, were a number of people with conflicting ideas as to what to do next. A decision was made about further road-making. I must look at the people who made it.

NOTES

1. *Medieval Islam* by Gustave E. von Grunebaum (University of Chicago Press, First Phoenix Edition, 1961), p. 5.

2. von Grunebaum, pp. 57, 58.

3. *Passion and Society* by Denis de Rougemont, translated by Montgomery Belgion (Faber, London, Revised Edition 1956), p. 107.

4. de Rougement, p. 103 fn.

5. *A History of Magic and Experimental Science* by Lynn Thorndike (Macmillan, London, 1923). Vol. II, p. 20.

6. *Oxford English Dictionary*, under *arithmetic*, provides the source for this quotation.

7. See *A History of Mathematics* by Florian Cajori (Macmillan, New York, 1919) where the diagram I have borrowed appears on p. 91.

PART TWO
Modern

CHAPTER 11

The Fish that Swam

I HAVE been watching the coming into being of some of the tools which, simply by being at hand, played a creative part in further westering. Men and instruments working together, making the Iberian Peninsula into a launching-pad for approach to a New World: that is what I try to comprehend – and first of all, what sort of men, what motives?

It was in April, 1492, that the contracts between Columbus and Ferdinand and Isabella, the Sovereigns of Spain, were signed and sealed. Under those Capitulations, Christóbal Colón was to set forth 'to discover and acquire certain islands and mainlands in the Ocean Sea'. (I shall rely on Profesor Samuel Eliot Morison[1] for many pleasing details). A main expectation was that Columbus might find, by sailing west, the easterly fringes of the wealthiest of Old Worlds, the Orient. He might arrive at principalities in which there was an established sovereignty ranking with that of the recently united Castile and Aragon, and therefore he was authorized to show a passport written in universal Latin – a document to indicate that Columbus possessed the full protection of his own rulers in sailing with three caravels 'toward the regions of India' (*ad partes Indie*). Columbus was further supplied with three identical letters of introduction, one to the 'Grand Khan' (the Chinese Emperor) and the other two with blank spaces so that the proper titles of other princes could be inserted. Contingencies were thought out. The timing of the signing, Eastertide, is significant. The endeavour was very consciously, a 'Christian' enterprise. So, and correctly, is this taught in some American schools: a school-history of the United States in front of me opens automatically with Columbus and a first chapter-heading: 'Christian Europeans Find a New World'.[2]

It took more than three months, or until August, 1492, for Columbus to complete his stowage for departure. There is still time for me to pause. I can hardly dodge that very central question – what sort of people were those Christian Europeans? What was the nature of 'The Fish that Swam'?

The Fish, the mystical Fish, *Der Heilige Fisch* as German Christians have called it, still comes readily to mind at Easter-tide. Why, for Christians, is 'fish' a holy symbol? The prominence of fish in the New Testament may well be connected with the answer. In the earliest universal language of the Mediterranean the very word in Greek

$$ΙΧΘΥΣ$$

was a mnemonic which could be interpreted as standing for:

$$Ἰησοῦς \ Χριστὸς \ Θιοῦ \ Ὑιὸς \ Σωτήρ$$

or literally in our tongue: 'Jesus Christ of God the Son Saviour'. That is the meaning of the word 'ichthys' as it is both written and pictured in the Catacombs and secret places of the early Christians of Rome, and on the many later seals, as in this example:

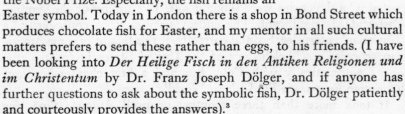

which affirms that the interpretation shall so stand from alpha unto omega.

In *The City of God* Augustine makes mention of 'ichthys' and its interpretation. At the present day that fish is not wholly forgotten. Allusion to the use of the symbol and its meaning did not render the novel *Barabbas* by Pär Lagerkvist so obscure as to prevent it winning the Nobel Prize. Especially, the fish remains an Easter symbol. Today in London there is a shop in Bond Street which produces chocolate fish for Easter, and my mentor in all such cultural matters prefers to send these rather than eggs, to his friends. (I have been looking into *Der Heilige Fisch in den Antiken Religionen und im Christentum* by Dr. Franz Joseph Dölger, and if anyone has further questions to ask about the symbolic fish, Dr. Dölger patiently and courteously provides the answers).[3]

But I do not suppose that it was in the early nature of Christian companionship as exemplified in the fish-symbol, as communicated by St. Paul or as expounded by St. Augustine, that the exploration by Columbus was promoted.

From Jerusalem onwards throughout the migration, some conception of the City of God has never been lost, but affairs of Church and State in Europe by the time of Dante were affording no complacency. Dante in his vision, looking down from Paradise upon 'the world endlessly bitter', the 'thrashing floor' where there was none, Pope or warrior, to govern well – 'none to govern upon earth' – makes one recall how more and more remote earth seemed to be from the Celestial City. It is not in anything so meek as the early Christian fish that one finds a symbol appropriate to the militant comradeship of the Crusader. The Cross, in its aspect of the straight sword with the straight guard-bar across the hilt, is closer to the martial spirit of the competing courts of Europe.

The cross worn by the soldier on his baldrick, shield or banner might be of any colour. Tradition hallowed white as signifying Faith, green Hope, and red Charity.[4] The phrase I used as chapter-title might therefore be misleading. The 'fish' that swam from the Iberian Pensinula was not the fish that symbolized the early Christian. The special symbol of Christianity worn as a banner by the fleet of Columbus was that other complex symbol, the Cross. The banner of the expedition showed in fact a green cross. The green cross represents the nature of 'The Fish that Swam'.

Yet the mystic fish was not wholly forgotten. There was another and altogether different 'fish' we have to consider – the little 'floating fish' – the mariners' needle. The magnetic fish was also in the swim, and how that happened I must have patience to discover.

I must look at the signing of the contracts between Columbus and the Sovereigns, against the background of the *Reconquista*, the recapture of Spain from the Moors. At the moment that Columbus presented his Plan for sailing westward to the Indies, it is clear that the paramount urgency for Ferdinand and Isabella was conceived as ridding the Iberian Peninsula of Moors, of Islam. 'Wait till the war is over' was several times Isabella's personal advice to Columbus. With the capture of Granada in January, 1492, that tedious ten years' war against the Moors seemed to Columbus to be over; how did it seem to Ferdinand and his Christian warrior companions? At such a moment of victory was Ferdinand weary of glory? Why not carry the meteor flag of Aragon against the Mamluke Sultanate of Egypt, seize Alexandria? Why bother with Columbus? Why bother at all with the Western Ocean? I shall have to deal with many things before I can see how the Sovereigns of Spain could ever begin to think about the West.

The 'long' Crusades to the Holy Land bring in the geographical fact that any sea-faring co-operation by fighters from the northwest of Christendom imposed a circumnavigation of the Iberian Peninsula. The thought I follow is that it was the circumnavigation of the Peninsula from the north which led on to the effort to circumnavigate Africa; which continuing effort was in its turn a prod to the voyages of Columbus and Magellan. To test that way of thinking I would go back if necessary to certain Normans in England – yes, back as far as Richard Coeur de Lion, Richard the Lionheart.

What I ask for is a quick glimpse of Richard, in 1189, setting off for the Third Crusade. A chronicler puts it that his desire was to find in the Holy Land 'Loode males' – the phrase means travelling-trunks – 'ful off ryche precious stones'.[5] That desire could combine with (for example) Sir Walter Scott's view of Richard, which stresses the 'military renown, which was the very breath of his nostrils'. If Richard had also believed that the Red Cross he wore signified Charity, the complex of intentions would not in any age be unusual.

I am concerned with the preparations for Richard's voyage. Customarily before 1189 there had been plenty of 'short' Crusades within the Peninsula, sometimes as substitutes for the 'long' Crusades. It is usual to say that the *Reconquista* begins with the conquest of Toledo by Christians in 1085. Fighters of many nations had found by then a 'thrashing-floor' in the Peninsula for old passions, ambitions, purposeful misunderstandings, hates, bitter memories and sometimes grudging respect for the enemy, be he Moor or other heretic. French, German and Italian knights fought in the capture of Toledo. English and German adventurers on their way by sea to the Second Crusade put into the mouth of the Tagus as a port of call, stormed Lisbon, and presented the port as a gift to the first King of Portugal. That was in 1147. Some of the English stayed there: one, Gilbert of Hastings, became first Bishop of Lisbon. That is what I need to note, that Lisbon became for sea-farers from the north a natural way-station. Portugal – the very name derives from 'sea-port'. Lisbon thus marks itself at once upon my map: an ocean-facing city – from her quays, as Morison observes, 'no long and tedious sail to blue water'.

The name of Hastings should have reminded me that English participation in Crusades began immediately after the Norman Conquest of England. Long-distance sea-faring or predatory naval action from England is not noticeable before the Norman Conquest and thereafter is suddenly noticeable – most noticeable indeed in the voyage sent off by Richard for the Third Crusade. His fleet consisted of upwards of a hundred ships. Consider for a moment the equipment needed for so many ships to cross the Bay of Biscay and circumnavigate the Iberian Peninsula. In the mind's eye you have to see certain advances in shipbuilding and gear, over the ships as pictured a century earlier in the Bayeux Tapestry. We are given to understand that this expedition of Richard's was carefully planned: the many ships were to sail together, all shipmasters were to show obedience to the king's ship, and from the mast of the king's ship each night a lantern was to be hung to guide the others 'as a hen gathers her chickens'. Further than that picturesque phrase I find no precise description of the equipment. The phrase does suggest that the king's ship was noteworthy for size. One has to guess that she had the best gear possible: she might have had a stern-post rudder. The guess-work about her gear makes me think of Alexander Neckam.

Alexander Neckam was foster-brother of Richard the Lionheart, suckled at the same breast. I don't know how many children Eleanor of Aquitaine had by her first marriage with Louis VII of France, but by her second marriage with Henry II of England she had eight children. Richard was the fourth son; she was happy to hand this child over to somebody else to nourish. Who the foster-mother was, with her own newly-arrived baby, is not known, except for the joke in Alexander's last name, or nickname, Neckam, (*nequam* = worthless, of less 'worth' in the code of chivalry). The foster-brother Neckam nevertheless made a name for himself: at once an Augustinian monk and a frequenter of the Court, a lecturer in Paris round about 1180, and after his return to England a man of respected attainments in the liberal arts, the two branches of law, theology, medicine and in particular, practical natural science. He was a leading authority in England on matters of importance to sea-farers: he wrote *De Utensilibus*, a handbook in which he discusses what things are needed in a ship's stores. Among these things he specifically mentions the mariners' compass. Neckam mentions the compass not as a complete novelty, nor yet as an instrument that is fully understood, but as an aid to be studied when by day there is no sun, or when by night there are no stars. The mention of the magnetic compass here, and in his other writings, is earlier than discussions of magnetism by Roger Bacon, Michael Scot, and Bartholomew of England, who soon after also begin to write about the needle.* Neckam writes of it as a utensil for seafarers.

I am not in the realm of certainty, merely of guesswork, if I suggest that in 1189 the chief ship of the expedition which was to sail across the Bay of Biscay, round the troublesome Peninsula and on to the Holy Land, was provided with not only a lantern but a magnetic needle. I am admittedly assuming that the equipment was as full and proper as possible; and indeed the only thing that I find noted as lacking to a proper equipment of a king's ship was the presence of the King himself. Richard preferred to travel overland.

It has been regarded as laughable that the title Lionheart did not endow Richard with the heart of a sea-lion. Neckam, though, expresses a general opinion of the period when he says that nobody of great worth should travel by sea if that can be avoided. Sir Walter Scott is also of opinion that Richard, as likewise his companion Thomas De Vaux, was somewhat a lover of good cheer and splendid accommodation. Richard's knights and men-at-arms, after tossing on the Bay of Biscay, put in to Marseilles for the rendezvous. They found that Richard and De Vaux had been there, but had gone ahead, overland, to Italy. It was in Sicily that Richard joined his ship.[6]

But returning to my subject of the compass needle, I make the guess that it was being studied on that voyage in the northern corridor of the Atlantic. For a better glimpse of compass and astrolabe at work

---

* A Viking method of finding the sun by using the optical properties of Iceland spar is discussed by Th. Ramskou in *Skalk*, the periodical publication of the Museum of Århus, Denmark (Nr. 6, 1966 and Nr. 2, 1967). This may have provided Vikings with a kind of 'sunstone' compass; perhaps a precursor of the compass called *matka* by the Pomors, or of Kollsmann's sky compass invented in 1948 for use in polar regions. But I follow Thorndike's assumption that Neckam was commending the magnetic needle.

on the Atlantic seaboard I skip from the court of Richard the Lion-heart to the lively royal household of John of Gaunt.

John of Gaunt (1340–1399), Duke of Lancaster, fourth son of Edward III, born at Ghent, interests all those who wish to trace the fightings for the Crown of England. My special interest in his household is different. The family trees which stem from John of Gaunt are complicated, for he was married three times. It is with the descent of titles through the male line that most heralds and historians are concerned. It is for his daughters that I watch him. As Regent of England he was much feared within England; yet what I emphasize is that for fifteen years (1372 to 1387), having married the daughter of Pedro of Castile, John of Gaunt regarded himself as King of Castile. It was not that Pedro's daughter came to him in England: John of Gaunt in his own person went to and claimed Castile. There was one child, a daughter, of that marriage. John of Gaunt assigned his claim to the throne of Castile to her, and it was through that line that Isabella, patron of Columbus, derived her title.

Isabella's father and mother were in fact both descendants of John of Gaunt. But the marriage which thus affected the affairs of Castile was John of Gaunt's second marriage. His first marriage, in England, had produced an English daughter, Philippa, and she married King John I of Portugal. Each of the five half-English princes born of that marriage was active in the maritime development of Portugal: the most famous of the brothers, Prince Henry the Navigator, became an example to those who set out to explore the Ocean Sea.

Now I am going to ask, where did Prince Henry's training and instinct come from? Or whence came Isabella's interest in the seafaring adventurer, Columbus? Some say that was because Columbus had red hair, blue eyes and ruddy complexion, and she had blue eyes and red hair too.* How Columbus, son of a weaver of Genoa, came by his red hair I don't know; Isabella, whose father and mother were

* Apropos hair colour and complexions it may be borne in mind that in the 15th century, as earlier, red hair and a sanguine complexion were often considered appropriate for men who were heroes or ladies who were high-born, and portraits were so painted. Mediterranean women often aspired to golden hair, to the extent of doing what could be done with gold wire; and some very dark-visaged gentlemen were pleased to wear goldilocks – look at Signorelli e Beato Angelico painted by Luca Signorelli, at Orvieto.

both descendants of John of Gaunt, came by her red hair understandably. A more important question leaps up to be tested, with regard both to Isabella and to Prince Henry. It looks as if in households that derived from John of Gaunt an interest in navigation was somehow in the air. At least it is worth glancing at normal goings-on in the ordering of John of Gaunt's own household during his first and second marriages.

It happens that no very difficult research is needed, for an Esquire of John of Gaunt's household was a certain sharp-eyed Geoffrey Chaucer.

Chaucer (1340–1400) was an exact contemporary of his lord and master, and if some circles have subsequently paid more attention to the squire than to the master, that's as may be. What I assume is that Chaucer's world was somewhat the same as John of Gaunt's world, and that by looking at the one you may see something of the other. By 'world' I here mean the physical world around the men, the geography.

It is with an estimate of what the geography was like at that time, that many commentators on Chaucer begin. If everlively Chaucer has not by himself enticed you to read him, a next best teacher to entice you is Professor John Livingstone Lowes; and Professor Lowes at once says that to enjoy Chaucer you must not only appreciate that his characters are just the same as those of people here and now, but you must also be prepared to see that the geographical stage on which the characters skip and prance is very different. The difference of the stage-setting, Lowes implies, may be easier to state than it is, in the 20th century, to feel; indeed, in order to *feel* the difference of Chaucer's world from ours, the difference may have to be overstated.

I am looking at lectures on Chaucer by Professor Lowes.[7] Perfect in their aptness and grace, the lectures begin with a reference to a gay little ballad from Chaucer 'to Rosamounde', which opens with a topographical compliment:

> *Madame, ye ben of al beaute shryne*
> *As fer as cercled is the mappamounde*

'Now Chaucer's *mappa mundi* – his map of the world – lay in his mind as a definite shape', says Lowes, and proceeds to emphasize the scores of medieval *mappamondes* wherein 'Europe, Asia and Africa lie folded close together, three cells within the circle of the Ocean stream, like the embryo of the later world.' To be very clear about this, and to simplify the image, Lowes says: draw for yourself a figure – 'draw a circle and bisect it north and south, and then bisect from east to west the western half'.

Professor Lowes' diagram is pleasingly reminiscent of Chaucer's

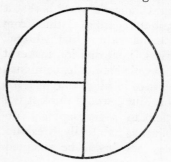

own exposition of 'the Astrolabie' for 'litel Lowis', his ten-year-old son. At the end of many paragraphs of that diminutive treatise Chaucer wrote the instruction – *And for the more declaracioun, lo here thy figure.* Similarly, as a visual aid Lowes uses his diagram which is to be representative of Chaucer's world:

Within the north-west quadrant, roughly speaking, will lie Europe; within the south-west quadrant will lie that northern piece of Africa which was all then known; while the whole of the eastern segment of the circle belongs to Asia. Precisely so, in fact, were many of the oldest *mappamondes* actually drawn, and an early treatise so describes them: 'a T within an O shows the design, through which in three parts was parcelled out the world'. There was as yet no *West*.

In Chaucer's world there was as yet no *West*.

That is an emphatic statement. But it is precisely what Professor Lowes was saying to his students of Chaucer. Outside of the circle as drawn there was nothing except what Gower had described as

> ... *thilke See which hath no wane,*
> *Y-cleped the gret Occeane*

and 'the gret Occeane' was totally unknown. East and south and north, no less than west of the circle, 'were bounded', so Lowes says, 'by the unknown'.

I am going to quarrel with my master, for I have come to believe that in so overstating the difference of Chaucer's world from ours Lowes is persuading his listeners into too much of a half-truth.

If I quarrel with my master, the tiff must be respectful: *Amicus Plato, sed magis amica veritas*.[8] Yet the tiff is a real one. I shall maintain that in the household of John of Gaunt, of which Chaucer was an alert and active member, the geography of the world was not at all restricted by the *mappamondes*. I assert that the representation given by Lowes is based too much on a playful literary conceit of Chaucer's when writing a happy little valentine.

One difference between our 'world' and Chaucer's world is that it has become with us habitual to separate and to regard as distinct from each other, two ways of looking at phenomena – a way that is literal, and a way that is symbolic or metaphorical. That division makes it difficult for us to share a 'world' in which people habitually combined or, as we might feel, confused, the two ways of looking. Into us it has been drilled that we must split our vision. But I would think it was more general in Chaucer's time to participate in geographical surroundings by a kind of fusion which we, just as habitually, break up. In *that* world we see the splitting process starting to be accepted. That, I think, is worth a pause.

It is clear to us what Professor Lowes means, when he emphatically says that in Chaucer's world, in John of Gaunt's world, there was no *West*. There were to them no physical Americas, or, granting as much literal truth as you like to tales about Phoenician voyages or to such reports as circulated about the Vikings, there was not much 'fact' about lands beyond the sunset for sober men to trust or believe. On what we tend to regard as a different level of consciousness, throughout the whole migration we have seen men always aware of some West beyond the visible horizon. Ocean did not lastingly engulf the sun: there were realms beyond the sunset. In what sense *real* realms? As real perhaps as death.

We saw that 'to go West' (signifying 'to die') was a metaphor older than Homer. A death-wish was not always unkindly. Sappho saw Hesperus, the Evening Star, as a covenant of homecoming.[9] The Hesperides of Greek mythology were not the same as the Fates who ruled you where you were. The Hesperides were the welcoming daughters of Hesperus, nymphs who at the westward extremity beyond the factual world attended, with the aid of a watchful dragon, the garden in which grew the golden apples. Those apples of the

Fortunate Isles, the Isles of the Blest, 'on earth like never grew, ne living wight like ever saw' – that was their essential nature. To earthly eyes the dragon might seem as fierce as Cerberus, yet at a moment of insight he would be seen as playmate and helpmeet of the friendly nymphs. Those Western Isles, with all of their additaments, are evident in the baggage we have looked at. Professor Lowes would have been among the first to say that on that level, the level of imagination, there was a West. The Hesperides were there. They were 'more nearly there' to Chaucer's world than to ours because as yet the literal had not been hacked apart from the metaphor, as with a cleaver.

Beliefs, illusions, are part of the stock in trade of all adventurers, and they are hardly to be dismissed, if they are what promote the adventure. Imaginary islands, imaginary lands, have their own importance, and have a factual importance too if they draw people to fact-finding. I spoke of different levels, that of the physical world and that of myth. The world of myth is not of the physical world but is engaged with it: the levels slip and slide, affect each other: merge, yet are independent. It may be the first duty of an imaginary island to remain imaginary. Plato almost did a disservice by making the island of Atlantis so nearly actual, so almost physical, so realistically populated, citified and organized for war. But he redeemed Atlantis for myth by having it swallowed up, leaving nothing behind except a shoal of mud, and the mud by good luck was never found. I say by good luck, for it was not at all always the duty of an imaginary island or an imaginary New World either to be, or to remain, blissful once it was found. Seneca (whom Chaucer read more closely than most of us do) winds up a bitter peroration at the end of the second act of his *Medea* with the jibe that when, across the waters of the Ocean Sea, a New World (*Novos Orbes*) is discovered, it will be laid open to the same original evil, and return that evil on its discoverers – the evil which destroyed Greece after the voyage of Argo:

> *How deerely was that wicked journey bought!*
> *Medea accurst, and eke the Golden Fleece,*
> *That greater harme than storme of seas hath wrought*
> *Rewarded well that voyage first of Greece. . . .*

Prescott remarks of Seneca's prophecy that it is 'perhaps the most remarkable random prophecy on record. For it is not a simple extension of the boundaries of the known arts of the globe that is so confidently announced, but the existence of a *New World* across the waters, to be revealed in coming ages'.* Columbus's second son, Ferdinand, marked the passage in his Seneca.† To those who meditate on Seneca's life and suicide in Nero's household the prophecy seems, as Prescott says, random, rather than pointing to any specific geographical expectancy; although we are reminded that Seneca's father and mother were both Spaniards from the Phoenician part of Spain (Granada), and there is no knowing if they carried any Phoenician blood, or conveyed any hereditary tale-telling of Carthaginian voyages into his nursery.[10]

Carthaginians? Am I going to bring them into this moment of geographical review? Not at all – I have given them up. Carthaginians are here only as a reminder that at one and the same time, or at different times and in different circumstances, the same land, an identical island, can be both imaginary and a physical entity. It is not a matter of choosing one truth or the other. The Canary Islands, for example, as soon as they appear in evidence, move with ease between the two realms, myth and physical actuality. Actual enough, we feel (with that great mountain-peak Teide, the peak of Tenerife, as sea-mark) to the possibly mythical secretive Carthaginian mariners: mythical enough, we feel, to that actual fellow Arnobius, with whom their name comes into our literature.

Arnobius (if he was an actual fellow) was a convert to Christianity in the time of Diocletian, and converts of the time were questioned as to their sincerity. Arnobius was required to write a treatise. In the treatise, circulated about A.D. 300, he mentions the Canary Islands (*canariae insulae*). These are assumed to be the same as those spoken

---

*   Quibus Oceanus
Vincula rerum laxet, et ingens
Pateat tellus, Typhisque Novos
Detegat Orbes.

† Columbus's first son by his marriage to Doña Felipe was Diego. After Columbus left Portugal and in the discouraging period in which he was seeking patronage from Isabella he met Beatriz Enriquez, whom Morison describes as 'a peasant's daughter'. They were not married, but Beatriz in 1488 bore him a second son, Ferdinand, who in due course became a squire at the royal court.

of by Posidonius (about 50 B.C.) as Islands of the Blest. At any rate
there they are – Fortunate Islands and Islands of Dogs – all in one
breath. Canary 'birds' we begin to hear about a great while later. The
canaries, those 'dogs' of Arnobius – in what sense had he *seen* them?
Were they physical flea-bitten dogs? – or the spiritual dogs that
Cerberus was transformed into, Christian animal-welcomers who
were to greet the Christian brotherhood as they voyaged toward the
Land of Behest? Is Arnobius talking about a group of real or imagined islands, and is some later chart-maker going to put dots in
fancied or real positions? This is a matter of importance, this is how
geography *begins*. May we then consult Arnobius to see exactly what
he says? No, we may not. The original treatise of Arnobius has never
been found. Nothing is left of the writings of Arnobius except the few
quotations that other ancients made – only the name Canary Islands.
The name floats up from Arnobius, and remains.[11]

In Chaucer's world, was there no *West*? There was as yet no single
West, for it was multiple. There were many wests of the same direction and they were mixed, and for the most part the mixture was
not mechanical (and so capable of being sorted out) but a more mys-
sterious chemical fusion. The myth of St. Brandon as set down in
The Golden Legend was familiar reading to Chaucer, in the French,
a century before it was Englished by William Caxton.[12] The voyages
of Brandon, that holy man of Ireland, are now entwined and filigreed
by other monks with symbols of piety; if you so wish, you may disen-
twine some of the symbols without particular damage – the direction
of the voyages is often changed towards the east (for that is toward
the Land of Behest), the duration is often the archetypal forty days,
and so forth. Yet the vision of the islands is so directly beautiful that
you do well not to tamper. Sometimes at finding a fair haven in an
island 'a fair hound' comes to fall at the feet of St. Brandon, and to
frolic in doggish fashion, and make him 'good cheer in his manner'.
Sometimes it is the birds which in their manner make him good
cheer:

> As God would, they saw a fair island full of flowers, herbs, and trees,
> whereof they thanked God of his good grace, and anon they went on
> land, and when they had gone long in this they found a full fair well, and
> thereby stood a fair tree full of boughs, and on every bough sat a fair
> bird, and they sat so thick on the tree that unnethe any leaf of the tree

might be seen. The number of them was so great, and they sang so merrily that it was a heavenly noise to hear, wherefore St. Brandon kneeled down on his knees and wept for joy, and made his prayers devoutly to our Lord God to know what these birds meant.

Actual touchable islands? Oh yes, more touchable than in the Irish poem about Bran, factually reporting:

> *There are thrice fifty distant isles*
> *In the ocean to the west of us*
> *Larger than Erin twice*
> *Is each of them, or thrice.*

Who can lead you to these islands? The first, most natural of all directional instruments, the birds.

Let us be *literal*. 'To know what these birds meant', as direction-indicators, was as important to a steersman as it might be in a mystical interpretation of St. Brandon's experiences. Intentional use of shore-sighting birds did not cease after that time when Noah sent the raven and the dove out from the Ark. In her book on *The Haven-Finding Art* Professor E. G. R. Taylor has discussed the part played by birds in human maritime discovery, and she remarks that birds as direction finders have been used in a twofold manner – pilots have carried captive birds and released them to spy for land from an altitude higher than the mast, and there has also been the observance by seamen of the flight and behaviour of wildfowl.

Ravens, carried by Northmen, provide an example of the one use: ravens come into the earliest reports of Viking voyages to Iceland and Greenland, and perhaps the term 'crow's nest', as used aboard later ships, perpetuates a memory of this. The annual migration of wild geese from Ireland to Iceland and Greenland and back is an example of the other use. This particular migration is possibly to be connected, as Professor Taylor points out, with whatever historicity is sought for the voyages attributed to St. Brandon:

> These noisy and conspicuous birds, the brent-geese, white geese, bar-nacle-geese and grey-lags, wintered in their tens of thousands in North-ern Ireland, and in the Shannon Estuary (which St. Brandon knew). They fly into their feeding grounds, coming in from the north, towards

the end of September and during the month of October. But ten days or a fortnight after the spring equinox they begin to leave. A large flock rises, and one long skein after another disappears over the northern horizon. A week or so later another flock departs in the same way, honking as they fly, and in four or five weeks' time the marshes are deserted – all have disappeared. They are on their way to summer breeding places in Iceland and Greenland. ... Commander Peter Scott states that there is nothing impossible in the monks' setting course by the northward migration, and keeping it by watching successive skeins of birds pass overhead. If the wind failed they could ply their oars, as St. Brandon's companions did, and in a week or less Iceland would lie on the horizon. The migrations, besides, both to and fro, coincide with the beginning and ending of the sailing season.[13]

I notice that there have been discussions of possible alterations in the course of the Gulf Stream, within perhaps the past thousand years, thereby affecting climatic conditions – perhaps affecting the behaviour of the wild geese also? – perhaps affecting human behaviour in Europe. I am however cautioned that it is easy to exaggerate the effect of such gulf stream alterations, and I accept the warning to avoid this distraction as if, in my own course, it were a Wandering Isle.[14] Southward I steer in the Atlantic and continue to consider the wild birds, and 'what these birds meant'.

Birds soon appear as of importance in southerly exploration of the Western Sea. The present name for the island-group of the Azores comes from the Portuguese word *açor*, meaning a hawk. The Portuguese historian Azurara relates that his countrymen, presumably having been attracted to the main islands of the Azores by the behaviour of the birds, went beyond the main islands to discover Flores and Corvo, lying 140 sea-miles beyond Fayal, because they noticed birds from the larger islands flying in that direction. The question rises, were the Portuguese the first seamen to visit the Azores?*

* In classical times there are allusions to islands farther out in the Atlantic than the Canaries.[15] I remain puzzled how to interpret 'farther out'. The 'farther' as used may not mean 'farther from the mainland nearest to it,' as we might naturally think, looking at a modern globe – the Azores would be farthest in that sense. I would think that for the ancients 'farther' might sometimes have meant farther in distance or sailing time from home, or from the Strait of Gibraltar – the Cape Verde Islands might in that sense be farther, though not farthest from the mainland.

Nobody that I have read mentions any Greek or Roman knowledge of those islands, yet the reading-matter available to well-read men of Chaucer's world included the Arabian geographers. Xerif al Edrisi of the 12th century and Ibn-al-Wardi of the 14th. After describing the Canaries, one or both of these geographers mention (according to the *Encyclopaedia Britannica*, 14th edition) a group of nine other islands in the Ocean Sea, which are assumed to be the Azores, since the number of islands is correct, the position more or less as estimated, and mention made of the 'hawks and buzzards'. Thus somebody must have reported with a measure of factual truth to the geographers – at least by the 14th century – the number and character of those islands. Somebody must have followed the crow onward to Corvo.

A good deal of stress is laid by the Arabian geographers on 'verification' of stories reported to them. There is in general more scepticism, or shall I say a more literal approach, among medieval Muslim writers than among Christian scribes of the time.* The dates of the reasonably literal-minded Edrisi are 1099–1166, or near enough. Edrisi was born in North Africa and surnamed 'the Nubian'; when he talks about the Ocean Sea and is in doubt he is apt to say so – 'no one has been able to verify' expresses his attitude.[16] So if he and Ibn-al-Wardi record what we call the Azores, I incline to believe there had been some scrutiny of the information.

Stress on the literal way of looking at things, stress upon verification of geographical details – the restraint in matters for which no objective measurement could be found, the interest in mechanical instruments which might assist attainment of objective measurement – this was all of the essence of the 'arabian' science then being raided by Europeans. The transcriptions reaching Europe might be purely speculative. There is for instance al-Asfihani, saying in the 13th century:

> I do not find a reason why there should not be on the other side of the water [the Atlantic] opposite to our side, another land. And as I find no reason why such a land should not exist, I find no reason why there

---

* At least one island of faith and imagination was spoken of among medieval Christians in the Iberian Peninsula: before there was a Portugal there was the Christian legend of a westward Island of Antilia, a refuge hoped for by those who wished to escape from the Moors.

should not exist on that land, animals, plants and minerals, such as those we have – or from other kinds and races.

The speculation is so reasonable as to be almost irritating. It is a deliberate heretical challenge to the taboo on Ocean. It was a statement at once too speculative and too heretical to encourage Mohammedans to go exploring. But in the last chapter we were watching the spread of heresies. There is at least one example in the 13th century of a southern European making organized effort to use the Western Ocean for a long voyage. This was the considered effort of Ugolino di Vivaldo, citizen of the Genoese Republic, who set out westward with two galleys in May, 1921. It is supposed that Ugolino intended to find an ocean-route to India. Which route, or what happened, is not known. Ugolino was posted missing.

It is likely that some of the Muslims may have remarked that what was defective in Ugolino's expedition was not his spirit, nor perhaps his seamanship, but his instruments. Mechanical instruments, with which to find position and direction: I cannot stress too heavily the importance of the idea of instrumentation, then beginning to take hold. To circumnavigate the globe was a not impossible thought, but you would need more aid than you could get from seabirds. Circumnavigation of the globe? Aristotle had mentioned it. Whether or no Abul 'Fida (1273–1331) picked up the notion from Aristotle, he had contemplated it to this extent: the world being round, if you wish to sail round it, that voyage is going to entail the loss or gain of a day, according to which way you go, whether the voyage itself is to occupy a short term of months or a long term of years. That was a 14th century remark (and 14th century Christendom was learning that you could find out where you were on the globe providing you had instruments. This was a learning that could apply to Ocean, provided instruments behaved properly at sea.

The lodestone had provided a mystery at which ancient Greeks had marvelled. St. Augustine recorded his astonishment that fragments of iron laid on a silver plate could be made to move at command of a stone held beneath the plate, not even touching them. Dr. Taylor (in *The Haven-Finding Art*) suggests that for an able magician a not very difficult next step was to call for a basin of water, on which model ships (with fragments of iron in them) could be put in motion, with the help of a concealed lodestone. If the fragments of iron were polarized needles, 'sooner or later it would be noticed that when the lodestone was removed the models turned north'. This odd behaviour of floating needles was recorded by some of the Chinese earlier than by anybody else; scholars find plenty of room for argument, but since the Chinese seem to have been the first to make the next remarkable step – the transformation of their floating fish into a navigational utility – one large tradition is that medieval Islam picked up the use of the mariners' needle from an eastern source, as readily as the Hindu numerals had been picked up. There is no particular difficulty of dates, to make it impossible to conceive that Muslims were using magnetized needles on their Central Sea in the 12th century. In the previous chapter I was expressing an unease, whether it would have been orthodox for the 12th century Muslim to play with magnetism for such a purpose. There is little to support the suspicion that the utility of the floating fish might have been irreligious, and little to prove that it was from 'Arabians' that Christians learned about it, except that the earliest Christian references to the sea-faring magnetic needle betray an ecstasy similar to that released by the acceptance of the eastern heresies that I was previously discussing. Guyot of Provins, in 1205 or perhaps a few years earlier, welcomes the needle in these terms:

> O that the Holy Father were unchanging, like the star that never moves! This is the star that the sailors watch whenever they can, for by it they keep course. They call it the Tramontane, and while all the other stars wheel round, this stands fixed and motionless. By the virtue of the magnet-stone they practise an art which cannot lie. Taking this ugly dark stone, to which iron will attach itself of its own accord, they find the right point on it which they touch with a needle. Then they lay the needle in a straw and simply place it in water, where the straw makes it float. Its point then turns exactly to the star. There is never any doubt about it, it will never deceive. When the sea is dark and misty, so that neither star nor Moon can be seen, they put a light beside the needle, and then they know their way. Its point is towards the Star, so that the sailor knows how to steer. It is an art that never fails.[17]

The North Star, the Stella Maris or Star of the Sea, had already been 'Christionized', and increasingly became the Star of Mary. A 10th century hymn invoked the Virgin:

Ave maris stella,
Dei Mater alma
Atque semper Virgo,
Felix coeli porta.

In the 12th century uprush of worship of the Lady, Alexander Neckam apostrophizes Mary as the Rose of Delights and Glory of Womanhood, and calls her the Star of the Sea and Queen of the Poles. 'Behold the Pole Star! – the apex of the north, shining out on high. The sailor at night directs his course by it, for it stands motionless at the fixed hinge of the turning sky – and Mary is like the Pole Star'. Dr. Taylor (to whom I am indebted for all these quotations) emphasizes the 'strange and interesting fact' that the compass in all early sea-charts is drawn or painted in the conventional pattern of a star. Each 'direction' had the name of a wind; between the 'winds' were half-winds, quarter-winds, eighth-winds; the pattern was one of star-rays. A further interest is that the name given to the pattern was not 'wind-star' but 'wind-rose'. Those early charts were (and still are) called wind-rose charts, the 'rose' referring to the Virgin.

The curious term *wind-rose* is, in effect, an assertion that the area to which the chart applies either belongs to, or can be reached by, the people faithful to Our Lady. It asserts Our Lady's dominion, nobody else's. The oldest surviving maritime chart of Western Christendom is the Carta Pisana (c. 1275). It is a remarkable, highly-sophisticated and beautifully executed piece of draughtsmanship, the product of a notable combination of skills. It is drawn on sheepskin; the skin is not so trimmed as to conceal its original shape, within which the area covered by the chart is the whole of the Mediterranean. The 'wind-rose' is projected diagrammatically into a geometrical grid which covers the entire area, so that bearings between any two points of the area may be found. The distances are drawn to scale, and the scale is shown in duplicate (one scale drawn vertically, the other horizontally), as if to guard against uneven shrinkage of the parchment. The combination of the skills exhibited is that of mathematical ingenuity coupled with knowledge of shipwork. My uninformed guess is that it was a chart for a shipowner, for head office. To read this large and eminently 'literal' *mappamonde* requires at least a moderate amount

225

of geometry and arithmetic, and a ruler and an accurate pair of dividers must be at hand.

I hope I am not being too fanciful in deriving an impression from the Carta Pisana that it represents a mature effort, and an effort not merely individual but representative of Christendom, to wrest away the Central Sea from Islam. The chart impresses me as an affirmation: 'This sea is ours'. Precision instruments for thorough routine mastery of all that sea were certainly improving in the 13th century, in all the seaports north and west of Sicily. The quivering compass-needle was now, by the more expert compass-makers, contained in a neat box (*buxola*). Islam was raided for some of those compass-makers: the King of Aragon had captured the Balearic Islands from the Arabs in 1229, and after that the Jewish instrument-makers of those islands turned to serve the ruling house of Aragon with astrolabes, time-pieces, drawing-instruments, almanacs and texts. Such brain-drain is a matter of record; also recorded is the competition, in the chart-making business, of Aragon's sea-faring rivals. Genoa, by the beginning of the 14th century, is outstanding for chart production. No less than seven charts from a single Genoese workshop, signed and dated between 1311 and 1327, still proudly exist. Chart-making itself compels attention to empty spaces on the sheepskin; and glancing at the early charts, a thought occurs, perhaps worth mention. In the Carta Pisana the draughtsman shows, by the exuberant projections of his grid into side-excursions, that he would be ready enough to fill in parts unknown, so soon as they were knowable. He does include a sketchy western seaboard of the European continent; but he has started out with the neck of his particular sheepskin pointed to the east. The emphasis, in the Carta Pisana is toward the east. Presently, other chart-makers, consciously or unconsciously, start off with the neck of the sheepskin pointing to the west. The chart-maker's choice, which way to point his sheepskin may be haphazard, or it may be significant. A generation later than the Carta Pisana there is much more detailed charting of an Atlantic coastline as far as the English Channel and Flanders; south and west Ireland and parts of Scotland appear on the Italian charts. More and more patrons of seafaring are thinking westward. Prince John of Aragon, in the 1380's, is conferring gifts and compliments on Abraham Cresques, a Jew in Majorca, spoken of by the Prince as a 'Jew of our house' and 'magister mappamundorum et buxolarum', master of maps and magnetic compasses. It was apparently from Abraham Cresques that Prince John had ordered, in the year 1373, a *Carta de Navegar* which was to show as much as possible of Ocean west of Gibraltar.

The Western Ocean is beginning to be mapped, by 1373, by Cresques and others. There is no knowing how the data was gathered, but I suspect that Ibn-al-Wardi was collecting his information from Catalans and the Genoese, not the other way round. In application of the instruments of knowledge, the competitive Christian princes have outrun whatever Islam could do. I remarked earlier that canonization of the sea-road by the Church would be an important factor in further construction of the Road West; an interesting, if trivial, detail of Church exerting influence, is that when Prince John comes to the throne of Aragon in 1387 and the Jew who was making a world map 'is dead', the unfinished work is handed over to, specifically, 'a Christian master'. Rivalry between Christian principalities, to obtain priority in the Western Ocean, is consciously beginning. Somewhen, on some charts and not on others, before there is other record to show they were officially discovered, the Madeira group of islands and the faraway Azores are pinpricked in. There they are on the charts, before the end of the 14th century. They were in the realm of the oceanography that John of Aragon was studying in 1373. I keep returning to that year because John of Gaunt, Regent of England, was then beginning to regard himself as King of Castile. In December, 1372, Chaucer had been sent to spend eleven months in Italy on his master's business. It seems that business took him first to Genoa and Pisa. I have no knowledge, to what extent the Western Ocean entered into whatever conversation went on in Genoa and Pisa. I would think it was a subject in the air, a matter of possible interest to Chaucer. Certainly John of Gaunt was interested in the control of the Atlantic corridor from England to the Peninsula. I am not supposing that John of Gaunt was peculiarly interested in Madeira or the Azores, those islands that appear in the Medici charts of 1351 and the Catalan charts of 1375. Presently, though, they are of interest to his family. We shall see them claimed and colonized by John of Gaunt's grandson, Henry.

Throughout the 14th century the many schematic *mappa-mondes* of the metaphorical style – the circle of habitable land surrounded by an unknown Ocean Sea – continue to be drawn. Any schematic map of man's world may continue to be so drawn, at any time, present or future; the metaphor it represents is permanent. I have not looked up the context of Gower's lines about

> ... *thilke See which hath no wane,*
> *Y-cleped the gret Occeane*

for the lines themselves tell you that 'thilke See' is that which is ever beyond the boundary of literal knowledge. But the boundary of factual knowledge can always be pushed outward. Side by side with the *mappamondes,* existing simultaneously in the 14th century, are the wind-rose compass charts; and they are speaking in a literal language. The *mappamonde* is reporting 'wisdom'; the chart is reporting 'knowledge' – impersonal geographical knowledge, verifiable by instruments. Verifiable knowledge – the word for it is *conoscenza* – has become a passion with an increasing number of Italians of the 14th century. It is a predatory passion; it looks for unknowns to look into; the wind-rose chart (the Virgin's chart) seeks virgin territory. The Mediterranean has been covered; the charts reach into Ocean. That used to be the *Mare Tenebrosum*; even the Mediterranean, for ancient Greeks, used to be 'wine-dark sea'; but Ocean now is 'blue'. Blue is the Virgin's colour; into blue water spread the wind-rose charts. (Verbal gossamer-thoughts indeed! Place no weight upon them. But *The Golden Legend* exhibits much gossamer word-play).

Looking back at the 14th century, we see two 'worlds' working simultaneously – 'working' in an old sense of the word, working as yeast 'works', as a ferment. We see them as if the world of the sea-chart and the world of the *mappamonde* were quite separate worlds; and sometimes they were, and sometimes they were blended. Sometimes we fail to see the Sea-World working in the minds of those whom *we* choose to class as '*mappamonde*-men'. I mentioned Dante. Attention is often paid to the cosmogony of *The Divine Comedy*, and I am not at all disputing the diagrams that illustrate Dante's method of geographical description, or the placement of Earth, Hell, and the Mount of Purgatory, all in general according with the world of a *mappamonde.* Yet if we look at Canto XXVI of the *Inferno* we can see a Sea-World also. In that Canto Dante's opening invective against Florence, his foreseen exile, his longing for another 'morning' ('and if it were already come, it would not be too early'), the mention of the fireflies (strange little flames), all leads on directly to the interview with whom? – with a larger flame – with Ulysses. I am very sure that none of Dante's 'placements' is haphazard. Who is this Ulysses to whom Dante listens? The message he is made to give to Dante is that no tie of home 'could conquer in me the ardour that I had to gain experience of the world, and of human vice and worth'. This is not Homer's Ulysses: this is a *new* Ulysses, shaping himself to Dante. You feel the touch of ancient flame, and yet it is different. Something old and something new, makes this Ulysses different. The difference is the new voyage, the voyage the old Ulysses did not make.

At the Pillars of Hercules, Dante's Ulysses speaks to his com- panions: 'O brothers! who through a hundred thousand dangers have reached the West, deny not experience of the unpeopled world behind the Sun. Consider your origin: you were not formed to live like brutes, but to follow virtue and knowledge.' Look at the Italian text: there is that word we noticed a moment ago – *conoscenza*, knowledge. Entering in what connection? In connection with navigation, sea- faring, exploration. This is a Ulysses pointing straight at the Western Ocean. The speech to his companions made them so eager for the voyage that willingly they turned the poop of the ship to the morning, her prow to the sunset. After long sailing they approached a new land (*nuova terra*). Alas, the voyage was folly, for from the new land a tempest rose and struck them. Three times round went their gallant ship, and the poop went up and the prow went down, and she sank to the bottom of the sea.

Was Dante thinking of Ugolino di Vivaldo? There is simply no knowing. To try to answer that question would be to dare 'the gret Occeane' of the unknowable that surrounds us all. With what instru- ments do you test Dante's thinking? For me, the Canto which opens with thought of exile, and leaving home, and finding a new morning, leads in a direct run to thoughts from the Sea-World. But the *mappa- monde* is in those thoughts simultaneously.

Now I am ready for the 'world' of John of Gaunt and Chaucer.

Dante was writing the Canto I have referred to at the very beginning
of the 14th century; John of Gaunt and Chaucer were busy in
the latter part and to the end of that century. By their time I am
fairly confident that the Italian rage for measurement, instrumentation, sea-charts – for *conoscenza* – had spread to England. From
what I have glimpsed of John of Gaunt I dared to say that sea
knowledge, particularly of the northern corridor of the Atlantic from
England to the Iberian Peninsula, was of importance to him. In
England of the 20th century the word 'peninsula' still tends to
connote the Iberian Peninsula. That connotation is in the blood. The
abbreviation for the famous shipping line, 'Peninsula and Orient' –
the 'P and O' – summarizes what had been in the mind of Richard the
Lionheart when he sent his fleet to circumnavigate the Peninsula and
to attack the East. P came before O in the alphabet of Richard's
shipmasters. It is the single letter P which seems to me to stand out in
the alphabet of John of Gaunt, with his daughter as Queen in Portugal and his own claim to the throne of Castile.

If the premise is admitted, that instrumentation may have been a
matter for rather special study within the household of John of
Gaunt, then a number of things begin to tie up. If compass and
astrolabe were, in that household, not regarded as oddities but as
utilities, we begin to see a place in the household for a squire familiar
with instruments, who could handle them and know what they could
do. Did instruments have limitations? Were they always trustworthy,
or where and in what circumstances might they deceive? If that was
a question of general interest, it might well have been all the more a
matter of special interest to John of Gaunt. But cut away hypothesis:
here is the story.

A certain friar, Nicholas de Linna (*Linna* standing for King's Lynn
in Norfolk) wrote an account called *Inventio Fortunatae*, in or about
the year 1364, of several voyages (Gerhard Mercator says five or six)
from Norfolk toward and beyond Norway, and also to the westward.
There is nothing unusual about the seamen of Norfolk in the 14th
century being venturesome: Fuller says of Norfolk that 'no county
doth carry a top and gallant more high' in maritime adventure, and of
the seamen, 'none to be offended if a friar be put before the mast'.
The second remark is taken to mean that navigating instruments were
used, and that a friar – a scholar – was needed to operate them. There

is little doubt about the availability of astrolabes in Norfolk; Lynn and nearby Blakeney were then both notable ports, and an astrolabe preserved in the British Museum is inscribed Blakene (Blakeney) 1342. The use of such astrolabes in bouncing ships at sea must however have been difficult. Observations of sufficient accuracy could for the most part only have been taken after landings; and even for experts, computations made without adequate star-tables (or decent chronometers) would seem to me to have been very baffling. That is perhaps the main point of the endeavour of friar (or frere) Nicholas of Lynn. He is reputed to have been a clerk of Oxford and to have been expert with astrolabe and compass, and to him must be applied that friendly remark, 'none to be offended', if he was put before the mast to see what instruments might do.

The voyage of the handy friar which has attracted most attention (and a comical story it is) is concerned not so much with the problems of using the astrolabe in sea-faring, as with the conduct or limitations of the mariners' compass. The story is that Nicholas as navigator persuaded the shipmaster to make a determined effort strictly to follow the compass needle and so to reach, no matter with what hindrance, the North (magnetic) Pole. The mariners' compass, by the time of Nicholas, had been greatly improved as an instrument since the days of Alexander Neckam and Richard the Lionheart. The compass was now in its box (the binnacle, then called *habitaculum* or *bitacle*), a lantern beside (fed with whale-oil), and whether the binnacle was aft or before the mast, Nicholas was concerned to be ever and most scrupulously watchful at the small sheltered housing, by night or day.

The report of the voyage was not fantastically embroidered either by Nicholas or by later scribes. A few maelstroms are mentioned, and nobody familiar with the Pentland Firth or the Norwegian Sea will be unduly sceptical. But what is presently of more concern, no matter where it was they had got to, is that the compass became sick. It had been the best of compasses, but as the ship went on the sickness was worse. The needle, poor thing, began to lose its sanity. I don't know the right name for its behaviour – possibly manic-depressive – and Nicholas could not put a name to it either. He and the magnet were equally distressed. The nearer they came to the Pole, where by all rational thought the compass ought to have been at its happiest, the more miserable the needle became. Into the spindrift Nicholas went on staring for sight of the upright naked mountain, black and shining, the Magnetic Pole itself – the needle's Delectable Mountain, the needle's very Heaven – renewal surely for its perfect life. The needle, on the contrary, the farther they went, grew worse. All the needle could do was to dip its head. It dipped its head most aimlessly and twisted sluggishly and most pathetically. Nicholas himself, staring desperately for the Reviving Mountain, was eventually so demented that he thought he saw it – or it may be some copyist who said he did. Leave it that he fancied he did. The fancied vision of the black and shining Pole had no beneficial effect on the needle. It was now useless, demented unto death.

Now the manuscript account of his voyages as written by Nicholas is no longer to be found, though copies of *Inventio Fortunatae* circulated for a long time after 1364. In the 16th century the narrative of this voyage was studied and seemed of importance to Gerhard Mercator and to John Dee, and from their quotations the tale may be pieced together. S. I. Varshavskiy, in his study of Nicholas of Lynn suggests that Nicholas may have got into the Hudson Strait, possibly into Hudson's Bay.[18] Wherever the ship got to, she was eventually turned back; and on the return voyage Nicholas observed and noted that the needle 'grew well again'.

The story has sometimes been dismissed as a fabrication, or as an example of foolish credulity, or as something to be greeted with a superior guffaw. I regard it as a true story – one that happens to be highly comical, and at the same time representative of a serious and spirited experiment. Everybody knows that the behaviour of the magnetic compass in the high latitudes is erratic, and that near the magnetic pole it is not to be relied on. Precisely – and who started that bit of *conoscenza*, knowledge? The discovery of the magnetic dip is nowadays recognized to have been a matter of immense stimulation to scientific thinking. Where *did* the power reside, that attracted the compass needle? The French crusader, Peregrine of Picardy, had written about the magnet in 1269; like Neckam, he believed the attractive 'virtue' resided in the sky – in Mary's star, the Polar Star. Roger Bacon thought otherwise, a magnetic pole on earth, and that was what Nicholas set out to find. It was not only John Dee and Gerhard Mercator who puzzled over the 'dip' that Nicholas reported;

it was also Dr. William Gilbert of Colchester, court physician to Queen Elizabeth, commonly called 'the first great English experimentalist' – unless you feel 'frere Nicholas' might have a share in the title. Mercator thought Nicholas had proved that the source of magnetic attraction was inside the earth; Gilbert made a spherical lodestone and pushed a tiny compass-needle over its surface; it behaved like Nicholas's needle; it dipped at either pole. Thus the earth was one large lodestone, and so perchance were other heavenly bodies. After Gilbert, magnetism became the archetype of action-at-a-distance, and, as Mr. Koestler points out, 'paved the way for the recognition of universal gravity'.

> Without the demonstrable phenomena of magnetic attraction, people would have been even more reluctant to exchange the traditional view that heavy bodies tended towards the centre of the universe, for the implausible suggestion that all heavenly bodies were tugging at each other 'with ghostly fingers' across empty space.[19]

Nicholas of Lynn quite clearly started something; but from that digression I return to the daily affairs of John of Gaunt's household.

It is about further appearances of a Nicholas that more serious doubts have been expressed. Some scholars have assumed or asserted (as for instance Dr. Varshavskiy) that the voyages of Nicholas of Lynn, and his expertise with astrolabe and compass, came so favourably to the attention of John of Gaunt that Nicholas was added to John of Gaunt's household as a squire; as, and for other abilities, Chaucer was added to that same royal household in 1369.

Professor Lowes uses a quotation to indicate what the occupations of a squire of a royal household might at that time be:

> These Esquires of household of old be accustomed, winter and summer, in afternoon and evenings, to draw to Lord's chambers within court, there to keep honest company according to their skill, in talking of chronicles of kings, and of other policies, or in piping, or harping, singing, or martial acts, to help occupy the court.

This comes from the *Household Book of Edward IV,* and the interests mentioned may or may not completely cover the range of

John of Gaunt's interests. Now Dr. Varshavskiy assumes (with others) that a friar who was fetched to and served at the court of John of Gaunt at the time Chaucer was there was Nicholas of Lynn; that Chaucer caught from Nicholas the importance of the astrolabe; and further, that in his irrepressible jocularity Chaucer used and made fun of this same 'hende Nicholas' in the *Miller's Tale*. The multiple identification pulses outward from the mention in Chaucer's prose treatise on the Astrolabe that he was intending to make use of tables compiled by 'frere N. Lenne'. Professor Lowes expresses himself in diametrical opposition to this: he will have nothing to do with the 'legend' of Nicholas of Lynn (or Linna), does not allude to a Nicholas having been at the court of John of Gaunt, and dismisses any identification of the Nicholas of Lynn with the 'frere N. Lenne' as resting 'on evidence far too shadowy to trust'.

I am primarily concerned with John of Gaunt's world, and to that end brought in Chaucer as a witness. Professor Lowes was eager to get on with his discussion of Chaucer's poetry and of Chaucer's eye for human characters. What I fear is that those to whom Lowes' lectures are beguiling may dismiss Chaucer's prose treatise on the astrolabe as exhibiting no 'human characters'. But as evidence of what Chaucer thought about his world, the world at Court, John of Gaunt's world, and how to get on in it, the prose treatise on the astrolabe is important. *That* treatise, happily, exists; is there in Chaucer's work, to be read. The pertinent question is, why should Chaucer at the age of 51 set out to write for his son of 10 a handbook about the instrument?

One human character is somewhat revealed in that prose treatise: the character of Chaucer himself. The character as there revealed is not that of a man whose sole world was that of the *mappamonde*. The treatise is evidence of the simultaneous existence at the court of John of Gaunt of the other geographical world. What caused Chaucer himself to pick up the instrument, to study it? Somebody taught him the fairly complicated procedure with the astrolabe and the augrimstones, and something impressed on him the view that instrumentation was a means of getting on, at least – this is my guess – with his particular master. I confess I am fully as partisan in my wish to bring Nicholas of Lynn into the court of John of Gaunt with Chaucer, as is Professor Lowes in his wish to keep 'frere N. Lenne' out of it. Shadowy indeed is the evidence; but what sort of evidence do you expect? Somebody taught Chaucer the astrolabe – and for the multiple identification, that the somebody was Nicholas of Lynn and also the 'hende Nicholas' of Oxford and the *Miller's Tale*; that the same somebody was a fellow squire whose special gift for scientific skills gained him perhaps some special favour at the court, where it may have been fair game to poke fun at him, yet not without grudging respect – well, what can anybody say to that amusing conundrum? We all know that Chaucer could take head, body, legs each from a different person and make them into one coherent figment, if he wished to tell a Canterbury Tale. I wouldn't dare to be too bold about the multiple identification. I wouldn't dare deny it, either. It is odd that in selecting a 'scientific' competitor the name Nicholas should come to Chaucer so naturally. One Nicholas of his, that astrolabist at Oxford, won his contest. Though 'hende Nicholas' was 'scalded in the toute', nevertheless, he had got what he wanted. An odd coincidence indeed that Chaucer should call that astrolabist Nicholas, and that he should choose to send his only son to Oxford to learn the astrolabe.

Whatever all this amounts to, Chaucer's action as regards the education of his son draws attention to the value placed on instrument work at the court of John of Gaunt. Of my Lord's private quarters – my Lord who claimed Castile, whose daughter married Portugal – I only provide a shadowy glimpse. On the long table in my Lord's chamber, I see sea-charts, not *mappamondes*. I see Nicholas of Lynn standing beside his master at that table, pointing at sea-marks, venturing to lecture. What was Nicholas's lecture? That in far northern or north-westerly seas the compass needle did not work. (In another language altogether, Dr. Dölger says that the fish in some waters was not *Der Heilige Fisch* but *Der nichtsnutzige Fisch*, the useless fish). The information – the behaviour of the floating fish – was that going to be useless to John of Gaunt, to Philippa and the grandsons? I cannot know, I cannot see, it may be only fancy that Philippa and the grandsons got the message. The message was: study the Sea-World, learn the instruments; the compass was mad only to the north-north-west: the other end was sane, which pointed south.

My ghostly glimpses may be only motes to trouble the mind's eye. Whether the five grandsons picked up the impulse from John of Gaunt or from other sources, they all, and in particular Prince Henry, paid notable attention to the Sea-World. Prince Henry in due course set up what Morison calls his 'combined hydrographic and marine intelligence office' at Cape St. Vincent, and that 'attracted ambitious seamen from all over the Mediterranean'. Many voyages probed westward, but the great tradition established by Prince Henry and mostly favoured by the Portuguese was to go south. The compass in the latitudes to which they sailed was behaving itself. South, until Africa had been surrounded – then east for India.

The glimpses have prepared us for Columbus.

Columbus arrived in Portugal in 1476 at the age of 25. In 1485, at the end of a nine-year period, and at the age of 34, he left Portugal for Spain.

He arrived in Portugal by accident, as a ship-wrecked seaman. A brother was already at Lisbon as a chart-maker; at first Columbus worked with his brother; then within a year he shipped on a Portuguese vessel in the North Atlantic trade, exchanging produce between the Azores, Ireland and Iceland. In the following year he captained a ship for merchants of Genoa for whom he had previously been a seaman: the advancement shows that his ability was recognized, and the voyage taught a lesson. Instructions were to purchase a cargo of sugar at Madeira and deliver it at Genoa. Columbus set sail before securing the money for the cargo; the producers at Funchal in the Madeiras refused to supply on credit; Columbus arrived at Genoa either without the sugar or without title to it. There was nothing to complain of in his navigation or his seamanship, but there was a tedious lawsuit about the sugar, which kept him in Genoa in the summer of 1479.

After the lawsuit it so happened that Columbus never returned to Genoa, though Genoa remained, in legal terms, his domicile; he ever regarded himself, and was regarded by others in Portugal and Spain, as Genoese. At the age of 29 he was back in Lisbon and was married to Doña Felipa Perestrello e Moniz, daughter of the captain of Porto Santo in the Madeiras, granddaughter of a knight companion of Prince Henry; Professor Morison emphasizes that she was 'scion of one of the first families of Portugal'. The marriage was a considerable step-up for Columbus, though it is possible it made the King of Portugal (Prince Henry's nephew) suspicious of him. 'A big talker and boastful' is an opinion which the King, or those about him, formed about Columbus.

The 'boastfulness' came from Columbus declaring his intention of winning the race to cross the Ocean Sea and reach the Orient by sailing westward. Professor Morison indicates that this hypothetical and in effect junior race, was not a wholly new idea. The senior race, for Portuguese, which had been started by Prince Henry and his brothers, was as we have seen to set off southward and circumnavigate Africa. The capture of Ceuta from the Moors in 1415 – an expedition blessed by Philippa from her death-bed, in which apparently all five of her sons were engaged – had started off the senior race in the triple aspect of a Crusade. The first aspect, as viewed from the court of Portugal, was as a crusade for military glory and for ready loot (part of the same heritage as Richard the Lionheart's 'Loode males'). The second was as a crusade for which complete and blanket authority had been applied for and received from the Papacy – to extend the Faith to peoples of any new lands discovered. For this the Portuguese had from the Pope the sole prerogative. The third aspect, emphasized by Prince Henry as of utmost importance to Portugal, a country poor in natural resources, was that of a trade-crusade, for planters to plant the flag and under its protection acquire produce.

For Henry, the capture of Ceuta initiated a succession of trading-posts along the west coast of Africa, way-stations on the way to the Indies. Since 1415, in this endeavour to establish an 'Africa and Orient' Line Portuguese seamen had been remarkably persistent. Each new station planted on the coast of Africa was a new farthest south; rounding the bulge into the Gulf of Guinea was a wonderful stimulus in this senior race: India, the main prize, just round that corner. But the Gulf of Guinea, though it gave a shipmaster the Ivory Coast, the Gold Coast, the forests of much-needed timber, also fetched him against the impassable and menacing obstruction of the country of the Cameroons. South, and apparently for ever south of the Gulf of Guinea, there was an intolerable amount of Africa to be circumnavigated. Competitors in the senior race kept plugging at it. But as years and years went by there was the more encouragement for thoughts about a junior race, Westward to Orient. Though it might involve a lengthy voyage without way-stations, it was the course that appealed to Columbus. It was the junior race that he was determined to win.

It is hardly likely that among seamen at the port of Lisbon, or among the King's councillors at the court of Portugal, there was complete agreement about the Westward to Orient cross-ocean sea-race being recognizably 'on'. The faith urged by Prince Henry was that Ocean, though unknown, was knowable; and one accepts that at the time Columbus was in Portugal, extension of the sea-charts was an established passion. Nevertheless, except to the most passionate, the literal sea-chart did not wholly sever itself from the metaphorical *mappamonde*. The emblems which fill in empty spaces in the old charts often represent both fun and fancy. In Humphrey's edition of *Old Decorative Maps and Charts* there are plenty of pleasing sea-monsters which lived on in many imaginations for centuries after Columbus. The whale, for instance, in the wild and distant seas where he rolled his island bulk: you see him in Ortelius (in the 16th century) making tracks away from Nova Zembla, and spouting with two spouts – or there he is, ubiquitous, off the East Indies – or you see Saxton's thin Cornish whale, or Wagenaar's pained Portuguese whale, or De Bry's Mexican puffer, Linschoten's African monster, or Mercator's Virginian beauty. All those whales are of the grand days when chart-making was the pride of decorators.

> *Who in innavigable seas*
> *Place mermen, whales, and what they please.*

In the sea-scape of those charts there is also something of

> *The backward look behind the assurance*
> *Of recorded history, the backward half-look*
> *Over the shoulder, towards the primitive terror.*

It is hard to believe that at the time of Columbus there was, even in Lisbon, general or complete exorcism of terror of the sea. Landscapes (as in an engraving by Dürer) could show the Christian man-at-arms in the dark wood, surrounded by foul fiends, all the more terrible if half-disbelieved; and in the unknown Ocean was Christian seaman less beset?

> *For all that here on earth we dreadful hold,*
> *Be but as bugs to fearen babes withal,*
> *Comparèd to the creatures in the sea's entrall.*

238

Not to all landsmen, not to all seamen, was the imagined whale a friendly animal; he or some other monster might be Leviathan himself, for whom 'what thing soever cometh within the chaos of his mouth, be it beast, boat, or stone, down it goes all incontinently that foul great swallow of his, and perisheth in the bottomless gulf of his paunch'. Ships go down at sea, and men come back no more; something swallows them. Bad seamanship, Columbus said; bad gear, or else bad navigation.

The school to which Columbus belonged was literal-minded; that is to say, it seems to have been completely cocksure as to what it assumed to be 'fact'. The fact was, the world was round; therefore the fact was you could sail west to the Orient. A fascinating medley of persuasive 'facts' was gathered to support the contention; no fact or fancy to the contrary was to be allowed to stand. For the first year or so of his marriage Columbus and his wife were quartered in Lisbon with Doña Felipa's mother. Within that household, when Christopher's brother Bartholomew and others of the 'West to Indies' school (or their opponents) were present, there must have been some fascinating conversations. Was the world really a sphere? Was there no danger of sailing to the edge of the plate and falling off? Wasn't the ocean too broad, the distance to the Indies too great, for the supply of food and water? What of the contrary winds, which had so far prevented anyone from beating far to the westward of the Azores?

Distance and winds – there is evidence that Columbus pondered these questions most seriously. After the time with Doña Felipa's mother, the young couple moved to Porto Santo in the Madeiras, where Doña Felipa's brother was governor. There their only child, Diego, was born. Later they moved to Funchal. Columbus in this period made voyages (Morison says probably two, on at least one of which he commanded a ship) to and from the Gold Coast. One would think it certain that he put into the Canaries, and probably into the Cape Verde Islands, for from his subsequent actions it is clear that he was studying all he could about what came later to be called the trade winds, and studying for a right point of departure, better than the Azores, for a voyage west. It was at this time that Columbus learned that Toscanelli, most learned, most reputable physician of Florence, had written to a Portuguese friend in 1474 urging a voyage due west to Japan – only 3,000 miles, said Toscanelli, from Lisbon. This was indeed a most exciting 'fact'. It fitted perfectly. Morison describes how eagerly Columbus wrote to Toscanelli, and how in 1471 or early 1482, Columbus received and prized an encouraging reply from the physician and another chart. 'The Toscanelli letter and chart were always', says Professor Morison, 'his Exhibits "A" and "B".'

So the Enterprise of the Indies, as Columbus called it, was born. Others had tried to find an island of Antilia west of the Azores, but what he would find was the Asia of Marco Polo. He was satisfied that prevailing winds would favour a start from the Canaries, 9 degrees west of Lisbon. Therefore he would refine Toscanelli's computation. The length of the ocean voyage from the Canaries to Japan would be 2,400 nautical miles. 'The actual air-line distance,' Professor Morison remarks, 'is 10,600 miles.'

Columbus collected other facts which supported his Plan, and the Plan was presented and argued in person to King John II of Portugal in 1484. It was at that time that the King came to regard Columbus as 'a big talker and boastful', and 'gave him small credit'. The King referred the project to a Committee. The Committee gave its decision, a flat negative, in 1485.

Doña Felipa had returned to Lisbon with Columbus and the child, Diego. In 1485, she died.

These blows in swift succession finished Columbus's career in Lisbon. In that same year he had the bitterness of seeing the King authorize two Portuguese mariners, Dulmo and Estreito, to set forth westward to discover Antilia if they could.

Columbus did not linger in Lisbon. Before the end of the summer of 1485, taking with him Diego (who was barely five years old) he went aboard a coasting vessel for Palos, the nearest port of Spain. He was not giving up his Enterprise of the Indies. In Spain would come another morning.

NOTES

1. Samuel Eliot Morison's classic work, *Admiral of the Ocean Sea*, appeared in 1942 in a two-volume edition (Little, Brown & Co., Boston). My references throughout this chapter are to his shorter work, *Chris-*

topher Columbus, Mariner (The New American Library, a Mentor Book, 6th printing, 1964).

2. *Conceived in Liberty* by Marshall Smelser and Harry W. Kirwin (Doubleday, Catholic Textbook Division, New York, 4th printing, 1957).

3. I refer to two volumes by Franz Joseph Dölger, *Das Fischsymbol in früchristlicher Zeit* (Tipographia Roma, 1910) and *Der Heilige Fisch* (Münster in Westf., 1922). The seal on p. 208 is copied from the cover of the latter.

The adoption of the mnemonic *ichthys* as a specifically Christian symbol is all that I am here alluding to. (The reference to Augustine is to *The City of God*, III, 249). There has been an enormous amount of scholarly attention to the Fish as symbol of life renewed and sustained, among peoples other than early Christians and in religions earlier than Christianity. Jessie L. Weston, in *From Ritual to Romance* (Cambridge, 1920) draws on Cumont for the special respect paid to the fish cultivated in ponds near the temple of Astarte (or Atargatis) in Babylon. She speaks (p. 126) of the belief of priests and initiates that in partaking of the fish as food on ritual occasions they were partaking of the flesh of the goddess, and she refers to the opinion of Eisler and others that familiarity with this ritual of renewal of life was gained and adopted by the Jews during the Captivity. I am not clear how the Jews in Babylon came to accept the same day (Friday) as the Babylonians for a Messianic Fish-meal, but Miss Weston's statement is explicit: 'From the Jews the custom spread to the Christian Church, where it still flourishes, its true origin, it is needless to say, being wholly unsuspected.' George Pitt-Rivers, in *The Riddle of the 'Labarum'* (Allen & Unwin, London, 1966) provides plates of the fish-symbol and the Chaldean fish-god, illustrating the reappearance of the fish-god's head in the Christian Bishops' and Abbots' mitres.

My mentor who introduced me to chocolate fish at Easter is David Morrice Low.

4. For traditional colours for Faith, Hope, Charity see for instance *Purgatorio*, xxix, 121–129.

5. The anonymous 14th century chronicler and the definition of 'Loode males' as travelling-trunks are found by looking up *Lode-male* (*loode* = *lode*) in the Oxford English Dictionary.

The references to Sir Walter Scott are to *The Talisman*. For the English Crusaders in Lisbon, see the introduction by William C. Atkinson to his translation of *The Lusiads* by Camoens (Penguin Books, 1952), and for Richard's fleet see Miss K. M. E. Murray's contribution to Austin Lane Poole's symposium on *Medieval England* (Oxford University Press, 1958).

6. Alexander Neckam may be pursued in Thorndike, *A History of Magic and Experimental Science*, Vol. II and in *The Haven-Finding Art* by E. G. R. Taylor. Professor Taylor tells the story of Richard's evasion of the sea-trip.

7. Here and later I refer to *Geoffrey Chaucer* by John Livingstone Lowes (Oxford University Press, 1934). The diagram on p. 215 I have copied from p. 32 and the remarks quoted from Professor Lowes are thereabouts.

8. *Amicus Plato, sed magis amica veritas* is the way Don Quixote chose to write the scrap of Latin, at the conclusion of his letter to Sancho Panza advising him how to govern the Island of Barataria. It is a very free translation of an expression of Aristotle in the *Nicomachean Ethics*, where he is about to controvert some of his master's opinions.

9. The famous lines of Sappho here referred to appear as Fragment No. 149 in *Lyra Gracca*, translated by J. M. Edmonds, Vol. I (Loeb Classical Library). In translation:

> O Hesperus ... thou bringest the sheep, thou bringest the goat, thou bringest her child home to the mother.

10. In the *History of the Conquest of Peru* by William H. Prescott, Seneca's prophecy is mentioned in a footnote (in my 1886 edition it comes at p. 90). The lines are often quoted or alluded to in books about Columbus, from Washington Irving to Samuel Eliot Morison.

The translation of the *Medea* by John Studley is in *Seneca: His Tenne Tragedies* (The Tudor Translations: Constable, London, and Knopf, New York, 1927) Vol II. The snatch I have quoted from Studley is from the chorus at the end of the second act. The lines given in Latin in the footnote on p. 218 form the peroration of that chorus. Studley so much softens the peroration that I have not quoted his version. Perhaps in England of Elizabethan times it was not politic, perhaps not believable, to exclaim that voyages across the Western Ocean might carry, or bring back, disaster.

11. For Arnobius, see Lemprière and the O.E.D. (under Canary).

12. *The Golden Legend*, compiled by J. De Voragine (floruit c. 1270) was Englished by William Caxton, who printed his version about 1483. I have quoted from The Temple Classics edition of Caxton's version (Dent, London) where the *Life of St. Brandon* appears in Vol. III, p. 48.

13. *The Haven-Finding Art,* pp. 76, 77.

14. Anyone interested in the Wandering Isles, and a full accretion of romantic trappings of Ocean, is probably familiar with (or if not will find pleasure in turning to) 'The Tower of Bliss' in Spenser's *The Faerie Queene,* Book II, Canto xii. This canto is given entire in Vol. I of *Poets of the English Language* edited by W. H. Auden and Norman Holmes Pearson (Viking, New York and Eyre & Spottiswoode, London, 1952).

15. *Geschichte des Zuckers* by Edmund O. von Lippman (Springer, Berlin, 1929) mentions that Posidonius provides the first reference to the Canary Islands as 'Islands of the Blest', and that the Canaries are so referred to by Plutarch (A.D. 40–120) and Mela (about A.D. 50), and Mela seems to speak of the Cape Verdes as 'Hesperides'. Pliny says that there are other 'Fortunate Isles' farther in the Ocean, and Juba speaks of the farther isles as 'Purple Isles'. Both of these 'farthers' may be the Cape Verdes. (For the colourful character Juba II, King of Numidia and Mauretania, I refer to Lemprière.) The term 'Purple Isles', also applied to the Canaries, was used by Horace as if both the Canaries and the outer isles provided dye-stuff. For this dye-stuff Lippmann uses the word *'Orseille-flechte'.* In English *orseille* is a variant of *orchil* (see the O.E.D.) and orchil means a red or violet dye prepared from certain lichens or special sea-weed. *Orchilla-weed* is mentioned in Cook's *Voyages* (1790) as supplied by the Canary Islands. Bancroft (1813) says *orchella* was growing abundantly at the Cape Verde Islands. It looks as if we may have to swing back to Carthaginian voyages and the search for a dye-substitute for the murex. Has Juba, of Numidia and Mauretania, retained memories originating in Carthage? *Encyclopaedia Britannica* mentioned that Carthaginian coins have been found on Corvo. If so, I would like to know who put them there.

  Lippmann gathers his references together in Chapter X, p. 401. The reference to Horace is to Epistles II, 2, 181.

16. At the beginning of *The Life and Voyages of Christopher Columbus* Washington Irving (in 1831) quoted a passage from Xerif al Edrisi to prove 'that at the beginning of the 15th century . . . a profound ignorance prevailed among the learned as to the western regions of the Atlantic; its vast waters were regarded with awe and wonder, seeming to bound the world as with a chaos, into which conjecture could not penetrate, and enterprise feared to adventure'. The passage quoted by Irving provided an effective opening for his book, though my interpretation of Edrisi is different. As to what was thought by 'the

learned' at the beginning of the 15th century, that is what I am struggling with in the text.

17. Taylor, *The Haven-Finding Art*, pp. 95, 96.

18. For the reference to Dr. Varshavskiy and for the courtesy of seeing a translation of the Russian text (Moscow, 1960), I am very much indebted to Mr. Gordon W. Creighton of the Royal Geographical Society. I have drawn on Professor Taylor's *The Haven-Finding Art* for some of the details about Nicholas of Lynn and about the compass of his time, but I have drawn even more upon the translation of Dr. Varshavskiy's study – specifically, for the quotation from Fuller, for the astrolabe marked Blakene, for the references to Gerhard Mercator and John Dee, and for the bit of the Irish poem which I quoted on p. 220. My respect for Dr. Varshavskiy and my sympathies as regards the 'multiple identification' of the Nicholases are indicated in my text; and I hope the English translation of his work may soon appear in print.

19. Arthur Koestler, *The Act of Creation* (Hutchinson, London, 1964). I am quoting from the edition of Pan Books Ltd., 1966, p. 670.

CHAPTER 12

Another Morning

I PAUSED at a critical moment in the story of Columbus. The year was 1485. The adventurer was setting foot in Spain at the small frontier port of Palos, above the mouth of the Rio Tinto, four miles upstream from the Franciscan monastery of La Rábida. The monastery stood (and stands) on the bluff where the river, coloured by mineral deposits, meets the estuary named Rio Saltés.

Nine years before, as a distressed Genoese seaman, Columbus had reached the thriving port of Lisbon, the port then in ascendancy above all others of the westward-facing Atlantic seaboard. There he conceived his ambitious Plan; but his career in Portugal had come to grief. He was now stepping ashore at an inconspicuous river-port on the frontier of Castile. He knew nobody in Castile; nobody knew of him. He was now a distressed sea-captain. He might be a master-mariner with a bee in his bonnet. He was also a stranger at Palos: a widower, short of funds, with a five-year-old child tugging at his hand.

Why did Columbus, in 1485, turn with confidence toward Castile? I assume his confidence partly from the fact that he brought the boy, Diego, with him. But why should Columbus have particular hopes of finding support in Castile? Nine years before, I doubt if gossip among professional seamen in Lisbon had dwelt much upon Castile. Unless something very dramatic had happened within Castile, Columbus's action in landing with Diego at Palos is difficult to understand. What had made Castile suddenly prominent in maritime affairs?

It is for specialist historians to analyse precisely the dynamics of the explosion whereby, within little more than half a century, the court of a relatively backward, poor and isolated part of the Peninsula came to rule the greatest empire since antiquity – 'greatest' in a geographical sense, or by other measures of momentary opulence or of temporary power over a wide range of unruly peoples, or by the measure of fear and envy accorded to the Court of Spain by other

Courts of Western Christendom. I have been preparing to be surprised at the sudden emergence of a spirit of conquest in Old Castile, but coming to it I remain astonished. Fortunately an English-speaking reader finds an increasing number of serious books which discuss the theme of Spain's swift rise to power: I turn for example to *The Spanish Seaborne Empire* by Professor J. H. Parry.[1]

I also turn to Lord Acton's *Lectures on Modern History*.[2] I need to refer to the contrast he conveys between the spirit of Renaissance in Italy and the simultaneous spirit of Reconquista in Spain. You cannot escape from the observation that within two societies of people not wholly dissimilar, not far removed from each other, there arose at the same period of time collective aspirations which are very different: in the one the emphasis on rebirth, in the other the emphasis on conquest. Acton reminds us:

> The one thing common to the whole Italian Renaissance was the worship of beauty. It was the aesthetic against the ascetic. In this exclusive study, that is, in art, the Italians speedily attained the highest perfection that has been reached by man. And it was reached almost simultaneously in many parts of Italy, Rome, Florence, Milan, and Venice.

Without elaboration, we agree that sometime after the time of Dante and on the 'thrashing-floor' of Italy there occurred a collective response to the notion of making a new way of living: 'new' in the sense of exhibiting a wider range of interests than other peoples had managed to exhibit since the flowering-time of the Greeks. A recognition of what some of the ancients had thought and done, the outburst of desire to 'make it new', the opening of the sphere of human sensibility 'for the delight, honour, and benefit of human nature' – one uses much later phrases to describe the rebirth, but each must describe or acknowledge the phenomenon – there was here the discovery of new purposes in living beyond the usual blind drives for affluence or power.

To point the contrast between what was exciting in Italy and what was exciting in the then contemporary Spain, it is not necessary to pretend that Rome was a city of sweetness, or to maintain that it had come to be on speaking terms with the City of God. Lord Acton is not hastily basing the distinction between the ideas dominant in Italy and Spain on moral values; yet he is eager to convey that as regards the behaviour of the two peoples there was in Italy a happy expansion of all kinds of activity, a wealth of fields of competition for diverse individual talents. Acton delights in the tolerance in Italian behaviour which was not a mere tolerance of apathy, of not caring. He remarks that Erasmus, who had no sort of clerical bias, 'warmly extols the light and liberty which he found at Rome in 1515, at the very eve of the Reformation'.

Spain of the same period presents a different picture. There is a feeling that the contrast is like that of Athens and Sparta. Before the accession of Isabella to the throne of Castile in 1474, what gambit had been made by Old Castile and León in the affairs of Western Christendom? In preceding generations we have an impression of Old Castile as of arid highlands, ruled by feudal castles, and with soldiery possibly more savage than those who in Italy developed the code of the *Condottiéri*. We accept that it was a rough country of hardships and hazards, at times a hunting-ground for bloody-minded fighters in coat-armour from any part of Europe, seeking adventure or seeking perhaps to be shriven at the shrine of Saint James of the Field of the Star (Santiago de Compostela) who, when vested with his red brocade, was also Santiago Matamoros, the Moor Slayer. We read that medieval cavaliers from Old Castile, for whom The Cid (with his famous horse, Babieca) was the exemplar, had long ago ranged from the highlands and captured much of the south. In the south was the New Castile, with Seville, after its capture in 1248, a residence of Castilian Kings. The southern land of Andalusia was a good land, with easy climate, and with the pleasures of luxurious and sophisticated life to be enjoyed in formerly Muslim cities, where an exciting architecture and graceful fountains and pleasure-gardens were visible reminders of the joy of being alive.

Professor Parry describes the drift of colonists from Old Castile and the north of Spain which went on for two hundred years after the capture of Seville: colonists attracted by the southern country 'and by the prospect of lording it over a Muslim population reduced by conquest to an inferior status'. Formerly Muslim cities (and Granada, which maintained precarious independence) kept up a reputation, each for special products – Toledo for arms and armour, Córdoba for leather-wear, Granada and Almería for silk, Málaga and Valencia for pottery. It was 'in the Andalusian melting-pot' that settlers from many parts of the Peninsula 'gradually lost their regional differences and became Spaniards', and that the Castilian language became a rich, flexible and beautiful instrument. It would seem that in the two hundred years preceding the period of Isabella there was in the New Castile of the south the possibility of economic stability and the development of a way of life within which Christian, Muslim and Jewish communities could live side by side, perhaps not loving each other, yet without such violent intolerance as would destroy a 'pax Hispana'. 'In Andalusia,' says Professor Parry, 'the Castilians developed their own domestic imperialism and formed the habits of conquest and settlement which they would inevitably, sooner or later, seek to exercise beyond the boundaries of Spain.'

Here I object to the use of that word 'inevitably'. What happened, happened: but why should it be regarded as inevitable that Spaniards and Italians chose, each in a collective way and at the same period, such contrasting views of what makes life worth living? – ways that are summed up in the terms *Reconquista* and *Renaissance*. The old disease of Reconquista did not emerge again in violent form until Isabella, with Ferdinand beside her, was in command of Old Castile; and how that came to happen is a story in which there were opportunities for people to choose between one way of life and another.

The story begins under circumstances as apparently absurd as those of comic opera. The red-haired ghost of John of Gaunt keeps beckoning from the wings. I intimated that Isabella's father, John II of Castile, was a grandson of John of Gaunt. For a time the Castilian strain of John of Gaunt's blood was relatively mild. Unlike the Portuguese grandsons, John of Castile displayed no outstanding ambition for empire, conquest or crusading. Very early in life it was made clear to him that affairs of state were to be managed by stronger hands: when he was eight years old there arrived at his court the remarkable Alvaro de Luna, the illegitimate product of a famous family of Aragon. John grew up in complete domination of Alvaro. The first wife Alvaro provided for John produced an heir to the throne, referred to (according to the whim of the historian) as Henry or Enrique.

It was a second marriage Alvaro arranged for John that unexpectedly resulted in Alvaro's own downfall. The second marriage was to John's Portuguese cousin (the princess who gave birth to Isabella), and that princess would not stand for her husband being dominated by anyone but herself. Alvaro had been in power for thirty years and held the highest offices; she demanded his removal. It was Isabella's mother who ordered Alvaro's public execution. John consented. Then John died, when Isabella was three years old. Her older half-brother, Henry or Enrique, became Henry IV of Castile. Isabella was now redundant: she and her widowed mother were retired to an inconspicuous country town (Arévalo) where the formidable mother is said to have lapsed gradually into 'a state of melancholy insanity'.

Thus towards the end of the 15th century affairs were going on in Old Castile: intrigues none the less violent for being remote. The highland castles 'perched on every suitable crag' were, as in medieval times, primarily fortresses. Feudal ties were loose, 'based upon personal loyalty rather than on territorial dependence or jurisdiction'. The economy of the northern *meseta* was still predominantly pastoral, 'based on the grazing of immense flocks of sheep, herds of pigs and half-wild cattle'. Professor Parry also suggests that the masters of flocks and herds fitted well enough into the migratory cycle of the open range; 'the peasant, conversely, tied to his land, was economically vulnerable and socially despised'. This picture of the still feudal heritage of northern Castile strongly contrasts with the lowland south, and when Henry IV of Castile showed himself even more inclined than his father had been to dally at Seville in preference to the rough life of the north, the blood of John of Gaunt seemed to be running even thinner. I can see that Henry's preference for the way of life in the south, his apparent pleasure in a peaceable integration of Christians, Muslims, Jews into one society, his predisposition to some of the impulses which were more galvanic in Italy – 'the aesthetic against the ascetic' – might easily, in the north, have aroused disgust; but I see as yet no expectation that from the north of Castile there was to come any world-shaking explosion of energy.

The way ahead for Castilians was not pre-determined. On either side of them, Italians were going one way, Portuguese were going another. What I do see is that John's display of interest in a 'cultural' way of life had been ineffectual. If he had been a man to seek out and encourage what Acton calls 'a generation of men remarkable for originality', he might have changed the story. But John was devoid of much spark; and if John failed to make a 'cultural' development seem lively and adventurous, his successor Henry more notably succeeded in bringing 'culture' into disrepute. I said that historians according to whim call this older half-brother of Isabella either Henry or Enrique: mostly he is recorded as Enrique the Impotent. Whatever the truth about his sexual impotence, the sneer was delightful to those who disliked him, and, by implication, wished to cast discredit on any way of life that he encouraged. Nothing comparable to the Italian Renaissance was likely to be fostered by a man so easily derided.

Like his father, Enrique left affairs of state to a court favourite, in this case Juan Pacheco. Pacheco, a 'New Christian' of Jewish descent, was the same age as Enrique, and nasty imputations were made as to their relationship. Manners at Court aroused the scorn of the feudal nobility, as being 'hedonistic and disorderly'. Yet there was nothing so excessive in the conduct of Enrique or, for that matter, in the temper of the nobles of Castile, as to cause his reign to be cut short. He was to die a natural death; and his legitimate successor would inherit the throne of Old Castile and León, including New Castile.

So far as concerned the rest of the Western world, these events might have been happening in Tibet. Even as late as 1474, when Isabella became queen at the age of 23, the story continues to have the unreal atmosphere of comic opera. Isabella had been born at a small country town or village with the musical name of Madrigal de las Atlas Torres; as a not much-needed half-sister of Enrique her formative years were spent as I said in seclusion with a reputed increasingly insane mother at Arévalo.[3] A very strict religious discipline, much employment upon needlework, a general absence of lavishness or such funds as might have befitted the blood royal – these give a picture of Isabella as a kind of Cinderella. Yet as the girl grew up it became evident that she might be heir to the crown of Castile. Progeny of her half-brother Enrique would take precedence, but was Enrique, or was he not, Enrique the Impotent?

It was said that Enrique's first marriage, made when he was a boy of 15, had not been consummated. He was married for a second time to Joana of Portugal, one of the lively princesses of which Portugal seems to have had a plentiful supply. Joana produced a daughter; but was the father Enrique? Among the courtiers at Enrique's court was one named Beltrán de la Cueva. Joana's daughter, as she grew up, was spoken of as La Beltraneja: not in Portugal, so much as by Isabella's mother. Isabella's mother does not seem to have been so demented as to neglect Isabella's chances. By 1468 the prospects of Isabella's priority over La Beltraneja were good enough for correspondence to be taking place between Arévalo and the court of King John of Aragon. Isabella was then 17, the young Prince Ferdinand of Aragon was 16.

In these dynastic matters 1468 was a critical year. Alfonso of Portugal (he had been king of Portugal for thirty years) was affianced to La Beltraneja on the assumption that she was heir to the throne of Castile. In 1468 La Beltraneja was 13. It was high time for Enrique to decide which of the girls would be his rightful heir. It was a decision about which he had often vacillated. Not that it mattered to Alfonso which girl was nominated: having been affianced to La Beltraneja on the understanding that she was legitimate, he had first claim to switch to Isabella if Enrique asserted she was to be the heir. Enrique, who knew nothing of Isabella's intrigue with Ferdinand, was reported to have indicated that of the two girls he preferred Isabella. Isabella snatched at the opportunity; she made public appearance as heir to the throne. Having thus appeared in public, then in private, and in secrecy, she was married to Prince Ferdinand of Aragon.

That secret marriage of two headstrong youngsters (aged seventeen and sixteen) produced the birth of a Spanish Empire.

The ambitiousness of the princess and prince was not widely noticed for another ten years. The secret marriage had been quickly revealed: that caused great indignation to Alfonso, dismay to Enrique, and differences of opinion among the hereditary nobilities of Castile. Each of these, in his own fortress-castle, preserved his independent rights. Some favoured war with Portugal and some did not; some were absentee landlords who, like Enrique, preferred the comforts of the southland. There, the Moorish kingdom of Granada could be regarded as an economic asset. Granada, with the productive irrigated terraces of the Alpujarra, with the cultivation of mulberry trees and silkworms, with handlooms in every village and factories in busy towns, was a hardworking dependency: Granada kept up good trade in silks with Italy, and the protection-money paid to the throne of Castile was useful. Throughout Castile there was no universal wish that the marriage of Isabella and Ferdinand should upset the status quo. Enrique with his mild temper (he forgave Isabella for her trickery) was despised by some of the nobles, but not by all, in his declining years.

Enrique died in 1474. Isabella was proclaimed Queen at Segovia. Portugal at once challenged her title. The 'Succession War' began. The outcome of that war was unpredictable – it was in fact a war that dragged on for five years – and presently it seemed to the King of Granada a plausible excuse for deferring payment of his annual tribute.

The Succession War seemed, to the outside world, a little war. In sea-encounters, Portugal had the better of things; yet in the peace-terms Portugal was forced to cede the Canary Islands to Castile. On land, it had been Ferdinand's activity that won the war. Even to those of the nobility who had distrusted him, the prince-consort had proved himself. During the war, the Queen, when not active in all other ways, had begun to produce children. Castile, victorious over Portugal in 1479, could preen itself and enter a new era – of what sort?

I glance at Italy of that moment, where the State had become, in Burckhardt's phrase, a work of art. Little wars between little Princes were expected, and were frequent. Princes (and Popes alike) employed professional soldiers, *condottiéri*. War itself, in de Rougemont's expression 'had grown civilized, to the full extent that such a paradoxical statement can be true'.

The *condottiéri* 'knew the price of a soldier'.

> The essence of their tactical practice was to make prisoners and to disorganize the enemy's forces. Sometimes — and this was their supreme achievement — they succeeded in defeating the foe in a truly overwhelming manner: they robbed him of all his strength by buying up his entire army. Only when this was not possible did they have to fight.[4]

When there was a battle, according to Machiavelli, it was not dangerous:

> Fighting invariably takes place on horseback, the soldiers being protected by arms and assured of preserving their lives if taken prisoner. ... The lives of the defeated are nearly always spared. They do not remain prisoners for long, and their release is obtained very easily. A

town may rebel a score of times; it is never destroyed. The inhabitants retain the whole of their property; all they have to fear is that they will be made to pay a levy.

No doubt such quotations over-prettify the condition of Italy in the 1480's. We know that killings, murders, violence, were not eliminated. But murder remains an individual affair; principalities remained unmilitarized. Power, for which there seemed to be plenty of competition, was (for that short 'halcyon season') defined by princes as power to foster the creative forces of each province, and hinder the destructive. So, for Italy, I could borrow the 'halcyon season' phrase from Guicciardini, or the phrase 'happy, immoral, and entirely peace-loving' from de Rougemont. But Castile, in 1479, was at a turning-point. The new Sovereigns turned it into a principality that was un-happy, moral, and organized entirely for conquest.

The fairy-tale ends when Cinderella is rescued by Prince Charm-ing. The real story is what happens then. Perhaps if Isabella's accession to the throne of Castile had been straightforward, easy and unchallenged, the temper of the new Sovereigns might have been milder. For them, the Succession War had been won by unremitting effort; it was for them no 'little war'; it had been a bitter struggle; it was they, as a team, who had won it. Coincident with that triumph, in 1479 Ferdinand's father died: Ferdinand, no longer the mere prince-consort who had won his spurs in Castile, was now also in his own right King of Aragon. This royal team was now and suddenly in competition with any of the largest courts of Europe. Theirs was no longer any small ambition. They had moved up among the Powers. A united Spain could play against France, against the Empire. Those were thoughts nursed by Isabella, Ferdinand and their confessors in the Spanish Church, in the decade after 1479. The Sovereigns of Castile and Aragon (still in their twenties) were far above such petty play as satisfied Italian princes.

The first to feel the severity of the new regime were the hereditary nobility of Castile. Their ancient feudal privileges were curtailed by the Cortes of Toledo; as soon as the enactments had been passed, the Cortes was dissolved. (It was not summoned again for 15 years). Power, in Castile, was now centred in the Royal Council, of which the Queen and King were members – and, before long, such dominant members as to be joint dictators. Recalcitrant nobilities found no redress by appeals to the Royal Council. If they resisted, their castles were individually attacked and razed. This happened something like fifty times; as Fernando de Pulgar records, 'the castles, the strongholds of power, were thrown down'. Soon there was no resistance to the Sovereigns from the nobility, and a visitor from Silesia observed in 1484 that 'the nobility fears the Queen more than the King'. In the meantime, action had been quickly taken to revive an ancient and distracting zeal. A blot to Spanish pride, a blot to Christian pride, was the existence of the Moorish kingdom of Granada. Granada, village by village, was to be blotted out. Systematic operations were begun by the Sovereigns in 1482.

Many motives for this 'last European crusade' have been discussed. Professor Parry summarizes:

> The Queen was inspired not only by her own intense religious conviction but also by the need to forestall the danger of a new Holy War. The Ottoman Turks had extinguished the new Byzantine Empire, and were engaged in conquering and unifying the Muslim states of the Levant. Already they were threatening the Christian kingdoms of the Balkans; in 1480 Muhammad II actually invaded Italy, and the invasion was stopped only by the Sultan's death. Castile could ill afford what in later Spanish history was to be called a fifth column. Isabella determined to press ahead with preparations against Granada. . . .[5]

Yet Italian princes of the period do not seem to have been specially perturbed by the threats of the Ottoman Turks. At times the Papacy had expressed alarm. Immediately after the fall of Constantinople, the then Pope (Nicholas V) had despatched a bull to the King of Portugal encouraging the 'round the Cape' plan of the Indies, partly because it might open, in the East, a second front against Islam. But at this late period, there was in Italy no general anticipation of a new Holy War. We read of clashes between Venetians and Turks; we read also of Venice's expansion of trade with Alexandria, of the effort to achieve a monopoly in spices, and of the fostering of tourist-traffic for pilgrims to the Holy Land.[6] As for the seizure of the port of Otranto by Muhammad II in 1480, that was a raid which might be played down. The south of Italy and Sicily were provinces of Aragon, and the raid might be a deliberate tweak at a moment when a King of Aragon had died, and his successor appeared to be busy in Castile. As an invasion, it was not pressed; as an affront to Aragon it could be played up by Ferdinand to inflame his people. Vengeance on Islam could be wreaked on hapless Granada. Everything, by 1482, conspired to fit the mood of Spain's new Sovereigns: the need to stifle restlessness within Castile and Aragon, the wish for unity of passion which is evoked by setting up a foreign foe, the ancient battle-cry at hand of *Reconquista*.

The war against Granada was not of interest to Columbus, but the rapid rise of Castile's Sovereigns to heroic stature – the power, energy and enterprise which had transformed Castile – made them (could he but get to see them) the obvious patrons for his Plan.

As regards marine affairs, an optimist in 1485 might feel that Castile was showing more enterprise than Portugal. The surrender of the Canary Islands had given Castile a good entry into the sugar trade – a chance to dislodge 'Portuguese sugar' from the monopoly it had acquired in northern seaports.

It is curious that in writings about 'The Age of Discovery' there is apt to be less emphasis on sugar than on spice. 'Sugar and spice' – in the nursery rhyme sugar comes first – but spices have run away with the fancy of many historians. The 'romance' of spices is easily justified. What spices meant before an age of refrigeration can be read, Miss Prescott remarks, 'upon the pages of any medieval account book or cookery book, and the reflective student of such domestic records may observe how here, again, the cook's ladle has had its share in ruling the world'. When H. A. L. Fisher (in his *History of Europe*) comes to the 15th century, he handsomely plays up the spice trade:

> As for the spices, they came indeed to Europe, but at what a price! First the Indians, then the Arabs and Abyssinians, who as early as the third century had closed the Red Sea route to the Roman navigators, and after these the Mamelukes of Egypt, exacted their toll before the precious wares reached the counters of the Venetian merchant. To eliminate the exorbitant profits of these oriental middlemen by the establishment of some direct means of contact with the east became an inevitable object of economic desire.[7]

The emphasis in English history books on the spice trade stems partly from a fascinating paragraph of Lord Acton:

The secret of Portuguese prosperity was the small bulk and the enormous market value of the particular products in which they dealt. In those days men had to do without tea, or coffee, or chocolate, or tobacco, or quinine, or cocoa, or vanilla, and sugar was very rare. But there were the pepper and the ginger of Malabar; cardamoms in the damp district of Tellicherry; cinnamon and pearls in Ceylon. Beyond the Bay of Bengal, near the equator, there was opium, the only conqueror of pain then known; there were frankincense and indigo; camphor in Borneo; nutmeg and mace in Amboyna; and in two small islands, only a few miles square, Ternate and Tidor, there was the clove tree, surpassing all plants in value. These were the real spice islands, the enchanted region which was the object of such passionate desire; and their produce was so cheap on the spot, so dear in the markets of Antwerp and London, as to constitute the most lucrative trade in the world.[8]

Lord Acton is speaking of the period after Bartholemew Diaz (in 1487) had rounded the Cape of Good Hope and after Vasco da Gama (in 1498) had brought his ships into the port of Calicut; after the distress of the Venetians at the loss of the spice trade was evident,* and the Portuguese, by capturing the supply at source, had done more than capture spices – they had started a new era – an era of forgetting about Islam and plundering the Far East. It is right that Actons' paragraph (and how artfully it is written, with Milton's music in the names) should express the romance of setting forth to barter for rare and precious cargo in faraway places, and right that it should emphasize the part 'Spice Islands' played. But I say it is also right to remember sugar. The loss to Muslim economy when the Near-East lost monopoly in spices was preceded by the loss, to the Arab, when Prince Henry the Navigator took away their trade in sugar. It was largely for sugar production that Henry attempted to colonize the Canary Islands in 1402, and a few years later, and

---

* 'When the news of Vasco da Gama's successful voyage became known "all the city of Venice was greatly impressed and alarmed, and the wisest men held that this was the worst news that could ever come to the city" '. That foreboding was soon borne out. 'In 1498 there was so much pepper in the Alexandrian market that the Venetian merchant captains lacked money to buy all that was there. Four years later, at Beirut the Venetians could find but four bales, and even in Alexandria there was little to be had. From this time onward that scarcity was to continue'. *Jerusalem Journey* by H. F. M. Prescott (Eyre & Spottiswoode, London, 1954), p. 17.

more successfully, colonized the Madeiras and the Azores. It was 'Portuguese sugar' that largely paid for the Portuguese voyaging.* Spices were part of the reward for sailing eastward, yet sugar has importance for the Road West. Sugar was the reason for Castile's seizure of the Canaries, and it was a Castilian shipowner interested in the sugar-trade who introduced Columbus to Isabella.

In a survey of human migration there is room to pause for the animals and plants which have moved along as chattels. Apart from all the economic aspects, the social story would be very dull without them. Thus Gibbon felt, when he interrupted himself to investigate those two companions, silkworm and mulberry tree. He was speaking of early Byzantium; there was a deal more patient coaxing after that, before the Arabs made the silk-tree stump along in their footsteps to a prospering home in Andalusia – that home which (at the point my narrative has reached) is about to be destroyed by Isabella and Ferdinand – and when Granada, which in Moorish times was 'a mine of silk which seemed to be pure gold', comes to be destroyed, I shall then see the need the Spaniards will have for other mines of other gold. The sugar-cane is another plant which ever since Arabs laid hold of it in Mesopotamia had everywhere followed their footsteps. 'Wherever Arabs went, everything sprouted' was in old times a proverb; that the proverb held true for sugar-cane is thoroughly proved by von Lippmann in his *Geschichte des Zuckers*.[9]

The sugar-cane is hard to grow from seed; therefore the distribution of the cane was not by wind or birds; the transplantation was step by step, by human carriers. In the long trek from Mesopotamia one notices that water-mills and windmills come into play, for crushing the cane; factory-production comes into being, and sugar (unknown to Greeks or Romans as a manufactured product) is a table luxury in much demand in Arabian Egypt. Round about A.D. 790 the Vizier Qafur is using daily a thousand pounds of sweets and two hundred boxes of spices; about 990 a great fashion is apparent for statuettes and figures made of sugar – apart from animals, castles and trees, policemen and judges are among the favoured shapes. The swampy soil around Palermo was seen to be appropriate for sugar-cane; Arabs had planted it in Sicily in the 8th century, as also in

* Sugar and timber. Madeira (as, later, Brazil) took its name from the timber it provided.

Spain; and as factory-production of the sugar-loaf continued in both of those provinces, it is assumed that by the 10th century there was a luxury trade there, as well as in Egypt and Syria, in sugary confections. Indeed, in earliest verbal references (in Persian and Sanskrit) the raw material and the finished product appear in words that are identical and indistinguishable; and how easily the Arabic term for sugar-cane and sugar candy dissolves into the medieval Latin *saccharum candi,* Italian *Zucchero candi,* Spanish *azucer cande* before, as *sugar candy* it reached England. Words which describe sweet things travel easily. The uncrystallized liquid drained from raw sugar slips into European language either as *syrup* (straightforward adoption of the Arabic) or as *molasses,* the new sweetening substance taking its name from what it replaced (late Latin *mellaceus*=of nature of honey). So also the medicines which Europeans take (or administer to their livestock) come to be surreptitiously identified with the sugar-coating in which they are administered: *theriaca,* which meant 'antidote for poisonous bites of wild animals', turns into the word *triacle* or *treacle,* and usage makes treacle the molasses-like inducement – that which conceals the antidote. Chaucer's phrase, *Crist, which that is to every harm triacle,* is a reminder of the insidious change that the syrups of the Mediterranean worked upon the language, as upon the eating habits, of northerners.

Crusaders to the Holy Land occasionally vied with one another for the capture of a caravan of sugar, but the feeling is that Europe's sweet tooth was whetted more by normal trade than by occasional crusaders.* Chaucer is noticeably fond of the word *sugre,* whereby I judge the substance was prized at the court of John of Gaunt. I have already suggested that it was much in the mind of Prince Henry the

* In the *Oxford English Dictionary* I find no quotation containing one or another of the forms for *sugar* until 1289, which is a hundred years after the crusade of Richard Lionheart. The word *spice* appears in 1225; the particular condiment, *pepper,* appears in Ælfric's grammar in the year 1000. I am not saying that the substances were not known in England before their names got into the vulgar tongue; but the spread of the name in the language may be some indication of the spread of the taste. I notice that after the substances came to England, the word *sugar* (with its derivatives and combinations) calls for 14 columns of quotations in the O.E.D. The word *pepper* (using the same count) calls for 8 columns, and 6 columns are sufficient to deal with allusions to the word *spice.*

Navigator to build up a Portuguese sugar-trade with England and with Continental ports. The foreseeable demand for sugar was limitless; Prince Henry did his best to supplant the Arabs in sugar production. After the first Portuguese effort with the Canary Islands (1402), Henry, in 1420, took sugar-cane from Sicily to Madeira – he took not merely the cane, but craftsmen experienced in factory methods of making the sugar-loaf. The cane in all of the Portuguese Atlantic Islands (Canaries, Cape Verdes, Madeira, Azores) prospered beyond even Henry's expectation; so (except on the Canaries) did the factories; and so did Portuguese shipping.

Prince Henry died in 1460, twenty years before the humiliating result of the Succession War, whereby the Sovereigns of Castile captured the Canaries from Portugal, and the shipowners of Seville and Cadiz could register that as a triumph over Lisbon. To the sugar-merchants of Lisbon there was one consolation in their loss. The islands that remained to Portugal had all been uninhabited at the time of their colonization; in developing their produce, there had been no hostile natives to contend with. The Portuguese occupation of the Canaries had always been hampered by the exceedingly hostile inhabitants, a presumably mixed breed of natives, known as the Guanches. Friendly relations with the Guanches had been impossible to achieve, and short of ruthless and complete extermination of the islanders there seemed no likelihood of profitable exploitation of the Canaries. By ceding the islands, Portugal was at least rid of an awkward problem. The first Castilian governor of the Canaries was Pedro de Vera, a name to be remembered. He went to the islands in 1480; in the ugly proceedings that followed, one of his tricks for the elimination of the Guanches was to use hunting-dogs. Thus the name anciently given to the Canary Islands by Arnobius, the Isles of Dogs, became fearfully appropriate.*

* The practice of using dogs against hostile natives was subsequently followed by Spaniards in the West Indies. Pedro de Vera, by his general conduct in the Canaries, earned such reputation for irresponsibility and cruelty that he was recalled to Spain in disgrace. I said his name is to be remembered, for later in my story (Ch. 15) his grandson, Cabeza de Vaca, plays a notable part. It took 15 years to exterminate all of the Guanches in all of the Canary Islands. Meanwhile the Castilians pushed ahead with their sugar plantations. In 1526 an English factor, Thomas Nichols, saw and

The moment Columbus set foot ashore at Palos, the alert spirit of the new Castile greeted him. It was of no consequence that he arrived as a stranger, a nobody. As the coasting vessel turned from the Rio Saltés into the Rio Tinto, he had noticed the conspicuous monastery of La Rábida. As soon as he landed, he walked with Diego the four miles back to the monastery to ask if Franciscans would take charge of his son. Two good friends of this part of the story are the friar Antonio de Marchena and the prior of La Rábida, Father Juan Pérez. They offered a home and schooling to Diego; they offered a home and counsel to the captain. Obviously Columbus should meet a ship-owner; the friar de Marchena knew the right shipowner – not just an ordinary shipowner, but the powerful Count of Medina Celi, the most energetic of the shipowners of Seville and Cadiz. Columbus was speedily introduced to the Count at Seville, and the Count, again, could hardly have been more friendly. Nothing, it seemed, could go wrong for Columbus – except that he might be pushing his luck too far. Morison writes:

> Medina Celi, of whom Columbus asked 'three or four well-equipped caravels, and no more', had almost decided to underwrite the enterprise when it occurred to him to ask permission of the Queen. He did so, and Isabella refused, believing that so important an enterprise as that of Columbus should be conducted by the crown. But this transfer from Count to Queen postponed Columbus's voyage some six years.[10]

The way I read it, is that it was Columbus who was pressing for more authority than the Count could grant. Nevertheless a personal interview with the Queen was arranged for Columbus. When they met, in the Alcazar at Cordova on May Day, 1486, Isabella was friendly. She at once appointed a commission under Talavera to examine the project. At that first moment, she could hardly have done more. 'We know nothing definite about the arguments', Morison observes, of this commission of men of learning; but by Christmastide 1486 the opinions of the advisers had become divided. Mendoza, cardinal of Toledo, and Ceza, afterwards Archbishop of Seville, were apparently in favour of Columbus's project; Talavera seems to have

---

counted the sugar-mills in the Canaries: 12 on Grand Canary, 11 on Tenerife, 1 on Gomera. At that time there were 16 on Madeira.

been more cautious, perhaps uncertain of the reliability of Toscanelli's calculations, perhaps uncertain of the reliability of Columbus.

If the Talavera commission remained of two minds as regards their advice to the Queen, they at least offered, and Columbus accepted, a retaining fee while they deliberated. The impression has sometimes been given that here was Columbus in a lethargic Spain, learning by experience 'the meaning of the phrase *cosas de España,* the irritating procrastination of Spaniards, who never seemed able to make up their minds, to carry out a plain order, or to make a firm decision without fees or favours'. That impression, that here was 'one of the greatest mariners, if not the greatest, of all time' compelled to make 'pitiable and protracted efforts to obtain a fair hearing,' over-dramatizes the situation, though I am sure it expresses Columbus's own view. For the year 1487 he managed to assuage his impatience among Genoese friends at Cordova, but the delay perpetually galled him. In 1488 he made a trip to Lisbon. Any hopes that he and his brother in Lisbon had of reviving the Columbus Plan in Portugal were dashed when they witnessed the three caravels of Diaz returning proudly to the Tagus. Diaz had rounded the southernmost cape of Africa – the 'Cape of Storms', he called it – and had made reconnaissance of 1260 miles of Africa's east coast. Diaz said that he would have gone on to India, except that his crew mutinied. King John of Portugal in his delight renamed the southern tip of Africa 'Cape of Good Hope' and was in no mood to listen further to Columbus.

Early in 1489 Columbus returned to Castile. His brother Bartholomew meanwhile attempted to interest the royal courts of England and France, with no success. In Castile the Talavera commission reported finally in 1490: the proposal was not recommended.

Isabella told Columbus that he might apply again after the war against Granada was over.

Sympathy with the frustration of Columbus need not obscure the fact that there were many pressing matters on the agenda of the sovereigns of Spain. Many pressures about which Columbus was ignorant were indeed working in favour of the Enterprise that he cherished. The War, the Church, the Inquisition, the forthcoming royal marriages – all come into the complex. Columbus is not the only man to think of. There is also a preoccupied converted Jew who had to deal with many things, the keeper of the King's purse, Luis de Santangel.

From the beginning of their reign, Isabella and Ferdinand had lacked and had demanded money. Between 1477 and 1482 the regulation of currency and increase of trade had multiplied the revenue of Castile nearly six-fold. The nation remained insolvent. It was during this period that application was made to Rome for the extension, to Castile, of the office of the Inquisition. The immediate purpose of this application was economic.

I am not condoning the Spanish Inquisition if I attempt to see the reasoning. In the 15th century there was a universal problem – a problem confronting any strict Christian or Muslim. Under either rule, true converts to the faith of the Establishment could claim all privileges, including tax-exemptions, which rigidly were not accorded to the unbelievers. What was the rule for false converts? – tax-evaders? Whether the call to faith and the allegiance of communal prayer was announced by the bell of the Christian or the human voice of Islam, there was the same question about the unwanted joiner, the suspect renegade.

With the Arabs, the existence of this problem had frequently acted as a brake on any desire to convert the heathen. Peoples they had conquered had been prompt to forsake their own lands, thereby evading land-tax. By seeping into cities, currying favour with one of the original Arab tribes and performing all outward observance of the customs of the faithful, unbelievers escaped the very purpose of military conquest. There was another and strong reason for the Muslim to dislike a convert. No Muslim could enslave a fellow-Muslim. The practice of Arabs in the 15th century was to go slow about conversion.

In Castile the office of the Inquisition for which Ferdinand and Isabella applied to the Papacy was to be under the direction of the Crown, not of the Church. The office was specifically for the purpose of raising money from individuals who claimed to be converts to Christianity. It was not an office for the investigation or conversion of heretics. Power to deal with confessed heretics was sufficiently established; what was specifically needed by the Sovereigns was power to investigate and if convenient to confiscate the wealth defended by

New Christians – The Conversos (former Jews) or Moriscos (former Muslims).

Popular feeling in Castile over the establishment of a Spanish Inquisition to exert itself against New Christians was almost certainly on the side of the Sovereigns. In Don Quixote it is a humorous matter for Sancho Panza frequently to assert that he is one of the 'Old Christians': no turncoat, and by implication an honest man, within his status a privileged person, no interloper. *Don Quixote* reflects a feeling against new converts milder than the feeling in Castile in 1480. When the office of the Inquisition was granted to the Crown, it gave the Sovereigns jurisdiction over New Christians. With the unification of all Spain, the Conversos of Castile, Aragon, Valencia and Catalonia became the special concern of Torquemada, the first and most notorious Inquisitor-general named by the Crown. After the fall of Granada, Isabella's confessor Talavera, soon replaced by her subsequent confessor Ximénes, extended Torquemada's methods against Moriscos.

The position of a Converso at the court of Isabella and Ferdinand, after the establishment of the Spanish Inquisition, was instantly difficult. Individual Conversos had from the beginning played an intimate part in the Castilian regime. Isabella's closest childhood friend had married a Converso; it was that married pair who effected the reconciliation of Isabella with her father, after her secret marriage to Ferdinand. Talavera, until 1492 the Queen's confessor, was himself a Converso. We are told that the war against Granada was largely financed by Jewish loans – the financial management at the beginning was in the hands of two Jewish members of the Royal Council, Abraham Senior and Isaac Abrabranel. What is not easy to discern is how far the Jewish loans were voluntary, or to what extent they were forced. I have just said that Luis de Santangel, Keeper of the Privy Purse during the time of Columbus's appeals, was a Converso. It is hard to balance the prominence of Conversos at the Court with some of the statistics that are flung around about the Inquisition: such as that Torquemada personally sent 10,220 persons to the stake and 97,371 to the galleys.[11] If Torquemada's licence from the Crown was restricted to raising money from the formerly-Jewish Conversos, by confiscation of the property of those condemned or by fines extracted for 'protection', figures so large as those quoted must be false. Yet there is little doubt of the fear of the Inquisition. The upshot of these considerations is that a Spaniard of Jewish descent might have been ready enough to back a war which would divert extortions on to the even more unfortunate Moors.

Meanwhile the conduct of the war against Granada, begun in 1482, was expensive. In a wide territory stretching from Ronda to beyond Almería there was, says Gerald Brenan, a defensive tower or castle built in every *alauz* or township. 'Yegen had one not a hundred yards from my house, and its site is still known as *el castillo*'.[12] The military operation is described by Ferdinand's pun: 'I will pick out the seeds of this pomegranate one by one' – *granada* means pomegranate. The picking of the seeds was a slow process: cheerfully begun, it had become exasperating. The war soon called for foreign mercenaries. One reads of the Englishman, Earl Rivers, and his company of English bowmen; and of another contingent of 2,000 Swiss pikemen. The ultimate result was never in doubt, but the progress, to Ferdinand and Isabella, was slow.

'Wait till the war is over' had been Isabella's advice to Colombus. Then, according to the wish of the most zealous churchmen, the plan against the Muslims (and a deferred plan against the Jews) could be succeeded by the Plan of the Indies. While the would-be adventurer was frustratedly sitting at Cordova, naming his illegitimate son Ferdinand, writing to Juan Pérez at La Rábida, or visiting Lisbon to see if he and Bartholomew could get a quicker bid from Portugal, England or France, it is not beyond belief that there were fanatical schemes of Spanish churchmen at high level working on Columbus's behalf.

The cautious Talavera had doubted the calculations, but to the most ardent of the faithful, what difference did a few sea miles matter either way? Men knew the world was round, men knew the Orient was just across the western ocean, men had the ships and instruments, and to use that *conoscenza* men had the most solemn of obligations. That same Toscanelli who had said that the Indies could be found by sailing west had been at Rome when envoys appeared 'from the Grand Khan, petitioning for missionaries to instruct his people in the doctrines of Christianity. Two such embassies were sent, but their prayer was not attended to'. I am quoting from Lord Acton to convey how Columbus's proposal, and the use of Toscanelli's name, could find support from Spanish Churchmen at the culminating moment of the Reconquista:

> Here were suppliants calling out of the darkness: Come over and help us. It was suitable that the nation which had conquered the Moslem and banished the Jews should go on to convert the heathen. The Spaniards would appear in the East, knowing that their presence was desired. In reality they would come in answer to an invitation, and might look for a welcome. Making up by their zeal for the deficient enterprise of Rome, they might rescue the teeming millions of Farthest Asia. . . . The conversion of Tartary would be the crowning glory of Catholic Spain.[13]

All this, Lord Acton admits, is 'somewhat hypothetical and vague'. Another ambition of the moment is more definite. A further crowning glory of Catholic Spain was to be achieved through the marriages of the royal children.

Of Ferdinand's and Isabella's five children only the second, the sickly but adored Juan, was a boy. The eldest princess, Isabel, was intended for marriage with Portugal, thus to unite the whole Peninsula. Juan was intended for the more ambitious marriage with Princess Margaret of Austria. The most ambitious of all marriages was talked of in 1491, the union of Isabella's third child Joanna with Philip of Flanders, heir to Maximilian – the Maximilian who was about to become Holy Roman Emperor.

Philip, the wealthiest of Europe's princes, heir to the greatest power, was the most sought-after of matrimonial prizes. I imagine one did not enter that realm of matrimonial bargaining without having prestige of one's own to offer, and a deep Privy Purse of one's own.

Luis de Santangel, Keeper of that Purse, thus comes into focus as a man upon whom there were extraordinary pressures. There were the King's expenses to be met. It is perhaps only a detail, but a detail to be thought of, that the mercenaries employed in a ten-year war against Granada had to be paid off: the matters mentioned of the 2,000 Swiss pikemen, and the English bowmen with Earl Rivers. At the fighting for one of the Moorish strongholds the English Earl had been hit in the mouth by a piece of rock hurled by one of the defenders. I do not suppose the loss of his teeth reduced the bite for his services. Now there were also ambassadors in parley for the proposed royal marriages. Such are expenses, among others, for which Santangel had to find the money.

The impression emerges of a Queen and King peremptory in expectations, and of a Keeper of the Purse, himself a Jew by descent, a Converso, worried about the money. Long before the end of the ten years' warfare it must have been clear that there would be no ransom for King Boabdil of Granada from distant Ottoman sources, and that he would have nothing left of his own. It must have been clear that systematic destruction of a formerly wealth-producing Moorish community was the destruction of any chance of its becoming once more wealth-producing. And if no treasure remained in Granada when it was captured, immediate pressure for funds would lash back mercilessly upon the Spanish Jews and Conversos.

So if some of the churchmen were keeping Columbus's Plan in mind for the glory of the Christian mission, I would think Santangel was keeping it on the agenda for the possible protection of his people. There was the bare chance that the Enterprise would pay. Santangel's kindred, said Acton, 'suffered under the Inquisition, before and after, and he fortified himself against the peril of the hour when he financed the first voyage of Colombus'.

Three events of the first months of 1492 appear then in natural sequence: the capture of Granada, the Edict to expel the Jews from Spain, and the signing of the Capitulations with Columbus.

There was no treasure in Granada. At the surrender the utmost ransom that could be extorted for King Boabdil was 30,000 gold castellanos. In the hope of gaining more, some lenience was promised to surviving Muslims. When it was clear that there was nothing more, the lenient clauses of the treaty were broken. Torture of Muslims and Moriscos produced nothing, and the disappointment (not unexpectedly) rebounded upon the Spanish Jews. By the edict which followed the fall of Granada in January, all orthodox Jews were to be expelled from Spain by August; they might take no property – property of Jews was confiscated. By a further turn of the screw, no formerly Jewish Converso was free to leave Spain, and any recent Converso could be handed to Torquemada.

Shortly before the fall of Granada the item of Columbus's petition came to the top of the agenda with remarkable speed. He had kept on pressing; now he was summoned. It was, to Columbus, a long-over-due recognition of his merits. Tardy though this acceptance seemed, Columbus took it as a personal triumph. To Santangel it could hardly matter what airs Columbus might assume, provided he brought back gold.

After the signing of the Capitulations at Easter, preparations for the first exploratory voyage westward to the Indies – a route there, and a route back – were made with speed. Columbus thought of sailing from Palos: there Pérez could help him to find the crews. The Queen, or perhaps Santangel, recalled that a penalty was due from Palos for some municipal offence: the penalty was conveniently compounded by commandeering two small local ships, *Pinta* and *Niña*.

Isabella, as all narrators believe, took special delight in the preparations. It was *her* Expedition. There were to be three ships. On the main truck of each ship there was to be hoisted, on departure or on entering or leaving any port, Isabella's royal ensign, the ensign of Castile and León. On the foremast or mizzen there was to be displayed the special banner of the expedition, a green cross on a white field. Green, we remember, was the symbolic colour of Hope. It may also be significant that the banner recalled the green cross of the Order of Alcántara: the Mastership of that Order had been an early presentation from Isabella to Ferdinand, in their younger days. Now, for the special banner, the crown on each arm of the green cross was further symbol of their union. Considering other mentions of Isabella's persistent interest in embroidery, I can believe she paid attention to the banners.

At Palos, Columbus found his third ship, a vessel slightly larger than the others: the *Santa María*, which he promptly chartered as his flagship. For the fleet of three small ships a total complement of about 90 men was recruited, almost all drawn from the neighbourhood of Palos. There was no soldiery. Each ship carried a few short guns to repel boarders, but none of them was a ship of war. There were no missionaries. There were a few specialists – a surgeon for each vessel, an official secretary, a royal comptroller, and one Converso. The reason generally given for the presence of the Converso is that he knew Arabic, 'which, it was thought', says Morison, 'would enable him to converse with the Chinese and Japanese'.

By August 2nd, the many preparations were completed. All hands were shriven at the church of Palos, all went aboard – Columbus himself embarked in the small hours of Friday the 3rd, to catch the dawn tide in the estuary of the Saltés. On that same ebb-tide, but without any banner, was another vessel, carrying away from Spain a last remnant of Jews.

Morison notes that as the ships of Columbus swung slowly into the Saltés and passed La Rábida close aboard, the seafarers could hear the Franciscan friars chanting their early Service. Whether or not Columbus could make them out the two figures of Juan Pérez and Diego watched his fleet depart. It was no great while since Columbus had arrived at La Rábida. The boy Diego, who was to become a governor in a new world, was as yet no more than twelve years old.

The outward voyage to the West Indies, as Professor Morison has been able to demonstrate, was practically a picnic.

All pre-Columbian Portuguese attempts to discover islands west of the Azores had failed, says Morison, because:

> In the first place, there was no Antilia, and no island nearer than Newfoundland; in the second place, to sail west from the Azores, as all these men did, one had to buck westerly winds in high latitudes. Columbus, in his African voyages, had observed the steady easterly tradewinds between the Equator and the latitude of the Canaries, and so chose the Canaries as his point of departure. That is the plain reason why he succeeded in finding something, even though it was not what he wanted.[14]

The Canary Islands lay astride of latitude 28° North, which latitude Columbus believed would cut Japan at the distance, according to his calculations, of 2,400 nautical miles due west. The first leg of the voyage to the Canaries was familiar. Since 1480 Castilian planters had made progress with the sugar factories. Pedro de Vera had killed most of the Guanches and all the main ports were in regular use. Columbus put in to San Sebastián, the port of Gomera (westernmost of the Canaries). Some necessary repairs to *Pinta,* which were effected at Las Palmas, held up the fleet for a couple of weeks. The time was occupied by filling extra water-casks and taking aboard further provisions. Columbus is said to have fallen in love with Doña Beatriz de Bobadilla, widow of the former Spanish captain of Gomera. This story Morison dismisses, pointing out that Columbus personally supervised the repairs to *Pinta* at Las Palmas, returned with her to Gomera, 'and on September 6th, 1492, the fleet weighed anchor for the last time in the old world. . . . Columbus himself gave out the course : "West, nothing to the north, nothing to the south" '.

The mariners' compass, improved since the time of Nicholas of Lynn, now took charge of direction; estimating the daily run of distance, even with half-hour glass and log-line with knots (the sailors' rosary), even with the printed star-tables of Regiomontanus, even with the latest astrolabes (still very difficult to use in a lurching ship at sea), was much more difficult. Columbus earns all the praise which Morison (who followed the same route under sail) gives him for navigation. Yet that praise is mostly for his uncanny gift for conning his ship, in currents then unknown, among the islands of the West Indies; and for the superb seamanship he displayed on the more difficult return voyages. Outward bound on the first voyage such trouble as occurred was psychological. For the first ten days the easterly trade wind blew steadily; then there were five days of variable winds and rain; there were false landfalls, but no land. The trade wind returned and drove the ships on, but still no land. No land for thirty-one days: there was talk of mutiny.

It is hard to know what such talk amounted to. In 15th century sea-narratives a mention of mutiny is common form: no reason to doubt that the threat of mutiny was often real enough, and equally, no reason to doubt that if for any cause a commander lost heart, to have mutiny mentioned in his log-book was a convenient personal excuse. Thirty-one days at sea with no landfall might have created mutinous feelings among the ships' crews; yet forty days of outward voyaging was regarded by seamen as canonical – forty days' search was so regarded by Dulmo and Estreito in their quest for Antilia. Da Gama, standing out to sea from the Cape Verdes, did not sight land again for ninety-six days; one does not read of mutiny. Da Gama's fleet was probably better provisioned than Columbus's; yet there is no mention of Columbus's men fearing shortage of food and water.

Columbus's chief worry would seem to have been that he had talked too much about the shortness of the distance to be sailed. In thirty-one days he had already overshot his expected mark. This doubt, that Toscanelli's calculations could have been wrong, was a worrying doubt indeed – possibly one not to be admitted, but to be so far as possible concealed. Morison finds in the record of the voyage that Columbus summoned his officers and 'cheered them as best he could, holding out good hope of the advantages they might gain; and, he added, it was useless to complain, *since he had come to go to the Indies, and so had to continue until he found them, with Our Lord's help*'. The italics are Morison's, and he stresses the passage as exhibiting Columbus's forcefulness in persuading falterers. It could also contain an element of self-persuasion.

October 10th is reported as a day of mutinous feelings, yet before that, although there had been false landfalls, there had also been signs of land. On October 7th birds in formation passed over the ships, flying west-southwest. Birds! – the earliest of direction-finders. Columbus altered course to follow the birds, which on subsequent nights were seen again against the moon. On the 11th, branches of trees with green leaves and flowers were reported as 'frequent'. By nightfall the following wind had freshened, and the ships, pitching in the roughest seas of the whole passage, were making 9 knots. *Pinta*, the fastest sailer of the three, was in the lead, half a mile perhaps ahead; and at 2 a.m. on the 12th Rodrigo de Triana, lookout aboard *Pinta*, sang out 'Tierra! Tierra!' Real land it was this time, one of the small islands of the Bahamas group, usually identified by a later name of Watling's Island, but now officially awarded the name which Columbus gave it when, by noon of October 12th, he had coasted round and landed on the leeward side – the name in honour of the Holy Saviour, *Salvador*.

Nobody has recorded the story better than Professor Morison: how the green cross of Hope first reached the islands of the 'Indians', how possession of a New World was opened to those who carried the royal standard of Castile.

NOTES

1. In this chapter and following chapters my constant and indispensable reference-book is *The Spanish Seaborne Empire* by J. H. Parry (Hutchinson, London, and Knopf, New York, 1966).

2. The passage on 'the aesthetic against the ascetic' occurs at p. 81 of Lord Acton's *Lectures on Modern History* in the original edition (Macmillan, London, 1906). The word *aesthetic* (introduced to the

English language I believe by De Quincey) was in Acton's time beginning to be tarnished. Even in his paragraph 'art' is exhibited as if it was something separate to be laid on, like icing on a cake. The word *ascetic* has somewhat similarly become specialized and dissociated from the original complex wherein (as noticed in the chapter on the Greeks) the connotation included athletic and military training.

3. I owe many details to *Historic Spain* by Alfonson Lowe (announced for publication, Daunay, London, 1967). The author, in private life a professional medical man, provides a very interesting discussion of the 'melancholy insanity' of Isabella's mother and of Enrique's 'impotence'; and he interested me more than that for his visual feeling for Spain and for Spanish history.

4. *Passion and Society* by Denis de Rougemont (Faber, London, 1962), p. 251. The passage from Machiavelli is quoted by de Rougemont, on the same page.

5. Parry, pp. 34, 36.

6. One of the best accounts of pilgrimage to the Holy Land in the 15th century is *Jerusalem Journey* by H. F. M. Prescott (Eyre & Spottiswoode, London, 1954).

7. *A History of Europe* by H. A. L. Fisher (Eyre & Spottiswoode, London, 1952), Vol. I, p. 412.

8. Acton, op. cit., p. 58.

9. *Geschichte des Zuckers* by Edmund O. von Lippmann (Springer, Berlin, 1929).

10. Morison (as cited in Ch. 11), p. 21.

11. These are figures stated in *Sex in History* by G. Rattray Taylor (Thames and Hudson, London, revised edition, 1959), p. 127.

12. *South from Granada* by Gerald Brenan (Penguin, 1963).

13. Acton, op. cit.

14. Morison, op. cit., p. 21.

CHAPTER 13

Brave Adventure

LOOKING back over the developments of any business or enter-
terprise,' Viscount Mackintosh remarked, 'one sees that
different talents are needed at different stages, but the real
glory is due to the man who first set out on the brave adventure.'

I regard the Spanish effort in their new world as an example of
large and complicated business enterprise.

The 'real glory' of which Viscount Mackintosh was speaking[1] is a
lonely glory unless the business is perpetuated. The tribute to Columbus on his tomb in Seville Cathedral:

> A CASTILLA Y A LEON
> MUNDO NUEBO DIO COLON

would seem less except for the instant team-work that there was in
Castile and León, and throughout Spain, to exploit the gift of the
New World.

The first voyage to the West Indies had amounted to a brilliant
demonstration, how to sail due West across the Ocean Sea, arrive
somewhere, and return. To the end of his life Columbus believed that
he had reached the fringes of the Orient, that the exotic civilization
reported by Marco Polo was to be found a little farther on. In the
meantime, in the famous 'Columbus Letter' written aboard ship, addressed to Luis de Santangel and forwarded in March 1493 on
Columbus's return to the Peninsula, there was an ecstatic and glowing prospectus for the fringe of territory that had been found.* Un-

---

* Columbus, on his return voyage, met with foul weather. He barely managed to put in for safety's sake to Lisbon. This visit to Lisbon, and the consequent interview between Columbus and King John of Portugal before he
could report to the Sovereigns of Spain, has always caused much speculation.
Morison gives good seamanly reasons for Columbus's putting in to Lisbon;
and in *Christopher Columbus, Mariner*, Morison prints in full his own anno-
tated translation of the 'Columbus Letter' which, together with a letter for
their Majesties, was forwarded (it is not clear just when and how) ahead of his

limited gold, innumerable naked natives, in a setting of unsurpassable loveliness and fertility, could be vouched for by the Admiral who had actually been there, who had obtained at least 'a look at it'.

Of the great island which Columbus christened *La Spañola* (Hispaniola, subsequently Haiti) the prospectus is particularly lyrical:

> Its lands are lofty and in it there are many sierras and very high mountains, to which the island Centrefrei [Tenerife] is not comparable. All are most beautiful, of a thousand shapes, and all accessible and filled with trees of a thousand kinds and tall, and they seem to touch the sky; and I am told that they never lose their foliage, which I can believe, for I saw them as green and beautiful as they are in Spain in May, and some of them were flowering, some with fruit, and some in another condition, according to their quality. And there were singing the nightingale and other little birds of a thousand kinds in the month of November, there where I went. There are palm trees of six or eight kinds, which are a wonder to behold on account of their beautiful variety, and so are the other trees and fruits and herbs; therein are marvellous pine groves, and extensive champaign country; and there is honey, and there are many kinds of birds and a great variety of fruits. Upcountry there are many mines of metals, and the population is innumerable. *La Spañola* is marvellous, the sierras and the mountains and the plains and the champaign and the lands are so beautiful and fat for planting and sowing, and for livestock of every sort, and for building towns and cities. The harbours of the sea here are such as you could not believe in without seeing them, and so the rivers, many and great, and good streams, the most of which bear gold. And the trees and fruits and plants have great differences from those of *La Juana* [Cuba]: in this there are many spices and great mines of gold and of other metals.

The mention of Tenerife was artful; it had proved profitable to take the Canaries from the Portuguese. The natives of the Canaries had been a nuisance; yet Pedro de Vera made slaves of some of them – that was a thought of potential value. Columbus does not hesitate to report that he had heard of some natives, in another island which he had not visited, who were 'very ferocious and who eat human flesh', and those cannibals were said to fight with bows and arrows. 'I make no more account of them than of the rest', Columbus said; but there

---

own arrival at Palos and his journey from there to Seville. It is from Morison's translation that I quote.

were thus included in the prospectus out-and-out idolaters as well as possible converts. The natives of his particular islands were all friendly and obedient; they 'might be made Christians and be inclined to the love and service of their Highnesses and of the whole Castilian nation'. 'All go naked', and are 'the most timid people in the world'. To prove that, 'I bring with me Indios as evidence'. Columbus mentions that on this first voyage he has already planted 'the town of Navidad', secured and well seated, with a garrison of his own men – 39 men had been left on Hispaniola to be busily collecting gold, to make a shipload of it which could be picked up. 'In conclusion', Columbus states that 'if their Highnesses will render me a little help' he shall give them 'as much gold as they want', and besides other products that he mentions, 'slaves, as many as they shall order, who will be idolaters'.

I am confident that Columbus believed everything he put into his letter to Santangel, which was enclosed in another letter for their Highnesses; and when I said that some of the points made were artful, I meant no more than that it was a letter to be read by people with different interests and he was putting in something to please everyone. I am sure he was convinced that as soon as his ambition to be Viceroy of the Indies was confirmed, everything that he promised could be made to come true. It was not altogether the persuasiveness, but the timing of the letter which made it instantly effective, and for reasons of which Columbus could hardly have been aware. The promise of 'as much gold as they want' and the prestige of extending the Christian faith and the realm of Christendom were incentives powerful at any moment; there were extra motives to make them especially powerful to Ferdinand and Isabella in the year 1493.

I do not think that I have harped too much about the strength that would accrue to Spain from the hoped-for royal marriages, especially from the proposal that Joanna should marry Philip of Flanders. Miss Eithne Wilkins[2] draws my attention to a detail which fits in. The detail is found in Albrecht Dürer's painting of the Festival of the Rosary, where the kneeling figure on the left of the Madonna is the Emperor Maximilian, portrayed with his strong craggy face in profile (and red-haired, of course). On the Madonna's right, beside the throne, a lily is shown above a black cappa'd shoulder – this is an indication that there stands the figure of Saint Dominic, the Spanish

Saint, Saint of the Order which had special charge of the rosary.* What makes one look twice is that it was in 1493 that Maximilian (whom Philip was to succeed) became Holy Roman Emperor, and Maximilian had ever been a most devout upholder of the rosary confraternities; and it was in Spain that they sang *'Viva el Rosario y Santo Domingo que l'ha fundado!'* Was it not of very special political interest to Ferdinand in 1493 to promote the marriage of his daughter and Maximilian's son by a prompt Spanish action peculiarly congenial to the Emperor?

I would neither exaggerate the detail, nor dismiss it. In 1493 any immediate Christian exultation at the capture of Granada was wearing off. The triumph over the Muslim was reduced to trivial actions. A mark of the faithful Muslim had been to wash publicly, before prayer, five times a day in the running water of the open fountains; to suppress the prayer, Ximénes prohibited the bathing. Lice were not to be eliminated; it was Christian for flesh to be mortified; lice were 'pearls of God'. Conversion in Granada on such points of conduct, and the drowning of the human voice of the Muezzin by the noisy ringing of church bells, and the pleasure of forcing Morisco and Converso alike to demonstrations of eating pork, brought the whole of Spain into unity with other kingdoms in Christian manners, but had not put Spain notably ahead of other kingdoms. In the Christian rivalry, conversion of the New World would unquestionably put Spain ahead.

Gold, important enough at any time, was also of special importance to Santangel in 1493. The grip of the Inquisition on the Conversos throughout Spain had not been relieved by the equally cruel but profitless grip on the Moriscos. To keep position in the royal marriage competition there was ever the need for the ambassador described in the saying, *poderoso caballero es Don Dinero*, a powerful gentleman is Mr. Money. For immediate military purposes the need

---

* The occasion for Dürer's painting was the grand fête held at Worms in 1495, where Maximilian was the guest of honour. This was 20 years after the first *Rosenkrantz* fraternity in Cologne, founded partly by the passionate Breton Black Friar, Alain de la Roche. Alain was sometimes a trial to his brothers in religion; he was *homo adeo rabiatus et furiosus*, 'a really frantic and crazy man'. Maximilian had been at the first ceremony of the *Rosenkrantz*, as one of the foundation members of the first confraternity. The 'indulgencing' of rosaries subsequently became a Dominican privilege.

for alliances and the need for money were in 1493 not less but greater than they had been during war within the Peninsula. Thoughts of Crusade in Africa had been given up, partly because Defence had become an operative word – defence of Italy against the French. Southern Italy *was* Spain; what use was it to have achieved a Spanish Pope in Rome (Alexander VI) if he were not defended? Alexander VI was impressing on Ferdinand that the invasion of Italy by Charles of France was imminent this year, next year at latest. Early in 1493 Ferdinand was busy at Barcelona with the raising and training of troops; warfare with the French in Italy, entailing mercenaries, entailing also expeditions from Barcelona across the Tyrrhenian Sea, additionally entailed the assistance of Don Dinero. The French had superior artillery; Spain must have superior artillery. I don't know what happened to Abraham Senior and Isaac Abrabranel who had managed the Jewish loans for the ten years' war against Granada, but if Santangel had been sorry for his people during that war, he had more reason to be worried in 1493.

Isabella's instantaneous delight at the receipt of the Columbus letter in Barcelona may be taken for granted. I have been lingering on explanations for Ferdinand's equal and equally quick excitement. The timing of the letter was so apt that perhaps Columbus need not have laboured to make the content in every way so glowing. Their Highnesses were prepared to supply their own enthusiasm. Their joint response was immediate. Columbus on his return had reached Seville, and there was notified in the warmest possible terms that he was to proceed at once to Barcelona. 'Inasmuch as we will that which you have commenced with the aid of God be continued and furthered', preparations for his second voyage were being instantly arranged. This was the message received by Columbus at Easter 1493, a short twelve months after the original signing of the Capitulations; and the message was addressed by the King and Queen so as to confirm Columbus in the highest possible of titles – 'their admiral of the Ocean Sea, Viceroy and Governor of the Islands that he hath discovered in the Indies'.

Morison narrates with zest how Columbus at Seville ordered new raiment and made dramatic procession overland across Spain 'with some of his officers, hired servants and six of the long-suffering Indians. These wore their native dress (largely feathers and fishbone-and-gold ornaments) and carried parrots in cages'. The court reception at Barcelona was spectacular. Preparations for the war in Italy took second place.

Columbus and the Indians remained at Barcelona for three months; during that period the six Indians were baptized; one was to remain on loan with the royal household (he died within two years) and the others were to return with the Admiral to Hispaniola. The public baptism of the Indians is worth mention. It was only the Pope who could authorize missions to the heathen: 'the Pope alone could allot to a particular Christian community – kingdom or religious Order – the exclusive right of proselytizing in a particular heathen area'.[3] The overseas activities of the Portuguese since 1441 (in the time of Prince Henry) had been formally covered by Papal consent. No kingdom but Portugal had been granted such overseas authority. Ferdinand (I continue to think that he was thinking of impressing Maximilian) had been very prompt to use the Columbus letter to remind the Spanish Pope that they were under mutual obligations; and Alexander VI did not hesitate to decide that a Spanish claim to lands west of the Ocean Sea in no way infringed the previous concessions to Portugal. The baptism of the Indians at Barcelona, conducted in state with King, Queen and the Infante Don Juan as godparents, was therefore a matter of political significance. It was a public announcement that Spain, and no other kingdom in Christendom, held authority from the Church in territories discovered by Columbus. Spain would carry to the Indies the rosary beads.

These high involvements perhaps exceeded Columbus's original reckoning, but he was clearly delighted. Morison notes that a curious rebus, reminiscent of the ancient Christian symbol $IX\Theta Y\Sigma$, was adopted by Columbus at Barcelona. The rebus and signature of Columbus are printed thus:

$$. \; S \; .$$
$$S \; . \; A \; . \; S$$
$$X \; . \; M \; . \; Y$$
$$:X\rho o \quad FERENS$$

'Many attempts have been made to solve the riddle,' says Morison. 'My own belief is that the initial letters stand for *Servus Sum Altissimi Salvatoris* Χριστός *Mariae* ῾Υιὸς, Servant am I of the Most

277

High Saviour Christ the Son of Mary. The last line is a Greco-Latin form of his Christian name, emphasizing his role as the bearer of Christianity to lands that never knew Christ. Even on such brief orders or chits as have survived he signed himself Χρο Ferens'.

Ferdinand's correspondence with the Pope rapidly proceeded to the question of where the new Spanish territories were to be delimited from those of Portugal. Portugal and Spain had each chosen its sea-routes for exploration, the one around Africa, the other due west-ward. A sensible suggestion was to draw a line of demarcation along a meridian of the globe somewhere to the west of the Azores – east of that meridian, Portugal; west of that meridian, Spain. Never was a momentous decision more rationally discussed. Columbus suggested the particular meridian at which he had observed the magnetic vari-ation of the compass needle to change from east to west. There was no objection to the principle that the behaviour of a mechanical in-strument might be the arbiter. John of Portugal objected only to that particular meridian as cramping his voyages in the South Atlantic, and suggested a line 370 leagues west of the Cape Verde Islands. Columbus advised Ferdinand that such adjustment would not affect his finds, and the political treaty between Portugal and Spain was easily agreed.

Without waiting for completion of the treaty Ferdinand permitted Columbus to set forth in June from Barcelona for Cadiz, where, again without any waiting, preparations for the second voyage had been going on for three months. Columbus himself in his full dignity was not required to hasten unduly from Barcelona to Cadiz. Morison notes that he and his five converted Indians made stately progression through Madrid and Toledo and took the pilgrims' road to Guada-lupe in the Estremadura. As the procession passed through Trujillo, Morison points out that it possibly aroused the admiration of a thir-teen-year-old boy named Francisco Pizarro, son of an army officer, though as yet of no other occupation than that of a swineherd; and on further progress to Seville Columbus 'passed through the little town of Medillín, where a small boy named Hernán Cortés must have seen him pass'.

The official in charge of the outfitting at Cadiz was Juan Rodriguez de Fonseca, Archdeacon of Seville, member of the Council of Castile, later to be Bishop of Burgos, and from these early days a figure of the greatest importance in the organization of the West Indies. Columbus in his new grandeur complained bitterly about Fonseca, but there is little doubt that Fonseca was being efficient about the fitting-out of the ships at Cadiz. One of the reasons why the minor port of Palos had been selected for Columbus's first voyage was that Cadiz, at that time, had been overcrowded with the compulsory deportation of Spanish Jews. In 1493 Fonseca made Cadiz aware that its main activity was the outfitting of a Grand Fleet of seventeen ships – 'this fleet', Columbus was later to say, 'so united and handsome'. The whole endeavour was to be bigger and better than anything ever attempted by Portugal, or by any other kingdom in living memory.

By the time that Columbus arrived at Cadiz the enthusiasm was general and contagious; Fonseca's main problem was that of coping with contradictory enthusiasms. It is hardly necessary to dwell on various efforts to make a good thing out of the expedition before it started. Morison finds a few instances on which to comment. There was skullduggery undiscovered until too late, about some of the wine casks. There was possibly no less percentage of graft and dishonesty, and possibly no greater, than in other enthusiastic national efforts. There were plenty of lively spirits, out for the adventure: Morison remarks upon one cavalry troop of twenty lancers. The troop was accepted for the expedition partly for their splendid horses, but before embarkation these troopers 'sold their fine Arab chargers in Cadiz, purchased some sorry hacks and lived high on the difference'.

Admitting such exceptions, the organization of the second voyage of Columbus exhibited efficient businesslike intention. 'The fleet carried few arms, and no trade goods other than small trinkets for barter. Its chief cargo was men – twelve hundred people, priests, gentlemen-soldiers, artisans, farmers – and agricultural stock – tools, seeds and animal: a whole society in miniature.'[4]

I pictured Dido as sailing from Tyre in the twilight, with the first stars beckoning. Not in twilight but on the bright autumn morning of September 25, with a light off-shore breeze, the departure from Cadiz is depicted. 'Every vessel flew the royal standard of Castile at her main staff on the high poop, and every skipper dressed ship with the big, brightly colored banners of the day. Waistcloths were stretched between forecastle and poop, and on them were emblazoned the arms of the gentlemen volunteers. A fleet of row-galleys from Venice, which happened to be in the harbour, escorted the ships and caravels to the open sea, with music of trumpets and harps and the firing of cannon'.[5]

Ten years after the bright morning of departure of the fleet 'so united and handsome' what, in the West Indies, was there to show for the effort? Twenty years after, or any time before Ferdinand's death in 1516, there was from the islands no very favourable balance-sheet, no reward that corresponded to Columbus's promises. Yet despite so much that failed, it could be held that the prestige-value of the Spanish Enterprise of the Indies paid off. I keep returning to that marriage of Joanna and Philip of Flanders. Isabella and Ferdinand suggested it in 1491: the project was, I would think, fostered by the events of 1492 and 1493; the wedding actually took place in 1496. Calamities then came upon the Spanish royal household with appalling swiftness – the death of the eldest daughter Isabel in childbirth; the death of the Infante Juan at the age of 19, childless; the death of Isabella herself in 1504; the premature death of Philip and the subsequent insanity of his widow ('Juana la Loca'). All these calamities nevertheless left Ferdinand with one young grandson, Charles, who through inheritance was to unite Spain, Austria, Burgundy and Flanders.

So far as the Enterprise of the Indies played a part in achieving the marriage which resulted in the grandson Charles, then, politically, the venture had served its turn. Apart from the existence of Charles there was little reward for Ferdinand in the Columbus venture. Even in Isabella's lifetime it had to be conceded that Columbus's promises had proved to be a mockery, and that was contributory to the sorrows that overwhelmed her. It had to be conceded that Vasco da Gama had out-navigated Columbus for the glory and reward of reaching the real India. It was 'Happy Manoel' of Portugal, not the Sovereigns of Spain, who awaited the wealth accruing from the Spice Isles. It was 'Happy Manoel' who could boast to his Pope: 'Receive, at last, the entire globe'. Yet under Ferdinand's rule Spain had proved strong enough, despite initial losses and the prospect of never-ending fighting, to eject the French from Naples and preserve control of wealth-producing Italy; and under the grandson Charles, to the other forces which could fight for Spain there would be added manpower (as happened after 1519) of the Holy Roman Empire. Italy and France were realities near to Aragon; the New World was distant. I think it was very remarkable for Ferdinand to have displayed the energy he did display in 1493 about the Columbus venture; after his death his energy was rewarded with what he had most wanted – Spain's military power in Europe.

In the excitement at Barcelona in 1493 Columbus, as Admiral and Viceroy of the new territories, had been proud to accept the three declared instructions from their Highnesses. The first object was the conversion of the Indians; second, the establishment of a continuing, self-supporting, profitable trading colony in Hispaniola; third, the exploration of Cuba to find whether or not it was a projection of the Asiatic mainland giving a landward access to the cities of Cathay. Ships were to be victualled at the Sovereign's expense for a round voyage of six months. All personnel were to be on the royal payroll except for the number (eventually about two hundred) of gentlemen volunteers. The Viceroy was to ensure that the Indians were 'treated very well and lovingly'. A number of priests (eventually six) were to accompany him.

I don't know if Columbus ever appreciated the incompatibility in the first two of the Sovereign's declared instructions. My impression is that Fonseca, at Cadiz, saw the incompatibility at once. It was all very well for the Admiral and Viceroy to be signing papers in a state of euphoria as Xρo FERENS. Fonseca, the ecclesiastic, was also a man of business. I think Fonseca saw from the beginning that the colony would depend upon slave labour. Both Fonseca and Columbus were men of the 15th century. Both knew that you could not enslave natives and convert them simultaneously. Even Columbus had known that – 'slaves', he had said in his initial Letter, 'as many as they shall order, will be idolaters'. When he got to Cadiz as Xρo FERENS I think Columbus was just hoping for the best of both contrary assignments: there would be plenty of slaves to do the work, plenty of converts to please the Queen. Fonseca, planning for a profit-making colony, foresaw slave-labour as the probable imperative, conversion of the natives a secondary and a doubtful matter – and he planned it so.

The passengers accepted by Fonseca for Hispaniola were

described a few pages back as 'a whole society in miniature'; but in two important respects it was not a 'whole' society. There were no women, and there were no unskilled workmen. The bulk of the men who were to set up the colony were technicians. But all were under the expectation that there would be a labour force. A peasantry would be needed for the clearing, planting, harvesting of new land. Factory work was envisaged: sugar-cane was to be transplanted from the Canaries, and sugar meant factories – not enormous factories, yet for each unit a gang of 30 or 40 workmen. Gold was going to need the manual labour of digging, washing, mining, or at the least transporting to the ships. The personnel accepted at Cadiz for the enterprise indicates that in the colony the peasantry, working-force, man-power for every unskilled task, were to be 'Indios'. That was the way the Enterprise was pre-arranged. Columbus had been very persuasive in his much-studied Letter. The Indian men were timid, obedient, innumerable; as Christians they would be pleased to fit into a Christian pattern of work; and 'the women work more than the men'. Fonseca was not so lightly optimistic. The natives might have to be forced to work. They might have to be treated as animals. Therefore they had better not be Christianized.

No society in this whole migration so far had been able to devise a way of life without some form of slavery. Always there were protests, not merely from the slaves, and the rules might change; but in any complicated society there had to be somebody to do the dirty work. The Latin word *servus* is mixed up with the verb 'to preserve'; Romans justified the preservation of prisoners of war for servitude as an improvement on the practice of slaying them. The word *slave* arises in the 8th century in eastern France 'at a time when princes and bishops were glutted with Slavonian bondsmen'.[6] At no time in the ancient world, or in the medieval world, was there any habitual identification of slavery with 'colour'. Within the Church in medieval centuries there were certainly efforts to accord moral value to acts of manumission for slaves and serfs; we cannot believe that laymen did not at times perform such acts sincerely, even if we also notice many who vied for the credit without actual disposal of the property. A sentence in Nathaniel Weyl's book[7] may carry a double meaning: 'In the 13th century, when Christians found it hard to find slaves to free on high church festivals, they bought pigeons and let them fly off'. By the 15th century there was a very general awkwardness about the irreconcilability of Christian behaviour and the rights of slaves; and if I look up the history of the words *rights* and *rites* they are at that time so intertwined that they can hardly be disentangled.

In Spain at the time of Ferdinand and Isabella the word slavery was loaded with religious weight.* We noticed that the problem of slavery was teasing the Muslim administrator no less than the Christian. Upon the matter of handing out the privileges of one's own Faith, the two great power-blocs of Christendom and Islam, facing each other across the breadth and length of the Central Sea, had come to an identical way of thinking. In the practice of proselytizing, the Muslim had learned to go slow. The system of the Ottoman Turks required an increase of Christian subjects, for the burdens which could be legitimately forced upon them – super-tax, or military service, or slavery. Within Spain, the more that infidels had been eliminated, the more the lack was felt of somebody to be coerced. The cruelty of the Spanish Inquisition is attributable in part to the exceeding exasperation of the question, what to do about Conversos and Moriscos. The fact of conversion gave them defence against the threat of slavery, unless the conversion could be proved to be false, or unless they could be forced to confess some other major crime.

So Fonseca was under strong unspoken pressure to go slow about conversion of the natives. Whatever mad priest converted them could protest for their rights as Christians; there would be unconscionable fuss. The first command of the Sovereigns might state that the prime purpose of the expedition was conversion; but the second command implied that the project was strictly business. Hasty business, too: ships to be victualled for a round voyage of six months allowed only about three months for the landing force to get started before the

---

* Tawney in *Religion and the Rise of Capitalism*, when talking of serfdom maintained that generally speaking religious opinion, perhaps into the period of which I am speaking, ignored the question. 'Whatever "mad priests" might say and do,' says Tawney, 'the official Church, whose wealth consisted largely of villeins, walked with circumspection.' I think the awkward question was always and everywhere ignored, so long as it could be. My impression is that religious concern about slavery began to stir among 'mad priests' certainly by the 1440's.

carriers would have to sail for home. A quick effective beginning was essential.

That the prime business of the West Indies was to be business, was I think Fonseca's interpretation of the instructions. The six priests accepted by Fonseca appear to have been lay priests, none passionately dedicated to conversion. For the expedition in 1493 I am sure that Columbus as Admiral was listened to; as Viceroy, I suspect he was less listened to, and that Fonseca could arrange matters pretty much as he pleased. After all, the Council of Seville had more than ten years of experience with affairs of the Canaries, and that was experience to draw on. Columbus's Indians might or might not turn out to be like the Guanches, but it was as well to be prepared to fight them, and to take along hunting dogs. (Diego Chanca, surgeon to the fleet, approved of that – dogs could be used as food-tasters for strange foods.) The Indians who had been converted at Barcelona seemed gentle enough; there they had been much experimented with as guinea-pigs. They liked to play with beads, they liked little tinkling hawk's bells, ladies of the Court enjoyed experimenting with them. At Cadiz hawk's bells were packed among the trinkets for trading, and glass beads in quantity – and bearing in mind Chanca's thoughts about food-tasting, gentlemen added to their own prayer beads some that were lucky, especially apotropous, blest with natural power to turn away any poison. Chanca does not seem to have been much worried ahead of time about the possible medical problems of one people mixing with another and communicating diseases. The exchange of plagues was later to be greatly noted, after the harm had been done.*

Harm! Was there to be any thought beforehand that the glorious

---

* Smallpox, measles, influenza are among the plagues communicated by the Spaniards to the Indians of the New World; of the plagues received the one most mentioned is syphilis. 'This subject', says Morison, 'is very controversial', but he follows and agrees with Las Casas, who stated in his *Apologetica Historia* (c. 1530) that syphilis was communicated to Spanish women in Barcelona by the six Indians who were brought there by Columbus in 1493. Las Casas (who went to the Indies in 1502 and spent most of his life working with and for the Indians) was convinced that the disease was one of long standing in the New World.

expedition might cause, or come to, any real harm? Twelve hundred men sailing from Cadiz – out of this old world, into a New! They were picked men, picked from the crowd of those who envied; they were off to the earthly paradise, rose-garden to the mystic, gold-mine to the adventurer. What if there were scratches in the garden, or struggles for the gold? They were the prestige men, they knew what they stood for: the pride of Castile. They knew what they would build, a handsome sea-port with suburbs, and the name of the port, it was rumoured, the Queen had decreed, would be Isabela.

The thirty-nine men already at Navidad, how much gold would they have stored? – they would have had nearly a year – their gold would be picked up, and all would be shifted to the site that they had been told to find for the great port of Isabela. Rumours, excitement, all the thrills before the sailing from Cadiz – as the date approached there is a phrase used by French scientists for what I want. The phrase (I know no accurate translation) is *passage de la frénésie*. It is used for certain moments in the insect world, when impulse gathers towards migration. The collective excitement is such that an individual grasshopper may completely change colour as he joins the throng, to share the colour of those already gathered for the passage. These were no grasshoppers gathered at Cadiz; these were men, many of them already proved for reckless daring – Diego Marques, Hojeda, Margarit – to join with such men, would not other men change colour? *Passage de la frénésie* indeed for such as Columbus's gossipy friend Cuneo, who was much *tincto d'amore*, 'dyed with love'. There were no women for Cuneo to play with in the ship's company, but for him and others there were thoughts of native girls in paradise across the sea. Cuneo did not know the name 'America'; but later John Donne was to put into words the luscious feelings with which Cuneo embarked upon the voyage:

> *Licence my roaving hands, and let them go,*
> *Before, behind, between, above, below.*
> *O my America! my new-found-land,*
> *My kingdome, safliest when with one man man'd,*
> *My Myne of precious stones, My Empirie,*
> *How blest am I in this discovering thee!*

The outward voyage was in accord with every optimistic promise.

The Admiral picked up the sugar-cane at the Canaries, and the course westward was then, in Morison's words, 'a sailor's dream of the good life at sea'. Landfall was perfect: the big, high island of Dominica, at dawn of a Sunday morning, November 3. Aboard the ships the men sang the services devoutly, 'very devoutly, giving thanks to God for so short and safe a voyage'.

There was a slight delay, scouting for anchorage. This was found on the lee of a small flat island; and though that island was in itself of no value and of no interest, it was a convenient platform on which to stage the first ceremony. Columbus in full dress as Viceroy and with attendant banners went ashore and proclaimed formal possession for Spain. Then before nightfall the anchorage was exchanged for a sheltered bay of the mountainous and wooded Santa María de Guadalupe: so named by Columbus. Riding at anchor beside the dense tropical rain-forest, under the southern slope of this superb island's mile-high volcanic peak, there seemed no reason to refuse the eager clamour for a shore party to have a day for exploration. That was arranged: Diego Marques the leader chosen.

On that morrow those who had cheerfully scouted and picnicked round the bay returned to their ships by nightfall, but Diego Marques and his exploring party failed to return. A matter of impatience, perhaps of no real anxiety; but when a second nightfall came with no signal from the party, there was a chill of fear. Diego Marques and the men with him had vanished. Rumour spread through the ships. This was the very island that the Indians with the Admiral, of the gentle tribe of Tainos, had told him was inhabited by Caribs, 'cannibals'. Four search parties, each of fifty men, soon found traces of Caribs. In villages which had been hastily evacuated they found evidence that the inhabitants had been eaters of human flesh, that in huts there were indeed tied up some captive Tainos, being fattened before slaughter. Two of the captive Taino boys and 'twelve very beautiful plump girls' were brought back to the ships; but no sign as yet of Diego Marques. It was nearly a week before Diego and his men were found – unharmed. Their story was that they had got lost in the forest.

There is no indication that Columbus was worried about the loss of time. At leisure the thirty-nine men whom he had left in the stockade of Navidad would be found. Pedro Gutiérrez, as their Highnesses' representative, had been left to count the gold, and Diego de Harana, cousin of Columbus's mistress in Cordova, had been in general command. Columbus appears to have been unworried about them. The fleet coasted onward through the islands of the Antilles. Toward the middle of the month, at the island which Columbus called Santa Cruz (now St. Croix), the planters aboard ship noted how the forest had been cleared by the natives and the land so intensively cultivated that it 'looked like one great garden'. Here the voyagers had their first actual skirmish with Indians: a native canoe was sunk, one Indian killed, one Spaniard mortally wounded; and Cuneo captured and raped his first native girl. The fleet drew away to explore the Virgin Islands and what is now Puerto Rico, before making the landfall of Hispaniola. That was on November 22. Five days more of ranging a coast that he had previously discovered, with landmarks which he and his converted Indians remembered, brought Columbus and all his fleet safely to the site of Navidad.

At Navidad there was no sign whatever of any of the Spanish garrison. Nothing remained.

From that moment on, little ever went really right for Columbus. There was no satisfaction in the story of what had happened to the garrison at Navidad, as elicited by his attendant Tainos from the frightened headman of their tribe. That *cacique* well remembered 'Almirante', was fearful of him, was faithful to him, and indeed continued to remain obsequious. The calamity had been no fault of his tribe. The *cacique* had given the Spaniards at Navidad the women they wanted, but they had wanted more gold than he could supply. Leaving but a small guard for their stockade, the Spaniards had gone inland, where other Indians had killed them; those other Indians from inland had then come to kill the remnant at Navidad. A sorry story. Fray Buil, the leader of the six friars, proposed that the *cacique* should be put to death. Columbus refused. Nothing could remedy what had happened.

Navidad could never have been a site for a seaport, and now that Navidad was best forgotten, there was urgency to find a suitable harbour. Eastward along the coast of Hispaniola the fleet set out upon what proved to be a most exasperating search. The trade winds were now against the Admiral: beating to windward against the trades and against a stiff westward-flowing current meant that in twenty-five days the fleet made good, Morison estimates, only some thirty-two miles. In all that time there was no sign of a harbour, no choice among the harbours Columbus had reported 'such as you could not believe in without seeing them'. The phrases of the 'Columbus Letter' were coming back to haunt him. It was not merely the loss of twenty-five days that was bad: it was also a most exhausting waste of effort, loss of livestock and morale. 'Frequent shifting of sail and constant wetting with salt spray wore the sailors down, exasperated the colonists, and killed a large proportion of the livestock'. Finally, in the lee of a peninsula which did give shelter (though not so much a harbour as a roadstead open to the north and west) Columbus 'decided to pitch his city then and there'. This was the city to bear the royal name of Isabela. From the start it was a site of discontent.

Superb as navigator, incompetent as Viceroy, now began to be the general feeling about Columbus. Except for the serious loss of livestock, the cargo and the twelve hundred men had been successfully transported to Isabela. They had enjoyed a halcyon crossing of the Ocean Sea; they had enjoyed the marvels of an island cruise; but now there had been a month which had begun with the bitterest of disappointments and had continued with frustration. They had a further short four weeks in which to found their city before the bulk of the fleet, under their deputy captain, Torres, had to sail for Spain and report what had been done. Torres had to sail not later than four weeks after the landing at Isabela, else his crews would run out of rations. On the whole voyage so far, and during the island cruising, the expedition had made merry with Fonseca's provisions and Isabela, perhaps surprisingly, provided nothing. The site, chosen in desperation, was ill-chosen. 'There was no fresh water handy', says Morison, and the place 'was swarming with malaria-carrying mosquitoes'. The site had nevertheless to be forced into providing a grandiose report, and had to be forced to do so quickly.

A town was laid out in classic form (for nothing less than a miniature Cadiz would suit the Viceroy) with church and governor's palace fronting on a square plaza. Men were set to work felling trees, cutting coral stone and digging a canal to bring water from the nearest river, and about two hundred wattled huts were built as temporary housing. But insufficient wine and provisions had been retained.

Workers fell ill of malaria, or from drinking well water and eating strange fish, although Dr. Chanca tried every new species on a dog before he would let any Christian touch it. Columbus, impatient to get things done, drafted some of the gentlemen volunteers for the hard labour, which caused great indignation; they had come out to fight or get gold, not to do menial work. When they refused, they got no rations, and that was considered an abominable way to treat a Castilian hidalgo.[8]

It was on January 2, 1494, that the landing had been made at Isabela. Alonso de Hojeda was one of the Castilian courtiers who had come out to fight and get gold. On January 6 Hojeda and an armed party went off to raid the central valley of Hispaniola. Parties, other than those employed on digging the canal and starting on the church and the governor's palace, were clearing the suburbs for planting and scouring the neighbourhood for spiceries – pepper, cinnamon, sandalwood. As the days ticked over, midnights came in which Columbus had to contemplate the writing of his report. There was not much that was good to be said about the Indians. The fiasco at Navidad had created mutual distrustfulness. I don't know what happened to the Taino converts who had seen the glories of Spain; they vanish from the account. The Indians of the swampy land round Isabela also seemed to vanish at the thought of doing any work. They might be tempted to pilfer; they had nothing to trade. As soon as the colonists in their 'miasmic dump' (Morison's phrase for Isabela) began to exhibit sickness which within the first weeks affected 'several hundred' of the Spaniards, Indians avoided them as much as possible. There were twenty-six Indians, some at least 'canibales' captured at St. Croix, that Columbus proposed to send to Spain by Torres, for their Majesties to decide whether they were suitable for conversion or for slaves. There were plenty of parrots that Columbus could send – when Torres sailed, he did take sixty parrots. The spices within reach of Isabela even Columbus had to admit were disappointing. Half of the four weeks passed without anything of substance to put into the 'Torres Memorandum'. Then, on January 20, Hojeda returned to Isabela with a considerable amount of gold dust and three sizeable nuggets. 'All of us made merry,' Morison quotes Cuneo, 'not caring any longer about spicery, but only for this blessed gold.' That had to be the great excitement of Columbus's report, for the next two weeks presented him with nothing but a list of supplies urgently needed.

The verve of the original 'Columbus Letter' is slightly tempered in the 'Torres Memorandum', but only slightly. Isabela is represented (Columbus hopes that Torres will amplify this orally) as almost already worthy of its royal name. The plantations started are already sprouting: the sugar-cane is doing so splendidly that the products are going to eclipse those of Andalusia and Sicily.[9] Fortunately there was a sufficiency of actual gold to be impressive, and Morison points out how, in imagination, Columbus expands the sample. 'He excuses himself for not sending more because many of his men have fallen sick, a strong garrison has to be kept at Isabela, and with no beasts of burden to carry the heavy metal the accumulation of a shipload would require much time'. He tucks in a suggestion that in the future a working force of miners from the quicksilver mines of Estremadura might speed up production. The confidence expressed by Columbus is so forceful that it makes it easy for him to plead that more medicines should be sent out urgently; and more provisions (wine, ships' biscuit, bacon, pickled beef); and clothing, shoes, firearms, ammunition; and livestock – sheep and cattle – and he particularly needs to breed mules.

Columbus must have sweated to make the 'Torres Memorandum' so enthusiastic. It is possible he need not have sweated at all, at this time. There was I think as yet a strong compulsion on both Ferdinand and Isabella to exhibit the expedition as a success already proven; their own prestige demanded that they should applaud everything in the memorandum that was optimistic, and even perhaps supply more glow than Columbus had thought of. The requests Columbus made were at once passed on (with very few exceptions) to Fonseca, with the order that they were to be promptly fulfilled. The only unwise item of cargo for Columbus to send by Torres was the consignment of Indians, and the only unwise item of the memorandum was the suggestion that this might be the beginning of a profitable slave-trade. The Sovereigns evaded this very awkward question; but from the orders to send the provisions and ammunition Fonseca might judge, I think, that the character of the expedition was according to the expectation – conquest was primary, conversion could wait.

After Torres with twelve of the ships had departed for Spain at the end of January, the Viceroy faced the problem of making his dreams of a prosperous Isabela come true; and that, with sickness, discontent and low morale at the 'miasmic dump', was difficult. His method was to leave the disgruntled colonists to improve under his younger brother Diego, a man who was peaceable and gentle, patient (as he had to be) to listen to complaints; and for Christopher himself and the more impatient soldiery to set off upon a march of conquest into the interior. This for the several hundred men who made it was a splendid introduction to the great valley 'so fresh, so green, so open, of such color and altogether so full of beauty' that Columbus named it Vega Real, the 'Royal Plain'. A fort was established on the Cordillera Central, and Pedro Margarit and fifty men were left to stay and hold it. Others ranged in the mountains and among native villages for any and every hint of gold. The expedition naturally involved rough work: 'On that trip,' Morison quotes Cuneo, 'we spent twenty-nine days with terrible weather, bad food and worse drink; nevertheless, out of covetousness for that gold, we all kept strong and lusty.'

Morison comments that 'those left behind at Isabela were neither strong nor lusty'. Or rather, there was the strong and discontented leadership of Hojeda, who was not going to stand idle garrison duty for Diego while others enjoyed themselves inland. So Christopher, on return, sent Hojeda with the largest possible number of trouble-makers (the number of Hojeda's force is mentioned as four hundred) to join Margarit, to roam and forage and prospect at will. Then, once again leaving it to Diego to avoid (if he could) further mutiny, the Viceroy sailed away on the third of his assignments, the exploration of Cuba.

If the Indians of Hispaniola had contrived to have any capacity for combination they might have repeated on a larger scale at Isabela what they had done at Navidad. There was, one deduces, no conception of unity within the native tribes, and no question among the Spaniards but that it was their destiny to rule Hispaniola as they pleased. Whatever risk Columbus took by sailing away from Isabela does not appear to have bothered him. He sailed off in April, to be away as it turned out for five months of cruising. How rations were divided between the Isabela-party and the Viceroy's sailing-party, I don't know. Columbus had, of course, full licence for the cruise in his instructions. He took the *Niña*, veteran of his first voyage, as his flagship, and two smaller caravels, and his gossipy friend Cuneo went along as passenger. Many and successful adventures (including the discovery of Jamaica) pleased the voyagers, and the seaport of Isabela was still there when they got back.

There was some good news for the Viceroy on his return to Isabela. His older brother Bartholomew had arrived from Spain with three caravels, and Torres was reported to be on the way with a further fleet and more supplies. In every way the Sovereigns were supporting the colony. But there was also bad news at Isabela. During the Viceroy's absence Margarit had returned from inland; Fray Buil had joined him in open revolt against Diego; and no sooner had Bartholomew arrived than the rebels had seized his caravels and made off for Spain.

This was more serious for the Columbus dynasty than any of the Columbus brothers appear to have appreciated. As soon as the rebels arrived in Spain, Fray Buil obtained audience with the Queen, and Torres, on the point of sailing from Spain with the promised supplies, was given a letter from the Sovereigns to their Viceroy. The letter suggested that it would be to their convenience if Columbus himself should wish to return with Torres for a visit to the Court. There was no direct command, no hint of criticism, no summons – though if Columbus had chosen to do so, he might have read it that way. Whatever his reasoning, Columbus did not accept the suggestion. Instead, he collected fifteen hundred Indian captives at Isabela and sent five hundred of them back to Spain with Torres (all that Torres' ships could carry) to be sold as slaves at Seville. This was a strange response to the Queen who had instructed him to treat the natives of Hispaniola 'very well and lovingly'; the more so as about two hundred of the slaves died on the voyage, half the survivors were sick when they were landed, and 'almost all' died soon.*

Columbus had not been convinced by his five months of cruising that there was gold to be found immediately in Cuba, Jamaica and the other islands he had visited; but Hojeda had learned how to get it out of the Indians of Hispaniola, and Christopher and Bartholomew

* Reverting to Maximilian's accession as Emperor in 1493, to his long and close association with perhaps the most fervent of the preaching Orders, and to the Festival of the Rosary at Worms in 1495, I feel sure that if Ferdinand and Isabella wished to have Maximilian's son for their daughter, the Conquest of the West Indies had better be not merely Conquest but Conquest in the Faith. The marriage of Joanna and Philip was still to be achieved.

agreed with Hojeda to use the quickest and most drastic methods to get the quantity of gold that would solve every problem.

For almost a year the Columbus brothers were occupied with subjugating and organizing Hispaniola in order to obtain as much gold as possible. Several forts were built in the interior, and armed men were sent to force the natives to deliver a tribute of gold, the alternative to being killed. Every Indian fourteen years old or upward had to pay four hawks' bells full of gold dust annually. . . . Even after the tribute was cut down fifty per cent, it was impossible, for the most part, to fulfil. Indians took to the mountains, where the Spaniards hunted them with hounds; many who escaped their torturers died of starvation; others took cassava poison to end their miseries. . . . By 1508 a census showed 60,000 of the estimated 1492 population of 250,000 still alive, although the Bahamas and Cuba had been raided to obtain more slaves. Fifty years later, not 500 remained. The cruel policy initiated by Columbus and pursued by his successors resulted in complete genocide.[10]

None of the three who signed the Capitulations lived to see the second phase of the Spanish overseas operation. Isabella died in 1504, Columbus in 1505, Ferdinand in 1516. The hopeless site of Isabela was abandoned in 1496 or 1497 with intent to make a better town of Santo Domingo, but few recruits displayed enthusiasm for Santo Domingo under Columbus's leadership. For Columbus's third voyage, in 1498, some of the colonists were picked out of gaol. Thirty Spanish women, though without official pay or keep, were given opportunity to work their passage on that voyage. In 1499 Columbus was deposed as Viceroy. In 1502 a very considerable effort was made to revive or replace the 300 or so surviving Spaniards in Hispaniola. Ovando, Knight Commander of Alcántara, was sent from Spain with a fleet of thirty ships and 2,500 fresh colonists. The business management remained (and for many years to come) with Fonseca. Hopes about gold in Hispaniola were diminishing, but there were hopes of other

---

Hence the ineffable stupidity of Columbus (from the Sovereign's point of view) in sending a consignment of miserable slaves to Seville at a moment when the slavery-conversion question was particularly awkward. I doubt if even Fonseca was much pleased at the arrival of those slaves at Seville: he had no wish to invite the religious Orders to become concerned about treatment of the Indios.

products, notably sugar and ox-hides. The eight years of Ovando's government, the subsequent government of Diego Colón, Columbus's son, are all within the first phase of the Spanish Enterprise of the Indies.

The second phase – if we wish to be arbitrary about a date – begins about 1519. Round about then a sweep of the telescope (or change of telescopes) is needed.

NOTES

1. *By Faith and Work* by Viscount Mackintosh of Halifax (Hutchinson, London, 1966).

2. I am referring to *The Rose-Garden Game* by Eithne Wilkins (Gollancz, London, 1969). The sub-title of this delightful book is 'The symbolic background to the European Prayer-beads'. Miss Wilkins traces many of the ways in which 'a rosary is both a rose-garden and a string of beads'. With the author's permission I was privileged to read the manuscript before publication, and was bewitched by its charm and excitement.

3. Parry, p. 45.

4. Parry, p. 47.

5. Morison, p. 72.

6. *The Negro in American Civilization* by Nathaniel Weyl (Public Affairs Press, Washington, D.C., 1960), p. 3.

7. Ibid., p. 6.

8. Morison, p. 84.

9. In *Geschichte des Zuckers* Professor von Lippmann quotes this report of Columbus's, and at a hasty reading one might assume that at the time of Columbus's writing the sugar-cane, and other plantings, were already in superb development. And so they were, in Columbus's imagination. I have indicated that he was under pressure to anticipate.

10. Morison, p. 99.

CHAPTER 14

Realms of Gold

A DISTANT money-market which soon had much to do with Portuguese and Spanish shipping was the Bourse at Antwerp. Ever since 1503 Antwerp (not Lisbon) had been the depot of the Portuguese spice trade. Tawney (in *Religion and the Rise of Capitalism*[1]) describes how rational and easy it was for a Portuguese government to accept a bid from Antwerp for pepper in bulk and to receive credit while the commodity was still on the water. It was the proud boast of 'Happy Manoel' of Portugal that after Da Gama's voyage he could command the 'conquest, navigation, and commerce of Ethiopia, India, Arabia and Persia'; but when Manoel's men had collected the goods the machinery at Antwerp took command. The machinery at Antwerp was housed in the new Bourse, with its dedication 'For the use of merchants of whatever people or tongue' (*Ad usum mercatorum cuiusque gentis ac linguae*) and there was rich reward for Antwerp when the Bourse was noisy over produce from the East. What 'Happy Manoel' found himself retaining from his ventures was only the burglar's share.

Spices were profitable, but what a burglar looked for first was gold and jewels. When Manoel appointed Don Francisco d'Almeida as first Viceroy of India, Malacca was already identified as a place to be looted; d'Almeida's ships carried cannon for the purpose of taking Malacca; and it was in the action at Malacca that we notice a name to be noted again – Ferdinand Magellan. The year of the Portuguese attack upon Malacca was 1509; the attack was wholly unsuccessful; d'Almeida died, the ships went home; but Magellan remained in ports of the East. He acquired a Malay partner from Sumatra whose native name was Trapobana – Magellan christened him Enrique – and Trapobana or Enrique also has a claim to be remembered. With the Bourse at Antwerp clamouring for Eastern produce, Manoel did not let d'Almeida's failure stand. Manoel sent Albuquerque as second Viceroy of India, and Albuquerque was soon surnamed 'the Great' for capturing Goa in 1510 and then in quick succession Malabar,

Ceylon, and Malacca. Magellan captained a ship in the second and successful battle for Malacca in 1511. He shared in the loot and after some years returned to Lisbon with Enrique in attendance. We next hear of Magellan in the service of Spain.

Spain's commercial policy followed the pattern established by Portugal with the Bourse at Antwerp. The 'first phase' of the Spanish enterprise is the period in which Antwerp is more interested in the real Cathay exploited by Albuquerque than in the inferior Cathay found by Columbus. The 'second phase' begins with the reversal of that situation by the Spanish exploits in Mexico and Peru. The year 1519 might mark the turning-point.

The condition of Hispaniola, around 1519, is indicated in a letter written at the time:

> That in farming, arable, grazing, and gardening culivation consists the future of Española is clear beyond argument, and so from such labourers the Indies receives much benefit, for the future depends upon it. But how to carry out the purpose is the difficulty, because your Lordship must understand that the labourers, and all those who go to the Indies, have in their minds a fancy picture of the grandeur and riches of the Indies, of which they have confused notions; and arriving and finding that they have no wine, and have to eat roots, and that the gold and silver they dreamed of is a fantasy – they soon abominate the country, and, imagining that the gold and silver is in some other part of the Indies, they run away there.[2]

Under the eight years of Ovando's government (1502–09), and under the subsequent governorship of Columbus's son, Diego Colón, despite the runaways and the labour problem, Hispaniola's trade increased. Professor Parry has collected the shipping figures: 'leaving out of account exceptional fleets such as those of Ovando, Diego Colón and Pedrarias', there were 66 crossings of the Atlantic in 1508; in 1514 there were 77; in 1520, 108. The increase is not spectacular. In Hispaniola there were seven incorporated towns in 1507, fourteen in 1514. Sugar and ox-hides appear as the main produce; and plantations and stock-farming become a larger factor in the extinction of the Indians than the previous ruthlessness of gold-hunters.

The seizure of Indian lands, the methodical round-up of as many Indians as possible, division of them into lots of roughly 100, and distribution of them in such parcels to remain in indefinite personal servitude to individual colonists – or to overseers managing for absentee owners – had become normal practice in Hispaniola. The practice was extended to Cuba, when that island was subjugated in 1511. To Fonseca and the Council of Castile the islands of the Caribbean had become no more than a larger version of the Canary Islands, and the native problem, though on a larger scale, the same as it had been with the Guanches. Fonseca was business overseer for the King; he saw his duty as not to be soft, but to produce revenue.

An industrial pattern for the West Indies had thus developed. The portion of the West Indians was death or slavery; what other portion was there? Spanish humanitarians (Las Casas the most active of them) flew at Fonseca. The Bishop of Burgos (as Fonseca had become) was no better than a vulture – the Indians were dying – in Cuba seven thousand children had perished in three months. Fonseca, in anger, made the famous retort to Las Casas: 'Look you, what a dunce he is – what is this to me, and what is it to the King?' (*Mirad, que donoso necio, que se me da á mí, y que se le da al Rey?*)

What, toward the end of his life, did the Spanish Indies mean to the King? Ferdinand had both more and less concern than Fonseca made out: he had some concern about the government, and less concern about the profits – for he had written off any great expectations from that quarter. Ferdinand, at the age of sixty-four, wrote his last letter to his grandson and successor, Charles, largely about financial troubles,[3] but there is no suggestion that he expected Columbus's islands to be of much material assistance. Charles, who on Ferdinand's death (in 1516) came to the throne of Spain at the age of sixteen, was closer to his other grandfather, Maximilian: and a new half-hidden persuader comes into the scene – Maximilian's bankers, the famous German banking dynasty of Fuggers. The Fuggers had an eye on the young King Charles; it might have seemed a benevolent eye, for they would help him to his main ambition, not merely to be King of Spain but to succeed Maximilian as Holy Roman Emperor. Others were claimants for that title; it was arranged to be a matter of auction; which, on Maximilian's death in 1519, was an auction won for Charles by the help of the bankers. Charles, nineteen-year-old Emperor in 1519, was at once in pawn to the Fuggers for millions. For his own pocket-money he took stock of what could come from the

Spanish Indies. Two items may indicate his opinion of them, at that moment. One item is that just before sailing from Corunna to attend his installation as Emperor, he stooped to pick up a small loan from Diego Colón. The sum was 10,000 ducats.[4] The deal was that Diego might now assume the title of Viceroy of the Indies, the title his father had lost. Ferdinand had never been willing that Diego should have that title, or, at the worst, that it should pass for so small a sum. For Charles, all that the title 'Viceroy of the Indies' appears to have meant, was ten thousand ducats.

Fonseca and Diego might work the islands and the islanders as hard as they could; their produce in 1519 was not ranking high at Antwerp. The second item that shows Charles's thoughts about the Spanish Indies in 1519, is that in that year he turned to Magellan.

Magellan has never captured the affection of historians so much as Columbus. With all of his faults there is something warm about Columbus; with all of his merits, Magellan is cold. Of the two, Magellan's is the hard-luck story. In the beginning Columbus turned up in Portugal as a shipwrecked seaman; he swam ashore, and then made his way with nothing to help him except his volubility and charm, his exuberant imagination and his tenacity. Ferdinand Magellan starts differently: a Portuguese by birthright, son of a family with some claim to nobility. Magellan appears in boyhood as a page in the household of the Queen at Lisbon – the Queen whose husband waved Columbus away. Nobody blames Columbus for taking his ambitions to Castile; nobody is drawn to Magellan for his transfer to Spain. How that came about is enigmatic. There is nothing to go on but the hint that Manoel, the Queen's youngest brother, had 'always loathed' Magellan,[5] apparently from the days when they were both of the same household. When Manoel had become King, and was admired as 'Happy Manoel', Magellan (at the age of 25) departed from the Court of Portugal and sailed as a 'supernumerary' in one of d'Almeida's ships. Seven or eight years later we see him on return from the East, at Lisbon again – this time with money in hand, and with the novelty of a Malay companion – but still disliked by Manoel.

Magellan believed there might be a direct route from Lisbon to the Spice Isles – a westward route, more southerly than the course

Columbus had chosen – south even of the 'island' from which the Portuguese were importing a red dye-wood, and consequently calling it *terra de brasil*. He suggested to Manoel that he could lead a fleet by that south-west pasage to the Spice Isles, but Manoel refused to listen. Therefore Magellan, and Enrique with him, moved to Spain. The moment was well chosen. Charles, bored with his own Indies, was ready for a raid into Portuguese treasure-land. The Fuggers might have shaken their heads, but there is mention of another bankers' agent, de Haro. The Casa at Seville, which administered the Indies trade, was over-ruled. Arrangements for Magellan's Spanish expedition were authorized with remarkable speed. There were some subsequent delays in the outfitting, but Magellan took departure from San Lúcar on September 20, 1519 with five ships. He set his course southwest.

Magellan's officers and men were Spanish; the Malay companion was with him. For a long time the voyage was dull. Quick summary can scarcely convey the tedium. The tip of Brazil, as claimed by Portugal, had to be avoided; but the whole length of the southern seaboard of South America was tapped without a sign of an expected open passage. There was trouble over rations, there was trouble with the inhospitable coast of Patagonia, there was persistent weather-trouble: one ship was lost in the gales at sea. By the end of the first winter at an entrance (as it might be, or might not) to the Strait which bears Magellan's name, morale was very low. One Spanish captain refused all further hazard, turned his ship back, and is no more heard of. It was not until the second winter of the exploration that Magellan with his three remaining ships (*Trinidad*, 110 tons; *Concepción*, 90 tons; *Victoria*, 85 tons) found a way through the Strait to the west cape, Cabo Deseado, Cape Desire. 'The Captain General wept for joy and called that cape Cabo Deseado, for we had been desiring it for a long time'.

At Cape Desire the wind was fair for a course north-west. Magellan hopefully named the Ocean the Pacific; he had no notion of its vast emptiness. Two winters of pounding against a coastline which had always impeded, may have made it seem incredible that one might set out and fail to find a landfall. On a course northwest from Cape Desire Magellan found no landfall. A month, two months – the ships moved quietly enough – there was no sight of land. Men were assured that they were moving, as measured by the stars; there was no other measurement. Under a burning sun one sees them, painted ships upon a painted ocean. In the three ships, how many men? Perhaps by this time a hundred – already on short rations. In the third month the food ran out. There were no more rats; in the account we read how men gnawed at oxhides, chewed their belts, sawed boards to eat sawdust; and died. Nineteen had died of starvation when the ships at last touched the Marianas. Natives boarded them, food was brought; hostility flared, the ships clawed off. Magellan reached a more friendly archipelago 110 days after departure from Cape Desire.

What Magellan had then reached were islands of the Philippines. In April 1521 the ships moved to Cebu. At Mactan there was the sudden skirmish in which Magellan was killed. Leaderless, the expedition was now divided. *Trinidad* made east for Panama; the other two ships continued westward. The story goes that at his homeland of Sumatra Enrique disembarked, and possibly resumed his native name of Trapobana. If the story be true, he was the first man to have completed a circumnavigation of the globe.

Victoria survived the round-world voyage to Spain, arriving in September 1522, two weeks less than three years from her departure. She had picked up some spice, and the sale of her cargo is said to have exceeded the money outlayed on the expedition by £200.[6] The share to Charles was I suppose the Royal Fifth. It was of no material help to Charles. The first circumnavigation of the globe had been an extraordinary exploit, but before it was completed, and after the death of the man who planned it, it was eclipsed by the conquest of the City of Mexico. I said that Magellan's was a hard-luck story.

Six months before Magellan sailed from Spain, Hernán Cortés had sailed westward from Havana. That was a private adventure which altered everything.

I should pause at this point, for taking a distant view of the whole long story of the road, the Conquest of Mexico, quickly followed by the Conquest of Peru, presents a sudden road-accident on an appalling scale. From a cosmic view, one migration which I have been watching as it moved slowly over land and water, is about to meet another which has been moving in an opposite direction. The collision which occurs on the western side of the Americas therefore has a significance larger than that of a calamity in which the particular Spaniards and Indians are involved. Cortés and his men happen to be the first and front-line soldiers who carry a European attack into the heartland of hitherto independent civilizations. I must watch the conduct of the Conquistadors: I must see them as Spaniards opening the second phase of the Spanish Enterprise; I must also see a pattern set, to be copied or varied in the behaviour of other European peoples. I should pause and look once more at European motives.

We glanced at the *passage de la frénésie* which took adventurers to Columbus's islands, and we saw the first frenzy wear off. It was not only the islands that had become lacklustre; those who had so far run farther to a westward mainland had fared worse. At Darien the actions of Pedrarias caused him to be called *furor Domini*. Peter Martyr has nothing to say of the affairs of Pedrarias 'because they were all horrid transactions, nothing pleasant in any of them'. Balboa got across the Isthmus, gazed upon a South Sea, managed even to build some brigantines, but was too gentle with the Indians, and his head was cut off by Pedrarias. (The soldier sent to bring Balboa for execution happened to be Francisco Pizarro.) News of that kind, but of no good kind, was relayed from the mainland – gold as measured by hawks' bells, but nothing to be translated into terms of startling benefit – until the news from Cortés about Mexico. Now for the first time even the most sceptical had to appreciate that the fabulous had really happened; and Pizarro was inspired to find yet another empire as wonderful as that of Marco Polo. This was news also not only of instant wealth, but of wealth that would continue. The gorgeous treasures of the treasure-houses in stone cities proved what reserves there were within the mountains. Pizarro, having murdered an Inca, was in his turn murdered; those deeds, it seemed, could be forgotten – what was important was the more and more new-built brigantines sailing from Panama. 'A fair wind for the navigator to Peru,' said Cieza de León, 'is that same wind that fans the smelting-kilns for silver.'[7] That was the *bonanza*, the weather that was 'set fair'; and the beckoning stars to sail by, were the fifteen thousand smelting-fires that lighted the night above the peak-tops of Potosi.*

---

* Baudin, in *A Socialist Empire* (p. 109) says that the smelting of silver (with a modicum of lead added to make the metal flow) was done in the follow-

What is then to be looked at is the suction machinery at Antwerp. The precious metals start off from New Spain for Old Spain, but Antwerp is the bullion-market. Bullion, because of its quantity, is cheapened, other prices rise, and he who comes off best in the exchange is not the Spaniard. The rising power in Europe of the early 16th century, as pictured by Tawney, is the merchant-banker. Erasmus, in 1517, might still be writing of Royalty as represented by the eagle, the bird to be singled out above all others as 'carnivorous, greedy, hateful to all, the curse of all, and, with its great power of doing harm, surpassing them all in its desire of doing it'.[8] Tawney prefers to single out the banking dynasties behind the scene, to whom the nominal Heads of States 'were puppets dancing on wires held by a money-power to which political struggles were irrelevant except as an opportunity for gain'. The young King Charles of Spain, in that view, is one of the puppets; having been lent the money to purchase the imperial crown, then, although he is King-Emperor, he finds himself rated by the Fuggers for the unpaid debt, 'in the tone of a pawnbroker rating a necessitous client'.[9] In other days it had been a Pope who might humiliate an Emperor; in Europe of the early 16th century, supremacy is with the banker. How to exert control of money-power, is the concern of moralists. Protestants feel the Church of Rome is far too lax in its control; there is Protestant indignation that the head of the firm of the Fuggers should have been permitted to die in the odour of sanctity, after seeing his firm profit as much as 54 per cent. in each of the preceding sixteen years. Calvinism, while giving a 'whole-hearted imprimatur to the life of business enterprise', at the same time tries to lay upon it 'the restraining hand of an inquisitorial discipline' stricter than that of Rome. There are 'seeds of discord', as Tawney points out, in the Calvinist morality, and the money-market of Antwerp is the seed-bed for them – very much a seed-bed when it

---

ing way: 'The ores were crushed with a stone and placed in kilns (*huaira*) shaped like flowerpots and perforated at the base. Charcoal was put on top of the ore in the kiln, and the metal, on reaching the point of fluidity, would drop into earthenware receptacles beneath. These kilns were set up on hilltops where there was a strong wind; and, if we are to believe the chroniclers, when the Spaniards began to exploit the mines of Potosí, it was an enchanting experience to see twelve or fifteen thousand fires lighting up the evening skies over the mountains'.

was once a year 'enriched with a golden harvest from the East' and once a year 'irrigated with the bullion of America'. In Antwerp, discord between greed and godliness shows up in the money-market; and in that realm Protestant moralists of Geneva find it difficult enough to impose 'inquisitorial discipline'.

Seville at the same period is preoccupied with a different facet of the economic matrix – with the problem of slave-labour. The stronger the demand in Europe for produce of the Americas, the heavier the pressure was on the Indians. That was of small concern to Antwerp or Geneva. It was a matter which roused strong feelings within Spain.

It had been a Spanish priest who denounced Pedro de Vera for his treatment of the Guanches in the Canary Islands, and the Sovereigns recalled de Vera and disgraced him. One of de Vera's institutions in the Canaries for dealing with captured natives was the *repartimiento* system of selling them in batches to the sugar planters. This was the system copied by Columbus in Hispaniola, in his last years as Viceroy; his control of the slave-owners was so ineffective that he was denounced and, though the rest of the original Capitulations were honoured, he was stripped of his titles and of further authority. If a modified *repartimiento* system of slavery could be condoned at all, it called for the owners of slaves to be under strict military discipline; and it was to impose such discipline that Ovando, Knight Commander of Alcántara, was sent with a fleet of thirty ships in 1502. Among the 2,500 men who enlisted to go to Hispaniola with Ovando were Hernán Cortés and Bartolomé de las Casas.

Ovando's expedition was a major operation, with the predominant purpose of establishing a well-governed Hispaniola. For many of those who enlisted, the choice was between service with the army in Italy against the superior artillery of France, or the life of the frontiersman. Whatever discipline Ovando might announce beforehand, there was ever the old idea of gold and naked savages, and the thought that the Indies would prove to be a land 'where there aren't no Ten Commandments'. What were scruples at home could drop off as soon as a ship crossed the 'Columbus Line', the meridian which divided the Old World from the New. Las Casas later on invented a parable to express that feeling. On shipboard, colonists would be aware of lice, he said, until they reached the 'Columbus Line'; as they crossed the line, the lice would disappear; but on any return voyage the lice could be expected to emerge from hiding at the same longitude 'in great and disturbing numbers'. In an age when lice as 'pearls of God' or pricks of conscience was a familiar metaphor, the parable was understood. Las Casas appears at once as one of the serious-minded volunteers. His father had been with Columbus on the original voyage of discovery; the son had been a student at Salamanca, where he took a licentiate's degree; and now at the age of 28 Las Casas was going to Hispaniola as a lettered man (*letrado*). Cortés, by comparison, had been signed on for the journey when he was a boy of 17, as an alternative of his going to Italy as a swordsman. His family may have found him troublesome. It was all signed up for him to sail with Ovando, but he missed that sailing – he fell off a wall at night-time after an amorous adventure, and the injuries caused a long delay. He was shipped out with a private merchant-venturer to join Ovando two years later.

By the time Cortés reached Hispaniola, Ovando had demonstrated that he had no intention of lowering the reputation of his knightly Order, a famous royal Order, with the green cross as emblem. Conduct under Ovando in the New World was to be in no way more lax than the conduct in the Old. The immediate discipline imposed on the colonists was much approved by Las Casas, whose temperament inclined him to become a lay-priest, a *clerigo*. As for the Indians, it was to be understood that they had exactly the same rights and privileges as the legally free peasants of Spain. This was the proclamation made by Ovando on his arrival, that Indians were all free men, that they would pay tribute only as did all other subjects of the Crown. There would be military compulsion to work periodically on royal service – gold washing or public works – but no individual Spaniard was to rob or harm them. The first crunch came over the interpretation of the word 'freedom'. For the legally free peasant in Spain (or anywhere else in Christendom) freedom did not mean 'freedom to be idle, to be left to one's own devices'.[10] But the Indians who heard that they were free men ran off into the bush. Within a few months the settlements were without food or labour. On the assumption that life in the settlements was to be the same as life in Old Spain, there was no solution except to round up the Indians and teach them to be Spanish peasants. The *repartimiento* system of collecting Indians and offering them in parcels to individual owners was therefore extended and legalized by Ovando; yet strict oversight as to proper treatment of the Indians was to be observed.

A second crunch came over the interpretation, what was 'proper treatment' for the Tainos of Hispaniola? They simply did not take to captivity; whether the captivity was kind or harsh, they died. In the eight years of Ovando's government, Las Casas estimated that more than nine-tenths of the Tainos perished. Las Casas placed the responsibility for this upon Ovando: 'he was a man fit to govern, but not fit to govern Indians'. Yet accusation of Ovando did not solve the problem; no man had as yet discovered one single mode of government that would make both peoples thrive. Ovando permitted some other experiments: the importation to Hispaniola of tribes from other islands, in the hope they might prove healthier slaves; the beginnings also of importing Negroes from Portuguese sources. Yet it was never Ovando's intention that the slavery system should be unrestricted. He kept the Spaniards' ownership to a better degree of order than other Governors had done, or were likely to do. Ovando was feared and obeyed by the colonists, though he was often scorned for his own lack of avarice. At the end of his term of duty he left such property as he had acquired on the island for charitable purposes; and 'when he left he had to borrow five hundred castellanos for his journey'.[11]

It was after the appointment of Diego Colón as Governor in 1509 that the dispute increased, at first in Hispaniola and then in Spain itself, about slavery. A crucial point was that there was further proposal to subjugate Cuba and to extend the same slavery system there, with (as some hoped and some feared) less control than Ovando had exerted. In Spain, Fonseca continued to be the Royal Councillor, in effect in complete charge of the Casa at Seville and of all the bureaucratic management of the Indies. What Fonseca had foreseen and fought against from the beginning, now happened: over the slavery question, other church-men interfered. In Santo Domingo the Order of Dominicans preached openly against the system, against the theory and against the practice. These were no outsiders speaking; these were loyal Spaniards; Diego Colón tried to silence them, but could not. Antonio de Montesinos, most outspoken of the preachers, was smuggled away to Spain to appeal direct to the King. So, to Ferdinand, the old and far from simple problem once more came up. His most experienced and powerful advisers were in violent disagreement. Fonseca was immovably against the Dominicans as trouble-makers: faithful old Ximénes (Isabella's confessor), although himself a Franciscan, supported de Montesinos. The compromise was a new and general code drawn up to govern the status and treatment of all natives of the Spanish Indies. This code was promulgated in 1512 and known as the Laws of Burgos. The naming of the code was a humiliation for Fonseca, for he was Bishop of Burgos, and had been determined to have no restrictions (except of his own) laid upon colonists and traders. The consolation he could draw was that although the code was moderately pious it was likely to be in practice unenforceable.*

Las Casas and Cortés both went with the expedition to subjugate Cuba in 1511. During Ovando's term Las Casas had not made himself conspicuous, but on the Cuban expedition he suddenly spoke up fiercely to the military commander, Narvaez, for his wholly unnecessary brutality. After the conquest of Cuba Las Casas and a business partner accepted their portion of Indians and worked them for farming and gold-washing 'with no more heed than others'. But, as he tells, it happened that for the Feast of Pentecost in 1514 there was only one other *clerigo* in the whole of Cuba, and nobody but Las Casas in his part of the island to say mass and to preach. In preparation, he turned to the 34th chapter of *Ecclesiasticus,* and he recalled the example of the Dominicans in Santo Domingo. The impossibility of reconciling his sermon with his own behaviour caused him to renounce his own slave-holding, to denounce the system, and to become a convert to the Dominican Order. To some he appeared frantic and crazy; though not to his business partner, who agreed with his scruples. The farm was sold. Las Casas set off to Spain to speak direct with the King. Ferdinand, feeling old and tired by this time, and not unacquainted with pestilent missionaries, nevertheless talked with and listened to Las Casas; and once again Ximénes (though also old and tired) was drawn in; and once again Fonseca ('ready, bold, and dexterous') fought against any restriction on slave-owners or on

---

* Subsequently, in 1514, Fonseca persuaded the King to entrust him with the separate royal seal for the formal authentication of all decrees and decisions pertaining to the Indies. (J. H. Parry, *The Spanish Seaborne Empire* p. 58.)

the slave-trade – he was already approving more licences issued by the Casa for the purchase of Negroes from Africa. It seemed that nothing much could be really altered.

The point of this excursion is to emphasize the division of Spanish feelings over freedom of enterprise in labour-relations, and to emphasize that by 1519 the coupling of labour-relations with race-relations seemed to some (like Fonseca) to simplify the problem, to others (like Las Casas) to render it impossible.

Ferdinand died; Ximénes was temporary Regent for the young King Charles; and Ximénes on his own death-bed authorized Las Casas to organize free villages for Indians and free reserves of lands for them in Hispaniola. At last, Las Casas saw hope – the Hope that Isabella's green cross of Alcántara had been supposed to symbolize. The hope was, there would be a resumption, with missionary assistance, of Indian self-government. After some years the result, Las Casas had to admit, was total failure. There were many causes of failure (smallpox contributed), but Las Casas felt the main cause was that everything in Hispaniola had been wrongly started. 'Bitterly disappointed in Hispaniola,' as Parry says, Las Casas in 1521 embarked on a social experiment of his own, the settlement of Cumaná on the coast of Venezuela 'of a community of Spanish farmers and artisans living a common Christian life under priestly direction, supporting themselves by their own efforts without recourse to forced labour'. The community was dedicated to the object of converting the unspoiled natives of Venezuela. 'It failed as completely as the free villages of Hispaniola; the settlers were massacred by the local Indians. Even Las Casas' spirit was crushed, for a time, by this disaster.'[12]

When Cortés sailed from Havana on February 10, 1519 his expedition consisted of 11 ships, the largest being about a hundred tons. The ships carried:

508 swordsmen		10 brass cannon
100 sailors	also	4 small cannon
32 crossbowmen		16 horses
13 musketeers		a number of dogs

and a quantity of powder, ball, crossbow
arrows and spare parts

It is worth listing the items as above (Mr. Maurice Collis does so in his *Cortés and Montezuma**) to emphasize the intent. On the evidence, it was a very formidable military force. It was enormous, for a private venture. Cortés had prospered in the islands; he was married, but a planter's life was not contenting him. He mortgaged his property and borrowed all he could to outfit this expedition. His initiative caught on; other proprietors of more or less his own age (which was then 34) joined with him, and rank and file according to capacity brought their own arms and equipment. At first the whole operation was furtive and as secret as possible. There could be no pretence of legality. They were, as Collis calls them, a brotherhood of adventurers; or, equally, a gang of brigands. The spirit inspired by Cortés was, however, to think of themselves as the King of Spain's men, and in their self-appointed adventure it was essential that of all spoils they would lay aside the Royal Fifth. They were emphatically not Governor's men, for the Governor of Cuba very properly attempted to arrest Cortés. By that time Cortés had more men than the Governor; and Cortés' men were, and mostly so remained, completely loyal to Cortés. 'The Alvarados, Puertocarrero, Olid, Escalante, all of us would have given our lives for Cortés,' said Bernal Díaz.

What shall I say of the conquest of Mexico that has not been better said a hundred years ago by the great Prescott, or by Sir Arthur Helps? Or possibly best of all, in the letters of Cortés himself, and the *Life* by his secretary Lopez de Gómara, and the marvellous eye-witness narrative of the old soldier who was there in continuous action, Bernal Díaz del Castillo? Who is so foolish as to attempt to retell the *Iliad*? It has sometimes been complained that no Spanish poet composed an epic poem on the Spanish conquests, such as Camoens composed in *The Lusiads* as a national epic of Portugal; but to read Bernal Díaz and Gómara (one has to read both of them[13]) is to feel the drama of Mexico at levels of tension and horror never touched by Camoens. In Gómara and Bernal Díaz is most of the epic,

---

* *Cortés and Montezuma* by Maurice Collis (Faber, London, 1954) is an excellent short study. As for the spelling, I follow the school which prefers *Moctezuma*. I have followed Mr. Collis, though, in avoiding the term 'Aztec'. The race which ruled Central America at the time of the conquest was called the Mexica, in its own language. 'Aztec' was a term later coined by Europeans and Mr Collis feels 'the time has come to forget it'.

and once their documents have been read, no gloss is needed. Characters (Cortés, Moctezuma, Falling Eagle, Doña Marina) and actions (the crossing of the causeway and the retreat, the rallying and building of the brigantines and final capture of the island City) – all these and all the minor actions (how Narvaez lost his eye, how Falling Eagle was betrayed) – are in those two Spanish chronicles, and in their living setting. It is a pity, granted, that no Homer has arisen, and each must make the epic for himself. But the matter is there; and what else can be said? (As, indeed, what can you say about Homer? – except, read him.)

Whether brisk Cortés would have started his private action in Ferdinand's lifetime is an open question. Clearly he had no fear of Diego Colón, and when it was only Narvaez who was sent to Mexico to put a stop to Cortés, Cortés laughed. But I can hardly avoid thoughts that have been rising while looking at the first phase of the Spanish Enterprise; and indeed it was a burden of thoughts from the beginning of the long road westward, that made me pause before looking at the road-accident to come.

From the cosmic point of view, what I have been speaking of as a road-accident is a collision that was sometime bound to occur, if two human migrations were drifting round the globe in opposite directions.

Palaeontologists explain this to me, as having happened. There is, for instance, a schematic 'minimum-evolution tree' which may be drawn after study of blood-group data of fifteen human populations. Most authorities agree upon an area of Asia as having been a region from which prehistoric tribes radiated. This may not preclude other beginnings of 'human' life in other places, but enough is 'known' about prehistory to postulate the tree that I am looking at, with its roots in Asia and its branches spreading outward. When that schematic 'tree' is mapped upon the globe to show the spread of the fifteen populations as studied by Edwards and Cavalli-Sforza,[14] I see the two branches which concern me, out-spreading from the same trunk and, after reaching round the world, coming into touch as geometrically neatly as if it were all a blackboard exercise.

I see that, but only as a reasonable blackboard exercise. The actual collision of two migrations of individual human beings is something different.

My narrative of westward journeyers began at a recent moment. I have been dealing with

> *Last week in Babylon,*
> *Last night in Rome....*

My journeyers, in whom I have felt proprietary interest, are now meeting with another set of travellers. What palaeontologists tell me is that originally their forebears ran off from the same part of Asia as mine. The meeting is a family reunion. The migrants, though, have travelled different roads, and that of itself makes them strangers. If my companions on the Road West, with habits such as I have been observing, meet with strangers whose beliefs are different, the chances are that there will be instant fighting. The surprise is that in spite of what we have been watching in Columbus's islands, and in spite of the spirit with which Cortés and his private army approached Mexico, the actual first reception by Moctezuma was not unfriendly.

A phenomenon which has been often discussed was a feeling among Mexicans, at the time Cortés approached, that there was likely to be a second coming of a white god who had been in Mexico before.

As reported by early Spaniards, as repeated by Humboldt at the beginning of the 19th century and as frequently repeated since, there had been steadily in Mexican tradition a primary and dark god, Tezcatlipoca (the Mirror that Smokes), associated with the night sky, also appearing in another aspect especially as a war god, defender of the tribe; and at one time there had come suddenly another god, Quetzalcohuatl (Green-feathered Serpent, or Eloquent Serpent). In the story repeated by Sir Arthur Helps, Quetzalcohuatl came among Mexicans in the mortal form of a white and bearded man, of broad brow, dressed in strange dress; he was a law-giver who recommended severe penances, lacerating his own body with the prickles of the agave and the thorns of the cactus, but who dissuaded his followers from human sacrifices. The teacher moved from Anahuac to the plains of Cholula and governed there with wisdom; then passed to a distant country and was not heard of, but remembered.

Thus far go Humboldt and Helps, and they mention the similar myths among other Indian peoples. In his more recent study Mr. Collis portrays the Mexican belief in a second coming of Quetzalcohuatl in precise detail. When in a distant past Tezcatlipoca had succeeded in driving out Quetzalcohuatl,

> He embarked on a magic raft on the coast near Tabasco and departed to an unknown region in the East. But before going he had uttered a prophecy: 'I will return in a One Reed year and re-establish my rule. It will be a time of great tribulation for the people'. This utterance was taken to mean that when he returned he would destroy the guardian god and punish the people for having abetted his expulsion. One Reed year occurred at irregular intervals. The year 1363 had been a One Reed; so had the year 1467. Quetzalcoatl had not come on either of these years. The next One Reed was 1519, the year we have now reached in this story.[15]

'This story,' which Mr. Collis very vividly retells, is the story of how a powerful ruler, Moctezuma (the Fretted One), meekly yielded himself and his city to the Spanish intruder who happened to come from the east to the port of San Juan de Ulúa [Veracruz] on Holy Thursday, 1519. Mr. Collis dwells upon the explanation: the arrival of a god was being awaited. Men of Cholula, men of Mexico, were expectant and watchful for the visitation of a god in the person of a white and bearded man. Moctezuma's tensions when he heard of the arrival and the vacillations of his conduct, are attributed to the power over the Mexicans of their own legend and to the apparently precise fulfilment of the prophecies of their own computations. The imagination shown by Cortés in grasping the situation and his dexterity in exploiting it is attributed partly to the advice of the remarkable Indian woman who had become his counsellor, his campaign-wife and his interpreter – the very remarkable woman named Malinche and known to the Spaniards as Doña Marina.

Certainly one of the most mysterious moments of history was the capitulation of Moctezuma, when he summoned the council in his palace 'which was attended by all the lords of Mexico and the country round, and either of his own volition, or urged by Cortés, he spoke to them in the presence of the Spaniards'. The speech is recorded by Gómara as told to him by Cortés, and Gómara comments:

Moctezuma could say no more, because of his tears and sobs, and all the people wept so bitterly that for a good while they could not answer him. They sighed and groaned so heavily that they even moved the hearts of our men; but in the end they said they would do as he commanded.

Then Moctezuma, first, and after him alike all his people gave themselves as vassals to the King of Castile and promised to be loyal to him (all of which was duly recorded with notary and witnesses), and each man retired to his own house, with God knows what feelings, as you can imagine. It was a notable thing to see Moctezuma and so many lords and gentlemen in tears, and to see how each one suffered. But they could not do otherwise, not only because Moctezuma desired and commanded it, but because it was rumoured that with Moctezuma not only would the line of the Culhúans end, but their rule also. . . .[16]

This first surrender of Mexicans to Spaniards was not a binding one. The fighting broke out in earnest – the fighting that made Bernal Díaz exclaim: 'I do not know why I am writing so calmly, for some three or four soldiers of our company who had served in Italy swore to God many times that they had never seen such fierce fighting, not even in Christian wars, or against the French king's artillery, or the Great Turk. . . .' That was even before Moctezuma's death, and after his death the fighting was harder, for the Mexicans had then chosen, as Bernal Díaz says, 'a brave king, who would not be so faint-hearted as to be deceived by false speeches like their good Moctezuma'. It was then that Bernal Díaz was candid to admit that he had had a bellyful of fighting. 'We stared death in the face', he says, and 'we decided to get out of Mexico'.

That is to say, Cortés, at that moment, so decided. How any leader but Cortés could have extricated his men across the causeway, or how any other leader could have rallied his small army and reorganized his Indian allies for the subsequent and final assault upon the City, are questions that can never fail to stir one's admiration for him. In the ultimate defeat of the Mexicans, sentiment turns naturally to that 'brave king' Cuauhtémoc (Falling Eagle) who had replaced 'good Moctezuma'. Falling Eagle was captured, and the summary account in Cortés' own letter to the King-Emperor Charles is: 'This lord having been made prisoner, the war immediately ceased . . .' After seventy-five days the siege of the City of Mexico was over, on August

13, 1521. The end of the fighting was so sudden that the absence of noise seemed very strange.

In an epic crammed with remarkable stories, the subsequent murder of Cuauhtémoc by Cortés is surely one of the most extraordinary: not the killing, but the method. Cuauhtémoc, when captured and brought before Cortés, asked for his death immediately. His words were: 'I did not surrender; I was taken by force.' Cortés endeavoured to embrace him, and Cuauhtémoc refused the embrace. Pointing to the dagger which Cortés had in his belt, he said: 'Stab me.' 'When he bade me stab him I enheartened him and told him not to be afraid,' Cortés wrote in his letter to Charles. Clearly it did not suit quick-thinking Cortés to have Cuauhtémoc dead at that moment; and clearly Cuauhtémoc ('not so faint-hearted as to be deceived by false speeches') knew that Cortés would have him killed whenever that was safe.

Nothing was safe for Cortés at the first moment of Conquest. The destruction of the City of Mexico 'filled everyone', says Gómara, 'with astonishment and dread'. Within the halls of Moctezuma a handful of Spaniards were setting up to rule uncountable Indians; Gómara goes on to detail the 'ambassadors' who promptly came to look at the Spaniards from large and diverse provinces, some of which 'were three hundred leagues away'. There were instant quarrels among the Spaniards over the looting of the City and division of treasure; there was for Cortés the vital problem of the explanatory letter to his own King and the despatch of a sufficiently impressive Royal Fifth of tribute. The Royal Fifth was sent off from Veracruz in three caravels. The accompanying letter was a remarkable composition. Cortés assumed the royal approval, petitioned that the land might be called New Spain, that his grants of lands and slaves to his Conquistadors might be confirmed, that friars be sent quickly, and farmers with herds, plants and seeds – but no turncoats (i.e. Conversos or Moriscos), and no physicians or lawyers.

Until there could be reply from the King, it was up to Cortés to exert a complete and martial authority over a New Spain of unknown size and of a population nowadays estimated to have been about twenty-five million. It was difficult to restrain his own captains from dashing away to set up independencies: Cristobal de Olid, for instance, sailed off with a fleet to capture a region eastward of the

Yucatan peninsula, now called Honduras. Such division of forces depleted Cortés bodyguard, and there was the constant threat of Indian 'ambassadors' eyeing him. Always, one gathers, Doña Marina was indispensable as an interpreter, confidante, and adviser. If Cuauhtémoc could not be won over, it was imperative at least to keep him alive and to make a show of his apparent subservience. I turn to a passage in Gómara:

> Cuauhtémoc was, as history tells us, a valiant man, and in adversity proved his royal heart and courage, in favour of peace at the beginning of the war, and in perseverance during the siege; at the time of his arrest, and when he was hanged, or was tortured to reveal the treasures of Moctezuma. (His feet were smeared with oil and exposed many times to the fire; but [his torturers] gained more infamy than gold). Cortés, indeed, should have preserved his life as a precious jewel, for Cuauhtémoc was the triumph and glory of his victories; but Cortés did not wish to keep him alive in such a troubled land and time. It is true that he thought highly of him and that the Indians held him in the same honour and reverence in which they had held Moctezuma; and I believe it was for this reason that Cortés always had Cuauhtémoc in his company when he rode through the city, or went on foot.

It is a passage to be read with the knowledge that Gómara was writing the 'official' *Life*. After Cortés towards the end of his life was living in Castile, Gómara was the secular priest of his household, lived with him and 'wrote nothing but what Cortés himself told him to write'. The picture that he gives of Cortés in the first years of the Conquest is the picture Cortés desired. It is a picture of Cortés fearing to make public appearances unless he had Cuauhtémoc (or, as my tongue finds it easier to say, Falling Eagle) with him. It is a picture of capturer and captive held together, for three years, in very uneasy bond. During that three years there were plenty of other pressures on Cortés; one of them domestic. Cortés wife, Catalina, arrived from Cuba. That was in the summer of 1522. Catalina's journey proved to be unwise. Doña Marina was the wife who had shared Cortés' campaign, and had borne him a son. Doña Marina was the great lady of Mexico. Catalina survived the climate of Mexico for three months, and then she died. Cortés was accused of her murder, and there was some sort of inquiry. Gómara provides no information; Bernal Díaz calls it a 'delicate subject'; nothing was proven. The 'troubled land and time' was beginning to settle. Officials were arriving from Spain to help (or to profit by) the administration. Priests were arriving to convert the pagans. Yet the picture remains, that Cortés did not regard things as being so settled as to permit himself to be seen, on horse or foot, without the presence of Falling Eagle. It can hardly have been a continuous companionship, but it was one that went on. It went on for three years, in spite of Gómara's other comment: 'Cortés did not wish to keep him alive'.

Olid's independency in Honduras was proving hostile. Cortés decided in 1524 to pay a visit, in person, to Olid. The plan for the visit was curious. Cortés chose to go overland, through the unexplored dark forests of what is now Guatemala. The manner of his setting forth from the City of Mexico is most impressive:

> Though going on a campaign to distant unknown regions, he took with him great services of gold and silver plate, three clerics to preach, a major-domo, a butler, a steward and a chamberlain. He had a doctor and a surgeon, several pages, eight grooms and two falconers. To keep his friends amused in the evening he brought five musicians, good both for wind and strings, an acrobat, a conjurer and a puppet master. Of his old companions he had Sandoval and Doña Marina. He also took Falling Eagle with him.[17]

The excessive ceremony of the setting forth, in October, is surely sinister. One knows beforehand that the journey is not going to be for amusement. It almost seems as if contrived to have been a journey into darkness. Once the armed force has got into the forests and is out of sight, little more is heard about the grooms and falconers, the gold and silver plate, the musicians, acrobat and puppet masters: they were presumably sent back. What one does hear about is one of the most extraordinary devices ever to be used for murder – a mariners' compass. Before the setting forth one feels that Cortés knew, and Falling Eagle knew, that there would be some opportunity of murder to come. For several months of the journey Cortés bided his time. There is no hint of murder. Then, as Gómara tells it, came a situation such as this: the Spaniards and Mexicans (for Falling Eagle was accompanied by other Mexican hostages – ten in all) 'were now in such a dense forest that they could see only the sky above them and the ground they trod, the trees being so tall that it was impossible to climb them and survey the country. They wandered about lost in it for two days . . . some thought they would die before reaching an inhabited place. Then Cortés brought out a compass and mariner's card. . . .' According to Cortés consultation of the compass, they 'opened a road by hand', and the road, 'after much hardship', brought them to the desired target 'squarely'.

Perhaps there were also other occasions on which, with careful ingenuity, it was impressed upon all the Mexicans that 'the mirror (which was their name for the compass)' could reveal all secret things, and that the mirror would not lie. When this faith was well planted, the mirror suddenly instructed Cortés that all ten of the Mexicans were guilty of treasonable thoughts. They were arrested, and there was no argument against the mirror. All might have been hanged – but if so, there would have been none to report Cortés' magic power. Cortés had only three of them hanged: Cuauhtémoc, Tlacatlec and Tetlepanquetzal. The execution took place at Izancanac during Lent, 1525. The death of Falling Eagle and of the two others was, Gómara says, 'a sufficient lesson to the rest'.

One other curious event which took place during the expedition to Honduras was that Doña Marina was formally married to a Captain Xaramillo. Gómara tells us that Xaramillo, at the time, was drunk; and that some thought Cortés should not have permitted his 'wife' to be married off.

Professor Simpson, introducing his edition of Gómara's *Istoria*, rightly speaks of the account of Cortés' march from Mexico to Honduras as 'heroic, tragic, and enthralling'. The two episodes which stand out to me are those of Falling Eagle and Doña Marina, and they stand out partly as illustrations of a peculiar kind of cunning. It is as if the problem of Falling Eagle had been transformed in Cortés' mind into something completely abstract – a wholly abstract 'brain-twister' – it is as such, that the use of the compass-box occurs to him. Consider how much he must have thought about it, and the kind of thinking, in those dark woods where it was dark in daytime. Not since Nicholas of Lynn have I seen anybody staring at the innocent compass-needle with such intensity; with Frere Nicholas it was an intensity of bewilderment, with Cortés the sudden flicker of the much-wanted answer. He could say to himself 'Eureka!' – and then make use of the device.

The exhibition of the mentality makes one look twice at the marrying-off of Malinche, the Doña Marina who had been indispensable. During that twenty-one months absence from Mexico was Cortés thinking ahead? What happened, when he did return, was that he set to work to expose the mismanagement of the officials who had been sent to replace him. He was able in 1528 to plan a visit to Spain, to present his own claims to the Emperor, perhaps to marry grandly and to return to New Spain as Viceroy. Some, though not all, of such a scheme succeeded. He was able to marry again; he was unable to become Viceroy. The later years of Cortés are restless rather than contented. The most contented old age of any of those who joined in his adventure may, perhaps, have been the old age of Doña Marina. I don't know what happened to Captain Xaramillo, but she lived on with a town house in Mexico City, a country house in Chapultepec, a garden in Coyuacan which had belonged to Moctezuma, and after her death she became a mountain goddess. There is a mountain near Tlaxcala where her name continues to be honoured.

The feature of Mexican life which most shocked the Spaniards was the practice of human sacrifice. It is probable that the shock to the Mexicans of the Spanish invasion was of itself a cause of the practice being exhibited at its very worst. Those who write in a detached way about human sacrifice, comparing rituals as practised at one time or another among many peoples – as, for instance, Frazer writes in *The Golden Bough* – recognize that the whole intention imposed its own, and sacred, restraints. 'Certainly nowhere does the custom of killing the human representative of a god appear to have been carried out so systematically and on so extensive a scale as in Mexico', says Frazer; yet in the examples that he quotes there is an undeniably intended dignity in the sacrifice. The act has to be awe-inspiring, and is made so by elaborate ritual. In sacrifices for fertility of the land, 'nature' imposed its own moments; other special moments were also imposed by deaths of kings or renewals of gods, and by calamities. There could hardly have been a worse calamity for Mexico than the incursion of the Conquistadors. In ancient times, Caesar had noticed that when he marched his legions into Gaul, some tribes in consternation constructed colossal images of wicker-work or wood and grass; men, cattle and other animals were put into the images; the images then set on fire, so as to burn up the living contents. The intimation is that this was a desperate procedure, traditional to the Druids as a last resort; as Carthaginian priests, when Carthage was threatened with destruction, called for the sacrifice of the five hundred children. It was in an extremity of grief and horror brought upon Mexicans by the Spaniards, that the ugliest of Mexican sacrifices occurred.

Nevertheless, even if I regard the practice of human sacrifice as something that flared exceptionally in the frenzy brought about by the Spaniards, I still have to face it as a ritual that was customary and established in pre-Conquest Mexico. The performances certainly shocked the Spaniards, with a shock not wholly due to the human suffering involved. It was not the incidental cruelty that caused the shock; nor is it that alone which shocks us now. I think that part of what we feel about it is that Mexican culture, in general, had reached a stage of development at which the practice of human sacrifice 'ought' to have been given up. The literalness of the act ought to have been discarded; had it become transmuted, we should feel better about the old Mexican civilization – it would be more in line with 'our' history. The offence, to us, is that Mexicans were retaining a 'primitive' practice in a culture which in other ways had become sophisticated. To a customary 'evolutionary' way of thinking, that is an offence unless it can be specially explained.

Special explanations for Mexican behaviour are not difficult to find. One thought, in line with evolutionary theory, is that at a prehistoric period when ancestors of Mexican peoples are visualized as migrating into the western parts of post-Pleistocene North America, they had no livestock with them, nor, in lands into which they wandered, did they find any large animals susceptible to domestication.

The absence of suitable wild species, and therefore the failure to achieve by domestication an efficient draught animal as an alternative to human traction and labour, was of profound significance in the whole development of the higher prehistoric cultures of the New World, from the Andes to New Mexico. We have seen that the production of the ox by castration was an event of far-reaching importance in the ancient Near East, and the lack of domestic oxen or their counterparts in prehistoric America can hardly be dissociated from the absence there of the traction plough and of wheeled vehicles. Such civilization as could be built was necessarily founded on a wasteful expenditure of human labour for which no alternative nor amelioration had been devised.[18]

Nobody is suggesting that the sharing of traction and labour is all that animals contribute to a civilization. St. Francis, if you so choose, may say that animals mean more than that; or so, in a very different way, may the disreputable soldier, Bernal Díaz. Scrounger that Bernal Díaz is (as any old campaigner should be) he makes you feel how empty Mexico seemed to the Conquistadors – empty of anything but people. The epic of Xenophon's march comes to mind, as you read of Cortés' men; and how important animals are, throughout the whole of the *Anabasis*; but when Bernal Díaz forages there is hardly anything to mention, except the ducks and chickens, and the big chickens that we call, oddly, turkeys. Without precisely setting out to do so, Bernal Díaz conveys that the absence of domestic animals has an adverse moral effect on the Mexican way of life. The keeping of wild animals, because they are kept 'wild', seems to him particularly 'hellish' – that is his word for the aviary and zoo in the City of Mexico. 'As for the horrible noise when the lions and tigers roared, and the jackals and foxes howled, and the serpents hissed, it was so appalling that one seemed to be in hell'. He disliked the snakes especially, the 'vipers in this accursed house, and poisonous snakes which have something that sounds like a bell in their tails'. The zoo is not hellish to Bernal Díaz because wild animals were ill-treated and unhappy in their captivity – far from that, the hellishness is that they are kept happy with human flesh. 'We know for certain, that when they drove us out of Mexico and killed our soldiers, they fed those beasts and snakes on their bodies for many days. . . .'

Another singularity is that the economy of peoples from the Andes to New Mexico had from earliest times been based on one particular food crop, maize. Baudin[19] writes about maize as a rather special mystery: the wild prototype of maize has not been identified; it is the only cereal whose origin is hidden; his feeling about maize is mystical, perhaps even anthropomorphic. He feels it should be stressed that for the American Indian the life of the maize is the life of the tribe. There is a special symbiosis. One of the myths expressive of this was used by Longfellow in *The Song of Hiawatha*. There, Hiawatha on his journey encounters his double who is the 'friend of man', and Hiawatha slays the 'friend of man' and buries him. From the grave, which is carefully cleared of weeds by the slayer, and which is warmed by the sun and watered by the rain, once again springs up the godlike maize. In the life-cycle of the Hiawatha myth there is a dearth of domesticated animal companions. There is no intermediary 'friend of man' to be offered to the corn-god, nobody but man's own double, man himself. The maize itself stands straight; it suggests a man; nothing else but man will do as a sacrifice for maize. Apart from the identification of man and the maize-plant, there is no intermediary animal to act as a substitute. The ram in the thicket spared Isaac, as the hind spared Iphigenia; but there is no ram or hind in Mexico.

Such explanations of the practice of human sacrifice are ingenious, but it remains a question whether our interpretations in any way represent a Mexican way of thinking. 'Soberness, restraint, a certain skeptical reserve in investigating the deepest emotions of the heart', is the advice given to writers of 'true' history by Johan Huizinga; and there is no phenomenon of cultural history more difficult, or involving a deeper complex of emotions, than human sacrifice. On such a matter I should not dare to theorize incautiously. Here, as perhaps in lesser matters, a theory based on western schooling might be fit to govern and yet, as Las Casas said, 'not fit to govern Indians'.

I turn with interest, though, to the presence of the llama in Peru; not as wishing to use the llama to prove anything, except that there is pleasure in him. In his studies of the empire of the Incas, Baudin makes much of the llama, which, along with maize, formed the basis of the economy of the Peruvian plateau before the Spaniards came. Spaniards, at a loss for a name for the animal (as Bernal Díaz had been at a loss over his 'lions' and 'tigers') spoke of the llama sometimes as the big sheep, sometimes as the small camel – the latter description is 'felicitous, for the grass of the puna (*ychu*) is all the food the llama needs to satisfy it, and it can go entirely without food and water for several days'. All of Baudin's passages about the llama are enjoyable: if one of these animals is mistreated, 'it defends itself by spitting into its enemy's face; when it is tired, it lies down, and no one on earth can induce it to take to the road again'.

The llama never did take to the road, in the sense of performing any heavy traction, or of being an animal to be ridden; one cannot

ride a llama. But all the same, the Spaniards found, and were astonished by, well-paved roads in Peru. 'Truly,' exclaimed Fernando Pizarro, 'there are no such fine roads to be found in all Christendom.'
'I believe,' said Cieza de Léon, 'that if the Emperor [Charles V him-
self] wanted to build another royal road equal to the one that goes
from Quito to Cuzco or the one that goes from Cuzco to Chile, he
would not, in spite of all his power, be able to do it'. The paved roads
of Peru spoke to the Conquistadors of a pre-existent and established
law and order as clearly as, in a much earlier time, the Roman roads
of Britain had spoken to the incoming Anglo-Saxons. In each instance
there was astonishment at the well-engineered roadways, and astonishment that they seemed little used and undefended. When Francisco Pizarro made his landing at Tumbes in May 1532 he was
prepared for much more fighting than proved necessary. As, in the
earlier example, Romans had withdrawn from Britain before the
Teutonic tribes moved in, so Pizarro's men found themselves in a
land where something had gone wrong: the ruling power was dis-
tracted, the Incas absent-minded, the people had forgotten how to
make war. The more they studied these strange 'Indians' the more
surprised the Spaniards were at the naiveté. Stone palaces and temples were all ill-defended, despite display of gold and silver; so were
the gardens and the terraces, despite their careful cultivation; and a
householder invited anyone to know his home was empty by placing a
little stick across the entrance as a sign that he was out. Perhaps the
strangest mystery of all was that the roads were paved not out of
kindness for any wheel to roll upon, but out of kindness only for the
feet of man and beast. Even in flat terrain a wheel was taboo; the
smoothness of the road was for the human and the llama.

In after times, and when the Inca way of life had been destroyed,
Baudin admits that many painted it as having been far too good to be
true. Though the taboo about wheels upon the roads does somewhat
please me, I cannot pretend that the roads were made for pleasurable
footwork only; that would be to forget wars, and soldiery, and tax-
gathering. A pleasing story is recorded, that in pre-Conquest days
tax-gatherers who used the roads were on occasion satisfied with the
payment of no more than the steam of a feather (I suppose a condor's
feather) filled with lice. That is repeated, as a piece of irony. Perhaps
I have granted to much affection to the llama. 'The regard of the

Indians for the llama passes the bounds of reason and clearly reveals their ignorance,' said Ulloa, who wrote about Peru in the Age of Reason. Yet though we do not have to credit that there was an Age of Innocence, we know that an Age of Reason may also be an illusion. Even a chromium world may turn into an old ruin that the winds howl through:

> And when I pay attention I must out and walk
> Among the dogs and horses that understand my talk.

If that is the way Yeats felt, I am glad the Peruvian Indian retained his llama throughout the Spanish occupation, and throughout later times. 'He is indeed the Indian's fitting companion', says Baudin: 'gentle, placid, grave, and a little sad, like him'.

Some of the original Conquistadors came to regret what they had done to Mexico and Peru. Many of the early chronicles were reviewed in 1638 by Antonio de la Calancha, and among them he came across the Will of a certain 'gallant captain', named Mancio Sierra de Leguizamo, who had been one of Francisco Pizarro's companions. Of Mancio Sierra, Calancha says that he 'performed great feats at Tumbes during the war, in Cajamarca at the capture of the Inca, at el Cuzco during the civil wars, and in the whole of Peru during the general revolt of the Indians'. Calancha also gives a more individual touch to Mancio Sierra as a person. 'He it was who seized the golden sun worshipped by the Indians in the temple at Cuzco, and gambled it one night, losing it before sunrise.' This episode, Calancha says, 'is the origin of the Peruvian saying of a person who plays for exaggerated stakes, "he would stake the sun before it comes up".'

Fifty-seven years later, Mancio Sierra made his Will ('executed at el Cuzco, 18 September 1589, before the public notary, Geronimo Sanchez de Quesada') including a preamble to the following effect:

> Before drafting my will, I declare that I have wanted for several years to make known a certain matter to His Majesty King Philip, our prince. . . . I have taken a leading part in the discovery and occupation of the countries we have seized from the Incas, who were the rulers, and which we have placed under the authority of the royal crown. His Catholic Majesty must know that we found these countries in such a

condition that there were no thieves, no vicious men, no idlers, no adulterous or evil-living women. . . . Cultivated land, mountains, mines, pastures, hunting woods and everything else were organized and shared in such a way that each one knew and owned his heritage; no one else could occupy or seize it, and there was no need to go to law. . . .

Everything, from the most important to the smallest detail, was planned and co-ordinated with great wisdom. The Incas were feared, obeyed, respected and venerated by their subjects, who considered them to be extremely capable rulers. . . . We subdued them and compelled them to serve God our Father, depriving them of their lands and placing them under the Crown, thanks to which, and because God our Father has permitted it, we have made the rulers who submitted to us into slaves, as the world knows. We were a very small band of Spaniards when we undertook this conquest, and I desire His Catholic Majesty to understand why I draft this account. It is to unburden my conscience and to acknowledge my fault. For we have transformed these natives, who had so much wisdom and committed so few crimes. . . .

The realm has fallen into such disorder that it has passed from one extreme to another. There was then no evil thing, but today there is no good, or almost none.[20]

In Mexico another remorseful old Conquistador dictated his reflections on the overthrow of the native Mexican régime, and the aftermath. His name was Alonso de Aguilar at the time that he served as a swordsman with Cortés, from the beginning until the achievement of the conquest. He was one of the older of the fighting men; he had turned forty at the time that they were all carrying arms and wearing their sandals by both day and night. After the warfare 'Aguilar received a fair allotment of land and Indians, and the privilege of a *venta*, or hostelry, situated on the highway between Puebla and the port of Veracruz. In a few years he became a man of considerable wealth. Then in 1529, at the age of fifty, he released his Indians and gave up all his possessions to enter the Dominican Order'.[21] From then on, and for the forty-two years for which he served his Mission, he was known as Fray Francisco. When he was more than eighty 'and nearing the end of my lifespan' he was persuaded to tell his story of the Conquest, and his remarkable chronicle has been translated by Miss Patricia de Fuentes, from whom I quote.

One gains an immediate impression of Aguilar as a swordsman who was brave and reliable at moments of pressure: workmanlike, and not noisy about it like the flamboyant Bernal Díaz. When the column of Spaniards marched for the first time over the causeway into the crowded City, into whatever unknown fate – of the multitude of Indians in canoes on the lake and on the rooftops of the houses, Bernal Díaz exclaims: 'No wonder, since they had never seen horses or men like us before! . . . What men in all the world have shown such daring?' Aguilar contents himself with the remark: 'To see such multitudes was frightening.' At the moment of the arrest of Moctezuma, Gómara does not play down the drama: 'Never did Greek or Roman, or man of any nation, since kings have existed, do what Cortés did in seizing Moctezuma, a most powerful king, in his own house, a very strong place, surrounded by an infinity of people, while Cortés had only four hundred and fifty companions'. Aguilar, one of those companions, does play down the drama: 'Then Captain Cortés ordered Moctezuma to go with him to his quarters, and he did so. He was seized because of the great fear the Spaniards had of him, and was taken to some chambers where he moved about freely without any fetters'. Aguilar was on the roster of those who guarded Moctezuma, when for a moment 'things were in a peaceful state, and we were free of strife and alarm'. Despite his quiet temper, Aguilar could revel as heartily as any in some moments of high spirits; as when returning from 'the boldness and fury' of the action on the coast against Narvaez they this time ran across the causeway, 'shooting off our cannon and muskets, running the horses and raising a gay clatter'.

Toward the end of his narration Aguilar is indignant that the men who achieved New Spain, who by themselves had been originators of that enterprise and at their own expense and effort had fought hard, had been little rewarded. Much of New Spain had been handed 'to many persons who had never heard or seen combat'; he felt the least of the Conquistadors 'was greatly deserving, yet most of them were impoverished'. Then, after his conversion, as Fray Francisco much of his indignation turns to the decay of the land itself and the depopulation, contrasted with the prosperity at the time when the Spaniards invaded. One of the provinces near Veracruz had been very rich in cacao, gold, cloth, fish and other products; it had supported formerly, according to his estimate, some eighty thousand houses: 'Now it has two hundred houses, or even less'. His recital of decay goes on: 'On the coast as well as inland there were large cities, towns and provinces, all of them thickly populated and very pretty, full of fruit trees; and now it is all deserted, with very few Indians.' Fray Francisco does not idealize (as we may feel that Mancio Sierra in his repentance did) the Indian social order before the post-conquest disintegration. The former 'abominable forms of worship to the Devil in this land', illustrated by his description of normal procedure of human sacrifice, are in no way glossed over; nor his horror of the Mexican 'priests' who had gone about 'very dirty and blackened, and wasted and haggard of face', with hair hanging down very long and matted, infested with lice –

> At night they walked like a procession of phantoms to the hills where they had their temples and idols and houses of worship.

And yet in those times:

> All the people, whether noble or plebeian, removed their sandals in the courtyard before they entered to worship their gods; and at the door of the church they all squatted on their heels and very reverently sobbed and wept, asking forgiveness for their sins. The women brought pies made of poultry. They also brought fruits, and paintings done on the native paper. In my opinion they were paintings of their sins. There was such a silence, broken by sobbing and weeping, that I was spellbound with wonder and terror.
>
> And now that they are Christians, and as though in retribution for our sins, most of them come to church by force, and with very little fear and reverence; they gossip and talk, and walk out during the principal part of the Mass and the sermon. In their time, therefore, great strictness was observed in the ceremonies to their gods, but now they feel neither fear nor shame. I could cite many more particularities; but to avoid verbosity, and because what I have said is sufficient, I shall say no more.

The suction of the Bourse at Antwerp made a strong return wind for the shipments from Potosi and Veracruz, and presently (forty years after Magellan's voyage) the annual treasure galleon from the Philippines was plying from Manila toward Acapulco, with its additional consignment. The effects of the shipments within Europe caused me to refer, at the beginning of this chapter, to Tawney's classic work. A general change of feeling had begun to show, I thought, in such matters as the divorce between the *mappemonde* and the mariners' chart. Tawney shows a change of feeling in full action when at first at Antwerp, then in Holland and in England, the rising world of business becomes a separate secular compartment. Tawney's key-sentence I take to be this: 'The theory of a hierarchy of values, embracing all human interests and activities in a system of which the apex is religion, is replaced by the conception of separate and parallel compartments, between which a due balance should be maintained, but which have no vital connection with each other'.[22] Such 'replacement' and escape from subordination would seem to slip rather easily into

> *The good old rule, the simple plan,*
> *That they should take who have the power,*
> *And they should keep who can.*

As soon as the Spanish roadway across the Atlantic had been constructed I am forced to watch what looks like a flashback to the very first westerly sea-route that was made in the Mediterranean. Even as Phoenician seamen returning toward a homeland citadel might wish to keep their traffic secret, so might the 16th century Spaniards have wished for secrecy; but even as Greek pirates fell upon the Phoenicians, so did other European pirates fall upon Spanish ships. The speed with which the attacks began is noticeable. When mentioning that Cortés despatched the first King's Fifth of spoils from Mexico in three caravels from Veracruz, I might have added that two of the caravels were intercepted by the French pirate Florin off the Azores. The French Court agreed to have Florin hanged for that action, but others intended to do better than Florin. So, when looking at affairs in New Spain, I must remember the increasing interference of interlopers. At first, Mancio Sierra and Aguilar were concerned only with the conduct of their incoming fellow-countrymen. Aguilar had died, I think, before Francis Drake put in to Veracruz to add to the distresses there. Mancio Sierra was an old man at Cuzco, with apparently sufficient troubles on his mind, when Drake came coasting northward along the seaboard of Peru.

NOTES

1. *R. H. Tawney, Religion and the Rise of Capitalism* (Harcourt, Brace, New York, 1926).

2. *The Spanish Conquest in America* by Sir Arthur Helps (John Lane, London and New York, 1890), I, 157, fn. 2. Helps is indispensable for details of the Spanish slavery system, which kept on being altered from time to time.

3. Helps, I, 339.

4. There is a reference to this transaction in *Rare Books and Royal Collectors* by Maurice L. Ettinghausen (Simon & Schuster, New York, 1966), Chapter IX.

5. *Ferdinand Magellan* by Hawthorne Daniel (Doubleday, New York, 1964) quotes the remark about Magellan ('the King always loathed him') as having been made by John de Barros.

6. Daniel, p. 275.

7. *A Socialist Empire* by Louis Baudin, translated by Katherine Woods (Van Nostrand, Princeton, 1961) quotes from the *Corónica* of Cieza de León (I, *cix*).

8. Erasmus, *Adagia* (quoted by Tawney, p. 76).

9. Tawney, p. 79.

10. Parry, p. 175.

11. Helps, I, 162, fn. 3, attributes this remark to Oviedo.

12. Parry, p. 179.

13. The famous works of W. H. Prescott, *History of the conquest of Mexico* (3 vols., New York, 1843) and *History of the conquest of Peru* (2 vols., New York, 1847), have been reissued in many editions. *Cortés, the life of the conqueror by his secretary*, Francisco Lopez de Gómara, has been beautifully translated and edited by Lesley Byrd Simpson (University of California Press, 1964). For Bernal Díaz I would refer particularly to the translation, called *The Conquest of New Spain*, by J. M. Cohen (Penguin Books, 1963). Nothing can beat reading *both* Bernal Díaz and Gómara. *The Conquistadors*, translated by Patricia de Fuentes (Orion Press, New York, 1963), contains eye-witness accounts by Cortés and some of his companions, and is especially welcome for introducing Fray Francisco de Aguilar.

14. The 'minimum-evolution' tree was pictured in an article by A. W. F. Edwards, *Studying Human Evolution by Computer,* in *New Scientist* (19 May 1966), with reference there to earlier work by Edwards and Cavalli-Sforza.

15. Collis, p. 54. There are various spellings for 'Quetzalcoatl'.

16. Gómara, p. 185.

17. Collis, p. 235.

18. *Prehistoric Societies* by Grahame Clark and Stuart Piggott (Hutchinson, London and Knopf, New York, 1965), pp. 172, 173.

19. Baudin, p. 280 (note on *Maize,* item 34).

20. This is translated from the Spanish text of Antonio de la Calancha: *Corónica moralizada del orden de San Agustin en el Peru (Barcelona,* 1638), I, xv, p. 98.

21. de Fuentes, p. 134.

22. Tawney, p. 8.

CHAPTER 15

Come, said the Drum

IN 1577 Francis Drake set out from England to use the sea-route that Magellan had pioneered. Drake, at that time in his late thirties, had achieved much experience of raiding the Spanish Main. In his early twenties he had commanded a ship in the Hawkins expedition which was thrashed by the Spaniards off Veracruz. He sought out a personal revenge in private buccaneering in the West Indies, and returned to Portobello and Veracruz with others for more successful raids. This seemed no more than minor robbery with violence; a more ambitious plan was to spy out the western coasts of Peru and Mexico; and, with more forethought than had been shown by the French pirate Florin, Drake secured several powerful courtiers and the Queen herself, as private shareholders in his Pacific expedition. Drake set out with three ships. In the Straits of Magellan he had much the same hardship as his predecessor; two of the ships were lost, and emerging at Cape Desire in the sole survivor, the *Pelican*, Drake changed his luck by renaming her the *Golden Hind*. The *Golden Hind* became so famous that her measurements have been scrutinized with care: length 81 feet between perpendiculars, with a 59 foot keel; her beam was 19 feet. As the small lone ship coursed northward along the coasts of Chile and Peru I do not know how many 'valiaunt mindes' there were aboard, but the change of the ship's name displayed their agreed intention. The dedication of the *Golden Hind* was to 'seek golde while sluggardes lye at home'.

Along the coast of Peru small treasures were not disregarded; the altar service of an unprotected Spanish chapel is mentioned in the narrative of the gentleman adventurer who kept the score. Another shore-party found 'a Spaniard lying asleep, who had by him thirteen bars of silver... We took the silver and left the man'. There is horse-play in the narrative, and presently much more loot – the *Golden Hind* became well ballasted with thirteen chests of royals of plate, four score pound weight of gold, six-and-twenty tons of silver, and a quantity of 'jewels and precious stones'. Drake then drew away from

Panama and coasted northward, with an eye for what was rumoured as a 'Strait of Anian'* or north-easterly passage home; with an eye also for safe harbour in which to career ship and clear her from barnacles and streamers of weed. In the summer of 1579 the *Golden Hind* had passed the unnoticed Golden Gate but found another harbour, safely remote from Spanish territory – the harbour which still carries the name of Drake's Bay.

In recent days a car driver picked up a brass plate in that neighbourhood which appeared to have an incised inscription. As Admiral Sir R. P. Ernle-Erle-Drax tells the story,[1] the finder and another man examined the piece of metal, 'decided it was useless, and threw it out several miles further east where it was picked up in 1936 by a man named Shinn. In 1937 it reached the hands of Professor H. E. Bolton, who proved beyond any doubt that it was the 'Plate of Brasse' which Drake had nailed to a stout post by the sea nearly 400 years before'. The inscription was made out to read as follows:

BE IT KNOWN EVEN TO ALL MEN BY
THESE PRESENTS
IVNE 17 1579
BY THE GRACE OF GOD AND IN THE
NAME OF HERR MAIESTY QVEEN
ELIZABETH OF ENGLAND AND
HERR SVCESSORS FOREVER I
TAKE POSSESSION OF THIS KING-
DOME WHOSE KING AND PEOPLE
FREELY RESIGNE THEIR RIGHT
AND TITLE IN THE WHOLE LAND
VNTO HERR MAIESTIES KEEPEING
NOW NAMED BY ME AN TO BEE
KNOWNE VNTO ALL MEN AS NOVA
ALBION.

FRANCIS DRAKE

The plate passed into possession of the California Historical Society and is now at the Bancroft Library.

Not having found a 'Northwest Passage', Drake made his home-

---

* 'Stockfish Strait' was another name for the hypothetical seaway; or, looking at it from the Atlantic side, 'Northwest Passage'.

bound westing round the world, and when he arrived the dividend paid on the investment was 4,700 per cent. From her share Elizabeth paid off her foreign debts, with handsome margin. 'Indeed', says Keynes in his *Treatise on Money*, 'the booty brought back by Drake in the *Golden Hind* may fairly be considered the fountain and origin of British Foreign Investment.'

It would be wrong, I am sure, to present Francis Drake merely as a pirate. The role into which he came to be cast, for Protestant Englishmen, was the role of Drake the Giant-killer – after it had come to be a matter of agreement that Philip's Spain was a giant to be in every way harassed, and killed if possible. In much-divided England a general agreement on this point was not reached quickly. There was more admiration than hostility towards Spaniards at the time that Henry VIII cemented the Spanish alliance by his first marriage with Catharine of Aragon; it was an admiration based upon a solid reason that appealed to all in England – the Spaniards were the finest soldiery of Europe – they, as no one else, had power to beat the French. No survey of English feelings should be so rapid as to overlook the pre-Elizabethan admiration for things Spanish, for Spanish blades and Spanish leather, Spanish dress and Spanish manners. When Mary, married to Philip of Spain, was Queen of England, the savagery of the religious burnings aroused an utmost fury among Protestants; yet again, cohesion among Protestants did not form quickly. In the scramble of passions that were on the loose in England, what impresses me most is the violence with which Englishmen were hating each other, and the virulence of mutual hatred between rich and poor. A phase of the internal fightings which calls for attention here, was the damage being done to England's all-important wool-trade by many men turned off the land and rendered 'idle' (a euphemism which meant unemployed and desperate) by the 'man-eating sheep'. The more violent of the unemployed retaliated against 'property' in any way they could; those whom I watch are the many who were whipped off the roads as rogues and vagabonds and forced to the seaports. There some were siphoned off into the fishing fleets (which Elizabeth, after her accession in 1558, did her best to expand) but others formed the crews of the numerous fleet of smugglers and sea-pirates. The number of English privateers at work in the Narrow

Seas in 1563 is estimated at four hundred. Some of those ships, when challenged, might claim to be Huguenot or Dutch, but it is clear that they were mainly English, and each as vindictive toward an English trading ship as toward any other. Who, indeed, was to challenge the privateers? Elizabeth's Royal Navy in 1559 amounted to twenty-two ships of size and speed and armament competent to cope with the sea-pirates. The privateersmen laughed, rejoiced at the discomfiture of their own countrymen who had once made England wealthy by shipping wool abroad. After the French re-took Calais in 1558 there was no outlet there, or in any other French port, for legitimate English traders. Antwerp had been more important for the wool-trade, but the activity of the English privateers was such that Antwerp was closed to all English traders in 1567. The ban continued, and Hamburg was closed to English traders ten years later.

The first of the tributes to Hawkins and Drake is that English sea-pirates were diverted by them from the Narrow Seas. It mattered little to the London merchant where the pirates went, so long as they went far away. Nor, as I see it, was it at first of any ideological significance that it was into Spanish waters that Drake led them. It was the gold that counted; and when such a neat dividend as 4,700 per cent was derived from Spanish gold, it was easy to supply other justifications for attacking Spanish ships. So Drake's drum led the way for anyone who had the wish to singe the King of Spain's beard, and a new and hearty camaraderie grew up, in which the approved sport was to 'bang these dogs of Seville, the children of the devil', and to be praised for it. Diversion of the 'idle' to this sport was highly welcome to English merchants and to the Exchequer, and political and religious zeal soon clothed the nakedness of piracy – so long as the damage was directed at Spain. The Netherlands had really suffered under Spanish military rule; the Dutch had every reason to fight Spain; England, it seems to me, had less excuse to turn against a former ally; except that England was seething with her own internal discontents, and the former ally was now a wealthy giant, growing wealthier and more gigantic. In an earlier time an English fleet would have joined with Spaniards in the final sea-fight with the Turks; but the battle of Lepanto, which ended Muslim sea-power in 1571, was fought without cooperation of any English crusaders. There was small acclaim in England for that Catholic triumph. The union which

Portugal made with Spain in 1580, whereby the port of Lisbon, the Azores, the slave-markets of Africa, and Portuguese trade-ports everywhere – Brazil, East Indies and the Spice Islands – passed wholesale to the Spanish Crown, drove home to English Protestants what a huge monster Spain had become. Now English privateers began to take on honours due to ancient knights of Chivalry. Sir Philip Sidney was the Protestant Knight *sans peur et sans reproche*, the 'light and ornament' of England's Court, the pattern of chivalrous behaviour. In 1585 he planned a voyage of piracy with Drake. The plan was precisely that of the pirate Florin who, a generation earlier, was hanged for it. Sidney and Drake were to lie off the Azores and, like Florin, waylay the Spanish treasure ships. The voyage, in fact, was not made; an earlier ambition of Sidney's was suddenly granted by the Queen, which took him to the Netherlands, and to the skirmish at Zutphen where his earthly career ended. Yet that Sidney had made plans to be a scavenging pirate shows how the code of English chivalry could change.

In her relations with Spain, Elizabeth might disown, if necessary, the actions of her privateers. As for Drake, 'the gentleman,' she said, 'careth not if I should disavow him.' But in February 1587, after much painful hesitation, Elizabeth had signed the death warrant for the execution of Mary, Queen of Scots: that execution of a crowned and anointed queen, and one regarded in the Catholic world as a martyr, was a direct challenge to the Pope and, even more, to Philip. It was a matter of months only before there would be outright war with Spain, admittedly the largest 'power' of the world. Spain had, it seemed, illimitable money, ships and men for any campaign. England, as Lord Treasurer Burghley impressed upon the Queen, was desperately short of money and could not possibly maintain a long war. Drake had the nod to set out in April 1587 to strike first and make the war a short one. He sailed direct to Cadiz, with well-trained privateersmen, and destroyed the Spanish fleet; then seized Cape St. Vincent, and rode at anchor off the port of Lisbon, immobilizing anything the Portuguese could do; and, when it pleased him, fetched home by way of the Azores, where he happened to pick up a rich carrack homeward bound from the East Indies, with a cargo to the value of £114,000. Philip had insisted that his own Armada should sail to punish England in that year, but Drake, 'El Draque', the dragon, had wholly disrupted it. 'Just look at Drake', the Pope mourned, with reluctant admiration. 'Who is he? What forces has he? . . . We are sorry to say it, but we have a poor opinion of this Spanish Armada, and fear some disaster'. The disaster came the next year, when the new Invincible Armada did reach the Channel, but never made the beachhead on English soil, toward which, as Philip planned, Parma and his invasion army could be convoyed from the Netherlands.

But Philip of Spain, master of the sea-world (except for a few pestilential hornets' nests such as the Netherlands and England), had to contend with one worry far more serious than any stings inflicted by the Dutch or English seamen. For Elizabeth, in very good health at the age of 55, the destruction of the 1588 Armada was of utmost importance: it united and inspired Englishmen, and let off such burst of confidence and pride and energy as had never been seen before. All England sang: 'this place breedeth courage'; and all seemed set (in the autumn of 1588) to go on singing. Yet galling as the joy of Protestants might be to Philip, and costly as was the loss of that Armada, these were griefs that could be borne if the whole round world, and in particular the Spanish Indies, continued to support him. Here was the hidden worry for Philip, now in his sixties, troubled with gout and a cataract in the eye, rigidly faithful to daily regimen of prayer and never-ending attentiveness to an enormity of business. His father Charles had abdicated from the press of imperial worries at the age of 56, to end his days in a Spanish monastery. Philip, with even more papers, minutes, orders waiting for his signature, innumerable Captains-General, Ambassadors and Viceroys waiting for their interviews, had no recess. The cataract was troublesome, yet Philip tried to read every paper that he signed. What he tried not to see was that the strength of Spain was now most heavily dependent on the life of the New World, and that the life of the New World was dying.

What I called 'road-accident', when Spaniards pushed the Road West to the Pacific coasts of the Americas, Professor Parry speaks of as 'demographic catastrophe', and he tells the story first of all, and quickest, in figures. The pre-conquest population of New Spain is put at twenty-five million.[2] Give or take a million from that estimate, the figure sets the scale which Parry scrutinizes. The table of Indian population in New Spain is this:

In 1519, 25,000,000
1532, 17,000,000
1548,   6,300,000

When he has studied those figures, Professor Parry expresses the catastrophe in terms somewhat more human than statistics.

> Here was what the *conquistadores* had been looking for: not only land, food and gold but an apparently inexhaustible supply of docile labour. ... Relieved of the drain of human sacrifice, indeed, and – once the conquest was accepted – of constant war, the Indian population, already vast, might have been expected to increase. Instead, just as it had done in the islands, it quickly began to decline. ... The Indian population in the early seventeenth century was probably less than one-tenth of what it had been 100 years before.[3]

The backlash of this catastrophe in Old Spain was more disheartening to Spanish Christians, and more serious to Spain's economy, than anything that English Protestants were crowing about.

In the narrative which Cortés dictated to Gómara, what stands out is his initial exultation at the potential wealth of all kinds in New Spain, and one cannot fail to see the admiration that he feels for the Mexican Indians. As for the development of New Spain, we saw him instantly asking his King for all that was to be advantageous – friars, and farmers with herds, plants and seeds. When he specified 'no lawyers' he was perhaps envisaging some sort of simple military dictatorship. The rule of Columbus's islands had, to Cortés' mind, been cursed by the existence of three independent instruments of royal authority: the governor, the *audencia* of school-trained lawyers, and the treasury – which in its turn had a triple-padlocked strongbox and was responsible to Fonseca's bureau in Spain. If I have said anything to Cortés' discredit, I must deeply applaud that he wished to quarrel (and did quarrel violently) with Fonseca. Perhaps Cortés was naïve about government, but I am stressing that he 'meant well' for New Spain – he did not view the land, or people, as simply to be pillaged. The wish was genuine, I think, that New Spain and its Indians should remain in good heart. An admiration for Mexican Indians throbs in

335

the pages of Gómara. Admittedly it enchances the glory of his conquest if Cortés makes out that his opponents were in no physical sense inferior; but Cortés makes a different point – he indicates that Indians were inhibited toward European warfare. They had a totally different conception of the purpose of a battle and of the rules. As had long ago happened between Greeks and Romans, as had recently happened between Italian *condottiéri* and the French, Indians when fighting with Spaniards were simply not playing the same game. Apart from disparity of weapons, there was disparity of idea. But at whatever game the Indians could agree on playing, Cortés expresses admiration for them. Consider the pre-fabrication of the thirteen caravels which Cortés ordered for assault upon the island City. The planking and fittings for the 'brigantines', as Cortés explains to Gómara, were contrived by Indian carpenters; they were carried for a week's distance from Tlaxcala to Texcoco on the backs of 8,000 men, escorted by 20,000 Indian soldiers, with 2,000 more bringing provisions. All this was as commanded by Cortés, but it was self-organized by his Indian allies. The procession entered Texcoco 'to the accompaniment of the greatest yelling, whistling, and whinnying in the world', 'to the sound of many drums, conches, and other musical instruments' – and the parade, which extended over two leagues of road, took six hours to make its entry without breaking line: all in order, all fine men, in feathers and clean mantles.

'All fine men, in feathers and clean mantles' – that is how they remain in Cortés's memory. It is not just the labour-supply that Cortés admired. He liked the looks of them. He liked them as men. Of course he also liked the work that, with their numbers, they could do. Hard work did not daunt them. There had to be a launching ditch and channel, so that the thirteen brigantines, when they had been assembled on dry land, could be put into the lake. That ditch was to be a quarter of a league in length; it was to be more than twelve feet wide; two fathoms deep at the shallowest part; lined throughout with planks and topped by a wall. Fifty days were allowed for the job. Eight thousand Indians were continuously digging, says Bernal Díaz. The task was completed. When the brigantines had been assembled, the ditch was there, and the 'navy' could be towed into the lake to play its part in the attack on the island City. What Cortés dwells on is the zest with which the work was undertaken – the energy of his Indian allies – their 'yelling, whistling, and whinnying'. The number of those allies, at that moment, was 200,000. 'It was a notable thing to be captain of such a host,' Cortés told Gómara.

After the conquest, it was an even more notable thing to be in command of the unnumbered millions of Indians in New Spain. It was inconceivable that if a small proportion of them were parcelled out in a *repartiemento* system of slavery, that would cause undue damage. Cortés proceeded to govern as Ovando might have governed, and so far as slavery was concerned, his system was confirmed when a Viceroy was later appointed. The slavery system of itself can hardly have been a major cause of the depopulation of Mexico, so soon and appallingly noticeable to the Conquistadors.

Exchanges of diseases was held to be a large factor in the catastrophe. Gómara reports that Indians regarded the smallpox that had been brought to them as 'the great leprosy', and remarks 'it seems to me that this is how they were repaid for the *bubas* (syphilis) which they gave our men'. Influenza may have been a plague as serious as smallpox. Perhaps the worst of the slow damages was the introduction of 'improvements' – the 'herds, plants and seeds' for which Cortés made early petition. Imports of livestock were particularly numerous, Parry points out, in the 1530's: grazing animals, horned cattle for the lowlands, sheep for the highlands, horses, mules and goats almost everywhere. All of these animals were new to the Americas of the 16th century and were introduced by Spaniards; they brought a new diversity to the economy of New Spain, but they caused a major revolution in the use of land. In a larger and more ruthless way, what happened to the Indians of New Spain is what happened to country people in England at a time when enclosures for the 'man-eating sheep' had an effect which some say was more severe than the Black Death.

Not physical factors alone, but psychic factors in the catastrophe, have been very much studied. In New Spain, far more attention was paid to the prompt conversion of the Indians than had been shown in the islands. Government was a matter of supporting existing customs with as little change as possible, but conversion, and the creation of a different way of life, meant the greatest possible demonstration of change. Cortés had removed Falling Eagle in secret, but it was thought best to destroy publicly the temples, the idols encrusted with human blood, the sacrificial stones. Elimination of the war-gods of Mexico might be the more explicable to Mexicans, because those gods had failed; but how was the ritual which hitherto everywhere governed every daily action to be replaced? The desired ritual for festival and ceremony, seed-time and harvest, domestic routine? It is impossible not to respect the earnestness with which Spaniards set about the religious transformation. Twenty-five million natives presented an educational problem which ran beyond the experience of any European nation. It cannot be said the Spanish rulers did not try to face it.

> The rulers of Spain throughout the sixteenth century without exception, were firmly devoted to the ends for which the Patronato was established. They used their power to send into the mission field men of outstanding ability, experience and zeal; men who – considering the smallness of the numbers and the magnitude of their task – achieved an extraordinary degree of success.[4]

Cortés had asked specifically for a Franciscan mission. Twelve Franciscan friars were selected, crossed the Atlantic in 1524, were received by Cortés with ostentatious humility, and set about establishing mission houses. Twelve Dominicans arrived in 1526. The original 'twelves' were multiplied. Augustinians arrived in 1533. Books followed. Zumárraga introduced the first printing press about 1534; he was much an admirer of Thomas More, and so was Vasco de Quiroga, who on the shores of Lake Pátzcuaro founded self-supporting Indian communities based on *Utopia*. The names of the early bishops dedicated to frontier service in New Spain indicates, as Parry emphasizes, that they could have been eminent in any court of Europe. From the beginning New Spain was served by churchmen of high ability. None who went out had more experience or more devotion than Las Casas – who in 1544, at the age of seventy, went to be bishop of Chiapa. Men of such calibre did not fail to attract some equally dedicated curates.

The very magnitude of the Spanish endeavour to convert Mexicans to the Faith, the proclaimed earnestness of the effort, contributed all the more to a bitterness of disillusion. In the islands only a small effort had been made, and made too late, and the Indians had died. In New Spain there were from the beginning strong missionary exertions, and Mexicans, although 'fine men', died just the same. For that tragedy there seemed to be no remedy whatever. It was not that Indians fought for their previous habits in an organized, spectacular, understandable way. They seemed willing to try peaceably, as at Lake Pátzcuaro, to work in communities such as Thomas More had thought of, at a time when all over Europe people made war against the Church, and in England More's head was stuck upon a pole above London Bridge. There was no such violence among Indian protestors. They did rebel against the new religion here or there: there were some 'hostiles', a mission house was raided, a priest killed, and there were sporadic fightings. Yet on the whole New Spain was unrebellious. There was an almost surprising readiness to accept, superficially, the Word. The irrational and awful horror was that the Word as given was not operative. It did not give the Mexicans fresh heart, fresh life. They died and went on dying. Much later on, this was a matter sanctimoniously held against Spaniards by other European peoples. Spaniards of the time were more aware than others, needed no others to advise them of their tragedy.

The backlash within old Spain is what I think of. To the rest of the European world Spain's power seemed at its mightiest. To an increasing number of Spaniards within Spain it was as if Philip, like Charles before him, was a landlord for whose foreign affairs Spain was depleted. The cost of servicing the never-ending wars and the empire seemed, in Spain itself, to mean a government of bureaucracy, office-holders, deputies, tax-gatherers: taxes were so appalling that most of life was tax-evasion. The long economic crisis and the very noticeable demographic change within Spain itself is a matter that Professor Parry comments on; he does not relate the economic crises and the demographic changes in New Spain and Old Spain as if they were cause and effect. He stresses that through their coincidence of timing, changes that occurred in Spain and in the Indies interacted very much to the disadvantage of both.

Yet I have failed to express what I mean about the spiritual backlash of the failure in New Spain. I must try to get closer to the actuality.

I made some superficial contrasts, between the ways of life shaped in Italy and Spain: the Italian apt to take or make more joy (in arts, for instance) than puritan Spaniards cared for or permitted. It seemed to me the Spaniard, on his way to rule the world, tended to despise the Italians as not as hard, or strong, or cruel to the enemy, as the Spanish fighter should be. I felt the Church of Rome appeared to many Spaniards as relatively diffident and indecisive, weak, soft, and not the real Militant and Triumphant Church, *Chiesa Militante e Trionfante*, that Spain would passionately wish. It seemed to me the pious Spaniard cared less for the cost and sacrifice it meant to him if it was his King who was putting down the disobedient Protestants – worse enemies indeed than Jews and Moors and Turks, for Protestants had been Churchmen once, and then turned traitor to authority. Charles, and Philip after him, as self-appointed military champions of the Counter-Reformation gave Spain the leadership in manifesting the rightful punishment, or so it seemed to many Spaniards. Rome, at the time Charles's star was rising, was powerless. Rome itself was sacked in 1527 by 40,000 wild and mutinous men (12,000 of them were Lutheran *Landsknechts*) who forced their way into the papal city, turned the Church of St. Peter and the Holy Palace into stables, and for eight days did every damage that could be thought of to churches, monasteries, priests and nuns. Two-thirds of Rome was in ruins at the end of the eight days. The barbarous invaders were some of Charles's own Imperial troops that had mutinied, but it was Charles who by degrees restored order. Charles, by 1535, had driven the French from Italy; he then had led an army into Africa and taken Tunis; he shone as the Defender of the Faith. By 1539 Rome, still physically showing scars of ruin, seemed little more than a dependency of Spain. You could not visit Rome at that time and feel from what you saw that Rome was a worthy symbol of a Faith to be defended.

Yet within fifty years after the sack of Rome a marvel had taken place. A new Rome had arisen which to the eye of the faithful, or to anyone with an appreciative eye, was trying to be a City of God in physical actuality. Rome, in stone and colour, had become a visual statement of official Christian faith, and a statement of such skill and draughtsmanship and on such scale, as none but Italian artists, and of their own volition, could have made. Foremost of many great men it was Michelangelo who 'by his longevity no less than by his genius, became the spiritual link between the Renaissance and the Counter-Reformation'. Perhaps only Michelangelo (I am quoting Sir Kenneth Clark)* 'had the energy of spirit to pull together the vast inchoate mass of St. Peter's', to re-erect that Temple of the Christian spirit, with the most commanding dome in the world, and, within, the most commanding portraiture of God, and Christ, the Virgin and the Saints, and of the sometime greatness and sometime horror of human behaviour. The whole of Rome's rebuilding was a positive, emergent expression of what the Church intended to mean, 'harmonizing, humanizing, civilizing, the deepest impulses of ordinary, ignorant people'. The resurrection of Rome after its degradation, a visible resurrection expressing the confident spirit of conforming Christians who happened to be supreme artists, had, I believe, immense impact in Spain.

Rome's revival emphasized Spain's failure in the New World. In a mere business sense, the decimation of the Indians was painful enough. In the first phase, the disappearance of the island-Indians as a labour force had knocked the gilt off the expected gingerbread; in the second phase in New Spain, the disappearance of the Mexicans really knocked out the ginger. A detached observer, no shareholder in the Enterprise, like Montaigne in his tower, might feel the appalling wastage in the loss of all those Indians on the other side of the world; Montaigne had read Las Casas, and expressed his grief and anger. It is worth looking into *Don Quixote* to see what Cervantes says, or perhaps what he refrains from saying, about the Spanish Enterprise of the Indies. I would not expect Cervantes to say much about it in an explicit way; as for any direct correlation between a mock-world of knight-errantry and a world of Conquistadors, Cervantes will not press that cap to fit except in so far as it pleases you. He draws incidentally on the Indies for the comedy of Sancho Panza wishing to be Governor of an Island; otherwise the Indies are scarcely in the tale. Yet despite their physical absence, I feel the presence of the Indies throughout *Don Quixote*, as the presence of a dream that is not much talked of, because that dream is over. There is no dishonour in talking of defeats, where there has been no surrender of spirit; but when the spirit is most deeply injured, there is little urge to talk. There is a noticeable contrast about the island Cervantes gives to

* *The Listener*, 10 April 1969.

Sancho Panza with Shakespeare's island in *The Tempest*. The one is a practical island: there is human wit and humour in it, but no allowance for miracles. The other is an untried romantical magical place where anything is possible.

But some of the younger Spaniards of the mid-16th century were not in the least resigned to failure of spirit, in the New World or anywhere else. To them (I am thinking of Loyola) the revival of St. Peter's in Rome was both a reproach and a stimulus. It was reproach, because Italians with their inspired rebuilding were doing more, as witnesses to Christian faith, than Spanish soldiers. I said the statement made visible (as in the Sistine Chapel) may be looked at as spontaneous and self-generated, a positive statement of axioms of the Church, and not such a mere defensive rebuttal as is implied by the phrase 'Counter-Reformation'. In Spain the century which produced St. John of the Cross, St. Teresa of Avila, and St. Ignatius Loyola likewise exhibits a spontaneity of spirit, not readily explained by outward circumstance. Among Spain's soldiers (again I think of Loyola as having started as a soldier) there was, one feels, more admixture of 'Counter-Reformation' than among Italian artists, and a more passionate desire to redeem soldierly defects. Later on, Philip as commander-in-chief, seems to have felt that one cause of defeats was that though Spain had been puritan it had not been pure enough. The Inquisition was revived; there were renewed actions to expel such poor Moriscos as remained; the failure of Philip's Armada caused him further spiritual self-scourging. Yet the spirit exhibited by Loyola's new-formed Society of Jesus was a militancy not so much of the sword as of the mind, and one feels that one intention of the Jesuits was to be a mobile force for expression of the same affirmation that was being shown in Rome's revival.

A recognition of spiritual challenge in the New World, a wish to make atonement for damage done to Indians, now become active forces in the extension of the Road West beyond the northern frontier of New Spain. Pressure to extend the roadway into wilderness is, and for some time to come, increasingly a religious pressure. In a study of road-making I must especially watch the endeavour of the Jesuits, the new religious Order initiated by Loyola. But there were other Spanish soldiers of Loyola's age-group who also turned, individually and independently, to some kind of missionary activity. One, whose adventures were of particular stimulus to the further construction of the Road West, calls for recollection here. His adventures were certainly extraordinary. Even his name, at first sight, is unusual. His name was Cow's Head.

The story of Alvar Nuñez de Vera Cabeza de Vaca has often been told, and is told especially well by John Upton Terrell.[5] The last part of his name (Cabeza de Vaca = Cow's Head) was derived on his mother's side from an incident in the very early days of the Spanish Reconquista, and it was a name of honour. The name of de Vera was not at all well regarded at the court of Ferdinand and Isabella. We saw that Alvar's grandfather, Pedro de Vera, had been, in 1480, the first Spanish governor of the Canaries; his conduct was such that he was recalled. An uncle of Alvar's, also a de Vera, was dismissed from the Court, and, to evade arrest, vanished. It was under the name of Cabeza de Vaca that Alvar (dropping the name de Vera) in his early twenties saw active service for three years against the French in Italy. He was wounded at the rout at Ravenna; returned and was married at Seville, when after a while he met Narvaez, just back from Cuba and Mexico.

'Narvaez with the long face, echoing voice, red beard, who lost an eye when we defeated him,' is the description by Bernal Díaz of the treacherous bully for whom no chronicler has sympathy. We saw Narvaez earning a special curse from Las Casas. When he attempted to capture Cortés in Mexico and Cortés captured him instead, Cortés laughed, and Narvaez' followers deserted to join the better man. But one cannot avoid a sneaking respect for the outrageous resilience of Narvaez when he turned up in Seville, with his one remaining eye fixed upon Florida. Cabeza de Vaca at that moment, though he was to become sorry for it, was taken in by Narvaez.

Ponce de León had sailed along both sides of the peninsula to which the name 'Florida' is now restricted. He had attempted to seize the land, had been driven out by the Indians, and had died of his wounds. For thirteen years Florida had not been seriously assaulted until Narvaez proposed to succeed where Ponce de León failed. Charles V accepted the petition. Narvaez was to be Governor; he raised five ships, more than 600 volunteers (10 wives among them), and Cabeza de Vaca accepted the King's commission as treasurer and provost marshal for the expedition.

The expedition sailed from San Lúcar in June, 1527. At Santo Domingo many deserted; there was a further lowering of spirit in Cuba; in April 1528 Narvaez, with Cabeza de Vaca and something like 300 men landed on the west coast of Florida, near Tampa. With no more than the vaguest of plans for rendezvous with his ships, Narvaez and his column of men in armour attempted to march toward a City of Gold. After four months they struggled back to the Gulf of Mexico, at the Bay of Horses (St. Mark's Bay). They had skirmished with Indians but had found no gold. At the Bay of Horses they did not find their ships.

Cabeza de Vaca called it the Bay of Horses, for that was where they killed their horses and built a flotilla of five boats, as best they could with improvised tools: the horse hides were for plating the boats, rigging, also for water bottles. At the end of September the five boats, each about 33 feet in length, carrying a total of 242 men, set out with whatever they could manage for oars and sails – for Mexico.

The wonder is that all the boats survived as far as somewhere near Galveston, where all (by then separated) were wrecked. A few of the shipwrecked men survived to become slaves of coastal Indians. In 1534 four of these men managed to come together – three Spanish soldiers and a Negro, a big African Moor who captures the fancy of all narrators. The white men were Castillo, Dorantes and Cabeza de Vaca; the black, who had been a servant of Dorantes, was Estevanico.

Six years – one has to repeat, six years – after leaving the Bay of Horses, the four men managed to get together, and escaped from the coast of Texas. They were in poor shape but set out to walk northward and westward across the rest of America. This ambition was achieved by the ragged foursome turning itself into a catalytic agent.

The scheme of travel was invented by Cabeza de Vaca, smallest of the Four in physique, quickest certainly in ingenuity. As a captive among the coastal Indians, he had served on occasion as a faith-healer. Early on this proposed walk to the Pacific, the Four arrived at an Indian settlement where they were offered food (including more venison and prickly pears than they could eat), and many other gifts, which they had the wisdom of first accepting and then returning to the donors. Perceiving that they were regarded as medicine men, Cabeza de Vaca exerted his powers; but, wishing to move westward, designed a method whereby the foursome might be floated from the first tribe to another.

The ingenious procedure was this: the first tribe – none knew its name, none knew its language, but call it tribe *A* – was persuaded by sign-talk to tell a next tribe *B* that if *B* were to assemble an adequate supply of worldly goods, *A* would bring the medicine men. When this was agreed, tribe *A* escorted the Four to *B*, *B* made its offerings to the Four, the Four with ceremony gave *B*'s offerings to *A*, and *A* went home rejoicing. The Four rewarded *B* by performing all healings required, and by the time it occurred to *B* to mourn for its possessions, the thought was induced that if a next tribe *C* put up enough goods, the Four would give *C*'s property to *B*, and so move on.

The method of being wafted from one tribe to another was not only ingenious; it actually worked. With astonishingly little friction the Four were handed on across the wide and abrasive territory from the uplands of northern Texas to the Sierra Madre Mountains of the far west coast. Not the least of the interests of the *Relacion* of Cabeza de Vaca is the way that the journey altered his own character. At first he feared he was performing hypocrisies; he then came truly to accept that when he and his companions prayed with sincerity, then, at the moment he made the sign of the cross, a healing spirit came from Heaven. The more that this was demonstrated by results, the more his own faith grew; and what at first had been little more than trickery to save their skins, was the means of his own conversion. He now moved onward, from one tribe to another, as, consciously, a Christian missionary. In the ten months of westward journeying he increased his efforts, in sign-language, to communicate his faith to Indians, in whom 'we found neither sacrifices nor idolatry'. Perhaps the method of journeying ensured that the Four were always passed from one friendly tribe to another. Even so, there were many hazards and emergencies. Cabeza de Vaca was shrewd not to overplay his healing powers, nor to outstay any welcome; there was often a motive for the Four to move on, in that Estevanico was dangerously free with Indian squaws. Ten months of travel brought the wanderers unscathed to the Gulf of California, then named the Sea of Cortés. There, in the mountains of the Sierra Madre, in March 1536, the worst emergency occurred. At long last, eight years after the expedition had reached Florida, Cabeza de Vaca met with a troop of Spanish soldiers, fellow-countrymen, speaking the same tongue. But the tongue was being used to different purpose. This troop of Spanish soldiers was slave-raiding.

The brutal fact was that by 1536 half the Indians within New Spain had died. Miners, farmers, road-builders, traders of all kinds, were in perpetual need of slave labour; the more the need was felt, the more legitimate slavery seemed. The Church compelled, the *Audencia* proclaimed, and 'good' Governors enforced, severe restrictions on licences for slaves. To those who craved for cheap labour supply, Authority was disgustingly restrictive; and Spaniards of New Spain (no less than other people when a Prohibition is imposed) did whatever was possible to bribe and corrupt Authority in the scramble for possession of the dwindling number of 'hands'. The Governor of the northwest frontier territory, Guzmán, has been reviled by most historians for using the King's forces to raid into open territory for new slaves. Guzmán could pretend to legality by asserting that all of his captives were hostiles who were attacking the province – a thin excuse, for which he was impeached before the time his troops, in the northern wilderness, happened to find Cabeza de Vaca and his three companions and their attendant band of Indians. By pointing out that there were strong pressures on Guzmán to supply slaves, I am not defending his character, which, in his own lifetime, few Spaniards openly defended. Cortés loathed him; his own Vice-Governor, Melchior Díaz, opposed him; his conduct was under investigation by the Crown; he knew that whenever the Crown lawyers got to his Governor's House at Compostela, his shrift would be short. It was for Guzmán, as it was for the quartet of wanderers, an exceedingly awkward moment when the slave-raiding troops ran across them and their Indians in the Sierra Madre.

The leader of the troopers, who had never heard of the Narvaez expedition to Florida, not unnaturally regarded the Spanish-speaking Four as madmen, and when Cabeza de Vaca asserted that his Indians were not for capture, there was an episode which, in the circumstances, was highly comic. Troopers were instructed to escort the Four to the Vice-Governor at Culiacán, but also secretly instructed to make sure that on the way they should be 'lost' and left to die in trackless terrain. This attempt was duly made, but it would have been hard to find any four men less likely to be 'lost' by being turned loose than those four; they found a way easily enough to Culiacán, and were promptly examined by the Melchior Díaz whose name stands out in frontier annals as that of a commander as generous to frontier Indians as Guzmán was unscrupulous. Five years later, as an officer on Coronado's expedition, Melchior Díaz lost his life in an impulsive accident; at the moment of meeting Cabeza de Vaca, Díaz was young, ardent to reform Guzmán's government, and instantly sympathetic to Cabeza de Vaca's missionary zeal. Before doing anything else, two months were spent by Díaz and Cabeza de Vaca, countermanding slave-raids, visiting and promising immunity to frontier tribes. On May 15, with twenty mounted soldiers, six unidentified civilians and five hundred Indians in attendance, the Four set off to make a triumphal parade from Culiacán to Compostela. Díaz had provided Cabeza de Vaca with ammunition for a stormy interview with Guzmán. The story of the Four had by this time circulated; they were public heroes; there was nothing Guzmán could do but listen to a declaration from Cabeza de Vaca and allow the heroes a further escort for a procession southward over El Camino Real from Compostela to Mexico City. There the Four were 'welcomed with joy' and were 'handsomely treated by the Viceroy'. They arrived on July 24, the eve of the great feast of St. James. They made a public appearance at the celebrations and enjoyed the ceremonies very much, except for the discomfort of wearing clothes and, especially, the discomfort of boots.

El Camino Real – an extra reason for me to take an interest in the procession which accompanied these four men to meet Mendoza, then the Viceroy of New Spain, is that the track on which it moved was already named and thought of as a 'royal' highway. Many another Camino Real, many another King's Highway, was constructed in New Spain; but this particular segment traversed by Cabeza de Vaca was the one which exhibited a power to grow, in four more centuries, into the present-day spinal route of California. The living forcefulness which pushed this particular segment of roadway outward into wilderness is what I am trying to analyze. In the complex of impulses something stands out which seems to characterize

347

the third phase of the Spanish Enterprise of the Indies – something which is apart from and distinguishable from the predatory impulses. It is perhaps unusual to find, as one of the impulses toward road-making, something that can be described only as a desire for ex-piation. Yet the more one examines the force which pushed the Spaniards into California, the more one is forced to consider one hard-working spiritual factor: the missionary impulse.

I must continue to bear in mind that the Indian population of New Spain at the beginning of the 17th century had dwindled to perhaps two million, and the white and near-white people settled in all the land numbered no more than perhaps 100,000. A percentage of the hundred thousand were explorers. In the first years after the Conquest, more wonders might be discovered at any moment. Cortés himself promoted exploration of the 'South Sea'; there might be land inhabited by Amazons, there must be passage somewhere from one ocean to the other which would make ship-traffic between Spain and 'the spice region' easy, short, and without risk. On the other side of the Sea of Cortés, Jiménez found Baja California. The outer western coast of Baja California was proved by Cabrillo in 1542 to continue unbroken for a long way; his two caravels put in to San Diego har-bour at the end of September; so far as his search was for a 'Strait of Anian' he might have stayed there, for the Indians were friendly and said no easterly seaway existed. Cabrillo, now in his fifties, had been one of Cortés' fighting men; he was not easily beaten; he coasted on to find how far the coast of Alta California did extend. On one of his landings he accidentally fell. His arm, broken at the shoulder, could not be properly attended to. He refused to turn back, and, when dying at sea, insisted the exploration should continue. The exploration did continue, although the coast of Alta California was nothing but a long lee shore. The two ships went on far beyond 'Drake's Bay'; they reached a farthest north somewhere about Rogue River, Oregon. By then they had had enough of searching for a Strait of Anian. They had found nothing that appealed to them in Alta California, and there was too much of it – too many entries in the log, recording simply: 'There are mountains which seem to reach the heavens, and the sea beats on them.'

If there was too much coastline of Alta California, there was certainly, to the north of New Spain, a daunting amount of singularly harsh wilderness for the earliest land-explorers to look at. Somewhere in all that wilderness there might be found the 'Seven Cities of Cibola', richer, and perhaps far richer, than anything imaginable. That was a hope which led to much questioning of the Four who had appeared, astonishingly, out of the wilderness. In 1536 what was uppermost in Cabeza de Vaca's mind, was that his long walk had been among Indians who were poor but on the whole friendly. He seems to have picked up that one Indian term for friends, or allies, was *techas*; his mode of travel had kept him among *techas*; and it is conjectured that is how Spaniards began to call the territory from which he started to walk, Texas.[6] Cabeza de Vaca sailed home to Spain in 1537, and seems at no time to have encouraged the hope that Cities of Gold existed in any territory he had heard of; but after Cabeza de Vaca had left Mexico City, I must assume that Estevanico (who remained in Mendoza's household) allowed himself to gratify a wish for travellers' tales. After Cabeza de Vaca's *Relacion* had been studied, an important large expedition was authorized by the Viceroy and organized by Coronado, which was to have many officers of experience – Alarcón, Cárdenas, and Melchior Díaz among them. I do not find it very easy to believe that Estevanico, three friars, and a retinue of Indians were officially sent into the northern wilderness a year ahead of Coronado, as a pilot-expedition to pacify the untamed tribes and undertake preliminary pathfinding. I think it more likely that Estevanico either persuaded or was persuaded by the lay-priests that he, ahead of anyone else, could find the way to the Seven Cities. At any rate, with or without the Viceroy's encouragement, in 1539 we see Estevanico dressed up with plumed head-dress, arms and legs decked with feathers, bells on his ankles, striding northward from Culiacán, waving a sacred gourd rattle to enliven any who might observe him and to enhearten the friars to follow. To add to the pomp and ceremony, Estevanico's personal servant 'carried four large green dinner plates on which his meals were served'.* The procession met with tribes who remembered Estevanico; they passed him on toward

---

* Terrell, *Journey into Darkness*, p. 281. Terrell adds that two lean greyhounds trotted by Estevanico's side, and that when Estevanico was killed, the Zuñis kept the greyhounds and the green dinner plates, but threw away the magic gourd.

the 'cities' he had promised to find. He far outstripped the friars who toiled after him; he sent back wooden crosses to signify his findings; the crosses were larger and larger. The end came when Estevanico with his gourd, his servant with the green plates and retinue of attendant Indians, appeared at a pueblo of the Zuñi and summoned it to surrender. The men of the Zuñi regarded Estevanico as tiresome, and with their arrows shot him and all but three of his attendants. These fled back to the friars, who, in turn, promptly retreated to Mexico; but there reported that the Seven Golden Cities of Cibola had been found.

Coronado's more professional expedition set out in 1540. Its achievements compel astonishment and admiration. There were accidents—the death of Melchior Díaz was one—but Alarcón successfully explored the lower Colorado River, Cárdenas discovered the amazing Grand Canyon, and Coronado himself marched north-eastward as far as central Kansas, the first white man to cover what later became known as the Santa Fé Trail. Meanwhile, and independently, de Soto had set out from Spain with a patent for the Florida which Narvaez had failed to capture, and with his small army marched from Florida westward. De Soto crossed the Mississippi in June 1541, and at one time he and Coronado came so close to each other that 'an Indian maiden, seeking to escape the attentions of Coronado's soldiers, fled for several days through rough desert country only to be taken by the second group of predatory Spaniards'.[7] 'Predatory' is, I think, a right word – probably for Coronado, certainly for de Soto, who had formerly been one of the Conquistadors of Peru. They traversed territory of immense potential wealth, but found no treasure ready-made for picking up. Coronado noted the great plains and the buffalo; de Soto noted that Indians grew yellow maize; they found no yellow metal, no gold. But Coronado started a renewed zeal for 'prospecting', and it was without going so far afield that four Spanish soldiers found, in 1548, in a mountain gorge near what became the city of Zacatecas, a silver lode of greatest richness. 'From this first excavation and the others that were soon opened throughout New Spain's provinces of Nueva Galicia and Nueva Vizcaya would come eventually two-thirds of the world's supply'.[8]

It was towards the end of the century that a new Viceroy of New Spain, Gaspar de Zúñiga, better known perhaps as Count of Monterey, felt there was too much frontier unless it could be populated, and that population by white settlers depended on a technical assistance plan for Indians. The silver of Zacatecas was the pull for a Camino Real to be extended from Mexico City toward the region of 'allies', Texas. In 1575, out of the hundred thousand Spaniards in New Spain, a handful of twenty families of pioneers had been encouraged to settle near the silver finds, beyond the narrow pass of La Angostura, in the Valley of Saltillo. That was a 'high land of many waters', where fields could be irrigated from springs 'as many as the days of the year'. The settlement prospered: maize, Spanish wheat, beans, fruit trees and an *estancia* with pasturage for breeding horses and mules, made it not merely self-supporting but a source of supplies for miners in waterless areas around Zacatecas and Mazapil. But the safety of such a settlement, and of mining camps, depended on the permanence of good relations with the Indians. Therefore Zúñiga's policy for the development of the 'silver' country was to encourage missions, mainly Franciscan, to provide outposts ahead of mining camps and settlements. Indians were to be tempted to visit mission houses by the offer of government gifts; the gifts were to be obtained by accepting missionary teaching; the teaching was to enable the Indians to make the wilderness productive for themselves and productive of supplies to sell to Spaniards.

Molasses from Campeche, butcher's knives, hoof parers, iron shoes for horse and mule, medicines, thread, cheese and dried shrimp were the weapons in the Spanish strategy. Sometimes arrows and death were the reward. But more often the Indians came docilely to the missions to learn how to assure themselves of plenty in this life while the missionaries taught them the *doctrina* of salvation for the next. They lived in *pueblos*, Indian towns set up according to Spanish law on specially assigned lands, with their own *alcaldes* and officers supervised by the missionary fathers.

In twenty years, 'peace by purchase' had quieted all of Nueva Galicia and much of Nueva Vizcaya. So astounding was the mission system's success in its initial phase that in the years to come the friars applied it unquestioningly as they moved along the *camino real*.[9]

Despite the smallness of their numbers, it seemed not impossible that a few Spaniards might establish a dominion over the whole vast territory that Coronado had surveyed. It was in Zúñiga's régime that

Oñate carried forward the red and gold standard of King Philip and, to the admiration of an attendant fifteen hundred Indians, set it up near Santa Fé in 1598. Within a few years the establishment of Santa Fé as capital of a new province of empire, New Mexico – as large or larger than New Spain – seemed proof of a conquest 'en lo espiritual'. The ancient quarrel between Las Casas and Cortés had been that Cortés said 'first conquer, then convert'; Las Casas had held that conversion should come first. In Nueva Galicia, the 'peace by purchase' as operated by Franciscans was successful. Zúñiga's hope was that at Santa Fé, as capital of all New Mexico, soldier and missionary would work hand-in-hand in government. So, for a time, they did; so long as there were very few of each, and until Pueblo Indians felt a strong desire to get together and stage a *reconquista* of their own.

The 'Great Pueblo Uprising' which later on temporarily destroyed the Spanish capital of Santa Fé, did not occur until 1680. When it came, it was to some extent a religious war. The Indians of Nueva Galicia were relatively docile; on the whole, they took to what the friars taught them and accepted that there were some advantages in the pueblos set up for them. But the peoples known as Pueblo Indians, such as the Zuñis and Hopis of the chromatic desert to the west of Santa Fé, or the Keres and Tewas along the Rio Grande, were so called because from ancient times each had a heritage of its own *pueblo*; and however their shared civilization might have faded from its golden age in the 13th century,* each people had its traditional proud religion, with elaborate ceremonials. Before the Spaniards came, Pueblo Indians had been able to defend their own communities against comparative newcomers from the north, such as the Utes, and against the raids of nomadic Apache hunters. After eighty years of tolerating the existence of Santa Fé, the Pueblo Indians were incited to make a concerted attack. The leader of the uprising was of the Tewa tribe, a man named Popé, whom some writers describe as a religious prophet, others as a medicine man. In the attack upon Santa Fé, four hundred or so Spaniards were massacred, including 21 of the 33 Franciscan friars. A number of Spanish refugees managed to reach El Paso but for two years no Spaniards remained in the province of New Mexico.

* That 'golden age' is a phrase accorded by those who have studied the Pueblo arts of pottery, turquoise jewelry and woven cloth.

Popé had the momentary satisfaction at Santa Fé of assuming the seat of dignity in the Governor's captured carriage; but the pleasure of having torn down the red and gold standard of Spain ceased when the horses for the carriage were stolen by Apaches. Apaches had respected Spanish arms, and horses were one weapon they had learned to steal, and this new weapon, gained from the Spaniards, they were quick to use. After eighty years of Spanish protection against Apaches, the Pueblo Indians were severely punished by that now-mounted enemy. After two years without protection, the Pueblos offered little protest at the return of a Spanish column of troops. From then onward the resumed Spanish government at Santa Fé was predominantly military.

Ignatius Loyola (Inigo Lopez de Ricalde) was the thirteenth son of a Spanish nobleman, born at the castle of Loyola in the Basque country. As a young man of the same age-group as Cabeza de Vaca, he was also, automatically, an officer in Ferdinand's wars against the French. Somewhat later than Cabeza de Vaca, at the age of 30, he was wounded. His wound was severe, and lamed him for life; but his spiritual transformation during and subsequent to convalescence places him firmly among the greatest saints of the Church Militant. If I bring Cabeza de Vaca and Loyola into a same paragraph, it is because they both happened to be Spanish soldiers of the same age at the same time, and from being debonair young officers both altered into men of serious religious intent. After Cabeza de Vaca's extraordinary adventure in North America, he was appointed at the age of 50 to be Governor of the province of Rio de la Plata, but he failed (as all others had failed) in the administration of that territory. It is perhaps unfair to him, to compare his stature with that of Loyola. Loyola's spiritual travail had been of deeper nature; his conversion may indeed be compared with that of Francis of Assisi; and his determination to be a soldier of Christ, expressed at first in extreme self-mortifications, then in pilgrimage and then in many years of fervent study, gave him the leadership, at the age of 43, of a group of seven who swore to vows of chastity and poverty, with intent of becoming a special Society of Jesus. Loyola's draft of his *Exercitia Spiritualia* and of the *Constitutions* for the 'Jesuits' has remained to this day the basis for the organization. In 1540 Loyola obtained the sanction of

353

Pope Paul III for his Society, and at the age of 50, Loyola was its first 'general'. Complete obedience to serve wherever and as directed by the Pope, complete obedience within the Society to the General, made the Jesuits an Order more flexible than older religious Orders, for the active spread of the revived spirit of the Church. There were no 'secret Jesuits'; the normal period of severe intellectual training was not less than about thirteen years; only after the full maturity of training were Jesuits to proceed to the solemn profession, involving a fourth vow, of going on missionary service. Of the original members, four of Loyola's companions (including Francis Xavier) were Spanish; but the Order was soon international, and, in addition to the spiritual message of the Church, the learning and culture inseparable from that message were to be spread wherever Jesuit missionaries were sent.

In 1566 Father Martínez, first of the Jesuits to be sent to 'Florida', was martyred by the American Indians. Father Segura and seven of his companions were likewise tortured and killed near Chesapeake Bay, not far from where Jamestown was planted by the English some thirty-six years later. The survivors of that Jesuit mission to the Atlantic seaboard were directed to join Father Sánchez, the first Provincial of the Order in Mexico City. The 'Black Robes' of the young Order, contrasting with the grey of the Franciscans, were soon in increasing number at the capital, and at the farthest outposts, of New Spain. In the burst of energy in Cortés' time, and under the first Viceroys, Spanish military posts had been advanced northward to great distances (measured by foot-travel or by horse) along the Pacific slope. Settlements were attempted in what seem nowadays the most impossible places, as in Baja California. In the beginning it was soldiers who first probed the wilderness; miners and stock-raisers followed; missionaries, so far as they could, caught up with predecessors. In the penetrations toward Texas we saw that the procedure was often reversed – Franciscans were used as pioneers, mission houses were planted ahead of other settlements. The northwestern frontier of New Spain became especially a Jesuit Land, for there the Black Robes began to penetrate often in advance of soldiery.

It was a colorful pageant. Black Robes moved into the wilderness beside or ahead of prospector, miner, soldier, cattleman, and frontier trader. Land travel chiefly was on horseback, muleback, or on foot, and land transportation by pack train or by Indian carriers. As the frontier expanded, here and there a town, a mining camp, an hacienda, a garrison, was pitched on the border of settlement. Still beyond, in the midst of heathendom, Christian missions were planted. As the Spaniards advanced northward, the Indians were reduced to sedentary life or driven back.[10]

For North American Indians, as they became involved in what I spoke of as road-accident, there was an equal loss of whatever they cherished as their own 'freedom', whether the collision that occurred was with a European in the gilded armour of a Coronado or in the black robe of a Jesuit. I suppose it might be held to make no difference, to a man who loses 'his' life, whether he has been run over by a tank or an ambulance. Nevertheless the difference of intention does make a difference to the historian of the accident. The intention of the missionary was, I think all must admit, to offer a 'better' life. I remember the feeling I had when (before this book began) I chanced to have a glimpse of the small white Spanish mission house near Tucson airport. Looking at that one remnant (still managing to serve an Indian 'reservation') no one could fail to think of the dotted line of such mission-houses, extending, as it once did, from Mexico City. Swiftly the eye went farther backward: the identification of Father Kino's mission house was for me not with Mexico City, but with the small white monastery in the desert below Mount Sinai, the one which had been planted by Justinian for Greek monks also on frontier service. Service, with what intention? The monastery at Sinai had been long ago placed there, because far longer ago than that there was supposed to have been a communication at Mount Sinai that men should try to build a City of God.

I felt it was worth the effort to watch what happened after that communication: that has been a main preoccupation of this survey. It was easier to aspire to build a Shining City than to achieve the building of it. Successive efforts made by different peoples provided some wonderful examples of inspired intention, and the Christian revelation was that the City of God was supernal, however transitory earthly efforts seemed. Always the physical roadways to and from a central city seemed to flex with dual purpose, to bring things from frontiers to the citadel, or to impress the ideas of the city on the frontiers. To some men, Christ's instruction was wholly unequivocal: when themselves thoroughly briefed in the message, and when trained in the 'best' that a city could teach them, to spend their lives upon a frontier, and there build better. I do not share the Jesuit's persuasion, and the conduct of the Order in the turmoil of wars in Europe is not within my theme. But I see that the ancient instruction to carry Christ's message to utmost parts, revived in New Spain, was what now gave a new extension to the Road West. One of the individual efforts which involved showing to frontier Indians the possible benefits of 'sedentary life', is seen in the story of the Black Robe who has just been mentioned, Father Kino.

I think of Kino mostly as he was in his later years, working as a 'father labourer' in the desert land of the Pimas and Apaches, far ahead of any protection from government or soldiery, but dreaming with incurable optimism of all the scrub and rock northwest of Mexico being turned into a Christian kingdom, to be called (in honour of San Francisco Xavier) the Kingdom of New Navarre. I think of Kino as a man of sixty-five at Tucson in 1710, talking alone with 'very many' Indians, he invariably in a black robe and they sometimes in feathers, strings of beads, bracelets, ear pendants and psychedelic face paints. Or I think of Kino on horseback, with a few of his household Indians, covering frontier distances that puzzle his biographer. Bolton[11] finds it was customary for Kino on missionary tours to make an average of thirty or more miles a day for weeks at a stretch, and 'out of this time are to be counted the long stops which he made to preach, baptize the Indians, say Mass, and give instructions for building and planting'. A large part of the effort was the encouragement of farming and stockbreeding.

The work which Father Kino did as ranchman would alone stamp him as an unusual business man and make him worthy of remembrance. He was easily the cattle king of his day and region. From the small outfit supplied him from the older missions to the east and south, within fifteen years he established the beginnings of ranching in the valleys of the San Ignacio, the Altar, the Santa Cruz, the San Pedro, and the Sonóita. The stock-raising industry of nearly twenty places on the modern map owes its beginnings on a considerable scale to this indefatigable man.[12]

'A Kino cavalcade was a familiar sight in Pima Land', with numbers of horses and mules varying from fifty to a hundred and thirty head. The 19 ranches which Kino supervised, and the attendant cultivations, were manned apparently almost without exception by Indians, and for the benefit of the Pima tribes; the operation was conducted as an extension and expansion, it would seem, of previous tribal custom. Supervision of the separate establishments entailed the hard riding that has been mentioned; Kino's desire to find new routes become a passion. 'One of his routes,' says Bolton, 'was over a forbidding, waterless waste which later became the graveyard of scores of travellers who died of thirst because they lacked Father Kino's pioneering skill. I refer to the Camino del Diablo, or Devil's Highway, from Sonóita to the Gila.'

Yet at each journey's end, after harsh, arid desert there was to be an oasis, and each oasis almost 'that shady city of palm trees' for which the Old Testament pilgrim had yearned from the beginning. The 'old promoter' refers to what had already been achieved at the oases within Pima Land:

There are already very rich and abundant fields, plantings and crops of wheat, maize, frijoles, chick peas, beans, lentils, bastard chick peas, etc. There are good gardens . . . vineyards for wine for masses, and canefields of sweet cane for syrup and panocha, and with the favour of heaven, before long for sugar. There are many Castilian fruit trees, such as fig trees, quinces, oranges, pomegranates, peaches, apricots, pears, apples, mulberries, pecans, tunas, etc.; all sorts of garden stuff, such as cabbages, melons, watermelons, white cabbage, lettuce, onions, leeks, garlic, anise, pepper, mustard, mint, Castilian roses, white lilies, etc.; and very good timber for all kinds of building, such as pine, ash, cypress, walnut, China-trees, mesquite, alders, poplar, willow, and tamarind.[13]

Pride for what had been achieved in Pima Land is but a spur to thoughts that go farther. Kino is confident of converting the Apaches – 'soon, in imitation of the rest, over here, they will be won to our friendship' – and 'by way of the same Apacheria' all that had been dreamed for New Mexico will be regained. Kino's vision was wider than that. His thoughts went from the Pima country 'northward to Gran Teguayo; northwest to Gran Quibira; and west to California Alta . . . and the South Sea, and to its great Bay of the Eleven Thousand Virgins; to the famous port of Monte Rey . . . and to the very renowned Cape Mendozino.' His thoughts ranged the whole continent: a dotted line of Jesuit missions to Canada would offer a short cut from Sonora to Spain and France 'only half as long as the road which we are accustomed to travel', the old way by the City of Mexico and Veracruz.

It does not seem that Kino ever lost his dream. The paragraph about the abundance of his plantations, the vegetables and Castilian fruits and timber, is bound to remind one of Columbus's euphoria at Isabela; but Kino's rosy picture is written after thirty years of frontier experience; and his enthusiasm, unlike Columbus's, refused to wilt. The carborundum of the desert wore down his body; he died at the age of 66; but he died fully clothed with his head on a pack saddle.

It is noticeable that in the 17th and 18th centuries many of the Jesuits who served on both sides of the Sea of Cortés and to the northward of New Spain, were northern Europeans.* The personnel of the Order had become international, but if the missionaries appear as a sort of Foreign Legion, what the legionaries subscribed to were the spiritual exercises and the constitutions of Loyola, and what they represented was the same civilization, or civility, by which Loyola had been stirred. The confident effort at Rome to create a style of expression, combining architecture, sculpture, painting into one panaesthesia of worship,† fits closely, hand in glove, with Loyola's more soldierly, more natively Spanish, effort. The term 'baroque', indeed, as it came to be applied by Northerners to the architectural style that was rising in Italy, suggests that there was felt to be something Spanish about it. Perhaps at that time there was a Northern fashion to identify as Spanish, anything that seemed aggressive, militant, or de-

---

* From the Jesuit annals for Sonora and Pimeria Alta, Bolton picks out 'the very un-Spanish names of Bentz, Fraedenberg, Gerstner, Grashofer, Hoffenrichter, Hawe, Keller, Klever, Kolub, Kurtzel, Middendorff, Miner, Nentuig, Och, Paver, Rhuen, Sedelmayr, Segesser, Slesac, Steb, Steiger, Wazet, and Weis. In California in those days labored Baegert, Bischoff, Consag, Ducrue, Gasteiger, Gordon, Helen, Link, Neumayer, Retz, Tempis, Tuersch, and Wagner, all of north European extraction'.

† 'I propose this name of *panaesthesia* to express "the totality of what an individual feels at a given moment",' McDowell, *Journal of Mental Science* (April, 1884).

signed to overawe with splendour; but be that as it may, the culture in which Jesuit missionaries were being trained was such as they could be proud of transmitting to the frontier. The baroque style of the churches built in New Spain was well calculated to appeal to native Mexicans; the number and size of those churches (despite the ever-diminishing labour-supply) is most impressive; no less impressive to me are the small mission-houses, almost invariably and individually beautiful, many of them put up by men of the foreign legion, who were themelves converts to Jesuit style.

The men, Spanish or un-Spanish, who penetrated into Sonora and Pimeria Alta, who built the desert mission-houses and drew roadways after them, must be thought of not as unsocial or unlettered; each one, before tackling the wilderness, was a graduate of thirteen years of college training. Romantic some of them had been, as boys – as Kino certainly was. Eusebio Francisco Kino, born in 1645 at Segno in the Tyrol, hardly knew whether to call himself an Italian or a German. The boyish desire that took hold of him, as he grew up in the Tyrol, was to go to China. His greatest hero, Xavier himself, although he tried until his death in 1552, had never achieved an entry into China proper. The Jesuit Matteo Ricci, who was received into the Middle Kingdom and reached Peking in 1601, attributed that success to the Chinese respect for a visitant who, even though a 'foreign devil', was an expert mathematician. Kino had a gift for mathematics, which he worked hard to improve, and year after year throughout eight years of his novitiate at Ingolstadt, he petitioned that when his preliminary training ended he might be trained for the Orient. His desire was such that he sought 'to live in the rooms of our college whose windows looked toward the East, so that I might be comforted, at times oft-repeated during the day, by the mere sight of the East'. Eventually Kino, at completion of his training and at the age of 35, was assigned to missionary work in Mexico. That assignment was a matter of luck. Kino and an equal Jesuit contender, both hoping for the Orient, were permitted to settle the 'devout quarrel' by drawing lots. The other drew 'Philippines'; Kino drew 'Mexico'; and the American Southwest thereby drew a most remarkable man.

Where Kino and other Jesuits went, roadways began to follow. Far up from Mexico City toward what is now the Arizona border, my atlas shows me the town of Magdalena; my atlas (small-scale) does not stoop to show the nearby village of Cosari, which Kino in his early days in Pima Land renamed Nuestra Señora de los Dolores. There a church was built. It had to have bells, so bells were sent, from Mexico City. 'Now they are placed on the little church which we built in the first days,' Kino reports. 'The natives are very fond of listening to their peals, never before heard in these lands.' The bells were important: their sound linked the rim of Christendom with the Eternal City. Later we see Kino repeating his request for a new bell for Dolores. Dolores had become mother of many daughter missions which had prospered; he had sent the money for the new bell for Dolores – a 'large and good bell' of, if possible, sixteen arrobas (400 pounds). I pause at that, for a bell of 400 pounds and its fittings (and counterweight) suggests there is already sufficient roadway for one of those early heavy carts with wooden wheels and loudly shrieking axle. The road for such a large bell may have grown only so far as Dolores, but Kino with his other mission-houses and his nineteen ranches is always seeking new trails into the Más Allá, the Farther On. To his procurator in Mexico he sends back bulls and horses; he sends silver; he sends three rather special bezoar stones, which interest him – they represent a very ancient heritage of Asian magic. Yet he sends things forward as well as back. He himself had pioneered an early trail from Pima Land to California. His continuing thought is that 'the Pimeria might lend a hand to California, her little sister beyond the Colorado'.

Jesuit missionaries in the north of New Spain soon found that trails, when made, attracted other men with other motives. Traders – Kino found them to be a trouble. Traders assumed a mission house was for their convenience, that an Indian community was easy game. When traders were warned off, they made complaints against the Jesuit Order. Settlers complained that Jesuits monopolized the best farm sites. Miners complained that their legal rights to Indian labour were usurped. The Bishop of Durango complained about his tithes: he might not collect them from Indians who were in the jurisdiction of the Order. Even as Kino was repeating his request for the 400-pound mission bell, his procurator warned him that the Bishop of Durango had demanded that all missions of the Society in New Spain should be suppressed, and the Bishop had the ear of the King. That warning by the procurator reached Kino in 1710, and I doubt if Kino liked the warning; he was at that moment building the mission-house where Tucson now stands. The totality of all complaints against the Jesuit Order within New Spain did in course reach the King, but in the general break-up of the Spanish Empire in the 18th century, partisan complaints from New Spain were not among the most serious problems of the Court in Europe. The universal expulsion of the Jesuit Order signed by Carlos III in 1767 was not prompted by the conduct of missionaries on the frontier. It was a political action in Europe (later rescinded); but so soon as the universal expulsion of the Jesuits was commanded, their frontier work perforce collapsed. Half a century after Kino's death, all Black Robes in New Spain were arrested, dispossessed of their mission-houses, hustled to Veracruz and deported.

Throughout the third phase of the Spanish Enterprise of the Indies, I am aware that my special attention to a roadway (now beginning to extend itself into El Camino Real of California) is merely the teasing of one single thread out of a huge dark background tapestry of history. The background tapestry, in all its size and complication, darkened by some centuries of age, presents its many patterns. In one large half-seen image which seems to represent the Spanish Seaborne Empire, I see in the tapestry the shape of an enormous though perhaps disheartened whale, who has been swimming to a new feeding-ground; and while he is gorged and floating, digesting or failing to digest, he is incessantly being attacked and pieces of his body gouged by a school of smaller killer-whales, ferocious *Orca*, all of which are equally ready at any moment to turn upon each other. This is the cartoon drawn by someone who reflects how the call of Drake's drum was heard at sea by many 'nationals' – French, Dutch, English, Danes. Come, said the drum, to one and all: Drake's raids at Veracruz were far outdone by others – the most notable massacre there was probably the horrible affair of 1683, conducted by de Graff, Van Horn and Gramont, operating under protection of the French, who were then holding Santo Domingo. A few years before that, La Salle had been the first white man to travel down the Mississippi to its mouth: the French incentive for La Salle's final expedition seems to have been the wish to capture the Spanish mines of Nueva Vizcaya. Drake's drum had of course drawn other Englishmen to the Pacific, among them Woodes Rogers, Clipperton, Shelvocke, Anson. Comedies sometimes accompanied their voyages – during Dampier's last voyage as pilot to Woodes Rogers (1708–11) their ship picked up the Scotsman Alexander Selkirk, who had been marooned. The ship went on to be beached, inside Baja California, for careening, and then, there is a picture of pure comedy. Selkirk, in the five years of solitude on his island, had forgotten most of his speech, but his joy at reaching the mainland could be proved to an admiring audience by showing how hard his bare feet had become and how fast he had been at running after wild goats. Captain and crew applauding, 'Robinson Crusoe' spent spare time at Baja California sprinting madly up and down the beach with wordless cries.

The cartoon of a tiring whale attacked by many killer-whales remains apt as a picture of the Spanish Seaborne Empire in the 18th century. At the beginning of that century, in 1704, we see the Dutch and English combining in the spectacular feat of capturing Gibraltar. By the end of the century, and largely as a result of maritime wars with England, Spain had lost effective commercial control of the formerly Spanish Indies. By 1808, as a result of the French military invasion of the Iberian Peninsula, the Indies are no longer under Spain's administrative control. Nothing, perhaps, could take away the pride of once having been a ruler of the world. That pride, like the pride of Lucifer, remained to Castile and Aragon; yet as to the future, there was loss of heart. Under the repetition of so many wounds to Old Spain in the 18th century, there was, except in one respect, a corresponding loss of heart in New Spain. The exception, in New Spain, is that the missionary effort on the frontier showed no loss of spirit. We saw the Jesuit Order summarily expelled in 1767; many of the Jesuit missions were secularized; but where the mission-houses were remote, as on the frontier, the missionary purpose was not lost – they were turned over to Franciscans. In New Spain toward the end of the 18th century, when everything else seems to be going from bad to worse, one item stands out for its vitality. The item is, new roadways in the Northwest. Whatever the changes in the rest of the world, for a long time there is no change in the pattern of frontier life, no loss there of energy. Black Robes have changed to Grey Robes, but on the way to Más Allá, to Alta California, the frontier missionary goes on wielding axe, spade and trowel, swinging the lasso, applying the branding iron, cinching the girths of horse and mule. The Franciscan missionary did not always have such store of academic training as the Jesuit; for urgent practicalities, and for pathfinding in the wilderness, he was no worse. Pathfinding for a continuous road from Mexico City to San Francisco Bay had been completed by the summer of 1776.

The pushing of a Spanish pathway all the way to San Francisco, at that time, I find astonishing. Silver and gold was not the drawing power. There was no particular trade purpose. There were two purposes: the lesser one was military. A *Visitador General,* José de Gálvez, had been sent direct from the King to oversee the banishment of the Jesuits and to improve Spain's percentage of revenues from New Spain. His function was like that of the English Henry VIII's Cromwell, to lay what iron hand he could on property of a proscribed ecclesiastical Order; and, at as little cost as possible, to defend King's rights. José de Gálvez displayed imagination; he listened to a rumour that alien white men – Russians – were landing on the coast of Alta California. All other nations were attacking Spain – and now the Russians! The answer that occurred to de Gálvez was to have a watch-tower at the far-off Golden Gate. How to provide for such a distant watch-tower and for communications to and from Mexico City, at minimum cost to his King, called for further imagination. Here, de Gálvez could count on the zeal of a fifty-five-year-old lame missionary, the Franciscan friar, Junípero Serra. Serra would not be bribed to make a mission trail for military purpose; but Serra was already, and of his own zeal, planning a chain of missions at a day's ride apart as far into California as possible. Where Franciscan missions went, a King's highway (at no cost to the King) would follow. José de Gálvez saw reason to applaud Junípero Serra's work for the particular mission trail which would in time become El Camino Real of California.

Soldier and priest together made a first pathfinding for a land-road all the way from Mexico City to the Golden Gate. The soldier was Bautista de Anza – 'one of the greatest of all Spanish frontiersmen,' says de Voto, 'and he had Garcés with him'. Garcés was the priest: we shall see him in a moment in action on his own. For their reconnaissance de Anza and Garcés used the overland route from the Sonora desert into California which earlier had been explored and marked by Kino. It was as harsh and hard a trail as any that might be thought of, but Kino had traversed it, and de Anza and Garcés refound it; they found some of Kino's markers for waterholes remaining as guides. Once into Alta California the going was not so difficult. In 1772 de Anza put up a first watch-tower at the Golden Gate, and the first thread of a road, though it would need much straightening, had been shown to be possible. In the meantime Junípero Serra had been at work on the coast of southern California. I said that he was lame. After arrival in New Spain he had walked from Veracruz to Mexico City; a spider bite on the way caused an incurable ulcer; the lameness never stopped his further walkings. Here is the picture of the beginning Serra made for the mission trail which was to stretch between Monterey and San Diego, and later, north to San Francisco.

The unpromising start to found missions one day's ride apart between Monterey and San Diego came on July 14, 1771, in the beautiful undulating country of the Santa Lucia's south-eastern valley where oak trees lined the San Antonio River. Junípero Serra walked seventy-five miles from Monterey to hang a wooden, metal-lined bell from a limb and cry out shrilly as he pealed: 'Hear O Gentiles! Come! Come to the Holy Church of God! Come and receive the faith of Christ!' A single curious native approached and at a distance watched the priest celebrate Mass on an altar of branches. The eighteen head of cattle allowed each of the newly found missions were turned loose to graze; olive and pomegranate seeds were planted.[14]

Serra was not put off by the unpromising beginning. Before the end of 1771 there were four little churches between San Diego and Monterey; orange trees and grape vines were planted; there was a connecting link of mule tracks, and by degrees each mission would have more tools and farm implements, more beads and coloured cloth to give the Indians, more vestments, altar services, fonts and statuary, and heavier and stronger mission bells. Not only Indians but colonists from New Spain came to support, or be supported by, the missions. Colonists came across the hard trail from the Sonora desert: de Anza led one troop and reached San Gabriel in January 1775 with 243 men, women and children, including infants born on the way. Herds of more than a thousand animals were brought across the desert to what Kino had spoken of as Pimeria's little sister, California. The planting of the missions one day's ride apart from San Diego to San Francisco was not a dream but an achievement; path-finding had become road-making; harvests were being gathered by the Greyfriars. Felix Riesenberg, in his book on *The Golden Road*, picks out of a priest's diary a note which indicates the start of granaries:

> And in a cage we carried from the Mission of Carmelo four cats; two for San Gabriel and two for San Diego at the requests of the Fathers, who urgently asked us for them since they are very welcome on account of the great abundance of mice.[15]

Garcés, the frontier missionary who had helped Anza to find Kino's trail from Sonora across the Great Colorado Valley, found that California, now that the mission road had been well started, was too tame for him. In 1776 he set out by himself from California, eastward, to find the Hopi Indians:

> Alone except for the guides who took him from tribe to tribe across the chromatic spectacle, he went from the mouth of the Gila to the Mohaves near Needle and from there across northern Arizona to the Grand Canyon country. So he found the Havasupais. That he could reach Cataract Canyon where they lived and descend its vertical wall is against reason but he did so. He spent five days with this remote tribe, who even today are no part of the known world. A gentle people, they responded to his gentleness and invited him to stay with them and forsake his foolish, heretical ideas. When he would not, they guided him to the south rim of the Grand Canyon; no other white man had seen it since Cárdenas two hundred and thirty-six years before. Gradually deserted by all his Indians except a child and an old man, he went on to the Little Colorado region and eastward across what is now the Hopi Reservation till he found the apostates he was looking for, at Oraibi. They would not listen to God's word but told him they would kill him unless he went away.[16]

This 'traverse of the unbelievable country', ending with the 'three weeks canto of thirst and weariness' that took Garcés back to the Mohaves, gives fuller meaning to the phrase De Voto used above – 'and he had Garcés with him'. The traverse by Garcés is coupled by De Voto with another astonishing traverse of the same year – the journey made by Escalante from Santa Fé up to Utah Lake and back through the Grand Canyon wilderness. Escalante forded the Colorado at what has ever since been known as the 'Crossing of the Fathers'. More than fifteen hundred miles of rough wild land was covered, and De Voto does not conceal his admiration for the feat – 'most of the route lay through country as difficult as any in the United States and some of it may be fairly be called the most difficult'.

To read of those exhibitions of frontiersmanship is like watching the appearance of flowers, blossoming at the end of an old vine, and blossoming against all expectation, for the root of the vine was severed, and by rights it should have been dead. Root, trunk, stem, branches of Spanish Enterprise in the New World had been so cut and bruised by 1776 that it is hard to believe sap is still rising on the frontier; but the effort of Garcés to convert the Hopi Indians and the traverse made by Escalante, flower just the same. It is half a century later that the tiredness of Old Spain is really manifest in California. In 1822 Mexico could no longer be held; or, if you prefer to look at things the other way, Mexico achieved its long-desired independence. This weakened California, but did not appear to incite the Russians, who were holding on to their Fort Ross north of San Francisco. No signs of aggressiveness from Fort Ross could be seen from the watch-tower at the Golden Gate; indeed, two more of the twenty-one missions were planted north of San Francisco Bay; the last of them was sited in the Valley of the Moon at Sonoma, in 1823. Franciscans had less to fear from the Russian fort than from the turn of opinion against them in Mexico City. The most insidious enemy of all was also beginning to appear in numbers on the Californian coast: foreigners in their trading ships, among them Yankee traders.

One need not be a Spaniard to pause with some nostalgia at what had been made of El Camino Real as a mission trail in its first half-century. A view of it must depend on what is looked for in a road. It was a dirt road, where there was earth or sand to make it so; where it had to scratch its way along mountain-sides it was little more than a mule-track. With seeming disadvantage it might be contrasted to many Old World roads, for Old World and New World were at that time exchanging status: it was in the Old World that there was a frenzied rage of new ideas; it seemed a function of the new Far West to preserve some of the old, out-moded thoughts. With the mission trail from San Diego to San Francisco, compare three other routes of the period, of roughly commensurate length. There was a roadway from Marseilles to Paris, along which a crowd surged, dragging a few cannon, singing the *Marseillaise*; very soon the whole idea of a Napoleonic roadway was to carry troops and baggage-trains with utmost speed. Speed was the dominant idea along the spinal road of Britain, linking London and Edinburgh; Britain, indulging Industrial Revolution to the full, was obsessed with 'speed'; a Scotsman (John Loudon McAdam) devised a new process of road-surfacing (macadam) to make the stagecoach wheels spin faster. The third route to compare with California's mission trail is the Old Post Road of America's eastern seaboard, from Boston to Philadelphia. Benjamin Franklin, as Postmaster for the English colonies, was as alert as anybody to the urge for speed. The first duty of all these other roadways was 'utility', and if that is the only quality to look for, the mission trail compares badly. But so long as New Spain lasted, haste, on a road from here to eternity, was not all that some of the friars were looking for. Possibly a respectable Mediterranean heritage persisted in El Camino Real of California. 'Is not the road to Athens made for conversation?' was Plato's remark. Italians had picked up that thought, and added beauty to it – the first duty of a roadway (as put into the first line of Virgil's first Eclogue) was to have shade in which to rest and be thankful. What was the equivalent philosophy for the frontier? *No se abure* – do not be in a hurry. The surfacing of a road, for the sake of speed, could wait; what had a priority, on that Californian road, were trees. In my opinion (which at this instant I will not stop to defend) it was Franciscan friars who brought the eucalyptus trees from Spain and planted them along El Camino Real.

But how that may have happened is another story and I leave such speculation for the moment. What is not speculative about the Franciscan trail is the growth of some of the missions in the first fifty years, and the pastoral beauty of the trees and farmlands which surrounded them. Most splendid of all, perhaps, was San Luis Rey, which through Father Peyri's exertions had grown from two rooms of poles and branches to a large building, said to have been a 'magnificent composite of Spanish, Moorish and Mexican architecture'. In 1827 a French visitor, August Duhaut-Cilly, wrote of it:

... we found before us, on a piece of rising ground, the superb buildings of Mission San Luis Rey, whose glittering whiteness was flashed back to us by the first rays of the day. In the still uncertain light of dawn, the edifices of a very beautiful model, supported upon its numerous pillars, had the aspect of a palace.[17]

San Luis Rey was a happy mission under Father Peyri; it had greatly prospered; the three thousand Indian *neophytes* employed there were healthy and contented. That was not always so at all times, among all of the twenty-one missions. Crimes, diseases, discontents are plentifully in the record of the fifty years. Not all friars were up to the standard of Junípero Serra, or his wise and courtly successor, Fermin de Lasuén, or Lasuén's protegé, Antonio Peyri. An early problem at some of the missions was that slowness could be dull: George Vancouver felt this when his ship made a passing visit in 1792. He thought that San Carlos Mission lacked vivacity, and gave the friars a music box. The frontier life outside of the missions, in the early years, also seemed dull to some of the officer's wives; we know at least that in 1786 the life of California was less to the liking of the wife of Pedro Fages than the urban excitements of Mexico City. Nevertheless, by the year 1818 there were some 3,000 whites in California and some 25,000 Indian *neophytes* at the various missions, and the physical conditions of the climate and environment seem just about perfect, if things had gone right, for the emergence of an interesting society.

The animals that settlers had brought with them showed almost embarrassing energy in their new and beautiful environment. On either side of the mission trail livestock bred faster than it could be slaughtered, and so many horses ran wild that herds of wild horses were a nuisance. A few individual men (Governor Vincente de Sola, Father Peyri) stand out for their abundant energy; perhaps there were too few of them? Perhaps not enough Spanish women would share a frontier existence? For any real fruition of Spanish life along the road, one returns to the feeling that the road had been severed too soon. The root, in Spain, had long been damaged; the branch, from Mexico City, was bent. The new régime in Mexico was certain to dispossess the Franciscan Order, as the Jesuit Order had previously been dispossessed. In 1818 notable French pirates, with two ships and four hundred men, made an attempt to land at Monterey; de Sola fought them off in commendable style; some friars played up well; but indirectly the invasion placed a burden on the missions. De Sola reinforced his soldiers, ordered each mission to train some of its Indians as archers, and to have available at all times a hundred mounts, ready for public use. The roadway itself, as a utility, began to improve; and this in the 1820s assisted what Felix Riesenberg describes as a 'parade of foreigners'. It was not at first a big parade. Occasionally the foreigner might be a 'mountain man', who appeared from the interior wilderness, weatherbashed and hungry, as Jedediah Smith appeared in 1826. He was a strange, lanky, blue-eyed character who caused no trouble to the missions, except that as he marched from south to north, in exchange for hospitality he would read aloud selections from his Bible, and would insist on expounding Methodism to the Franciscan friars. The big parade which altered the pastoral life of El Camino Real was started by a citizen of 'the United States of Boston', William Alden Gale. He wore spectacles and was called by the Indians 'Four Eyes'; and through his spectacles he very shrewdly saw the fortune Boston could make in 'California Bank Notes', as the hides of Californian cattle came to be called.

By the middle of the century the foreigners who followed Gale (Bostonians and others, sailing around Cape Horn) had carried away five million hides. The bartering for them had been initiated by Gale's principals, who sent the brig *Sachem*, well stocked with Boston 'notions'.

> Priests, soldiers, *dons* and senoritas came from great distances to examine the merchandize displayed on the *Sachem's* deck: Chinese fireworks, satins, music boxes, mechanical toys, chicken-skin shoes, gilt spurs, exotic foods, new tools, ornate furniture, stockings of red and black and flesh-coloured silk.[18]

A thousand other items were later and quickly added by rival traders – 'bolts of calico, green velvet, tooled leather saddles, silver buttons' – and Richard Henry Dana, in *Two Years Before the Mast,* makes special mention of 'bad wine made in Boston'. Sheltered at first by the missions and provided with mounts, the rival Yankee traders vied with each other to bring in new temptations. The change that came over the life of the road was now rapid, and hardly needs to be detailed. The expected secularization of the missions began in 1833: half of the holdings of each of the ten most prosperous missions was then confiscated by the State, the other half was divided 'among those Indians capable of living on their own'. Political appointees were to oversee the distribution of the lands and cattle, mission equipment and stores. Whatever the missions had failed to do for Indians, the Secularization Act ensured a worse mistreatment.

Some time before the Act was passed, Father Peyri seemed to be aging more quickly than expected. When visitors who knew him of old looked in to see him at San Luis Rey, rather than talk too much about the future of that 'King of the Missions', Father Peyri might propose a game of Spanish whist. He had watched the transformation of the mission trail: the 'Boston Riders' drumming up trade in the ranches and pueblos, and the increase of traffickers of lower grade. Grog shops, convenient for bargaining, gambling, smuggling, were now at distances shorter apart than the missions. When he knew that there was nothing he could do about the impending Dissolution, he accepted his orders to withdraw. He did not wish his return to Europe to be talked of; his determination was to slip away by night, so his departure might be unnoticed. Some of the Indians got wind and rode after him as far as San Diego to persuade him to come back. Two of the boys swam out to the departing ship. They climbed aboard and sailed to Europe to remain with Peyri.

NOTES

1. Letter to *The Times* (London), 18 July, 1964.
2. *Parry, op. cit.*, pp. 215–219.
3. Parry, pp. 214, 215.
4. Parry, p. 157.
5. *Journey into Darkness* by John Upton Terrell (Morrow, New York, 1962 and Jarrolds, London, 1964). Mr. Tellell's excellent book contains a very useful bibliography.
6. *Doomed Road of Empire* by Hodding Carter (McGraw-Hill, New York, 1963), p. 4.
7. Hodding Carter, p. 8.
8. Hodding Carter, p. 8.
9. Hodding Carter, pp. 11, 12.
10. *Rim of Christendom* by Herbert E. Bolton (first published 1936, re-issued by Russell & Russell, New York, 1960), p. 8.

11. *Rim of Christendom* is the classic biography of Father Kino. The details of horseback mileage are on p. 590.

12. Bolton, p. 589.

13. Bolton, pp. 578, 579.

14. *The Golden Road* by Felix Riesenberg, Jr. (McGraw-Hill, New York, 1962), pp. 38, 39. Riesenberg gives the reference for the exact words of Serra's invocation.

15. Riesenberg, p. 37.

16. *Westward the Course of Empire* by Bernard De Voto (Eyre & Spottiswoode, London, 1953), p. 290.

17. Riesenberg, p. 62.

18. Riesenberg, pp. 65, 66.

CHAPTER 16

Unfinished Business

ALEXIS DE TOCQUEVILLE, visiting the United States in the early 1830s, provides a famous outside view of the young nation. 'Anglo-Americans', as Tocqueville speaks of the people, showed an intense consciousness of nationality. Each individual State saw the wartime advantages of federation. At the same time Tocqueville noticed everywhere a strong and restless impulse for westward migration. Tocqueville's travels did not extend across the Mississippi, but he looked across that river and estimated that within about a century the whole continent would be parcelled into many more States than the original thirteen. Should the States hold together, should the people who were spreading over a vast territory continue to exhibit the same habits and manners, should they continue to be 'imbued with the same opinions, propagated under the same forms', Tocqueville had no doubt of the nation's rise to enormous power. The prediction that he placed at the end of the first volume of *Democracy in America* remains remarkable:

> There are at the present time [i.e. 1834] two great nations in the world, which started from different points, but seem to tend towards the same end. I allude to the Russians and the Americans. Both of them have grown up unnoticed; and while the attention of mankind was directed elsewhere, they have suddenly placed themselves in the front rank among the nations, and the world learned their existence and their greatness at almost the same time.
>
> All other nations seem to have nearly reached their natural limits, and they have only to maintain their power; but these are still in the act of growth. All the others have stopped, or continue to advance with extreme difficulty; these alone are proceeding with ease and celerity along a path to which no limit can be perceived. The American struggles against the obstacles that nature opposes to him; the adversaries of the Russian are men. The former combats the wilderness and savage life; the latter, civilization with all its arms. The conquests of the American are therefore gained by the plowshare; those of the Russian by the sword. The Anglo-American relies upon personal interest to accomplish his ends and

gives free scope to the unguided strength and common sense of the people; the Russian centers all the authority of society in a single arm. The principal instrument of the former is freedom; of the latter, servitude. Their starting-point is different and their courses are not the same; yet each of them seems marked out by the will of Heaven to sway the destinies of half the globe.

Thinking about the whole part played by the Road West in the rise to power of the United States, I would not be bothered by an initial quibble, that in a literal sense there has never been any one single physical highway across the continent which stands out as a one-and-only road. Thirty years before Tocqueville made his prophecy it had been proved that there would never be just one physical westward route. Before the Lewis and Clark expedition the old expectancy had lingered, that a direct waterway might be found to thread across the land mass from Atlantic to Pacific – one natural route that would predominate. The absence of such waterway exposed the whole width of land to exploration. Meriwether Lewis and William Clark gave 'the entire West to the American people as something with which the mind could deal'. The mind began to deal with it, unblinkered. The fur companies were quick to enter Oregon, and the 'mountain men' whom the trade developed 'completed the exploration of the West that Lewis and Clark had begun'.[1] The excitement of wilderness was re-inspired. It was upon the capacity of 'Anglo-Americans' to cope with wilderness that Tocqueville in part based his prophecy. It is possible to think of all the trails extending westward as comprising, all together, one great road – one shared arterial pulse extending to all capillaries. All trails made up one road, West.

A puzzle not explained by Tocqueville is how wilderness, of itself, would continue to unite a people into one single nation. The 'obstacles that nature opposes' had done little to unite, and perhaps had done much to divide, the Amerindian tribes. Among Anglo-Americans there were potentially different tribes of white men. From the beginning, frontier had been looked on as an escape hatch for many kinds of separatists. A 'common sense' of political unity among the States, which in the first days of the independent nation Tom Paine had talked of as 'the great hinge on which the whole machine turned', was not necessarily or persistently uppermost in everybody after national independence had been achieved. What wilderness then offered was common sense of possible escape from the machine. It was not so much a wish to expand the nation as to opt out of it that motivated Daniel Boone and the young Sam Houston. Once one had tasted wilderness it was not always easy to return to a restricted civil life; that had also been one of the discoveries made by both Lewis and Clark. It was the majesty of wilderness, the irresistible possessiveness of Nature's magnitudes and beauty, that (in Negley Farson's interpretation) 'destroyed them'.*

Samuel Parker found the mountain men of the far west helpful to him in the 1830s. Parker, himself a New Englander brought up to parsonage studies, had turned at the age of 56 to become a missionary to Indians in the Oregon territory. Carrying unfamiliar sidearms along with his Testament in Greek, he appeared, somewhat to their surprise, among the faraway fur trappers. By some of them he was accepted, and he accepted them, with respect. In his report to congregations at home, Samuel Parker excused some of the mountain men from 'conversion'. 'They appear to have sought for a place', he reported, 'where, as they would say, human nature is not oppressed by the tyranny of religion and pleasure is not awed by the frown of virtue'. That was his interpretation of an antipathy to democracy (*demos* = town-rule) which mountain men expressed in simpler rhythm. 'Darn the white diggins,' was the way Long Hatcher put it, 'while thar's buffler in the mountains.'

The carrying of a Testament in Greek almost suggests a premonition, on Samuel Parker's part, that the language once spoken by Homer was suitable on a frontier where all creation was seen, as once before by the Homeric Greeks, in fresh morning. The zest of living in a renewed Homeric Age had been expressed explicitly by young Sam Houston who, familiar with Pope's translation of the *Iliad*, identified the code of honour of the Cherokees with that which he admired in the Greek heroes. Sam Houston had been accepted by the Cherokees, and at times returned from captive white life to set his

---

* 'It is not without interest, or meaning, to note here that Clark died of drink; and Lewis, his mind allegedly unbalanced by the "unwonted quiet" of life after he returned from the magic expedition of exploration. so full of the sensual satisfactions derived from the scenes themselves, committed suicide. Nothing else, fame and money, could ever make up for it. It destroyed them.' Negley Farson, *The Sons of Noah* (Gollancz, London, 1949).

tipi freely beside theirs. His mood, though, vacillated. Since Houston was himself a multitude of different men in conflict, the momentary identifications of himself as a red man, real enough while they lasted, were, as it were, vacations. The point is that American wilderness was offering the opportunity of being tried out in various ways. The ways go on reminding us of the Homeric Era. At a time when Sam Houston oscillated back into the fold of white men, was reformed (except for his 'cussing') and was baptized by total ducking in a creek, the Baptist minister assured him the water had washed away his sins. 'God help the fish' was Houston's answer, in the exact and enigmatic spirit of an old Homeric jest. Audubon met Sam Houston at the new muddy little capital of Texas; the Alamo had fallen the year before, the battle of San Jacinto had been fought; and Audubon's sketch of Houston presents the man of that moment without embellishments – 'anxious, tired, angry, forced into a false pomp, disliking his tawdy regalia'.[2] The independence for which some of the Texans were fighting was independence not only from Mexico, but separate independence of the Lone Star State – independence from the Union, from Tom Paine's 'whole machine'.

The capture by the United States of its own frontiersmen is part of the story of the Road. The example of Sam Houston shows it was not always an easy capture. In a same year that Texans were asserting independence, Samuel Parker was observing that the mountain men of Oregon showed no wish for the Nation to come and catch them. Wilderness produced in them an affinity with some of the Indians, such as Sam Houston felt with his Cherokees. An Easterner's first impression of Joe Meek, when he happened to meet the famous grizzly bear killer (the meeting happened, appropriately enough, in Bear River Valley), was that 'in standing, walking, reading, in all but complexion, he *was* an Indian'. Of the even more famous Jim Bridger there is a description by David Brown, who went to the mountains in 1837, just after Parker had left. After noting with appropriate admiration Bridger's six-foot physique ('without an ounce of superfluous flesh'), his unquestionable bravery, horsemanship and skill with the rifle, Brown continues:

> His cheek bones were high, his nose hooked or aquiline, the expression of his eye mild and thoughtful, and that of his face grave almost to

375

solemnity. To complete the picture, he was perfectly ignorant of all knowledge contained in books, not even knowing the letters of the alphabet; put perfect faith in dreams and omens, and was unutterably scandalized if even the most childish of the superstitions of the Indians were treated with anything like contempt or disrespect; for in all these he was a firm and devout believer.[3]

It was an uncapturable 'Indianness' that Easterners first noted about the mountain men. The wilderness had made white hunters into red men, and no more than the red men were they likely to fit into Benjamin Franklin's idea, or Tocqueville's idea, of Americans in unified harmonious activity.

In reading David Brown's description of Jim Bridger, I must not forget that Brown was writing in a period of Fenimore Cooper's romances. Brown expected to see Bridger in the pattern of Leatherstocking; he expected to find the blood-brotherliness as between Natty Bumppo and Chingachgook imposed upon white and red huntsmen alike by the beauty, and the horrors and hardships also, of wilderness life. He expected to find Indianness, therefore he found it. To please or to shock the greenhorn a frontiersman might play Indian, even as Audubon 'showed off' on the Pennsylvania canal boat when it was leaving Pittsburgh for the east. Other travellers noticed that on a bench aboard the boat there was a bale of green blankets and fur. When passengers' names were called, the name of 'Audubon' went unanswered. 'It was called again. The bale stirred slightly, the furs moved, and turned over; the blankets sat up and from the top emerged a fur cap, a pair of keen eyes, a thick comical fringe of white beard. Audubon stood erect, in an Indian hunting dress'.[4] The onlooker reported that he was 'feathered to the heel'. But such an episode, toward the end of Audubon's career, was a mere and deliberate publicity stunt – pathetic, in that so great an artist was reduced to that kind of posturing. Leave aside Audubon trying to raise money in Philadelphia by parading in Indian clothes, leave aside Fenimore Cooper's Leatherstocking novels (stories which for the most part he concocted in Paris), the mountain men whose lives were on the frontier, the free trappers who lived and died there, the real professionals, rarely, if ever, went completely Indian. Indians of all variety were as much a regular part of wilderness life as anything else. Cohabitation was a normal matter; most of the mountain men found one or more

Indian wives: Kit Carson ('five-feet-four only but cougar all the way') killed a much larger but incautious trapper who attempted to rape Kit's particular Arapaho girl.* Mountain men often looked at the shared terrain with Indian eyes, saw and felt as Indians did, were closer to them in their thoughts and habits than they were to some fellow-nationals – and yet, no matter how escapist they might wish to be, the one thing they could never get away from, the thing that kept on keeping them different from the red man, was the Road.

The keelboats of the Missouri brought white men's tools. When Old Bill Williams, ex-circuit-riding Methodist, flung away his Bible and took to beaver-trapping, he hardly realized at first how trapped he was going to be by his own steel traps. Neither he nor anyone else could wholly escape from the trading post. Mountain men might balance the cost of necessities – tobacco (a dollar a pound) or liquor (straight alcohol, four or five dollars a pint) on occasion had to give way to powder and lead, or to personal hardware, the all-purpose awl and the equally all-purpose knife. The hunting and skinning knife is as good an illustration as any, how a hunter was not escaping from an unseen partner. The knife most valued in the mountains of Oregon bore the name 'Green River'. That was what the intials G. R. on a knife-blade spelled to the frontiersman. Jim Bridger and Joe Meek may not have known the whole of the alphabet, and their 'reading' may have been, as with Indians, entirely the art of 'reading sign', but both of them knew that 'up to Green River' meant up to the hilt, all the way, as far and hard as possible. There certainly was a Green River in Oregon territory, yet De Voto points out that the Sheffield blades from the England of Georgian times were customarily stamped G. R. for *George Rex,* and that long after Independence, American-made blades continued to copy the stamp. So the Green River of Oregon continued to be tied to an anonymous alphabetical G. R. Joe Meek's mortal hand-to-paw combats with grizzly bears (the tellings of which, when it was he who told them, reached a wonderful topmost peak of frontier humour) were not won by Joe Meek without something in his hand that he knew how to use. The knife, whoever made it, was handed to him by the Road.

* The bully's name, De Voto says, was Shunar or something similar. It is curious (bearing in mind Spanish experience) that there is little mention in the American frontier annals of venereal disease.

Daniel Boone is the prototype of American 'loners', path-escapers, who, if he saw behind him the smoke of another man's fire, moved on. Yet after Boone had gone on into Missouri territory, he touched back to the relatively populous Kentucky. It was in Kentucky that Audubon met Boone, and watched him load his rifle. It was 'a long heavy rifle'; Boone 'wiped it, measured powder, patched the ball with six-hundred-thread linen, and sent the charge home with a hickory rod'. Boone was still tied to civilized roadway by those six hundred threads, as Gulliver's threads had tied down Gulliver. But the meeting between Audubon and Boone symbolizes more than that. It was the meeting of two artists. Audubon's devotion to the wild – 'Mr. Audubon makes no more of tracking it in all directions than a shot star does in crossing the heavens' – is measured in the work which caused Sacheverell Sitwell to exclaim: 'Audubon is of the importance of Herman Melville, and *The Birds of America* is upon the scale of *Moby Dick*'. Boone's equal craftsmanship was not with brush but with 'long heavy rifle'. Contests usual among Kentucky hunters were 'driving a nail' by rifle shot, 'snuffing a candle' after dark at fifty yards, or 'barking a squirrel'. It was to the feat of barking a squirrel, which requires 'a greater degree of accuracy than any other', that Boone introduced Audubon. 'He felt proud to show me his skill' said Audubon, so the two men walked out together along the Kentucky River, Boone 'in homespun hunting shirt, moccasined but bare-legged', until they saw the squirrel crouched on a branch about fifty paces off, watching them. Boone pointed, said Audubon – 'He bade me mark the spot well, and gradually raised his rifle until the *bead* or sight was in line with the spot. A whiplike report reverberated through the woods and along the hills. Judge of my surprise when I saw that the ball had hit the piece of bark just beneath the squirrel and shivered it into splinters. The concussion killed the animal and sent it whirling through the air as if it had been blown up by a powder-magazine explosion'.[5] Audobon's praise for Boone's precision is the praise of one craftsman by another. His appreciation of Boone as an artist in the whole medium offered by wilderness was not confined to that particular piece of expertise. Audubon felt that the artist with a rifle could be as much of an artist as the artist with a brush; that it was in the nature of many Americans to appreciate only the art of the hunter; and that perhaps entered into the little episode I mentioned when, later in life, he dressed himself up for Philadelphia in frontier costume.

When Old Bill Williams announced his presence among mountain men in Oregon by saying that he could shoot higher and deeper, wider and closer, straighter and crookeder, and more rounding, and more every way, than 'ever a son of a bitch of them all', he was merely showing an entry card, in a respectably polished way, to an artists' club. To obtain a reputation as an outstanding club-member required mastery of more mountain skills, more wisdom in geography and in the management of Indians, than Old Bill Williams managed to achieve: at least De Voto, in *Across the Wide Missouri*, does not bother with Old Bill Williams. The many mountain men who rose to distinction as fur trappers were all, as De Voto describes them, 'necessarily fit instruments', but three of them in particular De Voto picks out as a cut above all others. Tom Fitzpatrick, Jim Bridger and Kit Carson are De Voto's choice as 'quintessential mountain men'. These he picks out because they 'added something else' to the courage and the craftsmanship in which others shared. De Voto speaks of Fitzpatrick, Bridger, Carson with the same homage that other critics might accord to 'old masters' of the Italian Renaissance. The feelings which support this praise are indeed exactly the same – praise for the men as artists and for the way they responded to a powerful outside patronage. The mountain men De Voto speaks of were not called on, as Michelangelo was called on, to rebuild St. Peter's Church. But after the Louisiana Purchase, the West was a rebirth of the Nation; the West was an American Renaissance; and these were artists who willingly acquiesced in the expression of a national assertion. No explicit commission was discussed, such as the Pope had discussed with Michelangelo; yet as the price for private employment dropped, Fitzpatrick, Bridger, Carson all became government men, and their performances for the patron-nation were just as much command performances as Michelangelo's. 'They are important historically,' says De Voto, 'because they were the best of a trade group, small and shortlived, who had a maker's part in extending the national boundaries and the national consciousness to continental completion.'

So, and because they were appealed to as artists, De Voto suggests the most notable mavericks could be roped in – though work for government meant destruction of what had been their mountain sanctuary. Parker showed no intention of converting mountain men; a War Department had less scruple. With the establishment of Fort Bridger in the summer of 1842 the wagon trail to the Pacific coast was much more clearly marked. Fort Bridger was a sign that the Road was going through the mountain barriers; the name was also a sign that the Road had corralled the escapists.

I am looking at Tocqueville as a man who was feeling the pulse of the great northerly arm of the road west from Europe. He and his friend Beaumont (both young French noblemen with liberal interests) had the wish to find out how 'democracy' was working out in practice, in the only nation where the processes were unimpeded by aristocratic traditions. The two magistrates from the court at Versailles believed that war-torn Europe, and in particular France, had much to learn from a study of the American experiment. Individual topics which the two men discussed together, and about which both wrote afterwards, included Religion, Women and Family, Conversation, Literature, Arts and Sciences, Negroes and Indians. What civil rights were to be possible for Negroes and Indians in the American society was felt by both men to be one of the sore points. Beaumont, after return to France, wrote a novel of protest (*Marie*) about the tragedy that a 'taint' of negro blood could mean in America; Tocqueville, in his own book, wrote with unusual bitterness about the white 'morality' exhibited towards Indians:

> The Spaniards were unable to exterminate the Indian race by those unparalleled atrocities which brand them with indelible shame, nor did they succeed even in wholly depriving it of its rights; but the Americans of the United States have accomplished this two-fold purpose with singular felicity, tranquilly, legally, philanthropically, without shedding blood, and without violating a single great principle of morality in the eyes of the world. It is impossible to destroy men with more respect for the laws of humanity.

This is one of the few comparisons made by Tocqueville between the northerly arm of the road west extended from Europe by Anglo-Americans and the southerly arm of the road as extended by Spaniards. Tocqueville is here reporting that Americans were showing, towards Indians, a morality which was all the more shocking in that it was condoned by 'the laws of humanity'. From Tocqueville's unwonted outburst I derive the impression that it seemed to him the laws of humanity were being drastically redefined all along the northern arm of the trans-Atlantic road west.

All along the northern arm of road across the Western Ocean there was certainly a new strong pulse-beat in Tocqueville's time. The two young Frenchmen went to America by sailing ship, 38 days from Le Havre to Newport, Rhode Island. At Providence they stepped aboard the steamer *President* to make the night trip through Long Island Sound to New York. The 'steamer' was an instant indication that Britain's industrial revolution had become a rage in New England. Nearly twenty years before Tocqueville's visit, three men at the Boston Exchange in 1813 (Francis Cabot Lowell, Patrick Jackson, Nathan Appleton) had met to set up a rival to England's 'dark Satanic mills' – raw cotton to be made into finished cloth by power looms, all under one roof at Waltham, Massachusetts. 'Mr. Madison's War' with England had made 1813 a propitious date to adapt New England as quickly as possible to the industrial pattern of Lancashire: Lowell and others were working as hard to that end as Arkwright had worked in the Old Country. If in addition to feeling the pulse-beat of the road from England to America one analysed the blood, there were now corpuscles in it; or, to put it more nearly in Tocqueville's terms, individuals on the Anglo-American road displayed uninhibited fervour to be implicated in a system in which Commerce was as God and polytechnic institutes were temples. At the wilderness end of the road a Daniel Boone might be exploring with his rifle, and the rifle linked him with that other artist at the Woolwich Arsenal, the Henry Maudslay who played such a notable part in developing machine-tools, and who had been expert at every metal-work but '*quite splendid* with an eighteen-inch file'. Along the whole length of the road there was an energetic peristalsis. At every pulse-point of the great tentacle one feels the pumping action. As from the eastern seaboard of America the heavy Conestoga wagons grind westward over the mountain passes, or as the flatboats steer down the Ohio toward its junction with the Mississippi, the men and women in them are at once escaping from Mr. Lowell's industrial system yet also drawing it onwards. The water-power of the first mills was being replaced by steam; steam in the 1830s was a symbol of the will-to-power; Tocqueville felt that, when he boarded the steamer at Providence. In

England at that moment a young steam-engineeer – Isambard Kingdom Brunel was a year younger than Tocqueville – was still in training. As soon as he was appointed (in 1833) to govern the short amount of mileage available within England for a Great Western Railway, he started to design the first steamship for regular trans-Atlantic travel. His eye was on the westward horizon; the announced purpose of his steamship was to extend his bit of railway 'a bit farther'.

Mr. Lewis Mumford, in *Technics and Civilization*, mentioned the year 1832 as marking a significant change in the efficiency of mechanical prime movers. He rightly warns against putting together thoughts which are not properly correlative, yet it is hard to deny that entirely different kinds of *passage de la frénésie* were combining to move in one direction. Brunel called his first steamship *Great Western;* within the United States there were at the same moment any number of independent and sometimes fantastic plannings for the westward expansion of the nation to continental completion. Plannings sprang up spontaneously, and some were grotesque. De Voto has fun in telling of 'General' James Dickson, 'a zany blown up out of nowhere for no cause', who was so fired by the Texas revolution as to persuade an army of sixty men to set off west from Buffalo, New York, on August 1, 1836. Among the dreams offered by Dickson was the capture from Mexico of all of the vast territories west of Texas. James Dickson and his sixty soldiers vanish from history – and yet, as De Voto says, he was only ten years ahead in his timing. Dickson had not foreseen that the annexation of Texas to the Union would be held up for most of a decade, largely by the slavery question. There would be no throughway to the far Southwest until the problem of the Lone Star State was solved. But throughways, and not just wagon trails but iron rails for iron wheels, were already being thought of. In England, 'the locomotive Monster' (as *The Creevy Papers* called George Stephenson's black and yellow *Rocket*) had been 'coming thro' every man's grounds between Manchester and Liverpool' since 1830. Earlier than that, Stephenson's first public railway from Stockton to Darlington in 1825 had much impressed some citizens of Baltimore, Maryland. Among them was Charles Carroll of Carrollton, last survivor of the signers of the Declaration of Independence; with the West wide open, imaginations in Baltimore were not confined to the trivial mileages of England, and land-grants of wilderness were more easy to obtain than between Manchester and Liverpool. The proud name adopted in 1828 was Baltimore & Ohio Railroad. Carroll as a grand old patriot celebrated the 4th of July of his 92nd year by participating in laying a corner-stone symbolic of the B & O, the 'O' as yet a vague quantity. A section of the iron road was operative in 1831; after twenty years of laborious engineering the rails did reach continuously to Ohio in 1853. But in the meantime Baltimore's initiative was copied by the Boston–Albany railroad line and the line from New York to Buffalo, both opening in 1842. The pressure for transcontinental railroads now had full head of steam behind it. Asa Whitney, for instance, was petitioning the Congress in January 1845 for an immense land grant for a railroad from the Great Lakes to the Pacific that would enable the United States to 'reach out one hand to all Asia, and the other to all Europe'.

On a policy of national expansion, James K. Polk of Tennessee won New York's crucial votes and gained the presidential election of 1844. The annexation of Texas (and, beyond Texas, the temptation of California) was the most lively of desires. Before Polk took office the annexation of Texas was agreed to by joint resolution of Congress; and as soon as Polk took office he sent about half of the national army (the total, at that time, was eight thousand men) to defend the border of Texas from Mexican reprisals. Diplomatic efforts to purchase from Mexico the territories of the farther West were abortive, and were soon unnecessary. By April 1846 an incident on the disputed border territory of Texas gave Polk occasion to ask Congress to declare war – Mexico had 'shed American blood upon the American soil'. In May 1846 war was promptly declared. Abraham Lincoln was one of few Congressmen who tabled a resolution that the war had been 'unnecessarily and unconstitutionally commenced by the President'. Whether or no the war was justifiable, more than ninety thousand volunteers soon enabled it to be fought on three fronts. The navy supported the landings near Veracruz for the direct thrust at Mexico City, and the navy's sailors on horseback did much of the effective fighting in California. A third campaign was the march of a volunteer cavalry regiment over three thousand miles of rough terrain from Santa Fé southward into Mexico – one who wrote of such campaigning was Captain Mayne Reid, an Irishman who had joined in the war for the fun of it. The point of remembering Mayne Reid (apart from the pleasure of recalling his boys' books) is that the pulse for extending the road west was felt by all kinds of adventurers. The 'little war', when it was ended, was found to have increased the area of the United States by about 50 per cent. All or part of the modern states of Arizona, New Mexico, Colorado, Utah, Nevada and California were ceded by Mexico under the peace treaty of 1848. But that was not all that was wanted for the new excitement of railroads. Five years after the treaty an additional tract of Mexican land, south of the Gila River, was added by purchase – as a right of way for one of the routes proposed from the Atlantic to the Pacific by rail.

The combat Tocqueville had been observing was between Americans and 'the wilderness and savage life'. It was a little trickier to add Mexico to the opponents and to destroy Mexicans as well as Indians without 'violating a single great principle of morality'. Yet if there is a feeling that moral laws were being bent, one is also forced to feel that a large and major culprit was the Road. It is the autonomous power exerted by pathway upon pathfinder that I continue to watch. A tendril of trail poking tentatively into wilderness displays small threat to its surroundings, or to its maker; but here the trail becomes iron-shod, a strong alteration. Dirt road, paved road, railroad, each shows progressive and increasing appetite, a stretching kind of appetite, the kind of appetite a dictionary calls 'orectic'. It was not President Polk who gave the road power to trespass; the gift was made the other way round. The first overland trails had indeed trespassed into California two months before the declaration of official war, when Captain John C. Frémont of the U.S. Topographical Engineers hoisted the Stars and Stripes over a makeshift encampment beside El Camino Real, not far from Monterey. Like the forgotten 'General' Dickson, Frémont had with him sixty volunteers; he was, at that time, chased back to Oregon; but the outstretch of his zeal was not reprimanded by those who served the road's appetite. And service to that appetite was offered everywhere along the road's length, from one end to the other. Brunel in England, working on his first iron steamship, was as much involved in pushing as Frémont was in pulling, to get the questing iron road to California.

Tocqueville chose the plowshare as symbol of the tool of conquest in America, but it was not the only symbol, even in his time.

True enough that the new steel plowshare invented by John Lane of Illinois in 1833, and the all-steel plow introduced four years later by John Deere, were powerful in breaking prairie land, increasing white men's food supply, and rapidly decreasing the food supply of buffalo and Indians. Yet among seemingly peaceable symbols I would also look at the ceremonial pick, spade, hammer and trowel which the Blacksmiths' Association gave to Charles Carroll of Carrollton for him to display at the festive start of the B & O Railroad. I have indeed decided to end my scrapbook with the scene at the completion of the first continuous railroad track from the Atlantic seaboard to the Pacific. That may seem to be regarding all that has happened in the hundred years since then as, simply, unfinished business; which, fortunately, is what it is. Adventures on our road since then, extensions to the air and to the moon or planets, do not alter the permanence of some questions which cropped up in an odd form at Promontory Point in Utah, in 1869. I confess, the oddness of the form in which the questions presented themselves at that time is partly what intrigues me.

It was in 1845 that Asa Whitney tried to get his land grant to finance a railroad by a northerly route from Lake Michigan to the west coast. It was in the same year that a ragged procession of Mormons was beginning to struggle across badlands between Illinois and an empty part of Utah.

The trek of the Mormons bounces me back to the beginning of this book, where I was watching a procession of another people, moving over other badlands, under guidance of a not dissimilar impulse. In the trek of the ancient Hebrews I accepted that their dominant wish was to set up a City of God. That was a motive which, in some or other form, has seemed permanent throughout this journey. I watched the aspiration as it became differently revealed, and as different peoples kept on moving westward. Religion was not the only motive for road-engineering, and yet at all times it remained a large one. The mariners' chart did not eliminate the *mappamonde*: they both stretched out. I saw that like John Donne I could not fetter nor imprison 'the word Religion'. Particularly after the Reformation and with the outstretch of the road into America I would have to attend to a considerable splintering of churches. I am singling out The Church of Jesus Christ of Latter Day Saints for a particular conflict that

385

arose, a remarkable conflict as it seems in retrospect, between a small and stubborn church and a large and stubborn nation. The First Amendment of the Federal Constitution seems very clear, that 'Congress shall make no law respecting an establishment of religion, or prohibiting the free exercise thereof'. But who defines religion or the free exercise thereof? So long as the Mormon Church was in an empty part of Utah, conflict with the Congress did not arise; but as soon as the trans-continental railroad chose to go through Utah a fight began.

I should pause for reminder how the Mormons and the railroad both got to Utah. I should have to recall the general emotional ferment in the thirteen colonies of the eastern seaboard on the eve of independence; exclusive attention to political history might make one forget what some religious historians speak of as 'The Great Awakening'. At an early stage of sporadic 'revivals', mass conversions resulted from preachings such as those of Jonathan Edwards, or George Whitefield, whose voice carried to as many as thirty thousand at one time on Boston Common. The 'great' awakening, spread at first mainly by Presbyterian, Congregational and Methodist evangelists, was not a ferment that ceased working; and in the 19th century as in the 18th, waves of religious feelings rose in the wake of Baptist preachers and lay exhorters. If the word 'religion' is not to be fettered nor imprisoned, it may have to be stretched to include hysterias sometimes released by the screamings, laughings, trances, visions and convulsions among Protestant converts, which at this period remind Professor Latourette (in his *History of Christianity*) of Flagellants within the Roman church of earlier times. Western New York State, roundabout 1815, was a frontier region which had been 'swept by revivals preached by itinerant or semi-itinerant Baptists and Methodists'. Professor Latourette sees Joseph Smith as a young man of old New England stock, 'self-confident, tall, athletic, witty, of distinguished appearance', who was at once profoundly stirred by the revival meetings and profoundly troubled by existing sectarian differences. The vision revealed to Joseph Smith and published in 1830 as *The Book of Mormon,* was one which could link people in America directly, geneologically as well as spiritually, with a family which fled from Jerusalem before its fall to the Babylonians. The power of poetic identification with ancient 'strangers and pilgrims on the earth' was as strong as it had been with the Pilgrim Fathers. It was when identification with ancient custom extended to polygamy that the church of Latter Day Saints aroused a most violent hostility from outsiders.

I see polygamy discussed in the fourth chapter of *Isaiah*, where it is not easy to tell whether it is one of the laments or one of the promises for 'them that are escaped of Israel'. But polygamy was not a practice adopted by the Mormon Church in its early days in New York State. The first urgency was simply to find a place for 'The Gathering'. Neighbours in New York State regarded Mormons as mad; no place for them there; their trek began. Brigham Young, four years older than Joseph Smith and one of Smith's first converts, appears with increasing prominence as Mormons moved on, first into Ohio, then into Missouri, then to Nauvoo in Illinois. As they moved, they preached. The wandering did not diminish, but increased, their number. At Nauvoo the troop had swelled to 15,000, and a newspaper screamed such hostility at the intruders as the Egyptian priest had screamed against the Hebrews. The Latter Day Saints retaliated by attacking the newspaper office; Joseph Smith and brother Hyrum were arrested and put in jail; a mob rushed the jail and Smith and his brother were killed.

It was after the fighting at Nauvoo that Brigham Young was elected President of the Latter Day Saints, and held out the daunting prospect of marching his people completely out of reach of any neighbours. It could mean marching as far as the unknown deserts of Utah. Should the only place of sanctuary be desert, never mind, said Brigham Young, there would be found the *deseret,* the Mormon word for honey-bee; and waste land, bad land to all others, should be made to blossom 'like a rose'. No crazier prospect was ever proposed than for fifteen thousand men, women and children, with hardly any equipment to make such a march. A minority of Smith's disciples did not follow Brigham Young, and small blame to them; under Joseph Smith Junior they moved from hostile Nauvoo first to Iowa, then to Missouri. The majority dared to follow Brigham Young into the farther and wilder unknown. They knew that in winter all the lands ahead might be covered in ten feet of snow, that in summer there could be blazing sun, perhaps no rainfall. Such rumours as there were about the trackless plains were bad: no trees, as in the wooded East;

the land itself, uninhabitable tundra; no tools would break the heavy crusted sod, therefore no crops; beyond the tundra, desert. Not rumour but certainty, said Brigham Young, that beyond all that were Delectable Mountains, and from them God would speak.

The first contingents bound for unknown Utah set forth in 1845 with a few ox-teams and a larger number of handcarts and wheelbarrows. The spirit of the first trail-makers was to plant a crop whereever they could, not for themselves to harvest, but to be harvested by those who followed. This journeying took two years, from 1845 to 1847; a feat as notable for courage as the voyage of the Pilgrim Fathers, and more so for endurance. It is said that when Young at length reached mountain territory he had some guidance from Jim Bridger, that 'atlas of the West'; of that I have no details; what I see in that two years of effort did result in getting a weatherbashed remnant of Mormons, not so many at the end as when they started, to a Salt Lake Valley that they could call their own. Almost as remarkable as the feat of the journey was the recuperation of the men and women when they had reached their Land. It was at that time, apparently, that Brigham Young legalized polygamy. The practice was as natural as it had seemed to *Isaiah*, and was in no way out of keeping with other identifications with ancient Israel, including that of working to build their City. Within four years they really had the desert blossoming, and Salt Lake City was formally organized by 1851 – a new City, sprouting in the desert, with temple and tabernacle to prove that the city was governed by a God-respecting Mormon Church.

A year before that (on May 1, 1850) the citizens of San Francisco had adopted a city charter, and elected a first American mayor to replace the Mexican *alcalde* of Yerba Buena (the township's previous name). As the stories of ancient Jerusalem and Tyre long ago intertwined, so do the stories of Salt Lake City and San Francisco: the pattern seems similar, City of God and City of Gold. We shall be seeing that when San Francisco became a gold-rush city the independence of Salt Lake City was doomed; what complicates the pattern is that it was some Mormons who played an effective part in the transformation of San Francisco into a gold-rush city. When Brigham Young had decided that the Mormon trek should stop at Salt Lake Valley, not all the Mormon men stopped there. Sam Brannan and others tramped on. It is possible that this departure of menfolk had something to do with the institution of polygamy at Salt Lake City; but what concerns me here is that as early as 1847 I see one energetic Mormon, Brannan, setting up as storekeeper in San Francisco, and others of his Mormon companions finding work at Colonel John Sutter's plantation on the south fork of the American River – New Helvetia, as the Swiss Colonel called it, or, as named by squatters, Sutterville. It was in the millstream that powered Sutter's sawmill that gold was noticed in January, 1848. There was no instant gold-rush. There was indeed an instant problem for John Sutter: his title-deeds were Mexican, he himself was Swiss, and throughout the first part of the war he had played more closely with the Mexican authorities than with the riff-raff of gringo adventurers. The war was just about over, and Mexico had lost, but no treaty had yet been made between the United States and Mexico. The cession of California to the United States was not in fact formal until February, and Governor Mason in Monterey, to whom Sutter had urgently applied to obtain a complete American land-grant for his holdings, did not immediately oblige.

Poor Sutter! Gold on his property, but no authority behind him to defend that property: the only hope of saving New Helvetia lay in keeping quiet about the gold. Faint hope! The very foreman whom he had sent to Monterey carried a buckskin bag containing six ounces of dust, which, wishing to be sure about, he showed at San Francisco to Isaac Humphery, a former digger in the Georgia goldfields. Humphery (or Humphrey) agreed to keep the secret, but lit out at once for the American River. Worse than that for Colonel Sutter, the Mormons whom he had hired told their Mormon Elder, Sam Brannan. Brannan, with more astuteness than most, collected enough merchandise to stock several stores in the gold country. When his stores were ready he staged a noisy entry into San Francisco, collecting a crowd to follow him to Portsmouth Plaza. There, at a dramatic moment, he whipped a bottle of gold dust from inside his long coat and shouted the words:

'Gold *Gold!* GOLD! from the American River!'

The date was May 11, and that was the beginning of the rush. A few, like Humphery, had been furtively trespassing on Sutter's land, but after Brannan's display more than a hundred men – almost a quarter of the male population of San Francisco – dropped what they were doing to race to the American River. Four of the Mormons carried away a bag of pure gold (said to weigh one hundred pounds) to show at Monterey: 'A thousand people surged north in a wave.' The 'entire garrison' at Monterey is said to have deserted for the gold rush; Commodore Jones wrote:

> For the present, and I fear for years to come, it will be impossible for the United States to maintain any naval or military establishment in California.[6]

In the later months of '48 there were ten thousand men at the diggings. Everything Sutter had at New Helvetia was expropriated; he was ruined. Some of the miners had a wonderful time, and so did Brannan. Commodore Jones was right, in that there was gold enough in California to keep that gold rush going for years to come.

Texas had become a State of the Union in 1845, without passing through the intermediate status of being Federal territory. California was granted sovereign statehood with remarkable speed on September 9, 1850. The Capital of the state was to be Sacramento, in the area of the goldfields. The speed of admission of California to the Union suggests a general recognition, not that California was ready to be a self-governing State, but that by its own efforts it would quickly have to be so. The ten thousand excited gold-hunters who had invaded New Helvetia in 1848, slaughter Sutter's cattle and felling his timber for their own use, was a foretaste of the first hundred thousand who from the world over streamed into San Francisco for the rush of '49. With miners and would-be miners came the hangers-on – 'speculators and promoters, gamblers, hoodlums, highwaymen, sharpers of every kind, fancy women and plain prostitutes' – and a notable contingent from Australia, the ex-convict 'Sydney ducks'. After San Francisco was incorporated as a city the Sydney ducks (with their hangout at the base of Telegraph Hill, spreading as 'the Barbary Coast') were strong enough to stage a revolution which city government was powerless to handle. That particular revolt was put down by the self-appointed Vigilantes of 1851 (Brannan prominent among them) who took it upon themselves to make 91 arrests and expulsions; four men were publicly hanged by the Vigilantes, one flogged, and fourteen deported to Australia.[7] Five years later, when another hundred thousand people had swarmed into California, robberies and arson were so frequent in San Francisco that Sam Brannan called for revival of the Vigilance Committee of 1851. A nucleus of seven hundred merchants swelled to a force of 8,000 Vigilantes in the Bay area. The movement to crack down on troublemakers easily led to false accusations; up at the goldfields the Vigilante spirit led to wholesale terrorization of any Mexicans who had dared to join in the diggings. Beatings and lynchings forced 'greasers' to join the other and revengeful criminals who, as highwaymen, caused the death-roll on El Camino Real to amount in the '50s to about five hundred killings a year.

Overland trails to California were so difficult, whether by Oregon or by Sante Fé, that it is wonderful that heavy wagons from the East could ever have been dragged all the way; and yet at the time of the gold-rush some of the great Conestoga wagons were to be seen in San Francisco. The teams of mules, and possibly some of the teamsters, were not those that had started the journey; and the initial red, white and blue of wheels, canvas cover and boat-shaped body were mud-encrusted, weather-worn and battered perhaps beyond further repair; yet enough of the wagons 'made it' to cause arrival to seem less miraculous. The Ox-bow route from St. Louis, dipping southwest to the Mexican border and joining El Camino Real at Los Angeles, was chosen by the New York syndicate headed by John Butterfield for the first stagecoach route of the Overland Mail; a hundred coaches were supposed to be in regular service by 1859; the baggage for each passenger for the month's journey was strictly limited to forty pounds, but Overland passengers were permitted to carry rifles, revolvers, Bowie knives, should there be Indian attack. Henry Wells and William Fargo, backed by Yankee capital (Butterfield was suspected of breaking trail for a secessionist railroad), were the rivals who were better favoured as the California goldfields began to yield to the further and tremendous rush to the Comstock mines in Nevada in '59. 'Wells Fargo' out-manoeuvred Overland in the express and banking business, and the name Wells Fargo stood for everything to do with traffic to the Old West, until the coming of the railroad.

The gold-rush fever was not diminished by the Civil War. Telegraph poles had been accompanying the roads toward California; their cross-pieces were interpreted by Indians (so jokers said) as intimation of a mass conversion of white men to the faith formerly upheld by Spaniards. It was by telegraph that Lincoln's call for Union volunteers was sent out in April 1861; by 1862 the first five hundred of California's fighters for the Union sailed to join the Massachusetts Cavalry; fully as welcome to Northern fund-raisers were shipments of gold, sent express by Wells Fargo. The contribution of California gold to the war chest (about $1,250,000) seems modest, in that after the Comstock finds Wells Fargo's San Francisco office was handling 3,000 pounds of treasure every day. Nevada was the new area for fantastic quantities of gold and silver, and the Union was happy to extend Statehood to Nevada during the war, in 1864. The other major goldfield of the Civil War period, and the one to Easterners of paramount excitement ('Pike's Peak or Bust') was in the Colorado territory. Kansas, in 1861, had become one of the wartime States of the Union; there was for a time contention between North and South over the wilderness territory of Colorado. For one day the Confederate flag was flown from dawn to dusk at Denver, but Unionist sympathizers were too many, and the Confederates were forced to retreat to fight the war from Texas. The major goldfields, though a major distraction of manpower, remained as a source of wealth to the Union throughout the war; and after the war Union power could show itself in the completion of a railroad all the way to California by Northern, rather than Southern, enterprise. After the war it was a practicable proposition, no matter how difficult, for the Central Pacific to be pushed eastward from Sacramento through the Rockies, and for the Union Pacific to be pushed from Omaha westward to meet it. The thought of one continuous railroad line had been in the air from the time that the Mormons were making their trek. There was an unforeseen collision when engineers devised that the meeting point for the lines of the Central Pacific and Union Pacific should be at a promontory extending into the Great Salt Lake of Utah – a meeting point in every way convenient except that it happened to be in territory which was governed by the Mormon Church.

The David v. Goliath contest (which is how I am picturing Brigham Young v. the rest of the Nation) was not much noticed in 1869 by Goliath. On Monday, 10th May, at seven o'clock in the morning, the Stars and Stripes was hoisted at Promontory Point in Utah, at the spot where the last two rails of the great Pacific road were laid. I am not sure that Brigham Young was invited to the ceremony, but everything else was thought out. Two locomotives, from East and West, were to approach to the absolute last yard of their respective rail-heads. Two ceremonial 'Last Spikes' were to be driven in – to be on the safe side, four spikes had been made, two of gold, one of a mixture of gold and silver, one of solid silver. When the spikes were in, the engines were to inch forward until their cow-catchers kissed.

A famous photograph was taken of the locomotives kissing, with the railroad officials, engineers and gangers in the foreground.* Out of the picture but discreetly in the background were four companies of the Twenty-First Infantry, to preserve decorum if need be. The loco-motives themselves were dressed for the occasion. The representative of the Central Pacific 'was a splendid engine, a Jupiter-60 with a giant six-foot-wide flared smoke-stack; the Union Pacific Rogers-119 with its six-foot-high, slender column-stack was no less splendid to behold. Their brasswork had been burnished till it shone like molten gold, and the multi-coloured paintwork was new and gleaming'. For those unable to be present at Promontory Point, a telegraph operator sat poised at a table beside the track, to flash the good news nationwide. The sight to be seen by all who were present was the stepping forward of T. C. Durant of the Union Pacific and Leland Stanford of Central Pacific, each holding one of the golden spikes to be tapped into the holes prepared in the inscribed final mahogany railroad-tie. Durant tapped in his spike with the silver spike hammer; there were cheers as he handed the hammer to Leland Stanford. Stanford missed with his first two strokes; the third drove his spike home; more cheers – and *Done!* was the single word flashed by the telegraph operator, at 12.47, eastern time. Came then the even greater moment: Jupiter-60 and Rogers-119 crept foot by foot forward, and inch by inch, until they kissed. Each driver broke a bottle of champagne on the boiler-front of the other's locomotive. The band struck up; the infantry fell in to guard the gold spikes as the engines backed away. It was a superb victory. New York celebrated the word *Done!* with a salute of a hundred guns. A lengthier telegram (thirty-nine words) was tapped

* The photograph has often been reproduced. It is included in *Union Pacific Railroad* by Garry Hogg (Hutchinson, London, 1967), an excellent history from which I have borrowed many details.

out to President Grant in Washington, and General William Tecumseh Sherman found appropriate words for an eventual reply. The great Pacific railroad was, he said, 'a work of giants'.

The completion of the transcontinental railroad was the culmination of long, hard, heroic contest with obstacles that nature opposes. The ceremony at Promontory Point was fittingly in the spirit of lions at play. The Infantry was needed, for a cheerful quantity of drink was taken; the ceremonial spikes were defended, but nothing could stop the silver-inscribed mahogany rail-road tie from vanishing in splinters; and flakes of iron, as further souvenirs, were hammered and gouged from the last pair of thirty-foot rails. Bret Harte, as poet-laureate, personified the locomotives, Jupiter-60 and Rogers-119, as hero-giants:

> *What was it the Engines said,*
> *Pilots touching, – head to head*
> *Facing on the single track*
> *Half a world behind each back?*

His verses were jocular. The conversation of the engines ('Spoken slightly through the nose, With a whistle at the close') was to the effect that they had met head-on, yet in perfect amity, 'without collision'. That is to say, the system of industrial organization that the giant locomotives brought along now, and without collision, ruled Utah Territory. No collision was to be thought of: Utah was to become a State of the Union, with the same advantages of every other State along the conquering railroad line. The process would be so automatic that nobody would question it. I watch the dates at which territories adjacent to the Salt Lake Valley became absorbed into States. To the west, the excitement roused by the Comstock Lode, and the Big Bonanza and other mining prospects, had much to do with the Union conferring statehood on Nevada in 1864. Some way to the east, the other wartime State, Kansas (1861), was gaining population through railroads; in 1867 Abilene, Kansas, had been chosen by Joseph G. McCoy as the first of the railroad cowtowns, and the age of cattle kingdoms (marking the accelerating urbanization of the East) had begun. Nebraska achieved statehood in 1867; Colorado (closer to Salt Lake Valley) was a State in 1876; Wyoming and Idaho (closing in on Utah on the north) were both States in 1890. But the

394

Salt Lake Valley, hemmed in now, still remained, stiffly and stubbornly, as 'territory'. Utah did not become a State of the Union till 1896. Even after the coming of the railroad, the Mormon Church was stubborn enough to defend its own rule in Utah for twenty-seven years.

The collision at Promontory Point in 1869 was not a physical collision. The Yankee locomotive and the California locomotive could converse in amity; they were allies; but the way of life they represented was not at all the way of life in Utah as asserted by Brigham Young. The collision of social philosophies was sufficiently dramatic to interest somebody so far from the scene as Jules Verne. One of his stories (*A Floating City*) is about fictional voyage to America in 1867. The main theme is to describe an Atlantic crossing in Brunel's third ship, the *Great Eastern*, but the 'amateur traveller' is alert to a large question – the American Republic has just come through the Civil War, and he is curious to see what American way of life will develop. Four types of American passengers suggest themselves for incidental comment: they are a Yankee, a Southerner, a Californian, and 'the Mormonite'. The spirited endeavour of the City of Saints has aroused Jules Verne's admiration; it is noticeable that he elevates the Mormonite somewhat above the other types. 'Look at his proud eye, his noble countenance, and dignified bearing, so different from the Yankee.' As for the practice of polygamy in the City of Saints, Jules Verne notes that plural marriage may be authorized, but is not obligatory. The practice is in no sense enforced; yet Jules Verne notes the hostility aroused in some of the other passengers by the mere mention of the word polygamy – a proposed lecture about the City of Saints is cancelled 'as the wives of the puritans on board did not approve of their husbands becoming acquainted with the mysteries of Mormonism'. Jules Verne conveys the impression that the proud Mormonite may be offering a civilization more to be respected than that offered by Yankee or Californian; but having lightly conveyed that impression, his amateur traveller of 1867 passes on to look at Niagara Falls.

But when the Yankee and the Californian ganged up on Brigham Young in Utah, Brigham Young had to fight for the City of Saints as David had to fight against Goliath. If he was to prevent the territory of Utah from degenerating into a State of the Union, as worldly-standardized as other states, he had to use a weapon that would startle the Union; and the best of the stones to use in his sling was polygamy. The wit that Brigham Young displayed does compel the admiration that Jules Verne felt. A moment ago I was expressing sympathy with Colonel Sutter, that Swiss disciple of the Age of Reason who, following Voltaire's advice, had tried to create a garden-estate in California and had tried to cultivate that garden. Sutter might perhaps have staved off the gold-rush for a time, had he announced that his New Helvetia was a leper colony. It was an announcement almost of that kind with which Brigham Young opposed the rest of the Nation. The Salt Lake Valley had suffered from intruders some years before the railroad came. There had been the 'Mormon War' of 1857, and Federal troops were still in Utah in 1863 at the time of a gold-rush in Bingham Canyon, just south-west of Salt Lake City. Ever since 1850 Brigham Young had fought against gold hunting. 'Instead of hunting gold,' he said, 'let every man go to work raising wheat, oats, barley, corn, vegetables and fruit in abundance that there may be plenty in the land.' The Bingham Canyon gold strike was a rich one and brought tough customers to Utah, but the City of Saints, unlike Denver City to the east, provided no saloons, brothels or gambling hells for the practitioners of three-card monte, the strap game, or thimble game. Gambler-desperados such as Tom Hunt and Charley Harrison (who in his day was the most accomplished gunman in the West) had to confess to being run out of Salt Lake City 'because of a little trouble with the Mormons'. They sought refuge at the 'Elephant Corral' in Denver. The Congress of the United States, happy enough to accept Colorado as a State of the Union with Denver as its capital (in 1876, the year before Brigham Young's death) could still be frightened off Utah because Brigham Young upheld polygamy.

Unless one feels respect for both combatants, the fight between the Mormons and the Republic does not seem very important. The larger issues are almost obscured by the peculiarity of the weapons used. A hundred years later we are given the opportunity of watching, as if we were spectators at an ancient Roman circus, one of the oddest of gladiatorial exhibitions: a railroad offered as an instrument of aggression, polygamy offered as an instrument of defence. The battle is more dignified than Conan Doyle suggested in *A Study in Scarlet* (first published in *Beeton's Christmas Annual for 1887*). It had a more comical aspect than Jules Verne's wit suggested: after Brigham Young's death (at the age of 76) other Mormon Elders, to preserve Utah from Federal interference, simply had to support polygamy, at no matter what personal inconvenience. Philistines seemed bound to win in the end – the gold at Bingham Canyon had led to the discovery of enormous finds of copper ore, mountains of it – and the railroad went on pouring more and more infidels into Utah. At last, in 1896, the fight was compromised. Utah, with Salt Lake City as its capital, became a State of the Union. The Mormon Church was forced to endorse a state constitution prohibiting polygamy. But the Congress in Washington did not come out of the battle unscathed. There are some who still feel that the Congress bent the Constitution of the United States by enforcing that the state constitution of Utah should prohibit a 'religious' practice. That is by now a distant debate, and by focussing too closely on the peculiarities of the collision one may lose sight of the larger issues. One large issue is, what sort of society, and with what room for psychic needs, was the Union trying to make?

NOTES

1. Bernard De Voto, *The Journals of Lewis and Clark* (Eyre & Spottiswoode, London, 1954), Introduction.

2. *Audubon* by Constance Rourke (Harcourt, Brace, New York, 1936), p. 280.

3. *The Book of the American West*, Edited by Jay Monaghan (Messner, New York, 1963), p. 76.

4. Rourke, p. 297.

5. John James Audubon, *Ornithological Biography*. Quoted in *Audubon, By Himself*, Edited by Alice Ford (Natural History Press, New York, 1969).

6. Felix Riesenberg, Jr., *The Golden Road* (McGraw-Hill, New York, 1962), p. 111. Much other information comes from *Here They Dug the Gold* by George F. Willison (Eyre & Spottiswoode, London, 1950).

7. *Committee of Vigilance*: Revolution in San Francisco, 1851 by George R. Stewart (Houghton Mifflin, Boston, 1964), p. 319.

CHAPTER 17

Sunset Gun

THE spirit of the nation that had achieved the power that Tocqueville prophesied was what I was thinking about in my preamble, if there is any such thing as general spirit, or any yardstick with which to measure. By making a road-survey I thought I might obtain at least some vague idea about our own condition. I had watched much road-construction before I reached a scene at Promontory Point in 1869, and there shut up my scrapbook. Topographically, Promontory Point is off my beat. I ought to wind up, according to intention, where I started, and where there are some loose threads to pick up. Yet Promontory Point delays me with its awkward question.

Eutopia was the composite word in Greek for the ideal spot on earth where all was well ordered for the good life, life good for both soul and body. By indulging in a neat word-play with the prefix of that word, Sir Thomas More (or his friend Peter Giles) emphasized another meaning – *utopia* signifies equally 'no place, land of nowhere'. Nevertheless, there were the many efforts to create utopias in the American continent. In the 19th century there was certainly much attention to the soulful side of life. I might have got off into social experiments, some of them deriving from Robert Owen and Charles Fourier. I might have looked at Brook Farm, where intellectual discussion and aesthetic discourse were to occupy leisure hours. I might have watched religious activities of every kind: the Great Evangelical Revival produced so much religious fractionalization that it is not surprising if, amidst soulfulness, there was a high percentage of zaniness, or worse.* Yet the frequency of opportunity for individual self-deception or for individual fraud shows only the wideness of the spread of psychic needs.

As it happened, the particularity which lured me into selecting the Mormon utopia for study was something which I have not so far

* *Religious Fanaticism* by Ray Strachey (Faber & Gwyer, London, 1928) remains one of the best short studies in this field.

stressed. It was, if I may make a brief parenthesis, the poetry of
Joseph Smith. If, in your general reading you keep an eye for

All the charm of all the Muses
often flowering in a lonely word

then you will sympathize that it was one word, as first used by Joseph
Smith, which woke me up. I had browsed in *The Book of Mormon* so
far as a story of brothers migrating into a quarter of wilderness where
men had never been. It was a story to look at, as one might look at any
other travel-story. There was a caption in echo of Biblical idiom, fair
enough to anyone with ear and eye accustomed to that idiom. I read
of the preparations for the wilderness-journey, and I came to this
(*Ether* ii. 3): 'they did also carry with them deseret, which, by interpretation, is a honey-bee'. *Deseret!* The charm of several Muses
flowered in that word. I've mentioned it before, but here I wish to
pick it out for admiration. The man who at that moment lightly
touched such a pretty conflation of meanings was a poet. The lonely
word is not to be found in dictionaries, nor is the name Joseph Smith
listed in the authorized who's who of poets; which is strange, for
when you regard his visions and pass from single word-calls to some
of his more extended performances there is much that will make you
put him somewhere in the company of William Blake. And that is the
point of this parenthesis: the kind of poetry tells you something about
the ethic of responsibility that Mormons carried with them. Utah
was God's country. The finger of God had pointed the way, and in
their book there are passages of superb intensity reviving the knowledge that the finger of their God was flesh and blood, and more than
that; and not a mechanical probe.

I cannot argue that because Mormons accepted Joseph Smith as
prophet, or that because he was a prophet who reminds me of William
Blake, that they would never have destroyed what scientists now call
the 'ecological repose' of their surrounding wilderness. I can, though,
argue that from the point of view of present-day conservationists the
madness of the poet Smith was far less crazy than the madness of the
poet Whitman. For Whitman the American continent was not so
much 'God's country' as, in his words, 'large unconscious scenery'.

There is little awareness of any responsibility toward habitat in Whitman.

> *Of Life immense in passion, pulse, and power,*
> *Cheerful, for freest action form'd under the laws divine,*
> *The Modern Man I sing.*

The cheerfulness is splendid, but there is a feeling that under his laws the land was there to be raped. What sort of relation of Modern Man with his environment? What sort of Life to develop as the continent filled up with 'infinite separate houses' and streets with 'throbbings throbb'd, and the cities pent-lo'? Whitman shared in the jubilation of Union when the railroad's mechanical probe touched Utah. Longfellow was more critical about the reflex that a railroad might exert; in 1865 he had written that 'the locomotive is the American Juggernaut'; and the choice of phrase suggests that he was thinking that excessive faith in mechanization would crush those who believed in it. Fables to that effect were only fables to most people; the possible backlash on 'Modern Man' of progressive technology was not felt widely until the 20th century. The general cheerfulness that had accompanied the coming of the railroad carried over to eager acceptance of the internal combustion engine; this had the additional advantage of conquering the air, and it was only a matter of time before men would put on space suits and do all things foretold by science-fiction. Technological progress in every department of life appeared to alter men's environment automatically; and two sentences about the change deserve italicizing. *'A weird aspect of this development lies in its apparently inexorable character. Each step appears as the inevitable consequence of the one that went before.'* Each 'forward' step seemed cheerful, until first one and then another total war revealed a brink that everyone was on. The sentences that I italicized were spoken by Einstein in 1950,* not about Hiroshima but about the further production of the hydrogen bomb, with the possible radioactive poisoning of earth's atmosphere and consequent annihilation.

It will be seen why I shut up my scrapbook where I do, for what our road has been doing since is still obscure. We should all prefer to keep the hydrogen bomb out of this conversation. So far as that

* *Variety of Men* by C. P. Snow (*Penguin Books*, 1969), p. 101.

enters, we are assured by most contemporary military scientists that it would be more difficult totally to eliminate the human species than Einstein believed. But the weaponry we have devised is not our only bogey. What is more difficult to dismiss is that the same apparently inexorable character of technological development which produces weaponry, interferes fully as much with such individual peacetime life as many of us wish for. There are creative qualities in-built in human genes; men are not faceless numbers; life is not mechanic. So in an ordinary daily life today there is much skirmishing; a civil war goes on to rid ourselves of being slaves to a mechanized civilization. Groans come to us by teletype; surprising, almost, is the variety of writers whose energy seems to derive from an obsessive hatred of the present-day civilization they depict. Herbert Read chose Faulkner, Graham Greene, Salinger, Vladimir Nabokov, Saul Bellow to illustrate that variety; and he put in Joyce, Eliot, Brecht, Beckett to strengthen the side.

So many groans from those who resent pollution of spirit – I shall not add to them. I would not let my survey of the road west open with a fanfare. The survey opened with a quarrel, and at this particular sunset gun it ends with one. Some road!

At the start of this road-survey I was looking at a Californian freeway, and it made me think about the Appian Way of Ancient Rome. I mean, that among the differences was this: unlike all that I had ever heard about the ancient Romans, present-day Americans were buzzing along on the right-hand side of the road. How come? There had to be an explanation for our particular custom of driving on the right. It is an old question, and a question not so vital as some that had bothered me as I watched men making roads across American wilderness – pathfinder, homesteader, trail driver, Indian fighter, railroad builder, Henry Ford – but there it is, one of the little questions that remains. The answer I like best was given to me with a great deal of humour and a great deal of beauty in *The Look of the Old West* by Foster-Harris, with pictures by Evelyn Curro.*

Mr. Foster-Harris told me (pp. 76, 77) that a Red Indian custom was to mount a horse or dismount from the starboard, or 'off' side. Whites followed the opposite custom. As a horse that was used to

* Bonanza Books: Viking Press, New York, 1955.

being mounted in one way was apt to act up at an opposite approach, that lent a pleasing complication to the general game of Indians or white men stealing mounts. A sufficient complication to add to the fun of frontier rumpus; sufficient in itself as a small sunset memory – but also leading on at once to the other little matter, the matter of the left-hand driving seat in automobiles.

I said a good deal in this book about the Appian Way, *regina viarum*, the queen of the Roman roads. I did not raise the question of the rule of that road – the driving rule – but that is what now crops up. I turn to Becker's *Gallus* for the impression that in ancient Roman two-wheeled curricles, when there were two seats, the seat of honour – the driving seat – was starboard. Becker describes a jaunt in one of the two-wheeled buggies (*cisium* or *essedum*) of which there were various models, and he pretty clearly puts the patrician driver sitting on the right, with his personal slave on his left (guarding what picnic fare they carried, also the bag of alms-money). The argument from this is that since the curricle had right-hand drive, the rule of the road was to drive on the left.

I don't know how to guess the speed at which vehicles might have approached each other on the Appian Way. Cicero speaks of the news of the murder of Roscius conveyed by *cisium* over a distance of 56 'millia passuum' in 10 of the 'short hours' of a summer night – there is no knowing how to translate these terms. Of Caesar's 'incredible' velocity in his four-wheeled *rheda*, Suetonius says he accomplished a hundred 'millia passuum' in a single day.

But the importance of discussing the rule on the Appian Way is that a rule established there was likely to apply wherever Romans subsequently built paved roads. On any road laid down for heavy traffic, anywhere in the Roman Empire, marching legions and baggage trains, if they were to meet and pass without confusion, presumably kept to the same rule. That rule, so the argument runs, was to keep to the left of the road; a rule obtaining then throughout the habitable world, wherever the Roman writ ran, including Britain.

The fact that people on the Continent of Europe nowadays drive on the right-hand side of the road is then to be ascribed to the French Revolution. Change for the sake of change, even as to rule of the road, and social and political significances of the change, are brought into the argument to explain that Napoleon for his troop movements reversed the custom of the Roman legions, and that by his rapid victories the right-hand rule of his armies was imposed in all countries that he conquered.

The conjecture is ingenious. Whether anybody has actually proved that Napoleon used right-hand rule for his troop movements, I don't know; but it is observable that the right-hand rule obtains in general on the roads of the countries which Napoleon, for a time, firmly conquered; and it does not obtain in the country which most notably stood up to Napoleon, namely Britain. The argument is that in England there was no desire to upset a rule of the road which had been used from Roman times, and Nelson drove (on the left) to Portsmouth, and Napoleon (and his right-hand regulation) stayed on the other side of the Channel.

But before I consulted Mr. Foster-Harris I had been puzzled how the right hand rule of the road had started in the United States. Mr. Foster-Harris has convinced me with his answer. One merit of that answer resides in its unexpectedness. Mr. Foster-Harris established that 'keep to the right' was an American rule of the road *before* there were roadways.

Some of the credit may be given to William Penn. It is said that Penn caused Flemish stallions to be sent to Pennsylvania to produce a special breed of horses for extra-heavy wagons. Such big covered wagons, in the beginning a speciality of Pennsylvania, were usually drawn by three teams (i.e. 6 horses) and where going was good the wagons would move maybe twelve to eighteen miles a day.

It was the big Conestoga wagon which measured itself first and famously against the overland hazards and long hauls to the West. There were rivals and successors (the somewhat lighter Prairie Schooner, for example), but it is the great Conestoga (deriving its name from Lancaster County, Pennsylvania) which Mr. Foster-Harris invites you to look at. It is worth looking. There was pride in that wagon, and superb workmanship. A typical Conestoga was 26 feet long, 11 feet high, weighing empty 3000 to 3500 pounds. It took four skilled men about two months to build it. The flooring and sides were nearly an inch thick. The bed of the wagon was boat-shaped, sloping toward the middle. Curving over the bed, some six to sixteen arching bows upheld the high wagon cover of white canvas or homespun. The cover was laced down to the wagon sides and at each end puckered, with a draw rope for opening or closure. Underneath, the vehicle was heavily ironed and strongly braced. Bolsters and axles were of hickory, the hubs of the wheels of black or sour gum, almost impossible to split. Rims of the wheels, according to terrain to be encountered, might be anything from 2 to 10 inches in breadth; a 4″ rim was a usual size. The front wheels were usually 3′ 6″ in diameter, the rear 4′ 8″. Iron tires heavily encircled the felloes. The wheels were secured to the axles by sturdy linch-pins. When new, the Conestoga wagon was always brilliantly painted, the running gear bright red, the body Prussian blue. The snowy cover completed the patriotic colours of the noble wagon.

This was the landrover which, before 1700 and into the late 1850s, carried the most of the freight and immigrants that went overland westward. And if you were teamster in charge of the big freight wagon, you did not mostly loll on the front bench to drive the horses: you hiked alongside. When your feet wore out or when the going was easy you caught a ride on one of the team horses, or on that feature of the Conestoga wagon called the 'lazy board'. The lazy board was a stout oak plank that pulled out from the port side of the wagon – always from the port side – that is the important testimony of the Conestoga wagon.

When the teamster hiked, he hiked to the left of the horses because, Mr. Foster-Harris says, 'if you are going to ride one horse of a team occasionally, as the freight-wagon drivers did, you'll choose the left-side horse because he's the one you can conveniently get on and off, mounting and dismounting, as you must, from the near side of the horse'. That 'must' of mounting a horse from his port side, is the custom that governs. The horses expected the teamster to be on their left – and therefore all else follows. If you are in charge of a Conestoga freight wagon you will con it from the left and 'you'll guide right and pass right so you can watch clearance'. And what a beauty it was to be in charge of – the red, white and blue Conestoga – you can see the teamster at this moment, standing on his portside lazy board – smoking one of those cigars named, from the name of his proud wagon, 'stogies'. Very convenient to have a rule for two such landships under high canvas, to pass each other portside to port, on roads or off. I heartily agree that the rule of the road in America was established indeed prior to roadways; that driving a car on the right de-

rives from freight-wagon tradition; and that the left-hand steering
wheel is a descendant of the Conestoga lazy board.

The eucalyptus trees at San Mateo? – and the tie-up with the
eucalyptus avenue at La Rábida in Spain – and all the people in that
story – especially the French judge, Charles-Louis L'Héritier? –
that's a loose thread that I have left hanging out. L'Héritier, *he* was a
character – notary namer of plants, and plants that were specially
stinking he chose to name after rival botanists of whom he disapproved. But he invented the good name *eucalyptus* when, in 1788, he
and it were refugees at Kew in England. When he was no longer
refugee, he took the tree to France. Remarkable transit that the tree
was making – Australia to Kew, Kew to the Mediterranean, Spain to
California. Is all, or any, of that story *true?* Well, this is not a place to
argue it. But the trees at San Mateo made a statement. Their statement was, their journey had been good.

The road goes on, or up. We think again of Dante's conversation
with Ulysses. Wise scrapbooks hold no prophecies. They record
hindsights of other men, like us, road-making, and in what spirit. I
attend to certain of the ghosts, for

> *what the dead had no speech for, when living,*
> *They can tell you, being dead.*

My scrapbook needs no other chord to end upon than that.

Index

Names of authorities have not been included in this index but are referred to in Notes at the end of each chapter.

INDEX

INDEX

Hanno, voyages of, 73, 78
Harrison, Charley, 396
Harte, Bret, 394
Hebrew: prophets, 50; writing, 64–6, 68
Hellenes, 35–9, 41, 80; alphabet, 65
Henry IV (Enrique) of Castile, 248–52
Henry the Navigator, 213–14, 227, 235–8, 256, 258–9
Herakles, and Melkarth, 69–70
Herakles, Pillars of, 69 n.; Phoenicians and, 39–40, 64; Greeks and, 84–6, 148; Romans and, 142–3, 148–50; Dante and, 229
Hercules, 70 n., 100; Pillars of see Herakles, Pillars of
Hermes Trismegistus, 94 n.
Herodes, trial of, 57 n.
Herodotus, 71 n., 83, 179 n.
Heron's Pneumatica, 155
Hesiod, 56, 77
Hesperides, The, 216–17, 243
Himera, battle of, 80
Himilco, 78, 82
Hippo, 165, 176
Hiram, King of Tyre, 34, 42–6
Hispaniola, 273–4, 277, 289–91; colonization, 274, 281–2, 287–93, 307; syphilis, 284 n., slavery and depopulation, 293, 296, 303–5; development, 296–7; Ovando's rule, 303–5
Hojeda, Alonzo, 285, 289–93
Homer, Herakles of, 69 n.; on Pillars of Herakles, 85–6, 150; edited at Alexandria, 146–7; influence at Rome, 147–8; reminders in America, 374–5; also, 25, 41, 128. See Iliad; Odyssey
Honduras, 314–15
Honorius, Emperor, 176
Hopi Indians, 352, 365–6
Horace, 74–5, 148–9, 243
Houston, Sam, 374–5
Human sacrifice, in Carthage, 76, 318; in Mexico, 317–20; in Gaul, 318
Humphrey, Isaac, 389
Hunt, Tom, 396

Iberian Peninsula, tin of, 40; conquered by Islam, 187, 201; circumnavigated by Crusaders, 210–12, 230; launching pad for Road West, Ch. 11; French invasion of, 362
Ibn-al-Wardi, 222, 227
Iceland, 196, 220–1, 236
Iliad, The, 37, 133, 146
Illinois, 385, 387

Incas of Peru, 320–3
Indies, Cape route to, 236–7, 254, 256; Westward route to, 237–40, 267–70; spices, 255–6
Ireland, 185, 220, 236
Isabela (in Hispaniola), 285, 288–93
Isabella of Castile, 248–53; John of Gaunt and, 213–14; interest in Columbus, 207, 209, 214, 260–1, 267, 276–7, 292; marriages of children, 265; death, 280, 293
Isaiah, 50, 387–8
Isis, 137–8, 170; in Golden Ass, 164, 168
Islam, emergence, 182–5, 187; impact, 182–4,186–90;navigational aids,185–6, 191, 202, 226; in Spain, 187–90; mystique, 191–4; science, 200–201; problem of converts, 262
Israelites, in Egypt, 25–7; Sinai, 27–31; Canaan, 31–3; impact of Tyre, Chs. 3, 4
Isthmian Games, 85, 87, 89
Italy, Hellenic colonies, 84, 95; Rome gains control, 97; identifications, 129; wine-traders, 131, 133; Renaissance, 246–7, 252–3, 340–1; condottiéri, 247, 252–3; silk trade, 251; Turkish threat, 254; Spanish period, 276, 280–1; influence of roads, 366

Jamaica, 292
Japan, Columbus' objective, 239–40
Jehu, King, 50–2
Jeremiah, prophecies of, 50
Jerusalem, City of God, 33–4, 41–2, 68; influence of Solomon's wives, 44; the Temple, 44–6, 56; court life, 50; sacking of, 52; interaction with Tyre, 68, 74; athletics in, 103; conquered by Pompey, 109; Paul in, 123, 125–7; destroyed A.D. 70, 160–1; captured by Saracens, 184
Jesuits, 353–4; missions, 342–3, 354–61; advancement of road West by, 356; North European membership, 358; expelled from America, 360–2
Jesus, Appollonius as rival to, 171
Jews, relations with Phoenicians, 34, 36, 41–2; threats to kingdom, 42–3, 46; kingdom divided, 50; Babylonian captivity, 52, 241; people of the Book, 68, 70; relations with Rome, 159, 161; in Spain, 262–4; expelled from Spain, 266, 268, 279
Jezebel, 50–1
Joana of Portugal, 250

411